R B M
Self-defence
&
Stress-defence

Andy Rees

Published 2022 by RBMdynamics

www.RBMdynamics.com

ISBN 9798780124979

© Andy Rees 2022

All rights reserved

This book is copyright. Subject to statutory exception and to provisions of relevant collective licensing agreements, no part of this publication may be reproduced, stored in a retrieval system, or transmitted in any form or by any means, without the prior written permission of the author.

Typeset in Garamond

This book is sold subject to the conditions that it shall not, by way of trade or otherwise, be lent, re-sold, hired out, or otherwise circulated without the publisher's prior consent in any form of binding or cover other than that which it is published and without a similar condition including this condition being imposed on the subsequent purchaser.

RBMdynamics

www.RBMdynamics.com

Preface

This book is not fear driven, nor simply an instruction manual on how to hit an attacker, look beneath the surface and you will see the intention to bring you far more than just another self-defence, or stress management concept.

The three phases of *RBM* are designed and structured to explain how your brain and therefore you, function under stress. Stress can be caused by a physical threat to your safety, such as a person with a knife, or by less obvious threats such as worrying thoughts, triggered by your perception of what's happening in any moment of your everyday life. Thoughts which often start the endless stream of anxiety led rumination.

Progressing through the chapters, this comprehensive information aims to ignite and support your growth to becoming empowered and confident within yourself. You will be introduced to the bigger picture, the core message throughout which is: *Empowered people make positive choices.* It will instill a mindset which enables you to become a dynamic problem solver, finding solutions to any threats of violence you may face. By changing your mindset, you lower your reactions to stressors, having an immediate and profound impact on your life by boosting your health and increasing your confidence levels, *you will start feeling comfortable being yourself in all situations*. Ultimately improving the quality of your time here on this planet.

You will be introduced to invaluable, ground-breaking concepts which challenge the beliefs many people hold about how to protect themselves, but also extend far beyond disclosing what to do if someone is about to attack you. It's the place for you to start your journey to becoming a more positive decision maker, learning that if your life is on the line, or you're feeling overwhelmed in life, *you have the power to positively influence the situation*.

You will hold the knowledge that if you're ever feeling scared or vulnerable you can find a sense of calm in the chaos, take charge of your emotions, and harness the power of your will to survive. You will see your self-worth elevate, forging a deep belief of; *"I am worth fighting for, and I deserve to be happy!"*

This information will change how you see the world around you and positively change how you see and value yourself. *RBM* is far more than just learning how to hit an attacker!

Foreword

RBM self-defence & stress-defence is education and training all in one place. Hard core science, applicable life information, and humour. There are books that you pick up, read, put down and forget, and those books you return to over and over, this is one of the latter. The heart and soul of Andy Rees is found within these pages, with valuable information that will "delay death" (since we all ultimately die). It contains information that transcends physical conflict, whilst providing the information to achieve a life of reduced stress. I highly recommend you purchase several copies.

Kenny Johnson, (BSc) Sports Science.
Founder of The European Institute of Combat Fighting.
8th dan Shito-ryu Karate, 6 times European Champion in Karate, 1st place at the Japanese Open Championships in 1985.
Master level in Kong Style Tai Chi.

A Big thank you to...

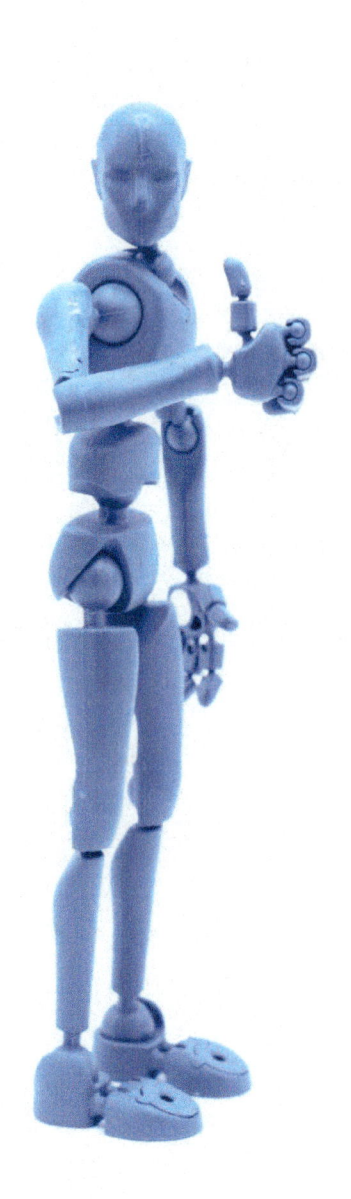

Lou, when I wanted to devise this realistic self-defence method & self-help strategy, inconveniently at a time when we had a young baby, you stood by me and kept saying *"do it"*, which says a lot about your strength, courage, and ability to have absolute belief in others, when it would be easier to play it safe. *A & F*, don't reach for the stars as you already hold them and remember you cannot add to perfect!

The *Tuesday night 'Lab Rats'* group, thank you for being willing to listen to the constant *"I have an idea to try"* and being open to it. But mainly, for questioning these ideas and being hyper-critical of everything, leaving me the challenge of adapting and evolving the principles to the point where you're satisfied with the quality and the validity of the data. The evolution of *RBM* could not have happened without you.

Kenny, for someone with so much knowledge, insight, and passion for the martial arts, you're an incredibly down to earth and generous person. I cannot thank you enough.

A big thank you to all the people who attended courses and were brave enough to ask questions. Every question asked brought out information which benefited all those who attended the course with you, information which wouldn't have necessarily been pencilled in to include. Courage creates evolution.

All information presented is protected by copyright law and may not be reproduced, distributed, transmitted, displayed, published, or broadcast without the prior written permission of the author. Self-defense training should always be undertaken responsibly, ensuring every available precaution for safety. Any content, instruction, or coaching provided by *RBM* should be used for educational purposes only. Although the author and publisher have made every effort to ensure that the information was correct at press time, the author and publisher do not assume and hereby disclaim any liability to any party for any loss, damage, or disruption caused by errors or omissions, whether such errors or omissions result from negligence, accident, or any other cause.

This information is not intended as a substitute for the medical advice of physicians. The reader should regularly consult a medical professional in matters relating to their health and particularly with respect to any symptoms which may require diagnosis or medical attention.

The information found here is meant to supplement, not replace, self-defence training. Like any moment involving speed, equipment, balance, and environmental factors, self-defence poses some inherent risk. The authors and publisher advise readers to take full responsibility for their safety and know their limits. Do not take risks beyond your level of experience, aptitude, training, and comfort level.

Trigger warning: whilst every effort, consideration and compassionate understanding has been applied to presenting this text in a non-fear based way, the subject matter may be potentially sensitive. Even though the purpose of this text is to provide information to enhance an individual's safety and well-being, the subject matter may include stimuli that recall or induce an individual's experience of trauma.

CONTENTS

Intro!
Info on Andy Rees & RBM..2
Why it's called RBM!..5
Questions I am asked first, answered first..7
- *Am I an 'Ex - Spurt'*...7
- *You don't need to train a thug to hit you with a club!*..............8
- *You aren't a Superhero*...8
- *Legality of self-defence*..9
- *A question of Morality Vs Ego*...11
- *Information validation*..13
- *Why do people just stand and film it?*....................................15
- *UK Government Crown Prosecution Service*.........................16

PHASE 1 - Ready!
The Mechanics of the Mind & Stress..24
- *The Butterflies & The Scaredy Cat*..25
- *The 'Grey Matter' & The Stress Response*.............................28
- *Fight or Flight*..40
- *The Feedback Loop from Stimulus to Response via Fight, Flight*......49
  or the pesky Freeze!

RBM! Development
- *Fight or Flight in daily life and how it damages health*..........63
- *Forget Guns, it's Cortisol that will kill you!*...........................64
- *Take your foot off the GAS*..66
- *RBM Pro-Active Stress Defence Drills*...................................68

Stay Safe and Feel empowered..69
- *Awareness is key, it's missile avoidance!*...............................72
- *Target Attractiveness*..79
- *The people you need to learn about*.......................................85
- *Signs it's time to dive for cover*..98
- *The POODLE Loop*..102
- *Drills in Spotting Danger & Developing Awareness*............105

RBM! Development 109
- Internal Proxemics 109
    - Stage 1 - Identify your location
    - Stage 2 - Pinpoint the location of the threat
        - Is the threat real or illusionary?
        - Think Tank - The Mental Spring Clean
    - Stage 3 - Move to a new location
- Target Attractiveness - Why does this keep happening to me? 115
- Are you living in 'OO' land? 117

Building a Bodyguard 119
- Human Demolition Services Ltd. 119
    - Don't feel guilty about learning how to injure someone! 119
    - Your two Crisis Responders 124
    - Meet the 'Thumping Thunder Fist Demolition Monkey' 127
    - How you train the Demolition Monkey 128
    - Tools of the Trade, The armoury of your 'Demolition Monkey' ... 138
    - The Rice Crispy Principle - Snap, Crack or Pop 146
- Where do you drop the Thunder Fist bombs 147
    - Hot Zones 147
    - Test Drive the Weapons Systems 170
    - De-escalation and Breakaways 172
- The Mental & Physical Obstacle Course 178
    - Be generous, and if they want a piece of you let them have all of you ... 178
    - The Moral Freeze 181
    - Surprise! Flinch 182
    - Colour codes of Scaling Flinch Response Recovery 184
    - There are No Blocks in RBM 189

RBM! Development 193
- Finding yourself in a psychological avalanche 193
- The bucket of self-worth & the shield of confidence 194
- Why taking time for you & learning new things, matters 200
- The importance of self-reliance 202
- De-escalation - take the power away from the enemy known as doubt ... 206
- Pick a target 208

PHASE 2 - Breathe!

And Breathe 212
- Box Breathing 213
- The Top Trump Breathing Card - Breathe like a Baby 214
- The back to front-ness of Tai Chi, Chi Gong, Yoga and Meditation 217

PHASE 3 - Move!

Data Loading 222
- Forest Gump It! 222
- Physical Chess - when you move, they must lose a piece 223
- "But I do Yoga" – The movement of joints and how to damage them, ... 226
  even in bendy people
- Identify the target, lock on, and get there no matter what is in the way 228
- Remember you have work tomorrow - The Safety Guidelines 233

Solutions to Physical Threats 234
- What to do when grabbed 239
- A Punch! 281
- A knife! 289
- Being Human, it's about doing the right thing 306

Looking after the organic motorhome 307
- Warming up head to toe 310
- Bodyweight exercises for core strength 322
- Train like a Demolition Monkey 336
- Warming down and loosening the body 339
- Over to you 355
- References 357
- Appendix 1 360

INTRODUCTION

Background info on Andy Rees & RBM!

To clarify from the start, I am against the use of unnecessary violence in any form. However, this doesn't mean I must leave myself vulnerable to an attack. I have information to use if absolutely necessary if my life is in danger, but I avoid violence and conflict at all other times. There is no room for ego in RBM!

It helps with your learning journey if you know about the person providing the information you're relying on if you ever find yourself in serious threat situation. You need to see credibility in the self-defence system you're being asked to put your trust in.

There were two keys points which started the process of creating *RBM*. The first, although unknown to me at the time, was in a single moment when I learnt violence doesn't follow the patterns and rules of the martial arts I practiced at the time. Starting in Shotokan Karate at eight years old, I was mesmerised by the lines of people moving up and down the dojo in unison, performing highly skilled kicks and punches. It was fascinating how the routines followed a set procedure, a pattern of self-defence, I completely bought into the martial arts, and what they taught. *Then key point 1 arrived;* and it was undeniably highlighted to me that violent attacks are not a choreographed pattern when as a teenager walking to school one morning, this revelation was delivered courtesy of me being grabbed by the throat and head butted by someone who I thought was walking past me. After seven years of training in Karate, I had no recognition of what was about to happen, no knowledge of how to see any warning signs and I was totally oblivious to a threat to my safety.

Having someone's head crashing into your cheekbone whilst grabbing you by the throat is not the Karate way! He was cheating, he didn't stick to the sequences, he just hit me, and all the feelings I had in my brain and body in that precise moment were alien to me, I was frozen to the spot. Luckily, the person left with me receiving only one hit, which was good news for me as I was powerless to do anything about it and totally unaware of what was going on. I clearly remember the feeling of shame afterwards, it was debilitating, and I can say from personal experience it's not great when your belief in your self-defence system falls on its backside when you need it the most, especially at 8:45am. This wasn't at night on a dark street, it was daylight, early morning, and in a city centre full of people, and it was totally unexpected, and I was completely unprepared for the reality of what happened.

This experience, and the questions I had about how everything could have gone so wrong started my search to find answers to what really happens in a violent encounter. Frustratingly, I wasn't being allowed to question the things taught in the various martial arts I studied, and when the hierarchy did give permission to ask a question, if it challenged the validity of the self-defence, then I found myself being palmed off with *"that's just how we do it"* when the sensei didn't have an answer. Not being able to question things from the very start of my participation in martial arts led to me owning a false confidence which crumbled under pressure, exposing the weaknesses in my self-defence training when I needed it the most. Thankfully, it wasn't a gang, or a knife attack which exposed the problem, as the consequences of this learning curve could have been far, far worse. The person who shone a light on my self-defence failings didn't use any fancy skills, only aggression. It was a simple grab and headbutt, yet the martial arts I learnt didn't prepare me for this, nor did they have answers when I asked the people teaching martial arts questions about this type of attack after the event.

Over the years I started to talk to people who had studied different styles and methods of self-defence and found that a vast number of people had also become disillusioned with the protection aspect of these systems. They either felt the things they had been taught failed them, or they simply remarked they did it for fun and fitness and would never rely on it if attacked.

After years of hitting dead ends with different instructors, I changed my game plan and I went to the top of the martial arts tree to Kenny Johnson of Shito-Ryu Karate, who's still highly respected in this field to this day. He spoke about how he had spent his life researching self-defence and found a lot of the answers I was seeking. My time learning Karate and Tai Chi from him was incredible, and I will always be grateful for his patience, knowledge and a friendship developed over many years, during which time I qualified to teach Karate, plus Tai Chi.

The other thing I learnt from him was close quarters, armed and unarmed combat for specialist groups. This took a long time, and I'm not talking about a weekend here and there, or training twice a week, but intensive immersion training. After which time, I successfully qualified as one of only ten instructors trained by him to deliver various facets of close quarters combat, including:

- Psychology, physiology, human body language & behaviour relating to combat & conflict violence
- Close quarter hand to hand, hand to weapon, weapon to weapon combat
- Blade edge & projectile weapon disarmament, retention, and usage
- Anti & Counter carjacking
- Urban threat awareness and counter measures

Finally, I had found the answers to a lot of my questions, and I started to teach these skills in the UK and across Europe to a wide-ranging client base. This was all going swimmingly until the second moment to have a huge impact on me happened, leading me to rip up what I was doing and start the process of developing *RBM* in its current format.

Key point 2; occurred when a person I had been teaching self-defence, and who became an incredibly good friend, tragically committed suicide. This raised many questions for me, the main one to be a thorn in my brain was *why put all your focus on learning to protect yourself from a violent attack if it's the pressure of life which most often kills you?* This led me to analyse the reasons behind learning self-defence, and to assess the whole basis of my teaching methods. I was determined to revolutionise everything I was doing to create something new, with a greater emphasis on how I see self-defence as a tool for helping people take control of their lives, and not solely focus on what to do if attacked.

"I wanted a system to assist in self-preservation for all of life's situations, and not only for when under the threat of violence."

Analysing my own experiences, I realised the sense of feeling frozen didn't only happen the time I was headbutted, but many other times in my life such as exams, big life decisions, being worried about changing jobs, all leading me to panic and essentially, freeze. Due to this anxiety, I didn't always make the best decisions, and when I did make a decision, it was promptly followed with rumination and excessive worry about the choice I had made, and the ones I didn't make. I identified and isolated the point when this mindset changed for me, it was after I had learnt the close quarter protection skills and learnt how to stop an attacker. It was this which changed me as a person and changed how I respond to all stressful situations, helping me manage anxiety more effectively, which in turn enables me to make better decisions, because *empowered people make positive choices.*

Fascinated by how this had a more profound effect on me than Tai Chi, Meditation and Yoga ever had, I decided to dig deeper, discovering what had changed within me was my thought process; positively effecting how I approached different problems in life and how I became far more versatile in finding solutions without letting stress and worry get in the way. I needed to harness this and form a structured way of delivering it to others who were looking for the same results, even those with no interest in learning self-defence. People want to learn protection skills to make themselves feel safe and secure, but I found the statistical chance of a person sustaining injuries through being physically assaulted is much lower than the number of people who've had physical and mental health problems through stress related illness and depression. It's anxiety most people are under attack from on a regular basis.

At the time of writing this information, more than half of my life has been dedicated to developing a fresh view of realistic self-defence. I had positive changes in my own mental health after immersing myself in the close quarter protection skills, changes which built my confidence in *RBM* being an authentic tool for people to use. The confidence gained from learning how to face an aggressive violent attacker will spread through your life and help you harness the courage needed to openly talk about mental health. Having a strong mental resolve doesn't mean you don't ever need to ask for help, being able to recognise the need for support and being brave enough to ask for help is what having a strong mental resolve is about. Mental health awareness in our society is moving forwards, it's improving, but it still has a long way to go, and the lack of value society places on this is evident in the amount of time children spend on this topic in school in comparison to other areas of learning.

Nearly forty years after I first walked into a Karate dojo, I have painstakingly blended information I was taught, with a vast amount of personal research and personal life experiences to present you with *RBM*. This is where, why, and how, *RBM* was shaped, developed, and formed. You can call it a realistic self-defence book, you can call it confidence training, empowerment principles, or you could say its stress management. If it works for you then call it what you like. I just hope this information has a positive effect on everyone who reads it, and makes your life a little easier, less stressful, safer, and of course, full of fun.

Why it's called RBM!

1. Ready!

Focusing on solutions, such as how to make a threat to your safety go away right now. Or on a day-to-day basis becoming adept at recovering quickly from setbacks when you are caught off guard by life's many surprises, rather than defaulting to ruminating on problems, causing further worry and stress.

2. Breathe!

Using breathing skills to directly influence the part of your brain responsible for monitoring stress and anxiety levels. Not complicated meditation, but simple breathing routines you can use anywhere, anytime, without anyone else being aware of what you are doing. Not that it should matter, but sometimes people feel self-conscious so skills which can be used under the radar are a good thing.

3. Move!

Positively programming yourself to have solutions to your worst fears of being attacked, building a new confidence in yourself, and observing as this confidence spreads through all areas of your life. Bringing with it the tenacity, inner strength, and drive to fulfil your goals to the absolute best conclusion. Stop standing still in life when you're frozen in panic or indecision. *Move,* and influence the situation for the better.

If you're ever unlucky enough to be attacked, ideally you'll be aware of the situation and be mentally ready. Next you'll breathe, as you understand the important & influential role breathing has on the fight or flight response. Then your brain will be loaded with information on what you need to do, so you will pick a solution and move. *Ready – Breathe – Move.* Perfect!

Yet, life does not always go to plan, so what if you're not ready? Well, you start at a different place in the loop and continue from there. It's not ideal but it's the reality of the situation, so you must deal with it. If caught by surprise, you will be startled and instinctively breath in. You follow this by moving off the spot and getting your mind into gear. This time the circuit is *Breathe – Move – Ready* and continue. If really caught off guard you will flinch which is an instinctive evasive movement, your brain will work out what is happening, then you'll inhale to get oxygen into the body to fuel the next movement. This time the circuit is *Move – Ready – Breathe* and continue.

You can start anywhere on the rolling circuit with each element supporting the transition to the next. By the time you finish reading this information you will understand perfectly how this simple format prepares you not only for when you're aware of a threat, but also for when you aren't ready and how to recover from this disorientation quickly. The application of this format is the same in any non-violent stress situations. You follow the same pattern regardless of where you find yourself starting on the loop, whether that be starting to feel worried or in a full-blown panic attack.

Whichever element of the *RBM* cycle you find yourself in when you become aware your fight or flight system is kicking in, this is your starting position. No matter how difficult it seems to move from here, whatever obstacles are in the way to a better situation, it's from here you follow the dynamic pattern.

Questions I am asked first, answered first

Am I an 'Ex – Spurt?'

It became clear to me over the years, when it comes to the topic of self-defence everyone seems to be an expert. It's quite remarkable such a high percentage of the population can confidently tell me what I should teach. *Punch them in the throat, kick them in the nuts, take them down and use an arm-bar, put your house keys in your fist.* I would do this, I would do that, yet when in the training room and placed under simulated attack pressure they do……..nothing! They freeze. All their grand plans evaporate, and that's okay, as it highlights the difference between the theory of knowing what to do, and programming yourself to do it without the need to think under stress. Mike Tyson famously said, *"everyone has a plan until they're punched in the face".* You need to learn what to do when you have no plan, and when you've been punched in the face!

People feel vulnerable with their lack of understanding of what to do in a hostile situation, and in establishing whether they should trust what I am saying they will fire off the question, *"am I an expert?"* Which is understandable and perfectly justifiable, people want credibility.

In my local area, if the word expert is used it's often met with the derisory response of; *An Ex is a has been and a Spurt is a drip under pressure,* so I am certainly not claiming to be an 'ex-spurt' in the field of self-defence. I did learn some specialist information, but so have many others. I'm sharing the things I have been taught, things I have researched and discovered, and things which make more sense to me than I previously believed to be the answers to personal safety and stress reduction. There will obviously be people who disagree with the information found here, and my view is that's great if it motivates their thinking to enhance themselves, or even reinforces what they believe by completely disagreeing with me. I'm not saying I'm an expert, I would prefer to say that I'm taking self-defence in a different direction to the other things I've seen out there.

With reference to the realistic self-defence aspect, I wasn't thinking of people who are highly trained and highly skilled martial artists, or people who have trained in combat when I created this strategy. It's not in any way suggesting you can walk into the *UFC* and challenge the elite athletes who ply their trade there. This information is for people who have little or no prior experience of violence and self-defence, have only read books on the subject, or have become disillusioned with the things they are learning. It will enable the reader to ask questions on what they see on YouTube presented as viable solutions to attacks, but I'm not entering the *'my style is better than your style'* debate which is so prevalent in this subject matter. I am not criticising any other system or person, as they all have their own space and benefits in the world. I'm presenting information on how I see things according to my experience to benefit those who are interested. Whilst I admire the skill set of the people in the martial arts and self-defence world and appreciate the hard work required for their athleticism, what I'm presenting is a method *you* can use today without all those years of experience, practice, and conditioning. A methodology which doesn't require you to be an elite athlete to stop an aggressor in their tracks, *RBM* is a system which increases your chances of staying safe without years of practice. It's written from the viewpoint, that statistically speaking, if you're attacked it will most likely be a person with unskilled violence, not using a spinning back kick or a submission hold, but a brick to the face, or a knife thrust towards your torso.

It's preferable for the average, everyday person to have principles which work now, for everybody, regardless of size and strength, and not to rely on a skill-based system, regardless of how good that system is. In a nutshell, neither you, nor I need to be an expert for *RBM* to work for you.

<u>You don't need to train a thug to hit you with a club</u>
What if someone dangerous buys this book or attends a course? This is another question people often ask, but if you conjure up the image of someone who fits your profile of a violent attacker, I think you'll agree it's hard to imagine them spending time and effort reading to learn how to stamp on someone's foot to break it. Their most likely way of using this book would be to hit you in the face with it. You aren't likely to find terrorists, rapists, drug cartels or muggers reading this, they will stick to the gang beatings, stabbings and shootings which have worked well for them so far.

<u>You aren't a Superhero</u>
Am I unbeatable? No! I am not, nor do I claim to be. *RBM* won't make you unbeatable in a physical assault, but you'll be more aware of threats before they happen and you'll know what to do if grabbed, and what to do if at the wrong end of a weapon, therefore improving your chances, but it will never make you untouchable. My belief is no system can, because the brick wielding thug can hit you on the back of the head at any time and you can be stabbed in your sleep regardless of any self-defence training you've had. *RBM* is in no way saying you're going to be immortal, but it will alter the percentages in your favour. Without seeing a threat, hearing a threat, or sensing a threat, you cannot do anything about it. What *RBM* is providing, is honest information to increase your situational awareness, awareness which not only includes seeing things

around you but also understanding what is happening on the inside, in your own mind and body.

Legality of Self Defence

"Will I get sent to prison if I use this information in the wrong way?"
If you use it unnecessarily, then yes, I hope so.

"I keep a baseball bat by the side of the bed, so why learn this?"
Good luck with that, see you in 15 years!

The term 'self-defence', how it sounds and how it is interpreted doesn't provide an accurate description of your legal standpoint. It causes confusion and uncertainty, and it's crucial for your safety you know where you stand legally. Any doubt centred around what to do if under threat can be detrimental, which will become clear as you read further through the information and get to the Feedback Loop section. *(Doubt is crippling and needs to be addressed).*

I believe the best place to look for information on this topic for UK residents is the UK Government Crown Prosecution Service, because they're the people who will assess what you've done, judge what you've done, and decide if any sentence needs to be delivered. To clear up any confusion of what you should or shouldn't do and have clear parameters of how you can protect yourself within the confines of the law, I have included the *UK Government Crown Prosecution Service* information on self-defence[1] at the end of this section. It relates to general self-defence but also self-defence for a home intruder. I have included this in its entirety, because cherry picking bits or condensing it wouldn't give accurate information, so you won't only find a section about punching a mugger, which tends to be found in most self-defence books. It must be in its complete form to cover everything and to give you the clarity needed, because this topic causes quite a lot of distress and concern for a high percentage of people I have taught. I apologise for the fact it's a bit of a slog reading the information, but it's worth doing this before you progress further, so you might want to put the kettle on and make a drink, then have a go at reading the *UK Government Crown Prosecution Service* information at the end of this section and return to this point before continuing. For readers outside of the UK, a simple internet search will find the relevant information on laws for your country of residence.

---

[1] UK Government Crown Prosecution Service Source: Information taken via the www.cps.gov.uk website for the UK Government Crown Prosecution Service.

The laws of the land exist to provide societal cohesion and to prevent people from running around doing whatever they want to, in theory. Percentage wise, most stick to the rules, some choose not to, and some are unable to. When laws are broken the police step in and take control, hopefully finding those responsible for the incident and with punishment given in accordance with the crime. This is the protocol you should adhere, for example, if there is a sound of someone in your garden, you call the police. If everything goes well, they turn up and either catch the person or scare them away with their arrival on the scene. Society functions well within this model and these rules, most of the time. If somebody steals your bag, you call the police, you may get it back with the police utilising CCTV or you may not. It's wrong, there's a sense of injustice, but it is not a life changing event, unless it affected you psychologically.

There are a few instances where things don't quite pan out this way, maybe the person looking inside your garden shed breaks into the house before the police can arrive. Perhaps a person grabs your phone out of your hand, and they stop, turn around and pull out a knife as they're an opportunistic sexual predator. Or a violent attack starts out of the blue, leaving you with no time to call for assistance. Consider it's not only the police response time which needs to be thought about, but also the medical response time if you sustain a life-threatening injury. An internet search for UK emergency service response times shows a drastic increase in time needed for emergency services to reach you when needed over the last few years alone, showing there is an advantage to learning how to limit the likelihood of you being injured because medical help may not arrive in time if you are bleeding out. CCTV is valuable, giving real time information as an alert for the police, if the people monitoring the screens notice an incident. However, it's mostly a tool for prevention and prosecution, being both a deterrent and a source of retrospective data, but not able to step into the fold to ensure your safety at the time, it's certainly not a personal bodyguard.

A question that society does not like discussing is, *"if you find yourself in what you see as a serious level of threat situation, and the police won't arrive quickly enough, then what do you do"?* This is the situation where you need to be self-reliant in your ability to protect yourself and your loved ones. What do you do if the societal safety net isn't there?

A question of Morality Vs Ego, and 'would you like the remote control?'

When answering questions relating to knowing when is the right time to use this information to strike somebody. The answer I give is:

> *"If you need to ask, it's not the right situation. When you don't have the opportunity to think of this question, then it's the right time, because you have no other choice. The will to survive supersedes everything as all you will want to do is focus on staying alive. Learn how to channel this desire for self-preservation and use it in the most efficient way. Being efficient in your ability to stop someone will for the greater part, reduce the severity of injuries and life changing incidents for all parties involved. If you do not act, someone may die, if you do, someone will most likely have a broken limb, which in time will heal."*

If a burglar is in your house but you don't feel under threat, let them take everything, you have insurance which covers theft. If they enter a room you or your loved ones are in, and you feel in danger knowing help won't arrive in time, accept the reality, it's time to act and you must come out on top. This often raises the next question, *but why should they get to take my stuff?*

The previous section *(if you read the information from the UK Government Crown Prosecution Service),* provided a clear understanding of where you stand legally in terms of protecting yourself, your loved ones, members of the public and your property. Prior to learning how to safeguard these things, you should establish whether you're doing it for the right reasons, reasons which are tremendously important to you. If you try to apprehend a burglar you see leaving your house, consider that whilst trying to stop them, a fight is likely to break out. The fight can turn from a scuffle to a serious altercation, and you may accidentally kill the person, or they may kill you. A very costly decision for you and your family over some item which could have been replaced. You on the other hand, are irreplaceable, as are your family.

This topic causes so much frustration when people first start learning *RBM,* but whether you agree or disagree with the law and the interpretation of these laws is irrelevant, it is what it is. Even if you consider it unjust, whether you think it's right or wrong, you cannot do what you want without facing consequences or taking unnecessary risks. Appendix 1 clearly covered the fact you cannot launch the first attack unless you genuinely believe to be under threat, and you must be able to justify this. You're within your rights to legally chase a person and use reasonable force to perform a citizen's arrest if necessary, but is it necessary? At this stage, the issue of the morality of self-defence needs to be addressed, because a question I often ask the people attending my courses is:

How much money would you ask as payment to break someone's ankle? To snap it the wrong way causing a compound dislocation, seeing the bones tear through the skin. How much money would it take for you to do this to another person?

The answers are always the same, *there's no amount of money*. Based on this sensible moral view, why would you risk getting into an altercation where this might happen for a TV? *"Because it's mine, it belongs to me"*. People start to sound like *Gollum* from *Lord of the Rings*, it's just a TV.

I am often questioned on what I would do if I heard someone in my home stealing my things, loading up 'my TV' into their car? The answer is always the same, I would only ask, *"would you like the remote control?"* It's because I don't care about the material things, I have insurance. There's going to be paperwork at some point, so I can fill out an insurance claim form which is uneventful going forward in life, or option two is filling in a police statement after an event in which I challenged a burglar. Or there is the 'accepting all realities' option, where my family have to fill out forms because I am no longer around. Remember, I'm not under the illusion I'm immortal because of this training, my common sense doesn't allow me to rule out the fact things may not go the way I want them to. (You won't read that soundbite of reality in many self-defence books on the market.)

Another aspect for consideration is if I decide to confront the burglar over some meaningless stuff, and a scuffle started, and I had to drive my thumb into their eye, I will then have to justify all this to a judge. A judge who likely lives in a different world to most people, and probably in their lifetime has never experienced the feeling of being threatened or faced a violent encounter. They will be deciding on my future with their interpretation of the events as to whether my actions were justifiable. If my life or health were under threat then my thumb would definitely be getting all eye squidgy, but not for items which could be replaced in a few weeks by the insurance company doing what I pay for. Risking everything for those things doesn't make sense to me, it's a no-brainer. Enjoy the new insurance funded replacements by letting the burglar take your TV and the remote, along with your ego, gift wrapped with a bow on top.

Don't overlook the fact you will need to justify your actions to yourself. If you cause serious injury to another person, you'd better be sure you knew it was the only option, otherwise it's going to play havoc with your brain. There is a psychological cost of injuring or killing a person, we know this from people who bravely served in the military on our behalf. So yes, you can chase a person and use reasonable force to stop them escaping with your stuff, it's more a question of whether you should, and what part of your personality feels that you need to. You're within your rights to do this but realise the situation you perceive in front of you can escalate into something far worse in a few heartbeats. If verbal or physical cues you're picking up make you feel under threat of physical harm, then you don't have to wait for the home intruder to deliver the first attack, you can use a pre-emptive strike. But could you alternatively take the option of retreating to a safer room and locking the door?

It's highly beneficial to sit down and work out what's important to you in your life. Decide what you would fight for with every ounce of your being, all the other stuff doesn't matter. If somebody is merrily helping themselves to your possessions in a burglary or a mugging, give them what they want. If they change their plan and move towards you or your loved ones and you sense a real threat, then it's a different matter, this is a game changer and where you fight with all the tenacity you have until everybody is safe. But avoid the famed 'red mist' from descending by making sure you can put the brakes on when the threat is removed. It's the unskilled, untrained person who's more likely to end up killing an intruder, because they've not prepared for the reality and the stress of the situation.

This is a difficult topic as it's centred around social justice, if nobody stands up for what's right, then what's right is lost. Do you stand by and watch people break the rules? Should you intervene and put yourself at risk? I cannot give you a belief system, nor would I want to impose mine onto you. However, what I can do is give you information to make decisions based on what is important to you.

Information Validation

Does this information really work if I am attacked?

It's helpful for you if there's some way to qualify this information as not being just theoretical. When I say it will work for you now, I mean right now. It's not about what you can do after practicing for decades, it's about what *RBM* can do for you, right now. Ben attended a one-day course many years ago. He didn't think he would ever need the skills, but just wanted to find out more, so he signed up.

> *"I was walking home, and I saw a guy coming towards me, staggering up the road. I thought nothing of it when he asked if I had any money. Suddenly, he grabbed my arm and shouted, "Give me your money". I realised he had a knife and was pointing it at me, this is when the information I learned seemed to kick in. The first thing I had learnt was, if possible, make a sharp exit, so as a car sped by me, I ran out into the road and legged it, yelling "help I'm being mugged". The car waited until I got out of the way and continued to drive at high speed up*

the road. My attacker grabbed me by the wrist again and attempted to pull me into a driveway. I tried to appeal one more time bringing what little change I had out of my pocket, but he threw it on the ground and grabbed me again. I realised; I was going to have to fight back. I grabbed the wrist with the knife and with the other hand I drove my thumb into his eye and pushed. Not the most pleasant thing in the world but I kept thinking "protect yourself, you have to stop him whatever way you can". He fell backwards, and I kept my thumb in his eye until I was kneeling on him. He tried to get his hand free and swing the knife at me, but I had his wrist and twisted it, causing him to stab himself in the forehead and hurting his wrist.

I realised I had neutralised the threat and there was no need to do anything else. I had the knife, and I was sure he would not get up and follow me, so I left quickly. My mobile phone was damaged, so I couldn't call the police, but the next morning I took the knife to the police station, made a statement, and handed over my clothes for D.N.A samples. The man who assaulted me was brought in for questioning and pleaded guilty. Apparently three witnesses came forward to identify him. I would like to know where they were at the time of the attack because they were not helping me. One of the witnesses even claimed I was the attacker, which I suppose is what I was in the end. The man received two and a half years without parole for attempted armed robbery and I got the confidence that everything I had been taught works.

So, what have I learnt from RBM? No one has the right to threaten you with bodily harm and if they do, you have every right to do whatever is in your power to stop them. I attended a full day course and after that night it changed my outlook on life completely, I'm not scared to walk down the street because I know I can defend myself, I'm quietly confident of my abilities, of what I am willing to do if someone threatens me or my family. I still hate violence and spurn aggressive behaviour but RBM! taught me that sometimes if threatened you can fight back. I have been shown how to neutralise a threat by swiftly inflicting pain to weak areas and then stop when there is no longer any threat. This training is not about becoming a 'have a go hero' or 'vigilante', it is about asserting yourself and not feeling scared of what is outside your front door."

Ben

[2] *For the actual article reporting on the incident please refer to:*
http://eadt.co.uk/1.191251

---

[2] *East Anglian Daily Times*: December 2008, Will Clarke, http://eadt.co.uk/1.191251

What I remember most from talking to Ben about this incident, was his annoyance at being referred to as a victim. He was peeved about it as he felt he was a target of knife crime but in no way a victim. His account is as expected for a violent attack and this is how violence functions, it's not choreographed, it doesn't always go to plan and you might mess things up, a bit like life really. It's how you react when things don't go as planned which is the element to focus on developing, utilising your ability to adapt and create solutions, having a versatility when facing challenges you're able to focus on seeking out and creating positive solutions.

What Bens' story does highlight is even though there were witnesses, nobody called the police or came to help. You must learn to look after yourself and have the confidence and belief in your ability to do so, developing a life skill of self-reliance, taking responsibility and ownership of your decisions. Something which certainly is not only relevant in self-defence situations.

<u>Why do people just stand and film it?</u>

I remember a TV program showing 90% of people will walk past you if you are being attacked. The disturbing reality we have today isn't people scurrying past and ignoring the violence, but filming others being attacked and doing nothing to stop it, they could at least call the police or an ambulance before making their movie to post online. Of even more concern, younger people are viewing violent attacks as some sort of live entertainment, you can hear the laughter in the background of the videos whilst the attack is happening. The sickening sound of a foot stamping down on another person's head muffled only by the collective sound of others egging on the violence, encouraging them to do more damage.

Society has morphed into a place where humour and entertainment is found whilst witnessing another human being beaten or stabbed. The screen seems to act as a psychological distancing tool as though they aren't directly involved in what's happening, a bit like watching a violent movie or video game, but that's a whole other debate which divisively splits opinions. Society is becoming more and more desensitised and accustomed to violence, with things people should find abhorrent, now becoming the norm. This is what I find alarming, and it's happening more frequently, but not everyone is like this so it's not all doom and gloom.

For your reference

UK Government Crown Prosecution Service Source: sourced via the www.cps.gov.uk website for the UK Government Crown Prosecution Service.

Principle

This section offers guidance of general application to all offences susceptible to the defences of:
- *self-defence.*
- *defence of another.*
- *prevention of crime; and*
- *lawful arrest and apprehension of offenders.*

Self-defence and the prevention of crime originates from a number of different sources. Defence of the person is governed by the common law. Defence of property however, is governed by the Criminal Damage Act 1971. Arrest and the prevention of crime are governed by the Criminal Law Act 1967. This guidance is particularly relevant to offences against the person and homicide, and prosecutors should refer to Offences against the Person, incorporating the charging standard, elsewhere in the legal guidance and Homicide, elsewhere in the legal guidance. In the context of cases involving the use of violence, the guiding principle is the preservation of the Rule of Law and the Queen's Peace.

However, it is important to ensure that all those acting reasonably and in good faith to defend themselves, their family, their property or in the prevention of crime or the apprehension of offenders are not prosecuted for such action. The CPS have published a joint leaflet with ACPO for members of the public making clear that if householders have acted honestly and instinctively and in the heat of the moment, that this will be the strongest evidence for them having acted lawfully and in self-defence. Prosecutors should refer to joint the CPS-ACPO leaflet - Householders and the Use of Force Against Intruders.

When reviewing cases involving assertions of self-defence or action in the prevention of crime/preservation of property, prosecutors should be aware of the balance to be struck:
- *the public interest in promoting a responsible contribution on the part of citizens in preserving law and order; and*
- *in discouraging vigilantism and the use of violence generally.*

There is often a degree of sensitivity to be observed in such cases; this is particularly important when the alleged victim of an offence was himself/herself engaged in criminal activity at the relevant time. For instance, a burglar who claims to have been assaulted by the occupier of the premises concerned.

When considering cases where an argument of self-defence is raised, or is likely to be raised, you should apply the tests set out in the Code for Crown Prosecutors, refer to the Code for Crown Prosecutors elsewhere in the legal guidance.

The guidance in this section should be followed in determining whether the Code tests have been met.

When considering the sufficiency of the evidence in such cases, a prosecutor must be satisfied there is enough reliable and admissible evidence to rebut the suggestion of self-defence. The prosecution must rebut self-defence to the criminal standard of proof, see Burden of Proof below.

If there is sufficient evidence to prove the offence, and to rebut self defence, the public interest in prosecuting must then be carefully considered.

Guidance

The Law and Evidential Sufficiency
Self-defence is available as a defence to crimes committed by use of force.

*The basic principles of self-defence are set out in (*Palmer v R, [1971] AC 814*); approved in R v McInnes, 55 Cr App R 551:*
"It is both good law and good sense that a man who is attacked may defend himself. It is both good law and good sense that he may do, but only do, what is reasonably necessary".
The common law approach as expressed in Palmer v R is also relevant to the application of section 3 Criminal Law Act 1967:
"A person may use such force as is reasonable in the circumstances in the prevention of crime, or in effecting or assisting in the lawful arrest of offenders or suspected offenders or of persons unlawfully at large".
Section 3 applies to the prevention of crime and effecting, or assisting in, the lawful arrest of offenders and suspected offenders. There is an obvious overlap between self-defence and section 3. However, section 3 only applies to crime and not to civil matters. So, for instance, it cannot afford a defence in repelling trespassers by force, unless the trespassers are involved in some form of criminal conduct.

Reasonable Force
A person may use such force as is reasonable in the circumstances for the purposes of:
- *self-defence; or*
- *defence of another; or*
- *defence of property; or*
- *prevention of crime; or*
- *lawful arrest.*

In assessing the reasonableness of the force used, prosecutors should ask two questions:
- *was the use of force necessary in the circumstances, i.e. Was there a need for any force at all? and*
- *was the force used reasonable in the circumstances?*

*The courts have indicated that both questions are to answered on the basis of the facts as the accused honestly believed them to be (*R v Williams (G) 78 Cr App R 276*), (*R. v Oatbridge, 94 Cr App R 367*).*
To that extent it is a subjective test. There is, however, an objective element to the test. The jury must then go on to ask themselves whether, on the basis of the facts as the accused believed them to be, a reasonable person would regard the force used as reasonable or excessive.
*It is important to bear in mind when assessing whether the force used was reasonable the words of Lord Morris in (*Palmer v R 1971 AC 814*);*
"If there has been an attack so that self defence is reasonably necessary, it will be recognised that a person defending himself cannot weigh to a nicety the exact measure of his defensive action. If the jury thought that that in a moment of unexpected anguish a person attacked had only done what he honestly and instinctively thought necessary, that would be the most potent evidence that only reasonable defensive action had been taken ."
The fact that an act was considered necessary does not mean that the resulting action was reasonable: (R v Clegg 1995 1 AC 482 HL). Where it is alleged that a person acted to defend himself/herself from violence, the extent to which the action taken was necessary will, of course, be integral to the reasonableness of the force used.
In (R v OGrady 85 Cr App R 315), it was held by the Court of Appeal that a defendant was not entitled to rely, so far as self-defence is concerned, upon a mistake of fact which had been induced by voluntary intoxication.
Section 76 of the Criminal Justice and Immigration Act 2008

The law on self defence arises both under the common law defence of self-defence and the defences provided by section 3(1) of the Criminal Law Act 1967 (use of force in the prevention of crime or making arrest). It has recently been clarified by section 76 of the Criminal Justice and Immigration Act 2008.

Section 76 of the Criminal Justice and Immigration Act 2008 provides clarification of the operation of the existing common law and statutory defences. Section 76, section 76(9) in particular, neither abolishes the common law and statutory defences nor does it change the current test that allows the use of reasonable force.

Section 76(3) confirms the question whether the degree of force used by the defendant was reasonable in the circumstances is to be decided by reference to the circumstances as the defendant believed them to be.

Section 76(4) provides that where the defendant claims to have a particular belief as regards the existence of any circumstances, the reasonableness or otherwise of that belief is relevant to the question whether the defendant genuinely held it. However, if it is established that the defendant did genuinely hold the belief he may rely on that belief to establish the force used was reasonable whether or not it was a mistaken belief and if it was mistaken, whether or not the mistake was a reasonable one to have made, i.e. the crucial test at this stage is whether the belief was an honest one, not whether it was a reasonable one. However, the more unreasonable the belief, the less likely it is that the court will accept it was honestly held.

Subsection (5A) allows householders to use disproportionate force when defending themselves against intruders into the home. The provision came into force on 25 April 2013 and applies to cases where the alleged force was used after that date. The provision does not apply retrospectively. It provides that where the case is one involving a householder (please see the section below for further details) the degree of force used by the householder is not to be regarded as having been reasonable in the circumstances as the householder believed them to be if it was grossly disproportionate. A householder will therefore be able to use force which is disproportionate but not grossly disproportionate.

The provision does not give householders free rein to use disproportionate force in every case they are confronted by an intruder. The provision must be read in conjunction with the other elements of section 76 of the 2008 Act. The level of force used must still be reasonable in the circumstances as the householder believed them to be (section 76(3)).

In deciding whether the force might be regarded as 'disproportionate' or 'grossly disproportionate' the court will need to consider the individual facts of each case, including the personal circumstances of the householder and the threat (real or perceived) posed by the offender.

Section 76(7) sets out two considerations that should be taken into account when deciding whether the force used was reasonable. Both are adopted from existing case law. They are:

- *that a person acting for a legitimate purpose may not be able to weigh to a nicety the exact measure of any necessary action;*
- *that evidence of a person's having only done what the person honestly and instinctively thought was necessary for a legitimate purpose constitutes strong evidence that only reasonable action was taken by that person for that purpose.*

*This section adopts almost precisely the words of Lord Morris in (*Palmer v R [1971] AC 814*) which emphasise the difficulties often facing someone confronted by an intruder or defending himself against attack:*
"If there has been an attack so that defence is reasonably necessary, it will be recognised that a person defending himself cannot weigh to a nicety the exact measure of his defensive action. If the jury thought that in a moment of unexpected anguish a person attacked had only done what he honestly and instinctively thought necessary, that would be the most potent evidence that only reasonable defensive action had been taken..".

Householder Cases

The definition of a 'householder case'

The heightened protection described above is only available in 'householder cases'. Subsection (8A) of section 76 of the 2008 Act explains the meaning of a 'householder case'.

Householders are only permitted to rely on the heightened defence for householders if:

1) They are using force to defend themselves or others (See(8A)(a)). They cannot seek to rely on the defence if they were acting for another purpose, such as protecting their property, although the law on the use of reasonable force will continue to apply in these circumstances.

2) They are in or partly in a building or part of a building (e.g., a flat) that is a dwelling (i.e. a place of residence) or is forces accommodation (see (8A)(b)). For these purposes, the definition of a 'building' includes vehicles or vessels (see (8F)), so that people who live in caravans or houseboats can benefit from the heightened protection. The reference to 'forces accommodation' acknowledges the fact that military personnel may spend lengthy periods away from home in service living accommodation such as barracks. The term 'in or partly in a building' is used to protect householders who might be confronted by an intruder on the threshold of their home, climbing in through a window perhaps. But householder cannot rely on the heightened defence if the confrontation occurred wholly outside the building, for example in the garden. The Government considered that the immediacy of the threat posed by an intruder is greatest when he is entering or has entered somebody's home and the heightened defence is only available to householders in those cases (see MOJ Circular No. 2013/ 02).

3) They are not in the building as a trespasser ((8A)(c)). Squatters, for example, could not seek to rely on the heightened defence. The fact that a person has gained permission to occupy the building from another trespasser does not stop them being considered as a trespasser for these purposes (see (8E)).

4) They genuinely believed (rightly or wrongly) that the person in respect of whom they used force, was in or entering the building as a trespasser (8A)(d)).

The definition of householder contained in subsection (8B) is wide enough to cover people who live in buildings which serve a dual purpose as a place of residence and a place of work (for example, a shopkeeper and his or her family who live above the shop). In these circumstances, the 'householders' could rely on the heightened defence regardless of which part of the building they were in when they were confronted by an intruder. The only condition is that there is internal means of access between the two parts of the building. The defence would not, however, extend to customers or acquaintances of the shop keeper who were in the shop when the intruder entered, unless they were also residents in the dwelling.

Subsection (8C) makes similar provision for the armed forces whose living or sleeping accommodation may be in the same building as that in which they work and where there is internal access between the two parts. The definition of 'forces accommodation' is set out in subsection (8F).

Pre-emptive strikes

There is no rule in law to say that a person must wait to be struck first before they may defend themselves, (see R v Deana, 2 Cr App R 75).

Retreating

Failure to retreat when attacked and when it is possible and safe to do so, is not conclusive evidence that a person was not acting in self defence. It is simply a factor to be taken into account rather than as giving rise to a duty to retreat when deciding whether the degree of force was reasonable in the circumstances (section 76(6) Criminal Justice and Immigration Act 2008). It is not necessary that the defendant demonstrates by walking away that he does not want to engage in physical violence: (R v Bird 81 Cr App R 110).

Revenge
In R v Rashford [2005] EWCA Crim 3377 *it was held:*
The mere fact that a defendant went somewhere to exact revenge from the victim did not of itself rule out the possibility that in any violence that ensued, self defence was necessarily unavailable as a defence.
*However, where the defendant initially sought the confrontation (*R v Balogun [2000] 1 Archbold News 3*)*
...A man who is attacked or believes that he is about to be attacked may use such force as is both necessary and reasonable in order to defend himself. If that is what he does then he acts lawfully.
It follows that a man who starts the violence, the aggressor, cannot rely upon self-defence to render his actions lawful. Of course during a fight a man will not only strike blows, but will defend himself by warding off blows from his opponent, but if he started the fight, if he volunteered for it, such actions are not lawful, they are unlawful acts of violence.

Use of Force against Those Committing Crime
Prosecutors should exercise particular care when assessing the reasonableness of the force used in those cases in which the alleged victim was, or believed by the accused to have been, at the material time, engaged in committing a crime. A witness to violent crime with a continuing threat of violence may well be justified in using extreme force to remove a threat of further violence.
In assessing whether it was necessary to use force, prosecutors should bear in mind the period of time in which the person had to decide whether to act against another who he/she thought to be committing an offence.
The circumstances of each case will need to be considered very carefully.
See Public Interest Use of Force against Those Committing Crime, below in this chapter
In R v Martin (Anthony) [2002] 1 Cr. App. R. 27*, the Court of Appeal held that whilst a court is entitled to take account of the physical characteristics of the defendant in deciding what force was reasonable, it was not appropriate, absent exceptional circumstances which would make the evidence especially probative, to take account of whether the defendant was suffering from some psychiatric condition.*

Final Consequences
The final consequences of a course may not be relevant to the issue as to whether the force used was reasonable. Although, the conduct of the suspect resulted in severe injuries to another or even death, this conduct may well have been reasonable in the circumstances. On the other hand, the infliction of very superficial or minor injuries may have been a product of simple good fortune rather than intention.
Once force was deemed to be unreasonable, the final consequences would be relevant to the public interest considerations.

Police Powers
Police officers are empowered by Section 117, Police and Criminal Evidence Act to use reasonable force, if necessary, when exercising powers conferred by that Act (Archbold 15-26).

Private Rather than Public Duty
Prosecutors must exercise special care when reviewing cases involving those, other than police officers, who may have a duty to preserve order and prevent crime. This includes private security guards (including club doormen), public house landlords and public transport employees. The existence of duties that require people, during the course of their employment, to engage in confrontational situations from time to time needs to be considered, along with the usual principles of reasonable force.

Civilian Powers of Arrest

Care must be taken, when assessing the evidence in a case involving the purported exercising of civilian powers of arrest. Such powers of arrest are dependent upon certain preconditions.

The principal civilian powers of arrest have been substantially amended by the implementation of section 110 of Serious Organised Crime and Police Act (SOCPA) 2005. The citizen's new powers of arrest can be found in section 24A, PACE 1984.

Members of the public (other than constables) may now only arrest for "indictable" offences.

- There are 2 conditions which apply:-
  - That there are reasonable grounds to believe the arrest is necessary for a reason specified and
  - It is not reasonably practical for a constable to make the arrest
- The reasons specified are to prevent the person in question:
  - Causing physical injury to himself or any other person
  - Suffering physical injury
  - Causing loss of or damage to property
  - Making off before a constable can assume responsibility
- Any force used to affect the arrest may be an assault and unlawful; and
- Any force used to resist the arrest may be lawful (see R v Self 95 Cr. App R. 42).

However in (R v Lee, TLR 24 October 2000), it was held that when a defendant was charged with assault with intent to resist arrest, it was irrelevant whether the defendant honestly believed that the arrest was lawful. Members of the public (as well as police officers) may take action, including reasonable force, to prevent a breach of the peace, which would not necessarily involve exercising the formal powers of arrest.

Burden of Proof

The burden of proof remains with the prosecution when the issue of self-defence is raised.

The prosecution must adduce sufficient evidence to satisfy a jury beyond reasonable doubt that the defendant was either:

- not acting to defend himself/herself or another; or
- not acting to defend property; or not acting to prevent a crime or to apprehend an offender; or
- if he was so acting, the force used was excessive.

Prosecutors should take special care to recognise, and ensure a sufficiency of evidence in, those cases where self-defence is likely to be an issue.

Public Interest

Self-defence, being an absolute defence, is a matter of evidence and is not in itself a public interest consideration.

In many cases in which self-defence is raised, there will be no special public interest factors beyond those that fall to be considered in every case. However, in some cases, there will be public interest factors which arise only in cases involving self-defence or the prevention of crime.

These may include:

- Degree of excessive force: if the degree of force used is not very far beyond the threshold of what is reasonable, a prosecution may not be needed in the public interest.
- Final consequences of the action taken: where the degree of force used in self-defence or in the prevention of crime is assessed as being excessive, and results in death or serious injury, it will be only in very rare circumstances indeed that a prosecution will not be needed in the public interest. Minor or superficial injuries may be a factor weighing against prosecution.

- *The way in which force was applied:* this may be an important public interest factor, as well as being relevant to the reasonableness of the force used. If a dangerous weapon, such as firearm, was used by the accused this may tip the balance in favour of prosecution.
- *Premeditated violence:* the extent to which the accused found themselves unexpectedly confronted by a violent situation, as opposed to having planned and armed themselves in the expectation of a violent situation.

Use of Force against Those Committing Crime

The public interest factors set out in the earlier section will be especially relevant where, as a matter of undisputed fact, the victim was at the material time, involved in the commission of a separate offence.

Common examples are burglary or theft from motor vehicles. In such cases, prosecutors should ensure that all the surrounding circumstances are taken into consideration in determining whether a prosecution is in the public interest.

- Prosecutors should have particular regard to: nature of the offence being committed by the victim;
- degree of excessiveness of the force used by the accused;
- extent of the injuries, and the loss or damage, sustained by either or both parties to the incident;
- whether the accused was making an honest albeit over zealous attempt to uphold the law rather than taking the law into his/her own hands for the purposes of revenge or retribution.

Apprehension of Offenders

There are two important but sometimes contrasting public interest points regarding the apprehension of offenders. On the one hand, the rule of law and the Queen's Peace must be maintained and violence discouraged. On the other hand, the involvement of citizens in the prevention and investigation of crime is to be encouraged where it is responsible and public spirited. The law provides a defence for those who act in extenuating circumstances. However, judicial comment has suggested that the courts should take a firm stand against illegitimate summary justice and vigilantism.

Prosecutors will need to balance these potentially conflicting public interest considerations very carefully.

Procedure

Once a case has been identified by the police as one involving difficult issues of self-defence, the police should be encouraged to seek pre-charge advice from the CPS.

Within the CPS, if it is felt that the case involves difficult issues of self-defence, the prevention of crime or the apprehension of offenders, and is likely to attract media attention, a report must be sent through line management to the CCP or DCCP for the relevant Area..

Where the case may be media sensitive, the Area Communications Manager should be informed. The Area Communications Manager should consider informing HQ press office.

READY

The Mechanics of the Mind & Stress

- The Butterflies & The Scaredy Cat.
- The 'Grey Matter' & The Stress Response.
- Fight or Flight.
- The Feedback Loop –Stimulus to Response via Fight, Flight, or the pesky Freeze!

RBM presents information without any restricting allegiance to an 'art' and without any ego involved, because if a self-defence method is to have any worth, it needs core principles and solid information which positively adjust your thought processes for the better. The information must be reliable, and comprehensive in detail when concerning knowledge of psychological and physiological responses to stress, because not having an understanding of what happens to your mind when under the threat of attack can leave you vulnerable and exposed to violence. It's important to shore up this weakness, and for this reason self-defence information must be practical and not just designed to blow smoke up your pipe hole, false confidence is dangerous, it could encourage you to engage in a confrontation you aren't equipped for.

Phase 1 contains the largest proportion of written information, explaining how the brain functions in both conflict and non-conflict triggered stressful situations. Exploring how your stress response works and proceeding to emphasise if you fail to change your mindset towards a more positive and solution seeking operating system, the consequences can be dire. Because if your mindset is skewed, you won't move off the spot when under physical threat, *no matter how skilled in self-defence you are, or how well you can perform the drills in a class.* Away from the topic of being attacked, not understanding the stress response will have negative impacts on your decision making in life, because being unaware of the cause and effects of stress makes it difficult to select the right decisions when under pressure. In these situations, you will remain frozen with a sense of being directionless and feeling mentally adrift, which is something most people can relate to.

Telling people how to kick an aggressor in the groin is easy, anyone can do that, but being able to do this simple kick when afraid for your life is a very different story. Which is why providing an understanding of how your mind functions when under threat is far more specialised, and ranks higher on the list of priorities than any physical movements.

In addition, there's the task of extracting the new, positive mindset gained through the *RBM* techniques and implementing it into your daily life. Sparking a positive improvement in your health and your life in general to maximise the positive change.

The Butterflies & the Scaredy Cat

I believe everyone at some point has found themselves in a situation where they've felt riddled with anxiety, and frozen with fear and worry. Perhaps it was the threat of violence and physical harm, or maybe having to speak in front of a large group of people. I'm sure you can relate to this, your heart starts racing and pounding in your chest, sweat beginning to leak from every pore, and you start breathing as though you've run a marathon in clogs. Your body starts trembling and shaking whilst standing on the spot, then comes the nauseating feeling not too dissimilar to being thrown around on a rollercoaster and the feeling of butterflies in your stomach kicks you in the gut like a cramp. Then you look for water, because your mouth is so dry you can't get your words out.

These physical reactions to stress if left unchecked and combined with an anxious mindset, will escalate to levels far exceeding what you require to be able to function effectively in a stressful situation. Quickly reaching detrimental levels, causing you to behave like a chimp on hippy crack, this is your stress response spiralling out of control.

The physical sensations synonymous with feeling scared and anxious are the symptoms of your natural responses to worrying situations, but at the right time, the right place, and to the correct levels, they are in fact a most valuable, functional tool. Negative issues only arise when the response levels exceed what's appropriate in relation to the stressor, as excessive levels can cause you to freeze when an immediate threat is about to physically harm you, like the person being attacked with a baseball bat who stands still and gets hit for a home run. Or another example is an excessive response to a situation, such as having anxiety about standing in front of an audience to speak, or maybe worrying about traveling to a new place. Many people are adept at keeping these feelings and responses to minimum levels, but for others, life feels as though there is a constant sound of an air raid siren in their head, with anxiety levels elevated so highly they find themselves set to a constant state of being on edge, or false alert.

An explanation of why your body responses and functions change under stress will positively and profoundly change how you feel about these sensations, and recognising them for their true purpose and functionality helps prevent you from perceiving them as negative. The heart will beat faster, and your breathing will become shallow and rapid, providing more oxygenated blood to the muscles to either escape or club something. Whilst the heart is beating faster and harder the coronary arteries will start to narrow, and this process is called vasoconstriction. The activation of vasoconstriction is to speed up the transmission of oxygenated blood and provide a safety net by minimising the chance of you bleeding to death if cut or bitten, because it helps stem the flow of blood from any wound. *(It's not uncommon for a person to survive being attacked with a knife but be unaware in the immediate aftermath they have been stabbed, due to the endorphin release acting as painkillers and vasoconstriction restricting blood loss.)* If the stress level is high enough you may get rid of any unnecessary cargo, possibly voiding your bladder and bowels to become lighter on your feet to quickly run away from a threat, or to catch what you want to hit. Plus, you'll make yourself smell pretty stinky to a mugger when you drop all of that in your pants. Without the medical advancements we have made in terms of IVF, all species needed to be able to reproduce to survive and so under attack, any testicles present in the conflict will withdraw up into the body for protection as an evolutionary reaction, highlighting why kicking to the nuts without proper commitment doesn't achieve the desired result.

The butterflies in the stomach are caused by blood rushing from non-essential organs, combined with the feeling of hormones being released in the body. Digesting food or eating isn't a priority when in a threatening situation, so saliva production stops and you will notice you have a dry mouth, making it easier for you to sink your teeth into the thing which is attacking you, but it's important to note at this point I wouldn't advise you to bite an attacker unless absolutely necessary, because you don't know of any infectious diseases they may have. Your blood is being moved, pumped to the arms and legs ready to spring into action and if this fuel preparing the muscles isn't being used to run away or bash something, then the body will begin to tremble and shake, so ensure you use this power early by doing something to burn it off.

Starting to sweat stops the system from overheating and gives the benefit of making you very slippery and hard to grab. Your pupils will dilate, letting in more light and increasing your peripheral vision, enhancing the type of vision needed in a conflict and for spotting an escape route. The hairs on the back of your neck will stand up and you will get goose bumps, which heightens awareness of air movement around you thereby elevating your sensitivity to attacks. Your brain's neurotransmitter activity will increase to enhance alertness through hearing, vision, and other senses, *but under extreme stress these will be dampened and become less efficient.* You will produce natural painkillers, chemicals called Endogenous Opioids or Endorphins, working with the brain's receptors to lessen, or completely shut out the recognition of pain, which is why you can't bop someone on the nose and expect them to stop, because it may not hurt.

When deployed in the right way, the stress response gives you everything you need physically to perform to your maximum efficiency in life-or-death situations. The ability to run faster, react faster and hit harder are fantastically enhanced attributes made available to you in a fraction of a second. Yet people have been led to believe the bodily changes/sensations which go hand in hand with these abilities aren't a good thing. Viewing these sensations and physical changes as a weakness, seeing themselves as a coward when experiencing any of these. It's a false belief, and changing your view on this is of upmost importance to your life. *I can't emphasise this enough!*

The bodily sensations and reactions to stress are your Limbic System and Brain Stem stepping up to the plate and winning Olympic gold in survival response performance. I believe if teachers and coaches would educate youngsters on this it would make a massive difference to many people's lives. Think of a child who is about to speak to their peers at a school assembly or compete at a sports day or swimming gala trembling with nerves. If a teacher/coach, asked who felt nervous and then proceeded to explain to those experiencing these sensations why they have them, and the reasons behind these feelings, it would be invaluable to them. Not only for that occasion, but for their whole lives, it would result in children being aware that when feeling nervous they were primed to perform at their best. Knowing this, and feeling and acknowledging the inner strength they have, whilst learning to direct this energy at a young age would be incredibly positive and I think life changing. Helping them to grow and speak with confidence and passion in front of people, run faster in competitions, swim harder, and throw further, instead of letting them carry on in life without knowing why these bodily changes happen when scared or nervous and crippling them with a sense of weakness, vulnerability, and inadequacy, which leads to further anxiety. Changing the understanding and stigma around these feelings would change everything.

Imagine if you could re-live your life without the negative thoughts, emotions and feelings of weakness and vulnerability associated with having butterflies. Imagine not feeling inferior or incapable when you felt your heart race with nervousness. Think how much easier it would have been if you could have valued the physiological changes of your stress response for what they truly are, the body's equivalent of a V8 engine roaring and ready to go, preparing you to perform at your best. This knowledge would have helped restrict irrational fear in your life, and limited the destructive seed of self-doubt and the negative physical and mental health implications it brings.

The great news is you're alive, which means it's not too late. You can work on changing your view about these body responses, reminding yourself when you feel nervous you aren't weak and feeble and in fact, when you feel the shaking etc. you actually have too much power, power which is unused at that moment because you haven't run or hit anything. You don't need more strength or more courage, you need to learn to use the fuel you already have, or to mentally take your foot off the accelerator and prevent flooding the system, this will be explained in more detail as you proceed.

In situations where drastic psychological and physiological responses aren't needed, basically when you aren't being attacked, knowledge of the stress response and confidence in yourself are key to improving your health by managing stress and lowering anxiety levels. Knowing why these physiological responses happen will change your whole perception of them, and adjusting how you view yourself and the situation you find yourself in will have a positive influence, because this alone helps to reduce any anxiety spiralling out of control. The confidence gained from learning how to protect yourself from a physical assault spreads through your life, weaving a self-assured web of calmness into all situations. You may feel a little nervous sometimes, but that's not the same as anxiety.

The 'Grey Matter' & The Stress Response

This section will explain the *'Brain Team'*, taking you through a brief description of how the relevant components of the mind work, and giving a solid knowledge base from which to move forward with an understanding of how this 'team' function and interact together. Hopefully in a way which is as straight forward as possible, whilst still aiming to comprehensively cover the whole mechanics of how you function in response to a threat, and what happens when placed under mental stress.

Initially the information reflects how the brain team functions in a hostile threat environment, because it makes the brain feedback process more tangible when described in a threat situation. Without relating the stress response to a physical threat, it becomes too abstract and difficult to explain, but even if you have no interest in the realistic self-defence facet of *RBM* and are solely focused on the stress management benefits, please persevere as this section will also paint the picture of what happens when faced with everyday stressors. The reactions are on a subtler scale when told you are being made redundant than when having a knife thrust at you obviously, but it's essentially the same response mechanism for you to learn about, and helping you become familiar with the signs of this system being activated as early on in the process as possible. There's a lot of information here about a complex topic because a brief bit of blurb won't cut it, this section must be in depth so by the end of Phase 1 you know the *RBM* Solution Loop is a good thing, and the misplaced focus of the Analytical 'Doom Spiral' Loop, as the name suggests, isn't beneficial to you.

It's over twenty-five years since I started delving into the world of the human mind, learning about the psychology of violence and the implications on those involved in a violent event. At the beginning, I was taught the *Triune Brain Model Theory developed by Paul D. MacLean*[3], and a lot of people in the martial arts and self-defence world use this model as it outlines a simple brain explanation. The concept suggests we have three separate parts to the brain, operating independently of each other. The theory is one part of the brain is a thinking section, which is the newest bit called the Neo-mammalian complex, the second part is the Paleo-mammalian complex, described as the primitive emotional center, and finally, the Reptilian Complex where fight or flight and survival is located. This theory is still used today in self-defence books and can also be found in corporate training courses where management strategists attempt to show an understanding of brain functionality. I can see where this triune theory came from as the brain in a physical and structural sense does seem to have three parts, but in terms of its operation this is not the case.

Western science has moved on since this theory was developed, and the general understanding of the functionality of the brain has expanded since I first embarked on my quest to learn about what happens in our minds when under attack. I started to research further, taking into considering the information we have available to us now and how this applies to self-defence and stress. It's taken a lot of time, effort, plus plenty of head scratching whilst working out what the hell the neuroscientists were saying, but eventually I arrived at the stage where I'm confident in my ability to explain the thought feedback loop in the brain and the stress response in detail, and importantly, in a way I haven't seen before when relating to self-defence and anxiety. This is a comprehensive, relevant, accurate and in great depth description of the stress/fight or flight response in relation to self-defence and anxiety. It needs to be if it's going to motivate and inspire you to make changes in your life, or convince you to put your trust in this when fighting for your life. So here goes with the grey matter!

---

[3]

Paul D. MacLean 1990: *The Triune Brain in Evolution: Role in Paleocerebral Functions*

> *"The human brain has 100 billion neurons, each neuron connected to 10 thousand other neurons. Sitting on your shoulders is the most complicated object in the known universe".*
>
> Michio Kaku[4]

As a species we have achieved so many wonderful accomplishments, with the best parts of humanity warming you to your core. However, there's a flip side, the things which would take you to the darkest abyss via the route of unfathomable actions. Humans have the potential to be both fantastically creative, yet on another level also incredibly creatively destructive. If you were to read *Atrocitology: Humanity's 100 Deadliest Achievements* written by Matthew White[5], as the title suggests, you would get the picture. How these contrasts can exist within one person, let alone in a society isn't relevant when a person is punching you in the face, however it's a good idea to be informed on how the mind of the person wanting to hurt you functions before you find yourself in a violent situation. Think of this section as a fact-file team sheet, learning about the main brain players, discovering the roles and tactics of the team and how they interact, because having a reconnaissance mission and getting to know your allies and your enemies, both internal and external prior to any trouble is highly advantageous and recommended.

Remove a human brain from its organic crash helmet, which we call the skull, and you would be staring at the most sophisticated system on the planet. The bits you would initially be able to see belong to what is called the *Cerebral Cortex*. Also known as; the Neocortex, the Neopallium, the Isocortex and the Cerebrum. Already it's getting complicated as there are lots of different names for the same bits.

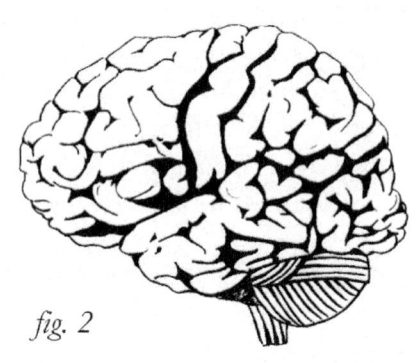

fig. 2

This recognisable grey matter is a thin layer found in all mammals, but it's not present in birds or lizards and it's the essential part of our separation from those species. It's the most recent brain addition in our evolution, hence why it is often referred to as the neo (new) - cortex. I think it resembles a pile of slugs, and the reason for these shapes is the deep grooves (sulci) and wrinkles (gyri) are needed to increase the surface area of the Cerebral Cortex, providing a space saving function. Enabling more brain to fit within the shape and the available

---

[4] Michio Kaku 2015: *The Future of the Mind: The Scientific Quest to Understand, Enhance and Empower the Mind*

[5] Matthew White, 2011: *Atrocitology: Humanity's 100 Deadliest Achievements*

space of the skull than if the surface of the brain was flat. More surface area equals more neuron space giving more bang for bucks in the processing department. These grooves and wrinkles form the most recognisable subsections of the brain, which we know as the two hemispheres.

The Two Hemispheres 'The Think Tank'
The Cerebral Cortex is split lengthways into two sections by the visible valley called the Longitudinal Fissure, creating the two hemispheres. This 'Think Tank' has two players, the Left Hemisphere, and the Right Hemisphere, as seen in *fig 3*. Both are connected by a thick cable of nerve tissue called the Corpus Callosum, enabling both halves to function as one whole unit. The hemispheres are involved in human thought process and activity.

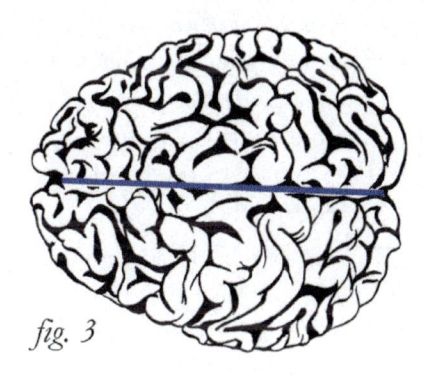

fig. 3

The Left and Right Hemispheres have a connection by way of the Corpus Callosum, (indicated on fig 3 in blue), allowing the integration of sensory input and functional responses from both sides of the body. The link between the hemispheres allows collaborative operations, but there are some jobs which are allocated specifically to one hemisphere or the other. The Left Hemisphere is responsible for controlling the right-hand side of the body, and the Right Hemisphere is responsible for controlling the left-hand side. Speech and language are located solely in the Left Hemisphere, along with logical thinking, analysis, and mathematical logic.

The Right Hemisphere is on duty for spatial recognition, face recognition, sense perception and creative artistic functions. Spatial awareness is the ability of a person to recognise themselves, their actions, and the effect these actions have on the picture of the world they are viewing, including the external factors of other people and objects. For example, when walking towards an object you will process the factors of direction, distance, and location, developing the relationship between the changes you are making and any changes in the external environment. It's a GPS system and a vicinity mapping feature, with radar thrown in for good measure. Spatial recognition has the very handy ability to fill in the gaps, completing segments of missing information by constructing a likely model of what will occur from the available information being processed. This neurological version of a predictive text feature is called *Coincidental Correspondence,* and is useful if a person is running at you primed and ready to hit you in the face with a bat, with you being able to estimate the flight path of the weapon based on information gained from seeing the early stages of the bat moving. You will be able to predict the arrival time of the bat at the destination of your face, which gives you the time needed to duck, rather than having to wait and see what happens and getting bashed in the face.

Facial marker recognition is another useful brain feature and in the section *Signs it's time to dive for cover*, you will learn about the non-verbal cues which take place, including facial changes, warning you of an impending attack.

Exploring further into the Cerebral Cortex you find the two initial structures of the Hemispheres become four areas called lobes, as shown in figure 4. The Frontal, Parietal, Temporal, and Occipital lobes, all performing different tasks which are your *higher functions*.

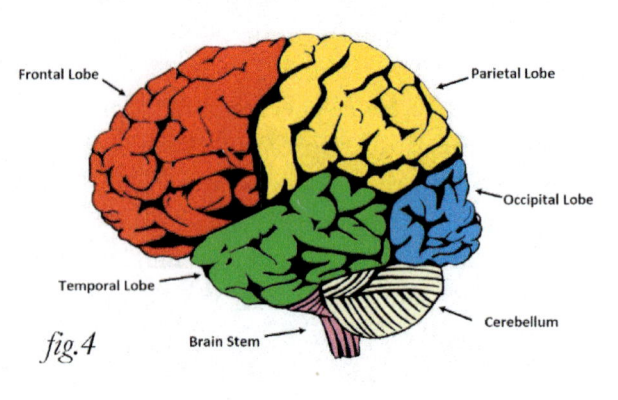

fig.4

The Frontal Lobe

> *"The frontal lobe makes up 50 percent of the volume of each cerebral hemisphere in humans. It initiates all motor activity, including speech; its most anterior divisions, the prefrontal lobes and supplementary motor cortex, integrate personality with emotion and transform thought into action".*
>
> Richard M. Restak [6]

Situated at the front of the brain, you find the pre-frontal lobe, at the forehead end of operations and spanning across both hemispheres. It's a biggie in terms of self-defence relevance, as it encapsulates most of the Dopamine Neurons in the Cerebral Cortex, which are needed for positive programming when learning new things. This lobe is also a major player involved in prioritising and planning. Utilising the spatial awareness ability in the Right Hemisphere, the Frontal Lobe will predict future events based on the current information available. The decisions you make in response to what the senses pick up in your vicinity will be heavily influenced by the social constructs you hold.

What I mean by this is throughout your life, your social interactions and experiences will have shaped your current belief system, which come into play when making decisions. This is relevant because your beliefs and personal

---

[6] Richard M. Restak, in *Brainscapes: An Introduction to What Neuroscience Has Learned about the Structure, Function, and Abilities of the Brain* (1995)

interpretation of what's right and wrong will influence the choices your brain will offer as viable responses if faced with a threat. *RBM* identifies how some of these conditioned belief structures can be a hindrance to your survival and may also negatively influence how you deal with stress. Explaining why it's important to update the information and the values which you hold, and dismantle the beliefs which keep you in harm's way, something often overlooked in self-defence systems. An example of one of these hurdles to overcome would be *'it's wrong to hit someone'*. You would be amazed at how many people have been attacked and didn't fight back because they had this rule drummed into them as a child, and as an adult even when they are in danger, they felt it was wrong to hurt another person.

Beliefs like these, which are correct outside of a life and death scenario, can render you powerless in the face of a serious threat, adding to the stress response levels of the situation. The potential knock-on effect is an increased stress response, one which has the potential to cause you to blow a fuse and override *all* your social beliefs. When this happens, you start to operate like a mad hatter and this is where the red mist comes in.

In his book *Base Instincts: What Makes Killers Kill?* Jonathan H. Pincus[7] researches the relationship between killers and their Frontal Lobe functionality. To summarise, and whilst trying not to do his work a disservice by attempting to put it in a nutshell, he presents the point that people with damage to the Frontal Lobe are able to kill because the social constructs which our present-day society holds to be right and wrong either don't register or are simply overridden. The acceptable behavioural constructs most of the population have in place to stop us from annihilating each other and wiping out our species within a week, exists in the Frontal Lobe, but if the lobe is malfunctioning, you're presented with a person without a 'brake'. No remorse, no conformity to the socially accepted values of what's right and wrong, presenting an Antisocial Personality Disorder, a person with no empathy.

How does this area of the brain come to malfunction? Some people are born with a glitch in the system, others suffer damage through abuse or injuries, an example of this is being shaken as a baby, an abusive parent can create a potential killer by damaging the prefrontal lobe and immersing a child into an environment void of love and care. Also, a factor called *desensitisation*, whereby through negative social conditioning, the function of the frontal lobe can be dampened, and the 'brake' system weakened. An example of this is children being recruited into child armies and being forced to execute family members including their younger siblings, with the sole intent of turning them into war

---

[7] Jonathan H. Pincus: *Base Instincts: What Makes Killers Kill?*

machines through over exposure to extreme emotionally disturbing violence. The control of the frontal lobe can also be weakened in a moment of extreme stress, resulting in the stress response spiralling out of control as previously mentioned, and can also happen through drug and alcohol use.

The Frontal Lobe plays a role in holding long term emotional based memories, which are heavily linked to the limbic system. This process of creating new memories can be manipulated to increase the efficiency of learning through a method of programming called Operant Conditioning, covered in depth in further chapters.

The *Parietal Lobe* is located at the top and towards the rear of the brain, it's involved in attention and motor control, processing spatial location and in perceiving pain, touch, and temperature. The sensory association cortex is located in this lobe.

The Occipital Lobe, located at the back of the brain is responsible for processing visual information such as colour, shape and motion with the visual cortex & visual association cortex also found in this lobe.

The *Temporal Lobe* is located just above the ears, and is involved in hearing and language processing, the auditory cortex, auditory association cortex, and part of the visual association cortex are found in this lobe.

Moving on to a different section of the brain we have The Limbic System, shown in Fig 5, and *is the hub for memories, emotions, and hormones.* Peeling away the recognisable slug like grey Cerebral Cortex, you would see the Limbic System. Found underneath the two Cerebral Hemispheres and above the Brainstem, it connects the parts of the brain responsible for high and low functions, bridging the gap between the thinking part of the brain and the automatic body functions controlled in the Hypothalamus, and linking the Spinal Cord and the Central Nervous System. It's the cog holding it all together. The Limbic section of the brain is composed of several parts to explore, first up is the almond shaped, captain of the survival stress team, the 'Amygdala'.

fig. 5

Septum

Hypothalamus

Amygdala

Hippocampus

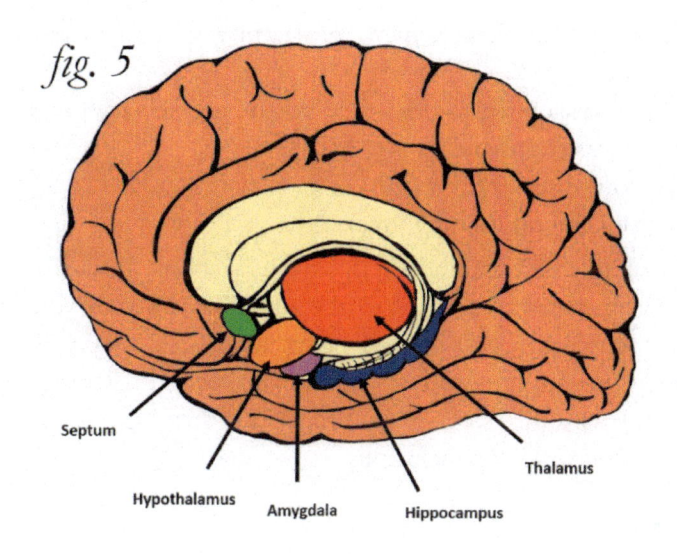

Thalamus

<u>The Amygdala 'Captain Amygdala - Operations Manager'</u>
The Amygdala are a collection of nerve cell clusters, forming two almond-shapes in the Temporal Lobe of the Cerebrum. Both clusters have a role in preparing the body for responses to emergency situations, working in conjunction with the Hippocampus in the storing and accessing of memories. Memories to be filed and used as a data bank for future use, and it's these files which are the resource used in the formulation of decision making. The Amygdala is vital for our survival by helping distinguish between one object to another, and as much as possible, preventing us from behaving totally irrationally. Without a correctly functioning Amygdala, you may find yourself eating this book rather than reading it.

The Amygdala can act as a 'thinking bypass'. *Let me repeat that part again as it's incredibly important; it can act as a 'thinking bypass'.* The Left Hemisphere is analytical and logical in its processing, but when your life is under threat the Amygdala can override this Left Hemisphere, instead triggering immediate automatic reactions to keep you safe. In a dangerous or stressful situation, the sensory stimuli (a trigger) will reach the Amygdala's basolateral complexes, immediately forming associations with memories linked to the stress stimuli (the trigger). As a response to this trigger, you will choose the strongest memory which has the closest fit to the situation.

Without a strongly associated memory (learnt response) as an option for a solution you would:
- either do what you did the last time this trigger occurred regardless of whether it was successful or not
- do what you've seen others do
- or stand still and do nothing, freeze!

The threat of an attack can induce this freeze response because you may not have any viable memories to apply to the situation you find yourself in. I've observed that people's biggest fear of being attacked is they will freeze, they never mention getting hurt, it's always about freezing. You may now be becoming aware why this section of information has high relevance to self-defence and is necessary in its inclusion.

<u>The Hippocampus 'Internal Hard Drive'</u>
This is all about the memory banks, the Hippocampus is important for converting data from short-term memory into long-term memory. First, the senses will build a picture using the information gathered from what's around you at any one time, this is the formulation of a memory base construct. Focus on the base construct now takes place with information passing back and forth between the Frontal Lobe and the Thalamus, with the Hippocampus transforming the information into a readable format and preparing this data to be stored in a file location, ready to be available the next time you try to access it. If you think about something often enough, or for long enough, the neural activity makes the construct/memory stronger by burning a deeper memory track, which is why repetition is used as a successful method when learning new things. When an emotional charge is added to a situation, such as trauma or fear, the Amygdala becomes more involved in the process. The extra input of an emotional link causes a stronger construct/memory to form and to form faster. Sadly, for a lot of people out there both young and old, in abusive home environments, war zones and other horrendous situations, trauma is a fast way to build a highly charged neural pathway, creating a hardened memory. The very use of the word trauma indicates these memories are not the ones you would want to hold onto.

Under stress, people will revert to type and repeat old patterns, using old information stored in the memory banks to solve problems. Negative outcomes from past confrontations will hamper a person's ability to defend themselves later in life. What's stored in your memory bank will come into play under stress/threat, so it's a very good idea to have new positive memories, solution-based memories, loaded in there to use as a response option in case you are ever under threat.

The Brain Stem, as seen in Fig 6, is the most primitive part of the brain and consists of the Medulla, the Pons, the Cerebellum, the Midbrain, the Hypothalamus, and the Thalamus. The Brain Stem sits above the spinal cord and is the house of the fight or flight activation system.

fig. 6

Medulla Oblongata - 'Quick, move'
Contrary to how it sounds, the Medulla Oblongata isn't a song from the movie The Lion King, but instead, an influential part of the brain located in the lower portion of the Brain Stem. Responsible for overseeing the roles of monitoring your heart rate and blood pressure and in charge of the reflexes in the body such as the flinch/startle response. There are twelve pairs of Cranial nerves weaving and webbing throughout the brain relating to brain function. Of these twelve, there are four cranial nerves whose nuclei are found in the Medulla Oblongata, one of which is of special interest to you and is called the Pneumogastric Nerve, otherwise known as the Vagus nerve. Starting in the Brain Stem and reaching the body through holes in the skull called Cranial Foramina, the Pneumogastric Nerve is one of the places to consider striking a person to stop them from being able to harm you. This will be explained in more detail in a later chapter.

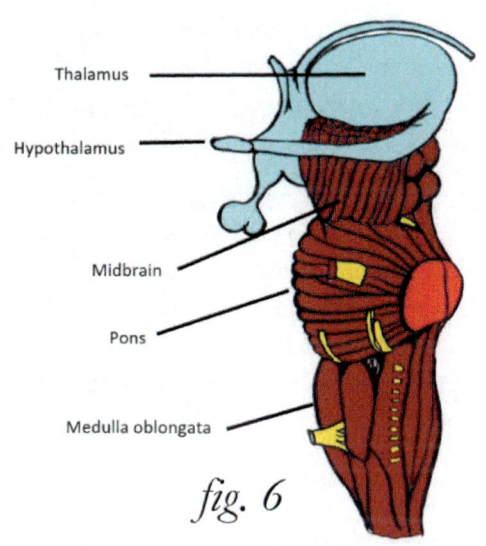

Pons 'Anxiety Alert - Panic Button Pusher'
The white matter which shapes the Pons contains nuclei, spending their time pinging signals from the Cerebral Cortex *(Big Brain)* to the Cerebellum *(Little Brain)*, along with using nuclei to deal with the autonomic actions of sleep, respiration, swallowing, hearing, facial expressions, facial sensation, eye movement, bladder control, and posture. Also conducting signals to the Medulla and carrying the sensory signals to the Thalamus.

Found within the pons is the *Nucleus Locus Coeruleus*, whilst being a great name for a gladiator, it's a key section of brain for the physiological response to stress, being the main area for brain synthesis of Norepinephrine, the hormone more commonly known as Noradrenaline. Epinephrine is known to pretty much everyone as Adrenaline, so these are the names I shall use to refer to these hormones throughout the rest of the text; Norepinephrine = Noradrenaline, Epinephrine = Adrenaline. Noradrenaline is produced mainly in the Adrenals, but a small amount is made in the brain for a quick evasive action. The Pons also regulate the change from inhalation to exhalation, something which will hold a larger significance to you as you read further.

Cerebellum - 'The Balancer'

The Cerebellum is the second largest part of the brain, and whilst it doesn't act as the ignition switch for movement it helps by sourcing information from the CNS and the sensory parts of the brain to regulate your movements. Ensuring good coordination, accurate timing, and balance. Without the Cerebellum, you wouldn't be able to get out of bed in the morning without face planting the carpet.

Midbrain 'Information Runner'

The Midbrain is your fibre-optic speed connection between the big brain and the little brain and works closely with the Pons. It's a back-and-forth information super-highway, working as a conduit between the Cerebral Cortex to initiate movements and the Cerebellum, with fine tuning movements for efficiency. The Midbrain has three main areas:

- *Cerebral Peduncle*, which sends motor skill information down the Brain Stem into the CNS to order movement.
- *The Corpora Quadrigemina* is the second area of the midbrain, it's the correlation and refinery information centre.
- The third is the *Cerebral Aqueduct*, a connective channel with fluid within it called Cerebrospinal Fluid (CSF), a clear liquid, cushioning the brain within the skull and serving as a shock absorber for the Central Nervous System.

The following two sections of the brain, the Hypothalamus, and the Thalamus, are so closely intertwined with the Limbic System they could have been included there as well as in this section relating to the Brainstem.

The Hypothalamus - 'The Dope Man'

The Hypothalamus is located beneath the Thalamus and is part of both the Limbic System and the Brain Stem, operating as a connecting center between the two sections. Monitoring pleasurable activities such as eating, drinking, sex, and influencing the Endocrine System *(the collective name for all the glands which produce hormones)*, the Hypothalamus has a busy workload, because on top of this it also controls the CNS. The Hypothalamus sends instructions to the body via the autonomic nervous system, giving the Hypothalamus total control of blood pressure, heart rate, breathing, digestion, sweating and the Sympathetic and Parasympathetic functions, which will be explained in more detail later in the text. This total control means it has the responsibility of regulating these systems in emotionally charged circumstances, like when scared about the axe whizzing towards your face.

The Hypothalamus has a sidekick called the Pituitary Gland, together they oversee the chemical release in the body, ordering the secretion of hormones in response to different emotions, stressors, and rewarding feelings, these hormones are essentially internal drugs. The Hypothalamus asks for a hit, and the pituitary gland along with the other glands, pump hormones into the bloodstream.

Anything with the job of controlling the glands of the Endocrine System and the release of chemicals in the body is a big, big player in a fight or flight threat situation responses, and in the responses you have to life's daily worries and anxieties. The Hypothalamus is an integral part of the brain when used for the reward-based training called Operant Conditioning, which is the hardwiring of new information into the subconscious.

<u>The Thalamus - 'Message Decoder'</u>
Found within the Brainstem, a high percentage of sensory input to the Cerebral Cortex goes via the Thalamus. It acts as a form of decoder, detecting and relaying information from your senses, and formatting these signals into a data file which has been prepared ready for the Cerebral Cortex, and ensuring it gets delivered to the right address.

* * *

That's the Brain Team, what they do and how they do it. The next section is quite complex, and the information will likely challenge the current teachings of many, if not all self-defence systems/personal development theories/meditation practices/and self-help courses and books. The data will continue to relate to the perspective of a person responding to the threat of a physical attack, staying with the consistent means of explaining the information. Following this, giving information on how the fight or flight mechanism, if overactive in its use, will have a very detrimental effect on your everyday health and how to limit, prevent and remedy this.

Fight or Flight

> *"We need defenses only when change happens in our lives faster than we can accommodate it"*
>
> *Vaillant, GE (1992)* [8]

The flight or fight response, also called the Acute Stress Response, was identified by Dr. Walter B. Cannon in 1915 whilst at Harvard University developing the theory on how animals responded to danger, with this theory later extending to human responses to threats. The study found when under threat and exposed to the stress of potential injury, humans will call forward the big guns to save themselves, which is the deployment of their inbuilt stress response survival tool called the Fight, Flight, Freeze response. (*There is another part called the Posture or Submit response, which will be covered later, but it's not immediately relevant here*).

A self-defence method will have the best chances of success if it fully explains what's happens to you during an attack, both psychologically and physiologically. It must ensure that as a safety method, its principles of application, the movements, and strategies are based solely around the factors of how you behave when your fight, flight, freeze response kicks in. This requires sound knowledge of your fight or flight system, and it begins with being able to distinguish between the two operating facets of this defence mechanism. You might be questioning the mention of *'two'*, but you do have two fight or flight systems which work together, a short-term fight or flight response, and a long-term fight or flight response.

<u>Short Term Fight or Flight</u>

If you are completely unaware of any threats and oblivious to any potential danger, then thankfully you aren't left entirely vulnerable and at the mercy of the violent and criminal element in the world around you, because there is a whole safety process taking place away from your conscious level of awareness. Happening within your subconscious mind and always monitoring your environment, is a system keeping watch for signs of danger. The watcher is the Pons, and at its disposal is the short-term fight or flight safety system called the Sympathetic Adrenal Medullary Axis, or SAM Axis for short, and it's continually running in the background and monitoring your environment like a radar, searching for any anomalies which may result in potential damage to you.

---

[8] Vaillant, GE (1992), *Ego Mechanisms of Defense: A Guide for Clinicians and Researchers*, Washington, DC, American Psychiatric Press

It helps to visualise the senses as a group of sentries; eyes, ears, nose, skin and to a lesser extent taste, all performing constant perimeter checks, keeping guard, and reporting back to the Thalamus. The Thalamus has the role of the officer in charge, decoding the messages the sentries are sending. Any potential threats are assessed and passed from the Thalamus up the chain of command to the chief anxiety monitor, which are the Pons.

Throughout your average day whilst you are relaxed, these sentries pick up on pings of minor interest which may need closer inspection. The Pons are receiving feedback from the sentries via the Thalamus decoder and will dismiss anything which is a deemed a false alarm. If there's nothing of note, or worthy of an alert, the Pons are relaxed. This processing of external data while you are in a quiet state of mind, with minimal stressors or potential dangers being identified, causes minimal activation of the neurons inside the area known as the *Locus Ceruleus Nucleus* of the Pons, residing in the Brain Stem. This stimulation will be at a minimum due to only a very low-level of potential danger, or no danger being identified.

This all changes in a fraction of a second if subconsciously one of your sentries picks up on a potential threat-level trigger, and this is where the SAM AXIS activation happens. This activation starts with a potential threat stimulus being identified by one of the senses, and the information being immediately processed in the relevant lobe. The Occipital Lobe for sight, the Temporal Lobe for sound, taste and smell, or the Parietal Lobe for the sense of touch.

This data moves through the sensory lobes into the Thalamus, the decoder, and from the Thalamus, the decrypted *potential threat* message is passed to the Pons in the Brain Stem. The Pons, *having a rather cautious characteristic with a tendency to swim in a pool of worry and err on the side of caution*, will spring into action if even a hint of a threat is registered. On sensing a threat, the Pons begins to sound the anxiety alarm, sending out warning flares. It's time to be alert, all hands to battle stations and this state of emergency orders the Spinal Cord to immediately initiate an evasive action protocol to avoid any incoming danger, with the objective of putting distance between you and any potential threat. An action which is completed without the need of conscious input from you. This *'get the hell out of there'* evasive movement is a subconsciously derived emergency evasion action called a Spinal Reflex, or a Polysynaptic Reflex, or a Withdrawal Reflex, but more commonly known as a Flinch Response. We also know it as jumping out of your skin with fright.

To perform this immediate physical recoil response, you need fuel to power the escape from the thing which made you jump, leading the Pons to send a signal ordering the Adrenal Medulla, (found in the brain), to release a synthesis of Noradrenaline. The Adrenals are usually responsible for meeting the demands of the production of Noradrenaline, but this contingency plan of a syringe of emergency rocket fuel in the brain to immediately power a leap away from the threat stimulus is evolutionary genius. The Adrenal Medulla has the laboratory required to produce an emergency source of the hormone, because in an extreme threat situation you cannot depend on one supplier delivering the fuel on time, every time. It's here the short-term fight or flight system gets its name because the emergency syringe for the shot of Noradrenaline is produced in the Sympathetic Adrenal Medullary, SAM for short, hence the name SAM Axis.

The SAM Axis evolved for situations where you're caught completely by surprise, by either a potential danger in close proximity to you, or a potential threat for damage such as an unidentified loud noise in the distance. Anything evaluated as an immediate threat to your safety will cause a subconsciously derived and executed evasive protective procedure, a flinch. It happens without the need of deliberate conscious thought, with no conscious interjection of a plan, and you won't have the opportunity to consciously abort this action.

It cannot be overridden, and you wouldn't want to override it even if you could, because it's the ultimate life preservation system for moments where you jump first, scream second, and get all jittery. This short-term fight or flight response is for getting you off the mark quickly, but if the threat stimulus turned out to be a real danger, after the initial evasive movement you wouldn't be able to rely on the SAM Axis, because you won't have enough fuel left. The one shot of emergency Noradrenaline won't be able to sustain moving full pelt for long enough to run away or to repeatedly hit the thing scaring you.

With the fuel tanks now empty and the evasive flinch movement doing the job of putting as much distance as possible between you and the thing which scared you, it's time for another system to come into play to look after the clubbing or running movements which will follow your flinch if needed.

The anxious Pons whacks the panic button over and over during the SAM Axis flinch activation, and this button hitting is sending signals asking for more back up. With the Pons extending its structural connections from the Brain Stem along to the Thalamus, the Amygdala, and the Spinal Cord, it uses these high-speed connections to send a message to the Thalamus telling those in charge over at battle planning to start the next facet of the fight or flight system.

Battle planning receive the request to start preparing the body to launch one of two options, first to 'floor it' the long-term flight plan of running away, or alternatively, fight for your life and club the thing which frightens you, which is the long-term fight plan. The signal is sent in preparation in case you need either option after your initial panic jump, and the backup request is sent whilst the SAM Axis activation is under way. It's all done mid flinch to ensure the system is ready for what might need to happen next.

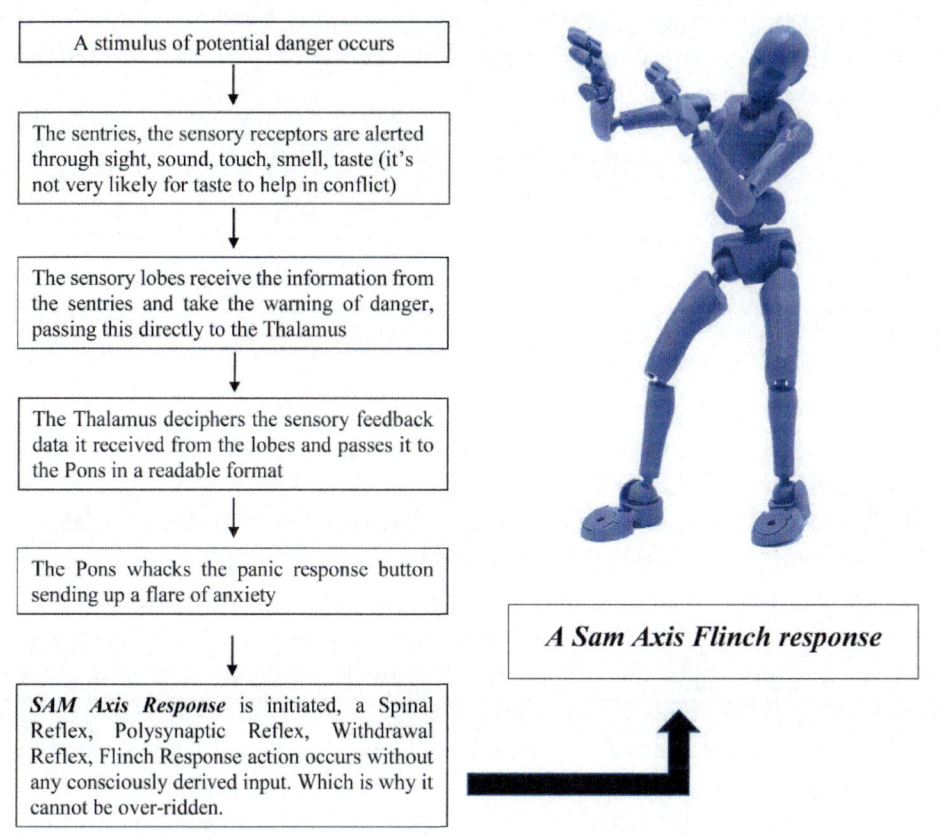

```
┌─────────────────────────────────────┐
│ A stimulus of potential danger occurs │
└─────────────────────────────────────┘
                  ↓
┌─────────────────────────────────────┐
│ The sentries, the sensory receptors are alerted │
│ through sight, sound, touch, smell, taste (it's │
│ not very likely for taste to help in conflict) │
└─────────────────────────────────────┘
                  ↓
┌─────────────────────────────────────┐
│ The sensory lobes receive the information from │
│ the sentries and take the warning of danger,   │
│ passing this directly to the Thalamus          │
└─────────────────────────────────────┘
                  ↓
┌─────────────────────────────────────┐
│ The Thalamus deciphers the sensory feedback │
│ data it received from the lobes and passes it to │
│ the Pons in a readable format                │
└─────────────────────────────────────┘
                  ↓
┌─────────────────────────────────────┐
│ The Pons whacks the panic response button │
│ sending up a flare of anxiety             │
└─────────────────────────────────────┘
                  ↓
┌─────────────────────────────────────┐
│ SAM Axis Response is initiated, a Spinal │
│ Reflex, Polysynaptic Reflex, Withdrawal  │
│ Reflex, Flinch Response action occurs without │
│ any consciously derived input. Which is why it │
│ cannot be over-ridden.                    │
└─────────────────────────────────────┘
```

A Sam Axis Flinch response

Long Term Fight or Flight

Whilst this SAM Axis, (all the fuel spent, dive for cover or jump out of the way action), reflex was running its program and launching a movement to jump away or shield yourself from danger, the Thalamus went into maximum overdrive. Transmitting the original message, which initiated the SAM Axis, the Thalamus will now immediately be sending out the second signal from the Pons referencing the threat and asking for backup.

This second message is to prepare the launch of the second phase of the defence protocol, a phase called the HPAC Axis Long Term Fight or Flight Response. If the situation is dangerous enough to warrant a call for either an evacuation plan, aka run like the wind, or alternatively a strategy to go on the offensive by bashing the thing which is a threat, you need to organise the fuel for whichever plan of action you opt to take. Plus, you need to co-ordinate the response action itself, so step forward the big boss of the Limbic system, Captain Amygdala - Operations Manager!

The Amygdala begins the initiation of the HPAC Axis by simultaneously sending signals ordering two operational commands, these will be referred to as Command Route A and Command Route B. (*Both of which belong to the HPAC Axis and are separate to the SAM Axis*).

The two command orders of Captain Amygdala.

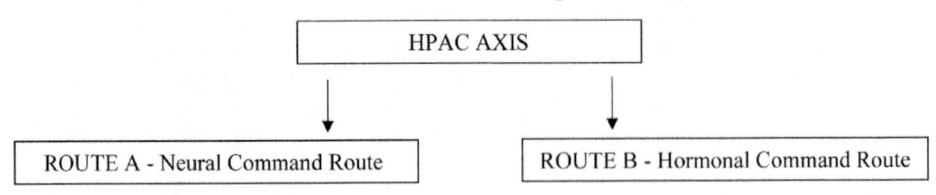

```
            ┌───────────────┐
            │   HPAC AXIS   │
            └───────────────┘
              │           │
              ▼           ▼
┌──────────────────────────┐  ┌──────────────────────────────┐
│ ROUTE A - Neural Command │  │ ROUTE B - Hormonal Command   │
│         Route            │  │         Route                │
└──────────────────────────┘  └──────────────────────────────┘
```

Both commands have the singular common goal of preparing the body and mind in case any further action is required after the initial SAM Axis activation. Preparation in case the flinch/jump/duck evasion wasn't enough, as even though you will have put a greater distance between you and the thing which may harm you, the threat might still be present. Route A, the *Neural Command Route* and route B, the *Hormonal Command Route* combine to create the incredibly fast process of the HPAC Axis, and *both command routes happen simultaneously*. Both commands happening whilst the leaping/flinching of the SAM Axis happens, the speed of this is astounding.

Remember, both routes A and B of the HPAC Axis launch individually but they both happen at the same time and whilst you are mid-jump in your SAM Axis reflex. The repetition of this fact is deliberate and necessary to hammer home the speed of brain processing of your fight or flight system because '*Will I be fast enough?*' is a commonly asked question. You don't need to train to be fast, you're already fast enough as this feedback and transmitting of information all happens in the middle of your flinching, in the middle of your SAM Axis, it's a phenomenal speed. Being aware of your brain processing speed limits doubt, and this will support you in building your trust in your ability to implement the effectiveness of this realistic self-defence method when under stress.

Route A - the Neural Command

Re-cap: Route A's beginning came with the initial danger signal picked up by the senses, and the information reaching the Thalamus. From here, the message was sent to the Pons (located in the Brain Stem) in the form of an anxiety level threat alert. The fight or flight system was triggered by Pons hitting the stress button due to the threat/stress stimulus, with the response being the SAM

Axis/Short Term Fight or Flight evasive action reflex being triggered. This superseded everything else, and jumping, flinching, or shielding, whichever one your instincts said was best for that moment.

This initial <u>neural command</u> doesn't end with the SAM Axis, it continues to exist through a lot of back of forth communication, until its presence is found in the HPAC long term fight or flight Axis. Like a military command centre directing an army under attack, relaying information in all directions at once.

- Pons *(Anxiety Alert - Panic Button Pusher)*, alongside hitting the panic button, relays a feedback message to Thalamus *(Message Decoder)* asking for backup
- This request passes from Thalamus to the Amygdala *(Captain Amygdala - Operations Manager)*
- As soon as the Amygdala has received the request to prepare for more back up, it tells the Thalamus to send messages to inform the; Cerebellum *(Watch your Step)*, Midbrain *(Information Runner)* and Medulla Oblongata *(Quick, Move)*, to prepare the body by firing up the CNS, ready for any further movement if required
- Amygdala's message to the Thalamus is get ready for a plan of action and it will ensure the body has the fuel needed.
- Thalamus delivers the message as requested, the proprio-receptors *(nerve endings in the muscles which initiate movement on instruction from the brain)* fire up all the engines, the muscles are alert and ready for any movement to be initiated when the order comes

What happens next in the Neural Command flow, is choosing the type of movement to be initiated. Who oversees the delivering of these orders and decisions to the body? Once again, it's *Captain Amygdala - Operations Manager*, the central hub for the fight or flight system.

After receiving the information about the threat stimulus, and whilst ordering the body to prepare itself ready for a plan to move, Amygdala will acknowledge the urgency of the situation and *override any logical and analytical interjection from the Left Hemisphere Cerebral Cortex*.

By shutting the door of interference from the Left Hemisphere, the Amygdala assumes command and takes control of crisis management. The message sent to the Left Hemisphere Cerebral Cortex is simple, <u>we haven't got time to analyse and philosophise about this, we need to move now. Do not open the Big Red Box of Doom</u>. Hopefully you recall this earlier piece of text: *The Amygdala can act as a 'thinking bypass'. The Left Hemisphere is analytical and logical in its processing, but when your life is under threat the Amygdala can override this part of the brain, instead triggering immediate automatic reactions to keep you safe.*

The choice of action you take at this point will be heavily influenced by your moral compass and is derived from information stored in the Hippocampus, which is the internal hard drive. The Amygdala, a busy bee in this whole process, will ask the Hippocampus for a solution because it has access to your memories at its fingertips and after super-fast scanning through the filing cabinet of memories for options, the Hippocampus will throw out an escape solution, (flight) also known as getting your Forrest Gump on. Or, if more appropriate an attack (fight) solution to bash your way out of trouble. Whether it's a fight or flight option which is chosen, the Hippocampus will send a solution plan back to the Amygdala, and upon receiving the message from the Hippocampus, relays the information via the Thalamus to the Brain Stem.

- The Thalamus informs the Brainstem of the selected response the Amygdala was given by the Hippocampus as the best option for the primed muscles to put into action.
- Hippocampus will have picked that solution as the best strategy based on recognition of the situation, and data available from previous responses to a problem of this nature.
- The Amygdala has established communications with the Hypothalamus about the hormone release and will ensure the troops are fuelled ready for the task in hand.

To summarise so far, you see or hear something which scares the bejesus out of you. You jump away from it before you even know what it is. This is the activation of the short-term fight or flight system, the threat avoidance *SAM Axis Reflex*. Your brain pre-empts the fact you may have to follow up with a running or hitting action. To prepare for this, the Amygdala asks the Hippocampus to choose an action plan. The Hippocampus searches the memory banks for a viable option and passes it back to the Amygdala. The Amygdala signals the Thalamus to tell the Brain Stem to get the body ready, get the proprio-receptors controlling the muscles all fired up. At this point, *Route A, the Neural Command* is almost complete.

Now what's needed is getting the necessary fuel into the muscles, and once this fuel is primed and prepared, the final stage is to give the order to execute a movement which is run or hit, or to abort all movement because the threat has passed.

Route B - the Hormonal Command

The multi-tasking role of the Amygdala in the fight or flight system is huge, alongside communicating with the Hippocampus, plus relaying with the Brain Stem via the Thalamus for starting *Route A - the Neural Command*, the Amygdala will also initiate and oversee Route B.

The first step of Route B is sending a signal to the Hypothalamus, carrying a message to release the long-term fight or flight hormones to get the body armed and into perfect battle-ready conditions. Running away from someone until they give up the chase requires the brain to give a cognitive instruction to move your legs quickly. The danger stimulus your sentries spotted is the synaptic starter pistol, but you depend on rocket fuel for energy to carry out this physical action of running. Bashing someone until they can't hit you back will also need fuel. Both actions can be over in seconds or even last several minutes, meaning a long-term fuel source needs to be harnessed in preparation for the worst. Step forward the *Dope Man*, the Hypothalamus who's your very own internal pharmacist. Using a close connection to the rest of the Limbic system and the Brain Stem, the Thalamus has the responsibility for managing the Autonomic Nervous System (ANS) function through hormonal release.

The ANS is a network of nerve fibres running through your body linking the brain with the organs, the glands (Endocrine System) and muscle groups. The ANS is primarily made up of two branches; the Sympathetic & the Parasympathetic systems, and both are largely subconscious in their operations. The Hypothalamus sends instructions to regulate hormonal levels appropriate for the conditions you find yourself in, also balancing both branches of the ANS in response to the external environment. Achieving the perfect fight or flight stasis by regulating hormones, which are our inbuilt drugs, and using the Neurotransmitters Dopamine and Acetylcholine. A huge breakthrough in my personal research and understanding of the fight and flight system, was becoming aware of Acetylcholine, which is released from Preganglionic Sympathetic Nerves to induce an increased stimulation of the Sympathetic Nervous System. This will be explained in far more detail at a later point in the text.

When anxiety levels/threat levels rise, the Hypothalamus stimulates heightened activation of the Neurotransmitters, which starts the cascade of the hormones Noradrenaline and Adrenaline being released from the Adrenal Glands, along with Testosterone from the Testes. These hormones hitting the bloodstream is exactly when you start to feel the catalogue of physiological changes covered in the *Butterflies & the Scaredy Cat*. This surge of Adrenaline and Cortisol alters the insulin level in the body, which is used to fast track glucose release into the bloodstream for more immediate energy, because it's handy to have an energy surge whilst under threat. Adrenaline release will increase heart rate, *(if it rises too high it will cause loss of motor skills, to be discussed later)* this allows more energy and oxygen packed blood to reach the muscles in preparation to fight for your life or break the land speed record whilst fleeing. Noradrenaline narrows the blood vessels in the extremities, *(the vasoconstriction of the arteries)* resulting in the redirection of blood to essential organs such as the heart and brain and increasing blood pressure.

Testosterone production will also be elevated during the fight or flight response, it's well-known Testosterone gives you super strength, which is useful if someone is trying to harm you. Testosterone is a naturally occurring steroid produced in the Testes or a combination of the Ovaries & Adrenal Gland.

The increase in the levels of the hormones being released is orchestrated by the Hypothalamus, via the Pituitary gland and the Adrenal glands, with a dash of Cortisol thrown into the mix. This is where the long-term fight or flight system get the name, the Hypothalamic Pituitary Adrenal Cortical Axis, or HPAC Axis for short. The HPAC Axis Hormonal changes happen so quickly the hormones/chemicals are already being released into the blood stream before any analytical thinking, *(housed in the Left Hemisphere Cerebral Cortex)*, has a chance to process the data from the initial trigger which caused your SAM Axis activation *(flinch)*. When you jump away from a spider which scares you, the movement is the SAM Axis, but the emotional and physiological changes of feeling your heart beating faster etc. are the beginning of the hormone release of the HPAC Axis. Taking place before you could even analyse whether the danger was real or not, you're prepared for fight or flight this quickly.

At this juncture, the Amygdala checks with the sentries (the senses), via the Thalamus, to have one last assessment to see if there really is a threat to your survival. Any reply other than a resounding *'No danger detected'* will prompt the Amygdala to communicate with the Right Hemisphere Cerebral Cortex, instructing it to push the button, and to begin deploying the physical action plan of fight or flight and you will now either run or hit. If no real threat was identified, no action would be required and therefore the system is powered down. Leaving you with a bit of a trembling, shaky feeling, and slight nausea while the fuel flushes out of the muscles and is processed ready for disposal. This is how the Sam Axis and the HPAC Axis run in perfect harmony with each other.

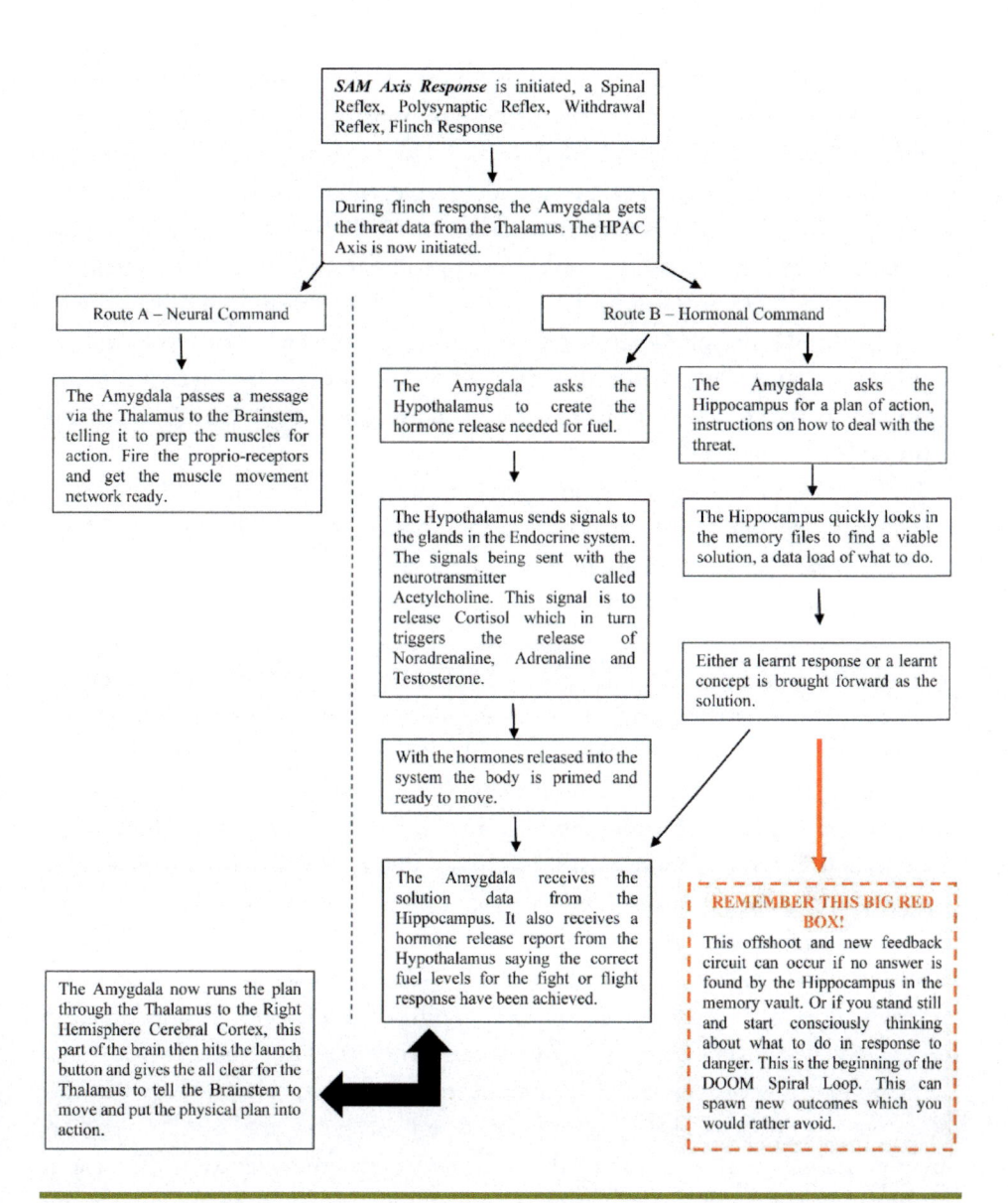

```
┌─────────────────────────────────┐
│ SAM Axis Response is initiated, │
│ a Spinal Reflex, Polysynaptic   │
│ Reflex, Withdrawal Reflex,      │
│ Flinch Response                 │
└─────────────────────────────────┘
                │
                ▼
┌─────────────────────────────────┐
│ During flinch response, the     │
│ Amygdala gets the threat data   │
│ from the Thalamus. The HPAC     │
│ Axis is now initiated.          │
└─────────────────────────────────┘
```

Route A – Neural Command

The Amygdala passes a message via the Thalamus to the Brainstem, telling it to prep the muscles for action. Fire the proprio-receptors and get the muscle movement network ready.

Route B – Hormonal Command

The Amygdala asks the Hypothalamus to create the hormone release needed for fuel.

The Hypothalamus sends signals to the glands in the Endocrine system. The signals being sent with the neurotransmitter called Acetylcholine. This signal is to release Cortisol which in turn triggers the release of Noradrenaline, Adrenaline and Testosterone.

With the hormones released into the system the body is primed and ready to move.

The Amygdala asks the Hippocampus for a plan of action, instructions on how to deal with the threat.

The Hippocampus quickly looks in the memory files to find a viable solution, a data load of what to do.

Either a learnt response or a learnt concept is brought forward as the solution.

The Amygdala receives the solution data from the Hippocampus. It also receives a hormone release report from the Hypothalamus saying the correct fuel levels for the fight or flight response have been achieved.

The Amygdala now runs the plan through the Thalamus to the Right Hemisphere Cerebral Cortex, this part of the brain then hits the launch button and gives the all clear for the Thalamus to tell the Brainstem to move and put the physical plan into action.

> **REMEMBER THIS BIG RED BOX!**
> This offshoot and new feedback circuit can occur if no answer is found by the Hippocampus in the memory vault. Or if you stand still and start consciously thinking about what to do in response to danger. This is the beginning of the DOOM Spiral Loop. This can spawn new outcomes which you would rather avoid.

The Feedback Loop from Stimulus to Response via Fight, Flight, or the Pesky Freeze

Irrespective of whether a stressor is a physical threat to your life, or it's a stressor such as a pile of bills, your goal is to be operating at appropriate and correct levels of this well-oiled, finely tuned stress response system. Working within the boundaries of the most appropriate level of response to any given situation will be referred to as the *RBM Loop*.

Seeing a potential threat up ahead, you feel the safety response engage and you become aware of it kicking in via the sensations of the butterflies etc. Your intuition of potential danger fired a low-level stress response, one which will often make you cross the road to avoid trouble, which is a good thing. The threat of death or certain injury, or sexual assault will push this safety response to a higher level, which is a positive and appropriate response to a dangerous situation. These examples illustrate how fear can be a positive motivator, and how you should accept the reality that if someone threatens you, you will be afraid. **Fear isn't the issue, it's the sense of uncertainty which is the crippling factor, because doubt is the psychological atom bomb resulting in total mental carnage.**

In terms of realistic self-defence, you can positively influence the efficiency of your fight or flight system by giving the Hippocampus *(Internal Hard Drive)* positive options to select from, and power these choices with a mindset always directed towards implementing a solution. The more positive you feel in the choices you have, the less opportunity there will be for doubt to creep in, because you're in control of your actions, limiting the negative psychological outcomes. The importance of this warrants a more expansive explanation.

Simple self-defence information with clear principles learnt through repetition is very important when in danger, with the data being retained and stored as a possible and viable option to use in a conflict scenario. The benefit of preparing yourself for the possibility of an attack, plus learning options that you have confidence in, not only gives you a physical advantage but also stifles the growth of doubt and panic in the mind. This limits any uncertainty regarding what you can do, should do, and will do, if attacked.

Having options is essential for restricting the likelihood of the dreaded freeze, which is every person's biggest fear when under threat. If you have learnt how to protect yourself whilst simulating being attacked, it makes all the difference, because choice is empowering, and it helps the HPAC Axis to operate smoothly. If you recall, the Amygdala asks the Hippocampus for a solution selected from your memory bank. When the Hippocampus finds the data files, it unlocks the options you have learnt through practicing self-defence and from this, it generates a solution based on what you've learnt. The response selected is passed from the Hippocampus to the Amygdala, and from here, this deployment strategy reaches the Brain Stem via the Thalamus. Command Route A is used to get the signal into the CNS, moving your feet rapidly away from the threat, or forwards to strike the threat. Command Route B is releasing the hormones into the bloodstream. The hormone release of the HPAC Axis differs in numerous ways from the SAM Axis emergency single shot of

Adrenaline. One difference is the presence of Testosterone in the HPAC Axis, but the biggest difference is the Hypothalamus (Dope Man), will use the neurotransmitter Acetylcholine to instruct the production of Corticotrophin Releasing Factor (CRF) which is a hormone responsible for firing the Pituitary Gland to produce Adrenocorticotropic Hormone (ACTH), telling the Adrenals to create Cortisol.

Cortisol revs the engine of the fight or flight system, preventing it from stalling because if you hit something with a club once, you might need to hit it again, so more surges of these hormones are advantageous. Each Cortisol 'rev' initiates more Noradrenaline and Adrenaline to be released into the bloodstream with the system releasing more fuel without restarting the trigger/launch process all over again.

The Hypothalamus instructs the recurring release of Cortisol to create a continuing loop of the long-term fight or flight chemical mix, but too much of anything isn't good for you, and whilst the thought of limitless Adrenaline, Noradrenaline and Testosterone sounds ideal, there is a downside to this fight or flight system if it's left to spiral out of control. This hormone release is of huge importance and far outweighs any martial arts skills or any weapon you hold in your hand in a conflict. But it's not as simple as just releasing a load of hormones, you need this chemical fuel in the right balance and at the correct levels to be at your optimum efficiency.

Hit the Brakes........
The Cortisol revved long-term fight or flight loop is stopped via the Parasympathetic branch of the ANS by activation of the relaxation response. The Parasympathetic branch instructs the halt of Cortisol release, slamming the brakes on the production of Noradrenaline, Adrenaline and Testosterone, in turn stopping the fight or flight battle station reactions. The halting of the fight or flight system is ordered using the neurotransmitter Acetylcholine, instructing the relaxation of the stress response system once the danger has passed. Being able to apply the brakes is an essential part of a self-defence strategy because you wouldn't want your heart exploding out of your chest. The ability to slow things down a little bit, or to stop the stress response is desirable, having a bucket load of hormones constantly being released into your blood system sounds great, but it's not quite as clear cut as this.

In his superb book *On Combat,* Lt. Col. Dave Grossman, with contributions from Bruce K. Siddle[9], presents fascinating information on the effects of too high a level of hormone release on a person when performing under stress. Grossman & Siddle show once there's a stress hormone induced elevated heart rate, due to the Sympathetic Nervous System, the effects on the body can be measured within the range of:

- 60 to 80 beats per minute is a normal resting rate
- 80 to 115 beats per minute, fine motor skills begin to deteriorate
- 115 to 145 beats per minute, optimal survival, and combat performance level for: complex motor skills, visual reaction time, and cognitive reaction time.
- Above 145 beats per minute, complex motor skills begin to deteriorate
- 175 beats per minute, cognitive processing deteriorates: vasoconstriction (reduced bleeding from wounds: loss of peripheral vision (tunnel vision): loss of depth perception: loss of near vision: auditory exclusion (tunnel hearing)
- Above 175 beats per minute, irrational fighting or fleeing: freezing: submissive behaviour: voiding of bladder and bowels: using only gross motor skills, running, charging, etc.

*This data is for hormonal induced heart rate increases, resulting from sympathetic nervous system arousal. Exercise induced heart rate increases will not have the same effect.

Grossman & Siddle

If the release of Cortisol, (resulting in spikes in Testosterone, Noradrenaline and Adrenaline) is happening too frequently or strongly, it will cause you to slide further along the scale. To many spikes and you begin to leave the desired performance survival zone of 115 to 145 BPM and slide further along the BPM scale into the negative area for function and performance. Interestingly, the neurotransmitter Acetylcholine, used to start Cortisol release when triggered by a threat, and also used to stop the release of Cortisol to relax after a stress event, is the same neurotransmitter when found at high levels creates the introduction of a new facet to your stress response. At high levels, Acetylcholine takes your stress response beyond fight or flight, and introduces the potential of the freeze response.

---

[9] Col Lt Dave Grossman, 1996: *On Killing: The Psychological Cost of Learning to Kill in War and Society*

To make this easier, and to put the hormonal induced changes into context, the visual representation of this data is as follows:

BPM	BODY	SENSES	COGNITIVE
60–80	**NORMAL RESTING HEART RATE**		
115	Fine motor skills start to deteriorate, fancy moves are no longer a viable option.	Senses are picking up all threat stimuli and continue processing any changes in your environment.	The brain is running the HPAC Axis and searching for viable threat solutions.
145	Optimum level for complex motor skills.	Optimum level for visual reaction time	Optimum level for cognitive function, providing you aren't working from a reactionary left brained thought-based system
175	Drop in efficiency of complex motor skills. Vasoconstriction has reached maximum level	Reduction in efficiency in all the senses. Depth and near perception are almost lost	Tachypsychia effects will begin. Cognitive process is switching to pigeon management.
	Gross Motor skills replace complex skills. You will now start to act irrationally, charging, involuntary running and actions which serve of no benefit to your survival. Voiding of the bladder and bowels will be actioned.	Auditory exclusion and tunnel vision have taken place. Complete sensory shutdown is happening.	Submissive behavior and the freeze response kicks in. The brain will engage in the emergency protocol of total cognitive shutdown to block out awareness of what is taking place to limit psychological trauma.

The freeze response is displayed as standing still in the hope the predator doesn't see you. It's the human version of playing dead, with pain killers released into the blood stream to numb sensitivity to pain. You feel as though you're frozen to the spot, whilst hoping the thing attacking either doesn't spot you, or if it attacks it gets bored and leaves. The freeze response partially shuts down areas of the brain responsible for processing neurological conscious awareness as a mental defence, and as a psychological aid protecting you against the traumatic event unfolding. Freezing like the resident of a morgue doesn't exactly conjure up the image of things going well, it's not very reassuring, or even sounding remotely like the situation is in hand.

Unlike in a human-to-human attack, playing dead or making loud noises are two different strategies advised if you find yourself in a bear attack. The advice given for hikers to avoid bear attacks is to wear little bells on clothing to make noise when hiking, because the bell noise allows the bears to hear walkers from a distance and not be accidentally startled by a hiker, which may cause them to charge. Walkers should also carry a pepper spray can. It's also a good idea to keep a look out for fresh bear droppings to give an idea if bears are in the area. You will be able to recognise the difference between black bear and grizzly bear droppings, as black bear droppings are smaller and often contain berries, leaves, and possibly bits of fur. Grizzly bear droppings tend to contain small bells, rucksacks and have the smell of pepper.

But jokes aside, like the difficulty in identifying different types of bears and which response to use, how do you distinguish the motive and threat level of a person attacking you? Are they going to leave you alone if you play dead? Or will your vulnerability ramp up their aggression levels? It's impossible to ascertain, so it's of no use employing the play dead tactic when a person is about to start stamping on your head.

Excessive hormone release isn't great for your survival efficiency, so having a brake system is an advantageous facet to this system. However, the brake system does have its own pitfalls, because as soon as the Parasympathetic branch pulls the plug on the stress response to stop you spiralling into an over stimulated hormone release, you will completely relax and shut down the fight or flight system. *What does this mean for you?* Well, it highlights where you may hit a little problem with serious implications, as smack bang in the middle of a conflict, any fight or flight hormones will be dumped out of your system, which is the same as a pilot dumping all their fuel mid-flight. Catastrophic!

This gives a clear picture of how you must strive to be in control of your fight or flight system in a situation where your stress response is triggered. You must limit the level to which the stress response is fired and activated because too much brings the system to an abrupt halt, dropping all your fuel mid-threat. This immediately creates the question of how to limit the levels to which the response is triggered? To solve this, it's necessary to investigate and identify the mental whisperer who causes the problems, the internal bogeyman.

Freeze, the Internal Bogeyman!
The surprise and shock of being attacked causes the release of the hormones via the cortisol revving, but there is something else which can cause the firing of the system, and if done excessively, result in a surplus of hormones and the problems this brings with it. The gremlin in the fight or flight machine causing things to go pear shaped is the rather familiar process we know as overthinking. If the Left Hemisphere Cerebral Cortex *(the analytical thinking part of your brain)*, starts to get involved whilst under attack, you begin consciously using cognitive analysis in thinking about the situation you're in, attempting to rationlise violence when you have no time to understand an illogical, chaotic attack which often has no rationality. Add to this any doubts you hold concerning your ability to protect yourself, or any worries about if you're *allowed* to protect yourself, or worrying if you will remember what to do, will all cause the left Hemisphere to swirl into action and over stimulate the Neurotransmitters. Once again, it's the over stimulus of Acetylcholine here causing the HPAC Axis loop to fly out of control, overloading the system and basically blowing the trip switch, causing you to freeze.

In this instance, it was an internal thought which created a triggered hormone release ultimately causing a freeze response, and you have forced the Parasympathetic branch to stamp on the brake and dump all the unused survival hormones, because of stress related over thinking. I call this opening the Big Red Box, and inside this cube of personal horror is the Doom Spiral Loop, where all the things to self-sabotage your survival exist. I know these are rather dramatic names, but they are truly representative of the impact it can have in this situation, because this box, once opened releases the least desirable outcomes for you to recover from. These can be mental or physical freezes, whereby you drop your fuel and flood your brain with distracting and consuming thoughts, worries and anxieties. You don't want to be practicing for the world musical statues championships if someone is holding a knife to your throat, so the freeze response is to be avoided at all costs and your self-defence method must cater for, and prepare for this potential eventuality. This isn't the same as flinching, that's a good thing, freezing is where you either mentally, physically, or due to a combination of both, come to a standstill.

What accelerates this overthinking?
Without any preparation in advance of what to do if attacked, when the Amygdala asks the Hippocampus to look in the folder for a suitable response, it will simply reply with *'sorry, I've got nothing on the internal hard drive'*. The result of this lack of data is often a threat being met with totally irrational movements which don't give you the safest outcome. Or the Hippocampus neurologically

shrugs with *'I've got no idea'*, a big problem when at the mercy of an unpredictable assailant during an armed and violent attack. But it can get even worse very quickly, as the uncertainty of what to do causes doubt, and doubt is the opportunity for the Big Red Box to open. The box opening is the window for the Cerebral Cortex left hemisphere, the analytical brain, to get involved. Intrusively sticking its head in, and starting to think about what's happening.

Too much thinking time allows the box to open, creating more problems and leaving a mess behind. This statement of 'too much time to think' often seems to perplex people, as they see no issue with having thinking time. Usually this is correct, but when faced with violence, in a time-restrained crisis management situation *the Amygdala overrides the Cerebral Cortex*. This override exists to limit the conscious analytical thinking input of the Left Hemisphere, ensuring mental focus continues along the most time efficient pathway available when a limited amount of time is afforded, which is using the HPAC Axis as a response to a threat stimulus.

Only if the Hippocampus isn't producing the solution needed, because the internal hard drive didn't have a valid option stored on file, will the Amygdala be forced to break away from this system and turn to the Cerebral Cortex for help. Realising the severity of the situation and being adrift without a solution, instead of the Amygdala delivering a plan to the Thalamus to pass onto the brain stem to move the body, it's now forced to report to the Right Hemisphere with *'we have nothing'*. It's at this point the Left Hemisphere steps forwards, sticking its oar in and deciding to have a strategy board meeting. The Big Red Box has been opened giving an unsettling introduction of *pigeon management*. Pigeon management is flying in, crapping over everything, and then flying off, which is what the Left Hemisphere does in this type of emergency situation, causing all sorts of problems and there's a variety of different triggers which can open the box:

Pigeon Management Triggers

REMEMBER - THE BIG RED BOX!

This offshoot and new feedback circuit can occur if no answer is found by the Hippocampus in the memory vault. Or, standing still and starting to consciously think what you should do in response to danger. This is the start of the DOOM Spiral Loop and it can spawn new outcomes which you would rather avoid.

| The Hippocampus could not find a suitable answer to the problem, causing indecision and panic. | A solution was given but you did not act immediately, allowing time for the Left Hemisphere to interrupt the positive feedback loop. | You have preconditioned beliefs preventing you from implementing the solution given by the Hippocampus, ie. 'it's wrong to hit someone'. |

THE BIG RED BOX IS OPEN

The DOOM Spiral Loop is in full flow, pigeon management negative thoughts driving this doubt filled emotional loop, continuing until you freeze, or submit. Or drop all the fight or flight hormones, exactly when you need them the most.

Your best laid plans for personal protection and threat survival are now a version of *Hitchcock's The Birds* all over the inside of your brain. A horror showing of bird poop, and a survival performance nightmare, with your brain flapping around in chaos.

When removed from the pressure of an immediate physical threat to your life, this left brained thought process relay wouldn't be called the Doom Spiral Loop at all, and is in fact a valuable tool when used correctly. If a problem pops up in life, sitting down with a coffee and having a brain storming session is exactly what this left brained relay is designed for and is the function being used in the correct manner. This is a subconsciously created, Right Hemisphere monitored ideas, using the Left Hemisphere to think about logistical factors. It's a highly productive means of operating, and the relax on the sofa with your feet up and mull it over loop has many benefits. Only when trying to utilise this process in a threat situation does it morph into the Doom Spiral Loop, because it's not appropriate for the job in hand, not when you're under pressure/stress, safety, and time limitations.

There are occasions where the Cerebral Cortex has caused the HPAC Axis fight or flight system to activate beyond what is deemed appropriate when logic is applied. This is known as an anxiety attack, a very real and unpleasant experience for anyone who has experienced this, as you feel totally out of control. To stop this slide into anxiety and to reset the brain, breathing becomes an important tool for re-balancing the mind and Phase 2 covers this in detail.

When under threat you want to use the fastest processor you have, and whilst the Left Hemisphere processing is by no means a slow process, taking 25 milliseconds, the subconscious HPAC Axis processing takes only 12 milliseconds. Neither are slow, but when under pressure to find an answer the fastest processor is the best processor. The data used as a foundation for the two feedback loop times of 12 milliseconds and 25 milliseconds are supported by information on the speed of brain schematics presented in the works *of Joseph Ledoux, The Emotional Brain: The Mysterious Underpinnings of Emotional Life, published in 1994.* Still the most referred to study delving into the world of neuroscience and the understanding of fear.

The quote, which opened this chapter;

> *"We need defenses only when change happens in our lives faster than we can accommodate it"*

Vaillant, GE [10]

beautifully sums up the need for the *RBM* Solution Loop. You depend on a realistic self-defence system when change in your environment happens faster than you can consciously process and respond to it.

Left Hemisphere Cerebral Cortex interaction has no place in your immediate defence mechanism to a physical threat because it doesn't function well in an emotionally charged threat level situation, and is out of its depth in this arena. The Left Hemisphere does have an important role prior to a threat situation, deciding on safety plans such as places to avoid, or the recognition of the need to learn methods to enhance your personal protection. In non-life-threatening situations, with no immediate threat to your existence, and not being emotionally charged it's fantastic, but these scenarios aren't the same as when a big old collection of knuckles is whizzing towards your nose and when the pressure for decisive action is on.

If you haven't prepared yourself for a nose shattering situation like this, there won't be any knowledge of what to do readily available to help you, and without this security and the comforting knowledge, you will start to worry and over-process, second guessing yourself, which eats away valuable time. This indecision causes panic, creating an internal stressor, triggering an internally driven stress response, and the negative hormonal release effects which come with it. Heaping more and more anxiety on top of the original stress level created by the external threat of knuckles impacting with nose. This secondary stimulation of internal doubt, drives anxiety upwards and because of this internal worry in addition to the external worry, the Pons are now in overdrive. The rate of panic button pushing increasing and more Acetylcholine activation being stimulated, with more and more Cortisol revving the hormonal system.

The HPAC Axis is going to spin out of control, it's been hijacked and bombarded uncontrollably by internal stressors at a phenomenal speed. Fresh hormones are released on top of the previously existing hormones, which

---

[10] Vaillant, GE (1992), *Ego Mechanisms of Defense: A Guide for Clinicians and Researchers*, Washington, DC, American Psychiatric Press

haven't been burnt away because you haven't moved off the spot. Your heart rate elevates even higher and as you slide up the Grossman & Siddle scale; you will lose all depth perception, lose fine motor skills, and the senses will start to shut down.

This slide itself causes more panic and exposes you to more anxiety, a very dangerous and unfamiliar territory to find yourself in and your body will know it must slow this process down, so you produce more Acetylcholine activity to stop the Cortisol production. Acetylcholine is also influential on how data is processed in parts of brain, and this overstimulation creates the mental *'Blank Zone'* which makes you phase out and become almost in a daydream state. Not so much playing dead, more like the walking dead. This is the mental freeze, Acetylcholine over stimulation will affect the linkage between the Cerebral Cortex Right Hemisphere, and the Cerebellum/Midbrain/Medulla Oblongata. The result? No movement will be initiated from any direct orders, and this is the physical freeze response.

Again, it's Acetylcholine involved, as it's also influential in the activation of muscle movement via Acetylcholine receptors found at the junction between muscles and nerves. Freeze is one likely outcome, but the same over stimulation which causes the Cerebellum/Midbrain/Medulla Oblongata collectively to do nothing (freeze), can also make them go into unsupervised work, doing a bit of free-styling and initiating movements without instruction from the Hippocampus/Amygdala. These unordered responses can be irrational fighting or fleeing, not ideal if you start irrationally running at the person with the semi-automatic rifle, or you run out of the house when your family are being held by intruders with knives, or even causing you to react in full red mist mode and kill someone.

Overstimulation of the neurotransmitters means if you do move off the spot, you will be fighting for your life without the movement refining skills of the Brain Stem, moving clumsily as though completely drunk in terms of direction, balance, and coordination. In addition to this, because of freezing or acting irrationally, this negative loop feeds another new 'Internal Threat/Stimulus' loop as the uncertainty of what is happening keeps tripping the HPAC Axis because of the anxiety caused by doubt and uncertainty. It's a complete disaster!

The Analytical Doom Spiral

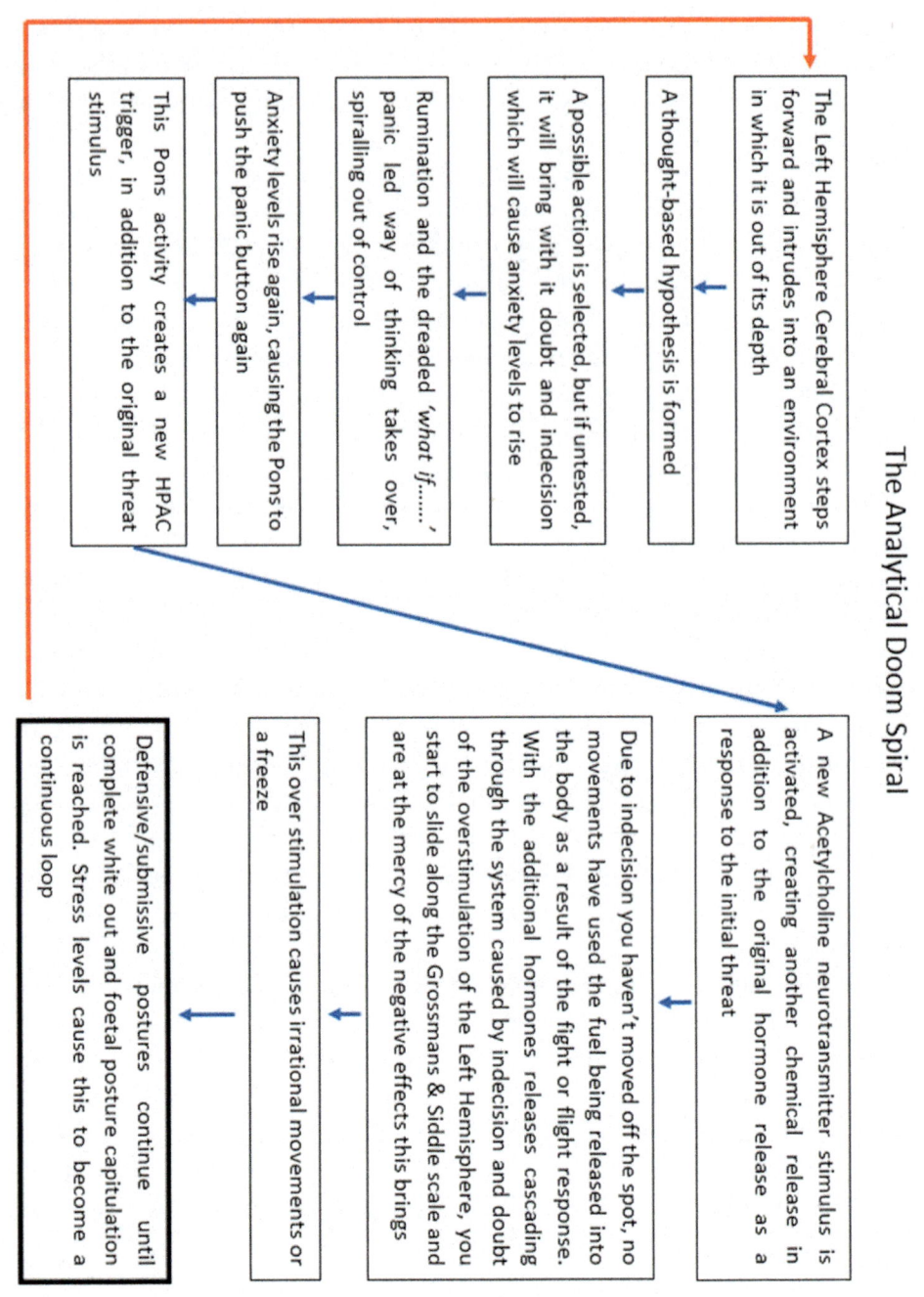

```
┌─────────────────────────────────────────────┐
│ The Left Hemisphere Cerebral Cortex steps   │
│ forward and intrudes into an environment    │
│ in which it is out of its depth             │
└─────────────────────────────────────────────┘
                      ↓
┌─────────────────────────────────────────────┐
│ A thought-based hypothesis is formed        │
└─────────────────────────────────────────────┘
                      ↓
┌─────────────────────────────────────────────┐
│ A possible action is selected, but if       │
│ untested, it will bring with it doubt and   │
│ indecision which will cause anxiety levels  │
│ to rise                                     │
└─────────────────────────────────────────────┘
                      ↓
┌─────────────────────────────────────────────┐
│ Rumination and the dreaded 'what if......'  │
│ panic led way of thinking takes over,       │
│ spiralling out of control                   │
└─────────────────────────────────────────────┘
                      ↓
┌─────────────────────────────────────────────┐
│ Anxiety levels rise again, causing the Pons │
│ to push the panic button again              │
└─────────────────────────────────────────────┘
                      ↓
┌─────────────────────────────────────────────┐
│ This Pons activity creates a new HPAC       │
│ trigger, in addition to the original threat │
│ stimulus                                    │
└─────────────────────────────────────────────┘
                      ↓
┌─────────────────────────────────────────────┐
│ A new Acetylcholine neurotransmitter        │
│ stimulus is activated, creating another     │
│ chemical release in addition to the         │
│ original hormone release as a response to   │
│ the initial threat                          │
└─────────────────────────────────────────────┘
                      ↓
┌─────────────────────────────────────────────┐
│ Due to indecision you haven't moved off the │
│ spot, no movements have used the fuel being │
│ released into the body as a result of the   │
│ fight or flight response. With the          │
│ additional hormones releases cascading      │
│ through the system caused by indecision and │
│ doubt of the overstimulation of the Left    │
│ Hemisphere, you start to slide along the    │
│ Grossmans & Siddle scale and are at the     │
│ mercy of the negative effects this brings   │
└─────────────────────────────────────────────┘
                      ↓
┌─────────────────────────────────────────────┐
│ This over stimulation causes irrational     │
│ movements or a freeze                       │
└─────────────────────────────────────────────┘
                      ↓
┌─────────────────────────────────────────────┐
│ Defensive/submissive postures continue      │
│ until complete white out and foetal posture │
│ capitulation is reached. Stress levels      │
│ cause this to become a continuous loop      │
└─────────────────────────────────────────────┘
```

Continuously passing along the Doom Spiral Loop when under threat causes a catastrophic carousel of hormone release, as round and around the stress response loop you go, potentially introducing you to a fourth facet of the stress response alongside fight, flight, and freeze, and it's called Submit/Posture. This is where you cover up to protect yourself, trying to appear submissive in the hope your actions may encourage some compassion from the attacker. Unfortunately, the attacker has the same brain system as you do, which means they will be in their Sympathetic Nervous System when behaving violently. You won't find a lot of sympathy in someone operating from their Sympathetic Nervous System, so this covering up and hoping for human kindness isn't a recommended tactic.

Submit and Posture usually occurs due to you not having a clue what to do when threatened, or from not giving yourself the permission to act, so submissive posturing is the last option when you've given up hope. This submit/posture facet can be seen illustrated as a vocal strategy as well as a physical posture. An example is the seemingly irrational response when people try to bond with the attacker hoping they will stop, attempting to appease the violent person who wants to turn your head inside out with their shoe. This is also evident when someone intervenes to stop an attack, and oddly ends up being assaulted by the person they tried to help, the immediate creation of Stockholm Syndrome by the victim to try and ensure their safety, safety by association of joining forces with the original protagonist.

As established, doubt is shaped and formed by your beliefs on how an event is unfolding and this is one of the biggest stumbling blocks to your efficiency in surviving an attack. One of the first tasks of *RBM* is targeting this doubt directly by changing your views on violence, and your views on flinching. If surprised by a random attack, your body will perform an evasive action without any conscious decisions from you, the SAM Axis does this for you and the reaction might be a flinch, or a run and cover response, or it might be grabbing the attacker. If you haven't trained to move from a defensive or evasive flinch response, then you may perceive what's happening as a negative outcome, a failed situation. But the flinch was in fact, a positive action, one which can be used as a springboard to yet another positive response movement, one for disrupting your attacker.

Let's look at it at face value, you're still alive. After the initial flinch used as a missile avoidance action, you will instinctively look towards the attacker, scanning for the next incoming missile. If at this point you believe you're failing, because you perceived your flinch as a weakness rather than a brilliant survival tool, you will slide into the Doom Spiral Loop, all because you have doubt and anxiety.

If your opinion of the feelings of butterflies in your stomach, heart pounding, sweating and body shaking are negative, and you view these as a sign of weakness and cowardice rather than being ready to fight, this will also cause the Doom Spiral Loop, because of doubt in yourself and doubt in your ability to perform under stress. These perceptions of flinching and the physical sensations in the body can open the big red box and speedily deliver you to a Freeze or even a Submit/Posture if left unchecked.

The Hippocampus looks at all memories, not just whether you have the memory of how to hit something. The social rules and behaviours which help us function nicely as a society are also stored in the Hippocampus memory banks and can end up causing confusion, opening the Big Red Box, and leaving you vulnerable at a time when action is imperative for safety.

If the indoctrination from your childhood of being told you shouldn't hit under any circumstances remains, you must change it and accept under threat it's okay for you to strike another person, otherwise you may find when fighting for your life this restrictive belief causes confusion and opens the big red box, causing you to freeze, submit or posture. The same thing can happen if worrying about injuring a person, or worrying about legal consequences, these barriers are born from uncertainty and create more doubt. Doubt will cause you to start the process of analysing what's happening and lead you down the path of thinking what you should do, rather than proceed with the solution of hitting the thing threatening you. Uncertainty causes a shift into the Left Hemisphere thought process rather than springing into action.

The *RBM* system conditions/programs your brain and your Central Nervous System to be able to fight back. Factoring into your defence system; the internal effects of stress, the stress responses, conditioned belief implications, and how to recover and move from the positive SAM Axis flinch postures. All of which are geared towards you moving smoothly into a pro-active HPAC Axis response when finding yourself on the back foot. It isn't necessary to live with people surprising you all the time like the 'Not now Cato' moments in the Pink Panther films, nor is it necessary to have people beating seven shades of you know what out of you in a self-defence class to prepare you for being hit. Stress response training means putting the mind under pressure whilst asking it to perform effectively and efficiently in response to specific problems, and to continue doing this until you can function outside of your comfort zone. Finding a calmness in the chaos, altering and developing how you respond to stress by strengthening the dominance of the *RBM* Solution Loop.

RBM Development

- **Fight or Flight in daily life and how it damages your health**
- **Forget Guns, It's Cortisol that will kill you!**
- **Take your foot off the GAS**
- ***RBM* Pro-Active Stress Defence Drills**

Fight or Flight in daily life & how it damages your health

The fight or flight system evolved to provide you with a fast release of hormones to move quickly away from, or towards a threat. It's a complex and fascinating system which has served you well for most of your life. The downside? It can be triggered in a low physical threat environment, via a distorted, *perceived high threat* level known as the Stress Response. To a degree, stress is normal, it's how you monitor the world, keeping an eye out for any changes but sometimes the radar system gets wonky, becoming over sensitive. Here's an example of where things go off piste:

> You leave your car and walk towards the house. Hearing a noise, you jump backwards, your heart is pumping a little harder with your brain telling you it's clearly a horde of the undead. You're breathing faster, you start to sweat, you're aware your mouth has gone dry and you're feeling anxious. It's as though with every step forward, you want to sprint twenty steps backwards. Getting closer to where you thought the sound came from, you spot something in front of you. You run as fast as lightening, then stop, turning to see what is chasing you. A cat disappears into the garden next door, and you realise you've been watching far too much TV.

If I've done my job in getting the information across to you, this all makes sense, and you are clued up on the fight or flight response theory. Recognising in this example where the SAM Axis and HPAC Axis feedback loop and hormone release took place. Identifying evasive actions, followed by flight or fight strategy formulation in the brain. Also, acknowledging how the Doom Spiral gets involved given the chance, because in your mind it couldn't simply be a cat, it had to be the worst-case scenario of a gang of the undead waiting for you. In this scenario, you activated the fight or flight response and immediately used up the hormone-based fuel source with the physical action of running, whilst trying not to poo yourself. Chemicals burnt and pants still clean, you're now slowing down your system, and chances are you won't think of it again, it's going to have little or no bearing on your life, passing as a non-event.

Now look at the stress response activation in a situation where there's no perceived physical threat, no response of running or clubbing, and it's all triggered by worry and anxiety:

- On the way to work it's bad traffic, a twenty-minute journey taking fifty minutes
- You hope your colleagues won't notice if you're late again
- Preparation for today's meeting didn't go well with disrupted sleep
- What if you were fired or made redundant?

The major difference in the outcome between the cat in the garden and the car scenario, is that when in the car there are no sudden bursts of movement made, i.e., to run away, this time you remained stationary. The stress hormones are not being used for fuel, not being burnt off. This is where the health problems begin.

I believe this hypothetical scenario is representative of how many people think throughout a run of the mill day with a variety of worries and anxieties instigating *'what if'* moments in their mind. What if this happens, what if that happens, but the worries you're focusing on are only potential outcomes which haven't happened, they are false realities. But even though they are fictitious, they are still powerful, and they do have consequences, because they will cause a release of cortisol which is incredibly toxic.

As a side note, have you noticed you don't ruminate about good memories? When thinking of happy times, you connect with the feelings you had at the time and enjoy the memories, you don't ruminate. Which is very different to the endless cycle of worrying thoughts, which once started, can seem to spin endlessly.

Forget Guns, it's Cortisol which will kill you

Why is it important to change how you think and how you see yourself in the world around you? The various elements of the potential stress triggers given in the example of sitting on the car highlighted how within a small timeframe there were several potential triggers to start the stress response system, each one initiating a low-level Cortisol release. The repercussions being the constant firing of the bodies endocrine system, flicking the switch and releasing stress hormones, eventually overloading the immune system until it blows, enabling all the nasties to get a foothold and you start becoming ill. For many people, and I used to fall into this category, a large part of each day was spent with constant rumination of *what might happen*. Thoughts mainly based on negative, worry driven potential outcomes for the future. If you function in this way, you're sitting in a freeze response in your mind, pigeon management's head office. The damaging thing is there's no limitation to these thoughts, no restriction on the number of things you can worry about which cause these stress triggers, as they're all created in the mind, and with no time limits to curb them. You can focus on these anxieties all day and at a phenomenally fast processing speed over and over again.

The fight or flight stress response system wasn't designed for this, it evolved for a very fast escape it or kill it action, then forgetting about what just happened and relaxing and carrying on with life. Nevertheless, modern day life is fast, with work, home life, emails, text messages and social media providing a constant, limitless stream of potential triggers for a low-level fight or flight stimulus.

Left unchecked, a problem focused, worry/anxiety thought process will trigger Cortisol, causing the immediate release of fuel by calling on the protein stores in the liver to provide glucose. Constantly worrying will trigger this reaction repeatedly, ending up with raised blood sugar levels, putting you at risk of diabetes. Cortisol is responsible for reducing inflammation in the body and in conflict is beneficial as it reduces swelling, enabling you to stumble, or drag yourself to safety before any injury starts to balloon leaving you immobilised and exposed to the elements. But this release suppresses the immune system and in doing so render you more susceptible to serious illness if the system is activated too often. For every Cortisol release, Noradrenaline and Adrenaline will also surge into the bloodstream, causing vasoconstriction of the arteries, over time this repeated narrowing of the arteries, combined with increased blood pressure, can lead to damage of the arterial walls leading to arterial plaque and increasing the possibilities of heart disease, and placing you at an increased risk of heart attack and stroke, not great for your long-term health. Long-term stress is linked to chronic fatigue, and the problems which come with it.

This misuse of the stress response and its health implications are a far more common occurrence than being grabbed, kicked, punched, stabbed, or shot at, yet it isn't spoken about nearly enough. Stress is a far more real and likely adversary to you than a mugger.

Stress is very personalised, different things create anxiety and worry at different levels in different people, and it's impossible to give a separate resolution to each individual worry, but it is possible to give one solution to every worry, and that solution is changing how you think. Safeguarding your health by altering your conditioned reactions to stressors, which is achieved by implementing a new protocol for how you think, how you feel, and how you respond. The strange thing is, I've found the best method of implementing this is through a realistic self-defence method and not meditation as most people would assume.

Take your foot off the GAS

> *"Every stress leaves an indelible scar, and the organism pays for its survival after a stressful situation by becoming a little older".*
>
> Hans Selye [11]

Hans Selye shared his *General Adaptation Syndrome (GAS)* theory in 1936, outlining the effects of stress on the body. He proposed stress is a major trigger of disease because chronic stress causes long term chemical changes in the body, resulting in the hormonal system being altered too frequently and for too long. He observed after the activation of the fight or flight response, the body would have to work hard to return itself to a natural hormonal homeostasis, with this workload becoming progressively more difficult with every stress response. The effort and resources needed to provide sustenance to this recovery takes its toll on the system, and the necessity to remove any fight or flight hormone residue is what Selye labelled the 'General Adaptation Syndrome'.

He believed people have a limited supply of adaptive energy to deal with stress, and through continued exposure the rejuvenating pool becomes depleted. Poor health then ensues, bringing with it the exhaustion stage, where stress has continued for some time and the body's ability to recover has been diminished or near depletion. Draining your energy levels and leaving you feeling washed out, this is often referred to as Adrenal Fatigue, Burnout, or Chronic Fatigue Syndrome. The individual has now become more prone to increased anxiety and depression due to the pressure placed on the CNS.

It's a self-fuelling negative spiral, as a lack of energy often drives to seeking an immediate source of energy, tending to be sugar based because the sugar rush creates a Dopamine and Serotonin feel good factor, and you are now programming yourself to become a comfort eater. Sugar intake places extra stress on the already tired, Cortisol punched Liver and Pancreas. Cortisol in high levels will involve Triglycerides used for relocating the sugar to visceral fat cells and the greater the sugar intake, the harder the body finds it to convert this into fuel. It ends up in storage as health-damaging body fat, so the larger the

---

[11] Stress and the General Adaptation Syndrome, by Hans Seye, M.D., Ph.D., D.Sc., F.R.S.C. Professor and Director of the Institute of Experimental Medicine and Surgery, Universite de Montreal, Montreal, Canada, *British Medical journal*, June 17,1950

stress and sugar combination, the more visceral fat you will have, which elevates blood pressure etc. giving further health issues.

Those suffering from stress exhaustion often feel as though they have had enough, often withdrawing into themselves and turning away from the challenges they are facing and forming a mental submit posture, they stop engaging in life. I think many people can relate to feeling like this to a varying level at some time in their life, and this is exactly why a positive response mentality can be of benefit to everyone. There is an abundance of information stating the physical effects of stress, but they fail to mention one thing, it might be so obvious perhaps there was no need to say it, but for me the glaring omission is the failure to highlight that living with stress is completely miserable, leaving you feeling isolated and adrift from friends and family. This really is the freeze/submit posture at its most devastating and it happens more frequently per capita across the globe than people being attacked.

RBM hits this head on by helping to create a bulletproof mental resolve. Constantly focusing on seeking out solutions which bring a positive outcome, using a reliable thought pattern to turn to when feeling as though life, or a person, is attempting to beat the will to live out of you. You may go a lifetime without ever being grabbed by the throat, but most people get punched in the face by stress every day. How you recover and respond is the key, stopping the negative loop from spiralling out of control, and this comes down to choice. It always has been about choice, because with choice comes hope, with hope comes empowerment, and with empowerment comes the strength to make positive decisions and changes.

Limiting these indelible scars helps to maintain as much credit in the bank account of health as possible, but to be able to make those positive choices you need confidence in yourself, belief in yourself, and a positive view of yourself, and this is where the self-defence aspect of *RBM* brings its rewards.

Stress Defence Drills

The first step towards taking control of how you act and respond to life is identifying whether your stress response is functioning as it's supposed to, or whether the left brain is running a coup d'état and overthrowing the intended use of this system. For one week, monitor your response pattern noting any instances where you felt any of these sensations:

- a person has 'made' you cross or angry
- you have feelings of butterflies in the stomach
- upon reflection, you've been over-sensitive to what has been said
- finding yourself pointing your finger towards another person
- problems with concentration, especially reading
- walking away from an argument, then going back to re-engage
- starting to sweat more than you feel you should be
- noticing more muscle tension in your body
- you have tension headaches around the temples and the eyes

Identify how many times you're having any adverse reactions/responses to everyday life. Most of the sensations listed, at a low level are perfectly normal, such as feeling a little nervous before an interview, but when they spin out of control exceeding the social environment around you, these are the times you should be taking note.

For example, nobody can make you angry, you can choose to react in that way as a response, but they didn't make you do it, that's absolving yourself of responsibility of your actions. Take back your power by taking responsibility for your actions and reactions. You can't control the outside world, but you can be in control of how you react to it.

Stay Safe & Feel Empowered

- Awareness is key, it's missile avoidance!
- Target Attractiveness.
- The People you need to learn about.
- Signs that it's time to dive for cover.
- The POODLE Loop.
- Drills in Spotting Danger & Developing Awareness.

We live in a world full of predators, who prey on the unprepared.
There are dangerous people everywhere.

Well, that's what you'll believe if you read the self-defence books telling you to prepare to be attacked. Conveying the message violent attackers are out there waiting for you and it's inevitable.

I've had an interest in martial arts and self-defence for a huge part of my life, and one theme which I've noticed is many instructors and authors have gone down the road of scaremongering with the theme it's odds on you will be attacked. The pictures on the front covers of books are of people about to be murdered or attacked with a knife in an alley. But let's be a bit more realistic, if people really were waiting around every corner to attack you, the very nature of living in a world like this would ultimately mean you would be ready for it.

To a degree, we are a product of our environment, if people are likely to be attacked every single day then they would always be in primed survival mode, and wouldn't be caught by surprise. Granted, violence is a real danger in our world and personal safety needs to be considered, but the reality for most people is far removed from this 'dark alley scaremongering'. It has to be, otherwise the population wouldn't be walking around with headphones on, texting as they walk and taking selfies for fear of being ambushed. If society really is as violent as some people say, then you would witness people moving around like a soldier in combat taking cover, not ambling from shop to shop.

The severity of violence does seem to be on the increase within the age group of young teens, it seems as though they've ramped up their level of aggression. I do think violence is happening at a younger age than previously with individuals of ten and eleven years of age being involved in knife crime, and I do think there seems to be a shorter fuse in people overall, with violence escalating faster than I have previously observed, but frequency per population occurrences are still low. Violence is in part, socially and geographically influenced and specific locations have seen more violence of late, with the increase of knife crime in London being an example of this, spreading from the epicentre outwards and effecting other areas.

It would be incorrect to say everyone has the choice to simply avoid violence, and way off the mark to suggest it isn't a very real part of daily life for some. But for most people, our society functions well and provides a safe and nurturing place for us to grow and interact with one another. Yes there is the worry of being attacked which exists for some groups of society more than others, for example currently it's teenagers, but on the whole, in the UK we are living in quite a safe world.

Ironically, it's the low frequency of assaults per capita which opens the door for danger because it lets people lower their awareness levels. Not accepting the reality of the potential for violent attacks in the world is what allows the opportunity for being caught by a surprise attack. Just the acknowledgment of this potential danger alone reduces the risk, because it elevates awareness levels.

Another factor which leaves people vulnerable is that nice people shy away from the topic of violence and therefore have little understanding of it, or what to do when standing face to face with it. Turning away from the uncomfortable truth that we do have some violent people amongst us, however rarely it happens, is partly what leaves people vulnerable. The topic of violence remains as an unknown entity if it's never discussed and conversations about violence are something which increases anxiety levels whenever it's raised for most people. But they need to take place, because awareness of the nature of violence will help to reduce these anxieties. Knowledge based around the topic and having self-defence skills leaves you better equipped to deal with trouble if it ever enters your life and this helps reduce the fear of the unknown. I am not saying you need to learn to protect yourself because the world is hunting you. My message is to *learn how to be safe so you don't hold any worries and anxieties about these things*. Learn to think differently so you can manage and reduce your stress levels.

Contrary to what some other self-defence books are conveying, the statistics in fact say for most of the population there's little to worry about, and the reality is some people are in the wrong place at the wrong time. When this happens and people do find themselves in the wrong place, they're unprepared for the situation, leaving them at the mercy of the attacker and it's for this reason there is value in the realistic self-defence phase of *RBM*, but please approach this from the viewpoint of *it's just in case*. Using a seat belt doesn't mean you're expecting to be in a crash every time you drive, learning to protect yourself doesn't mean you are constantly at risk of being attacked every time you step outside.

Hospital Episode Statistics Accident & Emergency Attendances in England 2018-19, the data shown in fig.14 highlights there's more chance of injury from playing sport than you have from being attacked: *Distribution of accident and emergency attendances in England in 2018-2019* [12]

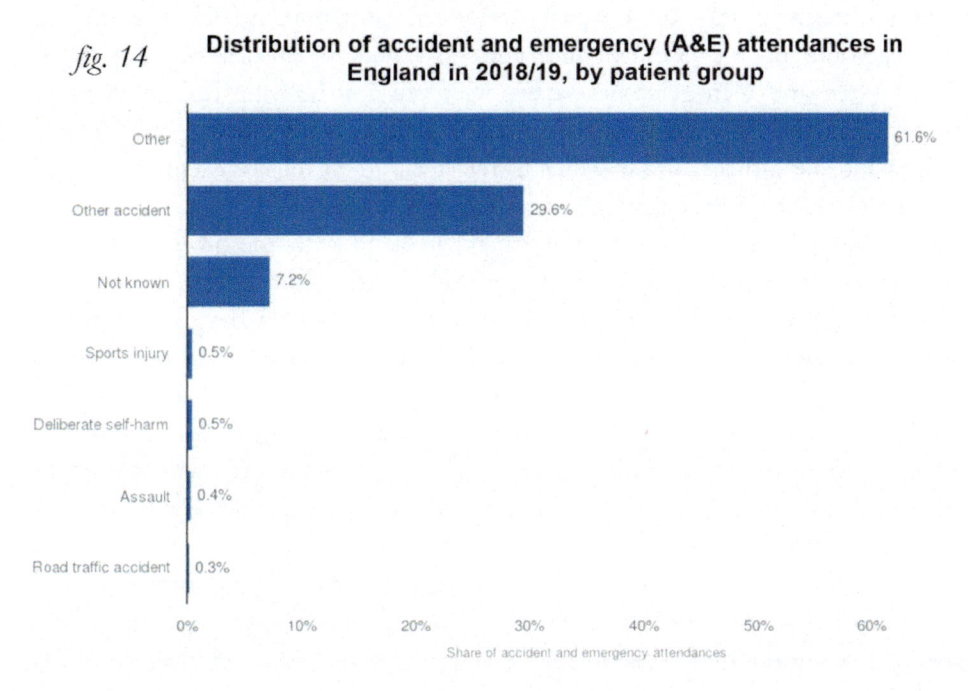

fig. 14 **Distribution of accident and emergency (A&E) attendances in England in 2018/19, by patient group**

Patient group	Share
Other	61.6%
Other accident	29.6%
Not known	7.2%
Sports injury	0.5%
Deliberate self-harm	0.5%
Assault	0.4%
Road traffic accident	0.3%

Share of accident and emergency attendances

I appreciate there's a large disparity between an injury sustained from sport and an injury from being attacked, with the potential outcome being poles apart. You don't tend to bleed to death from a swimming injury and it's not as physically or mentally traumatic as a stab wound, but based on frequency, there were more sports injuries recorded than reported serious assaults. There will be cases of assault which go unreported, so the numbers aren't exact, and it's important to emphasise there will also be injuries caused as a result of assault but not requiring medical assistance. This doesn't mean they aren't to be taken seriously, simply because they haven't been logged at A&E.

I'm not implying in any way that because they weren't recorded they aren't significant, as the anxiety and victimhood reinforcement they create and the emotional impact on an individual shouldn't be dismissed, but within this text any reference to a serious injury will refer to something which at best requires admission to the hospital and at worst the morgue.

Avoiding city centre pubs and nightclubs reduces your personal risk when noting high incident levels on Friday and Saturday nights. Alcohol and trouble

---

[12] Fig. 14 Accident and Emergency Attendances in England - 2018/19, Table 16

are best mates and it's a good idea to limit what you drink and keep your wits about you to lower potential risk even further. The figure I find alarming and one which is on the increase is the number of cases of self-harm, with recent data suggesting a significant rise in the number of teenagers admitted to hospital with self-harm injuries in the past two years, something in life has shifted, causing young people to buckle under stress. I hold a great deal of compassion for children and teenagers these days, with physical bullying becoming more brutal with children emulating the violence they are seeing in the UFC, music videos and the movies, and it seems to register in their minds as entertainment. Relentless psychological bullying via social media makes life even harder, and the rise in self-harm cases are going hand in hand with the growth of social media platforms. Bullying has been around forever, but I truly believe the landscape of bullying has changed, previously in the olden days of my youth before the internet, time away from school in the evenings allowed pupils to go home, prepare for the next day and get through it, giving time of respite. For children today it carries on out of school hours on social media with no down time, and no escape. Does the person being bullied switch off their phone and ignore it, or do they need to read everything being posted for any clues indicating what they are in for the next day? Stress, stress, and more stress. It's hardly surprising that along with the increase in self-harm is the increase in the number of teen suicides due to bullying, and it's shocking to see this curve matching the growth of social media.

Of equal importance as teaching children how to physically protect themselves, is helping them raise their self-worth to a level where what others say cannot deplete their belief in themselves. Society must wrap a compassionate arm around its youth and help where possible to avoid a mental health tsunami.

Awareness is key, its missile avoidance!

Learning how to keep yourself safe should be a positive and enjoyable thing and exactly what you're striving to achieve in *RBM*. Certainly not carrying an unhealthy level of paranoia and worrying about being attacked every time you step outside, that's not good for your stress levels, or your mental health and certainly takes the fun out of life.

I am presenting truthful information, helping to be alert to potential dangers, and helping to avoid them by increasing awareness. Turning up your level of street smart will help you in spotting 'potential' threats. A popular and useful tool to use for this is former marine Jeff Cooper's Colour Codes of Awareness[13], simplifying an outline of the mindset type and awareness levels you should be operating in during your daily life.

I have adapted Cooper's Colour Codes of awareness and included my own terms and explanations of the codes in the following chart:

Zombie: Unaware/unprepared	The operating state only useful for when you're asleep, or dead. Not when walking around, so ditch the headphones and the texting as you walk. Start paying attention to the world.
Prepared: Relaxed but alert.	*This is it!* This is your conscious level of awareness, the base level, not a state of paranoia but absorbing information about the world around you. It's very relaxing, not anxious or fear based, it's what modern self-help books call being in the moment, focusing on what's around you. Not letting your mind drift away and entering the zombie zone.
Ready: Switched on to a specific alert.	Something has drawn your attention subconsciously and you become consciously aware of it. Doing your best meerkat impersonation, your head shoots up as your instincts are telling you to keep watch on a specific variable in the picture, trust your instincts. Your HPAC Axis will fire in anticipation of fight or flight. When the peace vanishes, so do you, quickly!
Engaged: Leaving or eliminating a threat.	If caught by surprise the SAM Axis flinch reflex will fire, followed by the HPAC Axis and no conscious decision was needed for this. If you identify a threat by becoming consciously aware of it before it reaches you, but you aren't caught by surprise, the priming of the HPAC fight or flight system which occurred in zone *Ready*, when you were meerkat-ing, has turned out to be necessary. A pre-emptive firing for a potential threat has now become very real and necessary. You need a solution to the threat and must stay vigilant even once the threat has passed or been eliminated, do not drop to zombie after engaged, never assume it was the only threat or the only person presenting a threat. Think 'where's attacker number two?'

Once aware of a threat and in the mindset 'ready', it will be a threat which has a time or distance variable associated. How can I say this for certain? Well, because if a person grabbed you by the throat right now, there's no distance between you, both of you are connected by physical contact, it's happening now, with no time to avoid it. This would put you straight into the mindset

---

[13] Jeff Cooper, 1989: *Principles of Personal Defense*, Published by Paladin Press, a division of Paladin Enterprises, Inc., ISBN 0-87364-497-2 I

'engage'. Therefore, 'ready' must have the variables of time and distance, the time it would take them to cover the distance between you to grab you by the throat. If not, you would have been forced to move straight to 'engage'.

Not every *'ready'* level threat will escalate to an *'engaged'* level, it may be a false alarm. But how do you know for sure whether it's a real and legitimate threat you are facing, or nothing to worry about? This is essential information which needs clarification, because clotheslining a person you thought were coming in for the kill, when in fact they were rushing past you for a bus, isn't great for either party involved. You need some tools to help you identify real threats at distance.

<u>Location, location, location!</u>
You identify your location,
Pinpoint the location of the threat
Move yourself to a new location.

Proxemics is the term used when using a rough guide to split the space around you into zones, and it's achieved by sectioning off your environment at different boundary lines. This is nothing new, it's in nearly all self-defence books informing the reader when people move through these zones you should be aware of them, particularly as they move closer to the Intimate Zone.

What you don't find is a detailed explanation on how using proxemics can be a great dynamic tool for your awareness and threat identification, because it's usually only described in situations where one person at a time is walking through your zones, as though everyone else on the planet is at home asleep at that very moment. But for most of your life when you are out in public, you will find hundreds of people walking through these zones every day. Your priority is spotting the anomaly, movements which for some reason drew your attention, got your instincts firing.

Proxemics has the potential to be much more than a few nice diagrams in a book, and to achieve this potential it needs to become dynamic in its application. Think of yourself standing in the centre of a target, right on the bullseye as seen in *fig.15*:

(A) This point is your Intimate Zone of 1.5 metres.

(B) An area of 1.5 to 4 metres, which is the Personal Zone.

(C) The 4 metres to 12 metres area of the Social Space Zone.

(D) 12 metres plus away from the centre spot is the Public Space Zone.

Adopting your *Prepared* state of awareness, you will be observant of people moving around the social space zone (C) and the public space zone (D).

You won't be able to notice every person moving from the public space zone (D) into your social space zone (C) but if someone draws your focus then watch to see where they move next. It may be someone who is moving at speed through the zones towards you which draws your attention. Or perhaps other people in the crowd are parting quickly, telling you something bad is coming.

If a person entering the personal space zone (B) causes your intuition to get a little prickly, you should be hearing alarm bells if they're moving in a way which worries you. Such as loading their weight ready to throw a punch. You should be picking up this movement and being very aware of it, because if they make it into the intimate zone (A), you may have a problem which requires you to engage in a physical conflict.

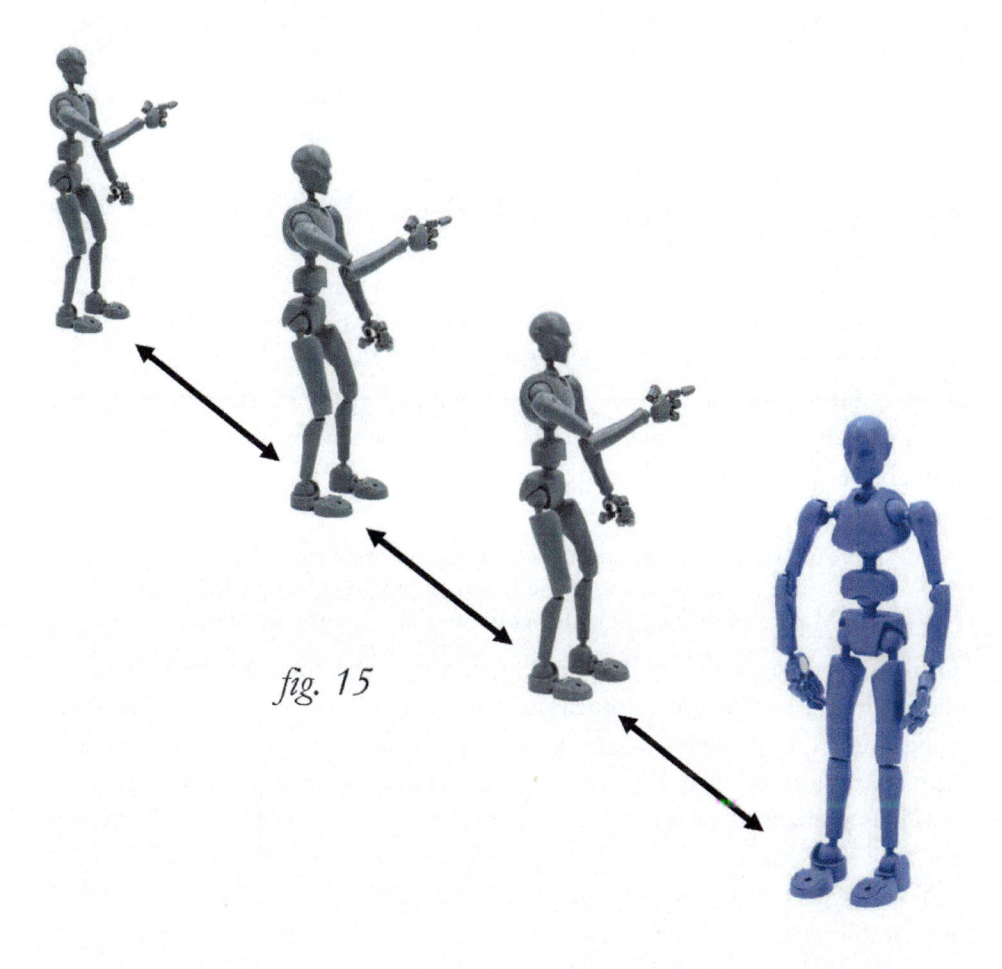

fig. 15

Regardless of what the self-defence world tells you, not everyone out there is an assassin with a contract on your head, you can't whack everyone who comes near you, what if they were going to pass through the intimate zone and straight out the other side without any problem? The reality is when standing in a crowd, people will be moving in and out of your personal and intimate zones without any intent of harming you and they will also be innocently navigating around other people and their zones whilst in these spaces. A plausible reason a person was walking so quickly towards you may simply have been to catch up with a friend who happened to be standing behind you, you mustn't live in the mindset of everyone is out to get you.

Not living with an extreme paranoia of being attacked but instead living with a rational approach to the world around you will highlight the natural flow of people in society. Yet this will also show how peoples movements does create a problem area for you which you need skills to overcome. You may have doubt and uncertainty as to why people are coming so close, are they a threat or not? You need to shore up your defences, and not leave yourself vulnerable to attack because this uncertainty opens the Big Red Box and then the chaos of doubt reigns supreme.

For this reason, this is where my explanation and understanding of dynamic proxemics will differ from other books and systems I have seen to date. A big principle to focus on here, *is the potential target area of the space you are standing in is not fixed*, the area of the bullseye with you standing at the centre can move, and this knowledge can be applied to clarify if a person is innocently moving through your space, or to determine if they a have a different, and sometimes hidden agenda.

If you have any doubt about why a person appears to be coming straight at you, <u>move the bullseye off the flight path</u>.
Make the proxemic zones come to life, become dynamic.

When you move, if the person heading towards you increases their pace, or adjusts their trajectory to compensate for your evasive manoeuvre and they change direction to track you, you know they are coming for you. You exposed them as a heat seeking missile coming straight towards you because their movements changed relative to yours, they changed to track the bullseye, the target, which is you.

You have immediately identified a threat and now you will be able to increase the distance between you and them, and if necessary and appropriate use some de-escalation techniques. If these options aren't going to work, you will already have your strategy of threat elimination in place. Which is quite simply, do whatever it takes to stop them from hurting you.

Step up your level of awareness

The next time you take a walk-in nature, see if you can spot a squirrel and attempt to walk towards it and try to touch its head. A difficult, if not impossible task to achieve and you'll be extremely lucky to get into its vicinity before it moves. It may not immediately bolt, it might scurry away from you a little to identify if you're a threat. If you change your direction, trying again to close in on it, it will burn rubber and dash off.

Now *I wouldn't advise doing this to people*, but in your local populated area, you would easily be able to walk around tapping most people on top of the head, entering their intimate space, and making contact before they realised what was happening. The contrast between a wild animal and people in our mainstream society is indicative of how low awareness levels have become. The general population are so switched off it's as though the zombie apocalypse is already here, people have let their senses become subdued through the knowledge they are safer far more than they are at risk. Which on the surface is obviously a good thing, as this is indicative of the fact society is relatively safe and provides the type of life we would always choose. But because of this safety people have become domesticated, which is a good thing, until you meet someone who isn't, someone who is violent and refuses to stick to the same laws and rules.

Observe people on a busy Saturday, all bumping into each other, oblivious to what's going on around them, it's no wonder so many people fall victim to pick pockets with their awareness levels set so low. People texting as they walk, not paying attention to the world as it unfolds around them, vast numbers walking in public with headphones on flooding one of the main senses. Nearly the whole of society walks around in awareness mindset *Zombie: Unaware/unprepared,* allowing people to move unchecked into their intimate zone and solely relying on other people not being violent as their safety strategy.

Aim to stay in a general state of *Prepared: relaxed but alert*, keeping your awareness switched on and monitoring movements through your distance areas, offering yourself the chance to evade trouble and leave early to avoid any confrontation. To develop this awareness, you will find development drills, avoidance techniques and de-escalation exercises for you to practice in a later section. But the first part of awareness is acceptance, the acceptance that illogical, irrational, and spontaneous violence can happen.

It's all about avoidance!
Previous attendees for *RBM* courses will all do anything to avoid having to hurt another person, not one of them would like to try out the things they have learnt, avoidance of violence is maximum priority. I was once given an exercise to complete which I always pass on, as it's a valuable exercise in awareness and

avoidance. Sit in a quiet space and think about what would you argue for and what would you die for. It's important to acknowledge an argument can easily tip into a fight and depending on how committed the other person is on causing you harm, can very easily spill into a situation where you have a person willing to kill you and you may have to meet them at that level to stop them. You now find yourself in a serious situation and one which may have been avoided if you didn't engage in the initial argument. The whole interaction doesn't have to be a progressive escalation either, it can leap from argue towards kill/die straight away if the other person decides to take it that far. If they shoulder charge you on a busy pavement and an argument starts, they can jump straight to plunging a knife into your chest.

How can this happen? Easily, and it may catch you unaware because you didn't think something this serious could result from a simple argument, you shaped your expectations on how the situation was likely to unfold based on your own belief system of what you think would be an appropriate response to the situation.

People fail to realise an aggressor's belief system has no correlation to their own, and the violent aggressor's reasoning of justified action enables them to go from a simple exchange of words to stabbing you faster than most can comprehend. Awareness of this disparity of beliefs, and acceptance of their capabilities is critically important. You should also consider that getting drawn into an argument can distort your awareness of what's happening around you, engaging in an argument draws your focus away from what's important, and in your fury and frustration, you don't see person number two come in from the side with a sucker punch to your face, plenty of people have been killed in this way. Over the last few years the one punch KO shown on the news and shared across social media seems to encourage more people to attack in this way.

Avoidance is a grey area and it's a difficult topic, because you need to decide when to stand up for yourself and when to let things slide, only you will be able to decide what's the right thing to do at the time. Decide carefully and I think you will arrive at the conclusion that rather than feeding your ego and arguing, it's simpler to let people think what they want about you and feel what they want about you.

Realise what they think about you is none of your business, those are their thoughts. If the situation doesn't threaten you with physical harm, let it be, they can have their moment of glory, winning the battle of the shoulder bump and you can carry on with your life.

Target Attractiveness

This is an important piece of information you must allow to stick in your mind.

For whatever reason a person may target, or had targeted you, whether it be for burglary, or making you the subject of a violent attack, domestic abuse, or a sexual assault, it is not your fault, you are never to blame for being a target.

I thought at this stage in our human evolution people wouldn't still be saying someone who has been sexually assaulted *'shouldn't have been drunk and wearing those clothes'*, as if fashion choices hold them responsible. People should be able to walk around naked with hypothermia being the only threat to their health. Dress sense and sobriety levels do not excuse violence. If you're in an abusive relationship, it's not your fault, the mental prison and control held over you makes it incredibly difficult to leave. If you leave your front door unlocked and you get burgled, it's not your fault. There are things you can do to limit the chances of you being selected, but even if you choose to ignore all the advice, the simple fact remains that if somebody commits a criminal act against you, *it's not your fault*. Victim blaming in our society needs to be addressed.

Target attractiveness is being aware of how you see yourself, and how others see you, within the collection of individuals forming the social environment around you. Identify what makes you stand out from the crowd, and if you want to stand out then you must know how to be prepared for this. Take responsibility for your own safety, because self-reliance is a big theme of *RBM* and you're the best placed person to look after you, so the more information you collect to be able to fulfil this job, the better.

There are key factors present in a criminal attack which apply to both you and the aggressor, making up the factors of violence potential. Let's explore these a little further.

Ability
The ability of the person to harm you, but also their perception of your ability to stop them will play an important role. The sting in the tail for an attacker is your hidden ability to protect yourself which will influence the outcome.

Opportunity
Are you proving to be a golden ticket by walking along a very quiet isolated path? Does the potential attacker have the option available of a quick escape? Have you had a little too much to drink and your awareness levels are low?

> **Awareness**
> Are you using headphones or texting by any chance? Are they aware you're unaware? Are you picking up the warning signs of aggression? Have you accepted the possibility that violence can happen?

> **Motivation**
> Do you have something they want, is it visible? Are you prepared and highly motivated to fight back if in danger?

What influences these factors and creates spikes of target attractiveness?

Your Ability

If untrained in realistic self-defence, and unfamiliar with how violence functions in our society, you'll likely have a low level of ability to protect yourself. You will always have the will and determination to survive, but find yourself lacking the ability to harness this. Sadly, the people you would rather avoid will be able to spot a lack of confidence, these people are predators, and they do this for a living.

Their Ability

Employing distraction techniques, intimidation techniques and rudimentary violence against you, along with the element of surprise. Possibly elevating their physical ability level by introducing a weapon into the fold, something which can potentially deliver more severe injuries faster. I say potentially as one punch can kill you, it doesn't always require a weapon to cause serious injuries. Generally, violent attacks are basic, and you're unlikely to see martial arts moves in street violence, but instead see simplistic, aggressive, and direct violence.

Opportunity

Are you walking alone on a quiet path? In a group but walking through areas unfamiliar to you? Maybe prior to visiting a city completely new to you, you neglected to research the area? Perhaps outside your home, you became engaged in an argument with someone? Have you had a little too much to drink, leaving you vulnerable. All opening doors of opportunity for violence to enter your life.

Your Awareness

Are you paying attention? Not paranoia but being observant of your surroundings and the people around you, or are you too busy texting to notice the people following you, or the car heading towards you? Are you aware someone is trying to distract you, whilst their friends position themselves ready to strike? Is there a way out, now?

Their Awareness
Have they been watching you and monitoring your routine? Have conversations with you previously given them what they need to know about your family environment? Attackers are often known by the target, so learn to spot people when they're strategically positioning themselves using conversation in their game of cat and mouse.

Your Motivation
Have you built a strong desire to fight until your last breath to survive? Learning how to stand firm on the frontline and protect your loved ones no matter what, because this will help to develop your mental fortitude. Increasing your own self-worth to the point where you see yourself as worth fighting for is also a way to increase your resilience. Will power is a strong weapon in your arsenal, trusting in your ability to protect is another.

Their Motivation
This is a tricky one, due to the many motivational factors of why violent crime occurs. To help clarify this, this chapter will delve further into causative motivational drivers for criminal acts, highlighting the things a criminal feels it's worth taking the risk for. Giving information which will help you ignore factors you can't influence, and how to manage factors you can control. For example, have you just withdrawn money and openly showed the cash before putting it in your wallet? Do you have a nice pair of branded headphones, the equivalent of walking around with £500 on your head? Do you have any threat history with the person walking towards you?

Observe people as you move through life, maintain a good level of self-awareness and environment awareness. This is all you can do at the first stage, concentrating on your decision making and how you present yourself to the rest of the world. Are you perceived as a target worth taking the risk for?

RBM increases your ability to protect yourself from a physical attack, and you will start emitting a new and real confidence in yourself, feeling comfortable in any environment you may find yourself in. The aggressor's ability levels will stay the same, but you learn how to stop them in their tracks, which again changes how you feel. You'll have practiced and perfected your awareness capabilities, becoming alert to the opportunities you may have previously been inadvertently providing people, and become aware of their ability to attack you. This leads to you modifying your actions, adjusting your social behaviour and your decision making, which by itself lowers the attacker's opportunity level and motivation level.

Is this right? Should you have to adjust how you act, and why should you have to learn this information because of the criminal element in the world?

There's a huge moral discussion on why you should have to change what you do, it's wrong you can't walk safely anywhere you choose to on the planet, it's wrong we worry about our children's safety when they should be free to explore and enjoy the world. You shouldn't have to spend one single thought about any of this, but until society progresses to a place where you can do whatever you want without risk of being attacked, it remains totally irrelevant, it is what it is, so sadly you need to learn how to deal with it until that change comes.

Until then, self-defence knowledge and awareness is necessary for how things are, right now to ease these concerns. You must deal with the reality of the world, not holding an idealistic utopian dream, and certainly not putting your head in the ground and ignoring the reality of the world in which we live.

Spending time making decisions about what other people are going to do is futile as this is out of your control, the only variables to concern yourself with are those under your control: will you walk where you know it isn't safe, will you learn to protect yourself prior to needing the skills?

How to Limit the 'Opportunity'

Understanding the motivational elements for criminals and how they act upon different factors will greatly assist your skills in danger avoidance. It's incredibly useful to able to construct a threat profile to pre-empt potential problems, and whilst violence can be random, often there are some pretty big signposts pointing out a likely fist in the face related visit to A&E.

Statistics are useful for constructing an image of the type of violence trends happening at a particular time wherever you find yourself in the world. There are core principles which apply as a response to all forms of attack, but they need to be presented in the right way for people to see how they relate to current worries about violence. If the stats show most people at a particular point are being attacked in a specific way, obviously your protection system should provide answers to these trends at that time. For example, with the recent surge in knife crime, most of the questions I am asked centre around this, and the self-defence solutions I am giving are focused on answering these questions. Yet these very same principles can be used to deal with a punch, or a grab, but people need to be shown solutions relating to incidents being reported on the news, enabling participants to gain a real confidence they can succeed against the type of violence seen being reported in their world. This transforms self-defence from being a non-specific routine, or an irrelevant set of moves into a pro-active method for aiding psychological preparation, as well as your physical readiness, for the most fear inducing and doubt creating violence.

I did originally include the latest crime figures in an early draft of this book, but instead elected to summarise the trends of violence and threats, but still covering the types of crime you will have seen reported. You require a summary of the trends of the statistics over the years as an information base, rather than what happened in the last six months. Realistically there are two main types of crime where the general population can find themselves face to face with an attacker. The first is the intrusive, violating act which often leaves people feeling unsafe in their own home, the criminal act of burglary. The second is physical assault, being on the receiving end of a person determined on causing you harm.

Burglary

Burglary is a global problem, with the type of theft falling into different categories, planned high end jobs or opportunistic acts. Whilst delivering *RBM* across Europe I found it commonplace for owners of nice cars to be worried about being followed home, held at gunpoint, and forced to give up their valuables. The weapon of choice in these organised robberies often being a shotgun or a handgun. They are timed for when the owners are at home which makes the security systems such as window bars, alarm system etc. all obsolete. In the UK, it's quite different as burglaries occur more opportunistically, and only one in five burglaries will end in a face-to-face encounter.

80% of burglars will be males aged between 16-24 years of age and there will be one or two of them.

Dave Putwain[14]

This is what you will likely face if you find an opportunistic burglary taking place at your home, one or two people in this age group. High end burglary is different, as it will be well organised and planned, like a bank heist, with more people involved and armed to increase the fear factor to reduce the time spent on site. Cases of professional footballer's homes being raided whilst they are playing games overseas have been reported on the news. When playing away games, the burglars work on the assumption that the most likely physically resistant person in their view who habitually lives there, the 25 to 35-year-old male, is absent *(this is stereotypical profiling and not factually based)*. They plan on facing the wife, children, and possibly grandparents.

---

[14] Dave Putwain 2012: *A Psychologists Casebook of Crime*

After a burglary, I advise you to put in place a security system, as burglars often return. Partly because they're familiar with the layout and what was missed last time, but knowing if they wait a short while you will have nice new shiny insurance funded replacements. Be aware that security systems can work as a deterrent, but also have the power to change the method the burglar uses. An alarm system turns what may have been a home burglary with the owners absent, into an aggravated raid, because whilst you're at home the systems will be deactivated. For this reason, you require personal protection skills alongside building security, because an alarm is a deterrent and not a safety net. However, this is only if they are really committed to getting into your home, the deterrents might make them pick an alternative target.

Assault

The second type of criminal act you're most likely to find yourself facing is that of physical assault, which is a situation of another human being placing a part of themselves or another object onto you, or into you, with the objective of causing harm. *The Offences against the Person Act 1861* is the law established to punish people for assault. I have included this in Appendix 1, defining the range of types of assault, and placed them in decreasing order of the severity in relation to the maximum penalty which can be dished out by the wigged one with the gavel. This law acts as a deterrent in society, but it doesn't seem to deter everyone and assaults can spring from anywhere, be it an individual, a gang, or crowd related. Looking at reported crime data over the past decade identifies the trends of violence over the years. It's these trends which are of interest, more than fluctuations in year on year numbers. What this data shows is that if you are attacked it will most likely be one or two people, probably male aged between 16 to 39. This isn't stereotyping or victimising any particular section of society, this is only presenting the raw data. Summarising the main weapons used in criminal violent assaults:

- Puncturing implements
- Knives
- Blunt force implements
- Stones
- Glass bottles
- Firearms
- The rest of assaults were without weapons.

Also, you're most likely to be grabbed and punched, and there is high value in learning how to disable more than one attacker, each of them with a weapon such as a club, knife or gun or a brick.

Practice in all rooms of your house, learning to protect yourself on the stairs, in the bath and in bed. Positions where you are restricted and in positions you think of as being vulnerable, like sitting down or lying on the ground. Practice in dimly lit rooms (but ensure the training environment is safe) as attacks do take place at night. Imagine being outside of the home and how this changes things by offering different advantages and restrictions. If your self-defence system doesn't include these aspects and you're only pacing up and down a sports hall hitting air, or pads then the benefits of your training are fun, sport and exercise based. It's providing a great social group and fitness program, but when it comes to the reality of a violent attack, you may find yourself short of information and in a bit of bother.

The people you need to learn about

Even though I'm going to talk about the part of our society capable of doing things which would take you to the darkest corners of your mind, it's not for you to be scared, or fearful. It's to enable you to spot potentially dangerous people and threats as soon as possible, shining a light on the dangers and avoiding unwanted attention. Knowledge and awareness, not paranoia and fear.

RBM is always encouraging you to focus on what you're going to do if ever facing a threat. Talking about the violent predators in society highlights the tactics used and helps prevent you being caught unaware, but it's not to switch focus and concentrate on their plan of attack or get drawn into their strategy and play by their rules.

Who are 'these people' causing the problems, who should you look out for while remembering not everyone is a violent murderer? It's beneficial to understand how violent people operate and accept a very small section of our society will use predatory characteristics to obtain what they seek. The definition of a predator as presented in the *Oxford English Dictionary* is [15]: *"an animal that naturally preys on others; A person who ruthlessly exploits others"*. All people engaging in a violent physical assault will utilise some predatory acts. It's important not to separate cases of rape from the category of violence, because at its core it's an act of violence and dominance, it's about power, control, resentment, and hatred.

Is the person attacking you a sociopath, psychopath, violent aggressor, rapist, gang member, mugger, or drunk attacker? If they are kicking you in the head whilst you're on the ground it doesn't matter how you label them, at that moment the only thing relevant is avoiding having a label hanging off your toe

---

[15] *Oxford English Dictionary*, OUP Oxford; 3rd edition (19 Aug. 2010)

in the morgue. Once an attack has started, the why, the who and all other questions are worthless, and your sole objective is to stop them, but recognising behavioural traits can help you avoid finding yourself in this position in the first place. For this reason, let's start by examining the world of the people with the characteristics, behavioural patterns, and the abilities of those commonly described as psychopathic or sociopathic, the most feared violent offenders in our society.

Sociopaths & Psychopaths
The psychiatric term for the people the general population would refer to as psychopaths or sociopaths, is Antisocial Personality Disorder. Welcome to the realm of the darkest abyss you can possibly imagine! If you don't fall into the category yourself, then this completely unexplainable world and their view of it will always remain beyond your comprehension, but hopefully after this section, within your knowledge base. There's a vast number of books detailing in depth the psychology of the people who've achieved notoriety, covering the mass murders, serial killers, serial rapists and so on. It's a huge topic and I've tried to give a tip of the iceberg explanation to provide the information relevant to you in terms of personal safety.

The question people ask after hearing about or witnessing the shocking crimes committed by people within this category is, *how did the person get to be like this, to be able to do these things?* The belief held by the majority of those in the current psychiatric field, points towards the view psychopaths are born and sociopaths are made. There are exceptions to this, whereby psychopathic behaviour has presented itself post birth, also the behavioural abilities of the born psychopath are associated with people who have had physical trauma to the Cerebral Cortex. Damage not from pre-natal circumstances but post-natal to the Frontal Lobe area of the brain which regulates self-awareness, self-control, and judgment. A point briefly covered in the section *Grey Matters – Pre-Frontal Lobe*.

MAOA or CDH13, is an enzyme responsible for breaking down Serotonin, Epinephrine, Norepinephrine, and Dopamine. Some research has found people can be born with lower functioning levels of this gene and that childhood trauma can influence these levels. Low levels of this enzyme lead to a build-up of these neurotransmitters leaving a person more disposed to violence, hence it has been labelled the killer gene. You may want to explore this for your own interest, but it doesn't warrant any more space here.

Additionally, any damage to the Amygdala would give an obvious explanation of how people are capable of things which seem callous to anyone else, as it's the processing hub for the emotions. An individual with damage to the Amygdala will often find life difficult because they are unable to express their emotions, leading to them becoming ostracised from the rest of society and causing further desensitisation to human connections. Trauma to these areas can also be caused by the environment in which a person lives, as life can be emotionally and psychologically damaging and exposure to severe abuse or exposure to the external stimulus of traumatic events can cause damage and limitation of processing in this area, leading to psychopathic traits post birth. So, there are instances where psychopaths can be created after birth but most commonly it's believed they are born.

The psychopath is often viewed by others as charming and most live a regular life. On the surface, everything seems fine with the person often being part of family life and working alongside others in everyday jobs, making their cold, calculated destruction of others even harder to comprehend. If you were to strip away the superficial story being outwardly projected, you would discover they're not authentically connecting with family and friends on an emotional level but viewing and valuing people as pawns in a game to be moved around and manipulated for their own needs. If they become violent, it will be within an opportunity which minimises risk to themselves and limits the risk of being caught. Data published by people who have researched in this field highlight a common theme of homeless people and prostitutes falling victim to psychopathic killers. The feeling conveyed by the psychopaths is it takes longer for people from these groups to be noticed as missing by their peers. They felt the police would not search as vigilantly for homeless people and prostitutes if reported missing as they would for a person who is a member of a different group of society, meaning the target attractiveness increased. It also seems as though they use these target groups as a training ground, refining their killing skills before moving onto their preferred, specific target type. The psychopath is far more emotionally disconnected than the sociopath and combining this emotional void with risk aversion means they often go on to create far more accumulative damage, most killers who achieve notoriety for long term sprees of murder are psychopaths.

In contrast, a sociopath will in most cases be impulsive and less careful about the risk of being caught, tending to be more transparent than the psychopath in the shallowness of their connectivity to others and far more restless in aspects of family life, friendships, and employment. They are willing to engage in violence without any thought, feeling, or concern of the consequences for themselves or others, giving little credence to the outcomes which will occur when they 'blow their lid'. Sociopaths are more likely to be caught earlier in a spree of indulgent mass killing than a psychopath, because they will take more impulsive risks. Sociopathic people who flipped and went for the onetime big kill are the disassociated teen who embarked on a school shooting, aiming at what they perceive to be the symbol of a society which they felt ostracised them, or the person shooting at a crowd in the street, or the radicalised extremist suicide bomber. They seem psychopathic, but they are in the sociopathic realm.

Stop, look, and listen!
It's worth exploring the psychopath and sociopath to build up a profile of the people who are walking around in society next to you, standing in queues with you, and possibly living next door to you. The similarities between the psychopath and the sociopath are:

- A lack of concern for the rights or welfare of others
- No respect for laws or socially acceptable behaviour
- Seemingly devoid of feelings of remorse or guilt
- Violence and the threat of violence is used to obtain what they want
- Constantly lie and deceive others
- Very, very skilled at the manipulation of others

Observing people around you and teaching yourself to spot these behavioural traits at low levels, especially when people are acting in ways which don't quite match the situation, will massively increase your awareness of potential dangers. There have been plenty of times when I've met people who just didn't seem to act in a manner which seemed appropriate and raised some warning flags, and you must learn to spot these signs.

Equally important is changing how predators see you, because the eerie thing is, no matter how hard you try to cover any insecurities and weaknesses you may have, if you try to hide these from a sociopath or psychopath, they can still see you, because *how you act is a form of camouflage.* Everybody walks, talks, and behaves in a way which hides their vulnerabilities, with this body language and behaviour patterns used as a shield, attempting to hide weaknesses by projecting a different persona.

There is a growing belief that the psychopathic/sociopathic predator can see straight through this shield because they're proficient hunters, skilled in spotting weaknesses in people regardless of attempts to conceal them. Irrespective of what you say, do and act, if subconsciously you don't believe in your ability to protect yourself, or hold a lack of confidence, they can see straight through the façade. Spotting the vulnerability and seeing the chink in your armour, they're now on the scent, as weakness increases the opportunity and can elevate the motivation spike. This may lead to a spontaneous, risk discounted, sociopathic attack immediately upon spotting the vulnerability, or a low-risk opportunistic psychopathic attack when the time is right. They strike when they see a weakness, this may be a lack of confidence, or even over confidence driven by an insecurity, or a false confidence. Trying to hide a feeling of vulnerability could be the accidental worm on the hook, catching something you would rather avoid.

A psychopath can patiently manipulate the environment they share with other people, such as the workplace, or they conjure up reasons to share an environment with a chosen person like syncing shopping habits. Sometimes they're closer than you realise and the time shared could be family get togethers. Spotting vulnerabilities in an individual's personality such as low self-esteem, people pleasing, or the need to avoid loneliness all contribute to creating a potential target. With time on their side, and once in a situation they can manipulate, they will start moving themselves into a place of trust, exploiting this in the future if desired. It's important to educate yourself to spot behaviour anomalies, because to rely on *why* they choose a target is unreliable, the reasons for target choices are unbelievably far ranging in variables, and nigh on impossible to identify and manage.

Some examples of why and how people have been chosen: *Richard Chase aka the Vampire of Sacramento*, a notorious serial killer who drank the blood of his victims. His method of selection? Simply whether the front door was unlocked, as in his mind an unlocked door gave him permission to enter. Then there's *Edward Leonski*, who targeted women by the sound of their voice. *Ahmad Suradji*, who killed 42 women aged between 11 and 30 years of age for the belief drinking their saliva would be his saving grace.

I've read all sorts of advice such as: don't have your hair a certain way, don't wear certain colours, don't drive a specific type of car, because these are the things the predators go for. Excuse the expression, but it's all bollocks. You may never know what catches the attention of a specific predator and this is exactly why we have talented profilers to help the authorities catch these people.

You can reduce the motivation level of these predators by elevating your ability level, as with this comes an increased sense of real confidence and you can limit opportunities by keeping your awareness high. A psychopathic tendency means they're unlikely to risk letting the world see who they truly are, and as risk limiters, they may not select anyone who could elevate this risk. If you walk with a real confidence and look as though you would fight back, then these factors can restrict your chances of being selected. They don't remove them, because you will never be able to apply logic to this type of attacker, but it will change the odds to your favour significantly. Remember, false confidence is an attention-grabbing flare to the psychopath, instead hold a confidence you can truly believe in, gained by having a self-defence method you trust will not fail you. Then the camouflage dissolves, and with it the sense of vulnerability diminishes, and instead of drawing attention from the most dangerous people in society you fade into the background, falling off the predator radar.

Antisocial Personality Disorder – The Psychopathic Predator

Opportunity: Don't be in places where you feel vulnerable. It sounds bleeding obvious, but people often say they felt vulnerable at night walking along the secluded lane and after having this feeling of vulnerability, they wanted to learn some skills, but the first skill would be not to walk where you feel in danger. Also don't endanger yourself for fear of being rude, if someone makes you feel uncomfortable, trust your instincts and leave, but leave safely and not rashly, potentially isolating yourself and putting yourself into deeper waters.

Ability: A psychopath can act in a way you will never be able to understand, capable of doing things you would never conjure up in your own mind. Unfathomable thoughts, abhorrent to most of the population yet in the mind of the psychopath, are neither right nor wrong. With no brake system, and no rational emotional or moral compass, these thoughts can be turned into physical action. Without genuine human connection being able to be formed between you and the emotionally numb threat, you will not be able to reason with them.

Motivation: Research carried out by *Radford University/FGCU Serial Killer Database*[16], shows out of 2527 cases, 48% of the murders were committed for enjoyment. There's not much you can do about this motivator other than to increase your ability to stop them, improve your awareness and restrict opportunities. Other than for fun, the reason for selection of prey seems random to everyone, except the predator in question.

Awareness: You fit the bill, for some reason you have drawn their focus, something is telling you to leave or stay clear - trust your intuition. You probably wanted something a bit more tangible, but don't underestimate gut instinct. If something doesn't feel right, if it seems a little off, listen to your instincts. When there's an internal screaming to stay away, have faith that your sensory systems are picking up cues subconsciously and making you want to get out of there, never stay to see if you were right!

---

[16] Radford University/FGCU Serial Killer Database

Antisocial Personality Disorder – The Sociopathic Predator

Opportunity: You just happened to be there, at that time, and at that place. You might have said or done something inadvertently to start the violence or done nothing at all. There's little concern shown by them for being caught attacking you, even in busy populated areas which you would perceive as being safe, there's still a risk. A far greater spontaneous element is being described here than with the psychopath, and less fear being shown of the risks involved, they are like a volcano capable of erupting at any time. An example would be road rage, not immediate rage but the person driving after you for two miles and then attacking you. Most people would have calmed down and disengaged by this point. The sociopath wouldn't care about consequences, whereas the psychopath would probably stalk you for a few months and then act, with less risk.

Ability: The same as the psychopath, using physical, emotional, and psychological attacks with a cold, empty emotional void towards others.

Motivation: Anger or resentment towards a group, or a person. Uses violence, sexual dominance, or intimidation to empower themselves.

Awareness: The same as when referencing the psychopath, trust your intuition, stick to what your instincts are telling you. If you think a violent storm is coming, get out of the area. If a person is making you feel uncomfortable, but you can't put your finger on why, get out of there. We're all pretty good judges of character if we follow our intuition. I have only refused access to *RBM* courses for two people because they just 'didn't feel right', my gut instinct was saying keep your distance. One seemed a little off, perhaps because he was a little too charming. The other, a fitness instructor who raised flags because of his happiness to receive adulation from others, the two people from his class following him around like groupies everywhere, yet he did nothing to discourage this was a flag.

With both of these people, it was a gut instinct, and they were both politely told this program wasn't what they were looking for. I didn't see either of them again apart from in the local newspaper. Mr. Charming had murdered his girlfriend, burning and dumping her body and Mr. Adulation executed a woman he was infatuated with who spurned his advances, killing her in front of her children with a bolt gun. They both murdered people years apart in two unrelated cases, and as far as I am aware, they were unknown to each other, all in a small and quiet town where extreme violence is a rarity.

Trust your intuition, it can be a finely tuned warning system if you learn to listen to it and don't ignore it when it's screaming danger at you. If you feel uneasy in any situation and it's safe to do so, leave immediately if possible. If you can't leave and things take a turn for the worse, then it's time for you to open a can of whoop-ass!

Ways that Predators Open the Door of Opportunity
People aren't always hit with a club and thrown into a van, the APD (Anti-Social Personality Disorder) predator directs, manipulates, and controls situations to gain the upper hand. Stories of these predators will often contain elements of manipulation in the build up to an attack, but if the level of opportunity is low, how do they create a door of opportunity? When looking back, a common occurrence prior to attacks by these prolific violent offenders, is that they used dialogue as a weapon:

- Enforced teaming is when a person uses specific language to manipulate a situation, building a construct of a common goal or a common problem. This artificial common ground creates a neutral space where they can meet you to gain your trust.
- Enforced teaming via physical action, is establishing a relationship based on acceptance. Achieved by manipulating a situation to get you to willingly receive something from them. For example, passing something to you which you take/accept lowers your resistance, your caution.
- Refusing to take 'no' for an answer.
- Very charming beyond the point of what is necessary at the time, like a desperate salesman. The question you should be asking is why the persistence, *what's in this for them?*
- Too many details! Embellishing the story with too much information, details which smell of a cover up, concealing their true intentions.
- Making a promise, with this pledge being delivered as a smokescreen, "I promise you will be safe" meaning exactly the opposite.

(For more information read 'The Gift of fear' by Gavin de Becker)

An example of how it fits together as a plan for creating opportunity would be something like this; your car breaks down and unbeknown to you, driving past is a person with an APD. For some reason you drew their attention, you caught their eye, they may have driven past another twenty people not giving them a second thought, but with you it was different. Their motivation is ignited. They see you as a high level of target attractiveness or one worth taking a risk for. If they offered to give you a lift, you would say probably no, and the offer would spike your alertness. So how do they get around this?

They spin a web to draw you in; "Would you like some help, it happened to me a few weeks ago, it always happens to *us* in the worst places." ***(Enforced Verbal Teaming)***

"*We* could just drive to the garage up ahead if you like, I know there are crazy people around these days, but <u>*you will be okay*</u>". ***(Smokescreen Promise)*** You say no, yet they keep persisting "it will be fine, I know *we* should be careful as *we* don't know who's out there, but you will be fine. You can use my phone if you like". ***(Enforced Teaming through verbal communication and accomplishing this by you physically receiving something from them. In this instance a phone, forcing the issue of accepting help)*** All this happens whilst carrying out what innocently appears to be trying to hand the phone to you. Remaining in their car limits the appearance of a physical threat, also allowing them the chance to leave quickly if someone else comes along. You take the phone ***(The team is now subconsciously formed)***. You start thinking they are no risk, otherwise why would they give you a phone, a thing perceived as a lifeline to the world. They seem nice and friendly, wanting to help, as even when you said no, they kept offering to help.

This may be a genuinely nice person trying to help, doing the right thing, or it may not be. Trust your instincts.

To summerise: Overusing the words; *we*, *us*, and grouping statements, such as '*I know we should be careful,*' are used by predators to construct a togetherness, a team. The false promises '*you will be okay, it will be fine*', may be reassurance from a kind person or they could be lies to conceal other intentions. If your instincts are screaming at you, listen, always trust your instincts! Pay attention to the language people use to manipulate you. Learn to spot this so it becomes more recognisable. It's not a nice way to have to view the world as there are nice, genuine people out there who just want to help. It might be perfectly innocent, but trust your intuition.

Leaving the dark world of the Anti-social Personality Disorder (APD) and moving onto the next category of physical assault potential dangers, you meet the familiar face of what will be referred to in this text as the *Aggressor*.

<u>Aggressors</u>
The *Oxford English Dictionary*[17] defines an aggressor as: '*a person, country, etc. that attacks first*'.

---

[17] *Oxford English Dictionary*, OUP Oxford; 3rd edition (19 Aug. 2010)

Note this doesn't state a physical attack, it's any act, or threat of an act, in verbal or non-verbal communication which you can justifiably say causes you to fear for your life, or safety. Not only who throws the first punch, or who grabs first. Aggressors are people who through social desensitisation have a tendency for violence which can bring out characteristics resembling the behaviour associated with the APD sociopathic predator. The people I refer to as aggressors aren't the ones who get a little rowdy on a Saturday and get into minor scuffles, but the people you see on the news captured on CCTV running through the streets hunting people who are desperately trying to escape. If they catch them, they senselessly beat them unconscious, or stab them to death. My use of the word 'senselessly' wasn't accidental, they are so hyped up in the moment they are becoming senseless. Don't underestimate them, they're a most dangerous entity and can be younger than most people would expect.

An individual with APD lacks empathy for other people, enabling them to function in the world of violence without any need of self-justification to be able to act with aggression. They can strike you without any reason other than you became the target. For the aggressor, the part of the brain monitoring and self-judging still works, it might not be functioning in the way we as a society would like because it's been negatively conditioned, but it still fires and works as a violence brake, which is something they must overcome. They often need some symbol of self-justification to engage in a violent act, however small this may be. Orchestrating an argument, pushing someone who pushes back, eye contact, being part of a different group or gang, are all enough to self-justify the attack. Peers egging them on gives another justification, as will alcohol, drugs, social dynamics, all contributing to the dampening effect of self-regulatory judgment and emotional centres in the brain. Each time they engage in violence the need for justification is lessened and the result is the brake is weakened and their ability to cause harm is elevated.

"What are you looking at……", is a widely used self-justification opener for a fight which has been around for as long as I can remember. Their focus zooming in like a laser, you're the target, they're in your face, shouting at you, questioning you, kick starting your Left Hemisphere Cerebral Cortex and getting it to engage as you try to be logical, you're trying to work out what to do about the verbal assault. They're abusing and emasculating you, all whilst revving up their own engine of violence. They sense you're caught in a state of flummox and they strike. Sneaky, nasty, and effective.

Fast track uncontrollable Psychopath – the 'Chemical Fruit Loop'

A study by the Global Drug Survey found that the UK has the highest proportion of legal high users in the world. One in ten of the 7,000 Brits polled admitted to taking legal high substance. That's double the global average.

Wensley Clarkson [18]

Drugs and alcohol dampen the self-regulation activity of the pre-frontal lobe, loosening the handbrake of what society, though our morals and laws, deem to be right or wrong. The *'Head Shops'* selling drugs under the label of plant food and the like, were legally able to occupy spaces on the high streets and were successful in getting these cheap drugs into mainstream usage. Since changes to the law, they've been shut down but cheap hits are now embedded in the psyche of the population and are in high demand, no pun intended! Now sold illegally these drugs are still out there, and it seems they are here to stay.

This particular band of drugs which are mainly made in China and increasingly produced across Europe, are almost impossible to stop. They are traded on the dark web and bought by people through encrypted text apps on their phones, they are everywhere. They sell for around £7 to £10 making them accessible in terms of cost and availability, and are perfect for those seeking cheap quick hits, especially younger teens. Most reported cases of these drugs going wrong tragically tell of the user dying, but there have been many cases of psychotic outbreaks. The most well-known is that of Rudy Eugene in the USA, who after taking a concoction called Mephedrone, *(commonly known as M-CAT, White Magic, and Meow Meow)*, decided to start eating a homeless man's face. Then there is Michael Daniel, also from the USA, who after taking the now notorious drug called Spice, opted to eat his housemates' dog whilst it was still alive. These highs don't only make you irrationally hungry, they can cause everyday people to become psychotically violent, an average, everyday person suddenly becoming an uncontrollable killer, a Chemical Fruit Loop!

The non-eating related incidents, some of which took place in the UK, are Sheldon Woodford who while high on Clockwork Orange attacked and mugged a ninety-year old woman. Clockwork Orange played a leading role in the case of the young woman, twenty-two, who burst into a house and attempted to strangle the families' nine year old daughter with a TV cable, and then proceeded to threaten to kill the younger son. The woman was understandably taken to a mental health unit afterwards, with her father blaming the high for causing this episode and insisting his daughter has never previously displayed aggression.

---

[18] Wensley Clarkson, 2015: *Legal Highs - Inside Secrets of the Worlds Newest and Deadliest Drugs*

Violence is exploding inside prisons in the UK due to cheap highs being smuggled inside. These chemical highs and the global problems they bring are not going away anytime soon. If you would like a glimpse into the darker side of your town or city centre streets, look up videos of Flakka, Spice or Monkey Dust on the internet. Only for the purpose of understanding the reasoning behind needing to cause structural damage to a person who may be attacking you, because if they are on this stuff, a punch to the nose isn't going to register.

The time-bomb which society failed!
A factor which I believe to be very relevant to threats of violence in society is the change in social care provision. Following conversations with people who work in this field, the story told was that current provision, or lack of provision of health care service in the UK, is playing a major role in potential outbursts of violence.

It's important that people with mental health issues are not stigmatised, and there is a strong need to reinforce the fact not everyone with APD or Schizophrenia is a risk, because not everyone has violent tendencies with these illnesses, and many are more likely to harm themselves than others. Many people with mental health issues who do have the potential to become violent due to illness, can function well in everyday life with medication. The real problem in the UK, is constant cuts to the funding of healthcare and the care workers who provide the support. Leaving resources spread too thinly and resulting in the people who are best monitored, often being left to self-medicate. The monitoring level has been reduced to a level where if people decide to stop taking their medication this will go unnoticed, and the potential for a catastrophic event has now increased without the level of care they need.

Part of the problem is not so much identifying when someone is becoming unwell but being able to get them admitted to hospital due to the reduction in beds. People are being sent home without the help they need and some people in the profession report there is a risk-taking culture presently which didn't exist 5 years ago. The medical profession would have previously been over-cautious with people, and that was probably better, as with mental illness you never quite know how it's going to develop and what event may trigger a psychotic episode.

When taking into considering the cheap highs available and the people left to self-medicate, I find the self-defence systems on the market whose message of *'if someone attacks you crush their throat'* to be abhorrent. Paying no regard to the fact there is a human being in front of you. The viewpoint of *'if they attack you just crush them, go for the kill shot'*, for me is horrendous. Obviously, when under threat you aren't going to have the luxury of time to ascertain if the person threatening you is usually a decent person and someone who forgot to take their medication for a few weeks, or someone who had a bad reaction to a recreational drug. In harsh reality, if a person is committed to harming you, you will need to injure them to stop them. But not knowing the reason for the situation and taking a blanket approach of doing as much damage as you can, I think is immoral. Do what is necessary whatever it may be but nothing more.

Legally, minimum force is what you are told to do, but also remember you're about to strike another human being. It may be a member of society who has been failed and left to self-medicate. It could be your child or family member who is a genuinely loving and caring teenager who went psychotic after a high was dropped in their drink by someone else for a laugh. This isn't your concern to try and fix, or endanger yourself trying to work out, but just consider if you are ever forced to take a step towards a person to strike them, make sure you are doing it only to save your life, or the life of others. When assessing the threat level, if you feel you have no option but to strike, then be effective in safeguarding your life but have compassion for the other person.

If your current belief is to get angry, seek payback, they deserved it, crush them, kill them, I suggest you stop reading this and spend some time assessing your views before you continue. It's not the message I condone, nor believe will serve you well. Not that you need my approval or permission, but you will be judged by your own conscience and the law. So, do what's necessary and what's right to ensure your safety, but learn ways of effectively and efficiently stopping an aggressor which doesn't default to kill.

From this point forwards all persons posing as a threat to your safety will be referred to as 'Aggressors'. This will be inclusive of individuals and groups known and unknown to you prior to an attack.

Prior to the event its useful to distinguish between the different types of threats to give you a heads up with potential warning signs, a reality of what can happen and the awareness to spot trouble. But when the attack is under way, treat everything the same because when on the receiving end of an attack, the type of person delivering the threat to you is irrelevant, getting out of there is the only goal.

Signs it's time to dive for cover!

What makes you turn and look when you sense the danger of violence around you? It's because you pick up on small non-verbal triggers indicating somebody has the intent to cause another person harm. Just like the gazelle at the watering hole looking up when the predators start licking their lips and thinking about dinner, you too pick up on cues, warning triggers.

Being consciously aware of the signs often seen in the build up to a violent attack enhances your ability to spot danger earlier, hopefully soon enough to get out of there before it happens. These warning signals will be referred to as Violence Indicators, and have been split these into three categories, the *Ignition*, the *Revving* of the engine and the *Full Throttle*, I thought it was apt to incorporate throttle in there, as by that stage it's exactly what they are thinking of doing to your windpipe.

A trigger is needed for the fight or flight system to launch, but if they're the one initiating the attack, there's no external threat to cause the system to fire, meaning there's a need to pump themselves up, working themselves into a frenzy to self-trigger. The aggressor uses different methods to cause a self-induced fight or flight hormonal release as they light the fuse on their own fight or flight system, and hope to simultaneously intimidate you to cause a flight, freeze or submit/posture, making you easier to hit. There will be various indicators of this happening, as their body language will be reflecting the release of rocket fuel that's happening in their body.

It doesn't chronologically always have to progress through the stages I've identified. The aggressor may be influenced by either psychopathic or sociopathic tendencies, stimulant use, or socially conditioned factors, which can enable an aggressor to jump straight to the full throttle stage as a fast track. It's worth noting some of the signs from the ignition list can be done internally, for example you will be unable to hear the aggressive threats being said in their own mind, ramping up their aggression levels and planning what they intend to do to you. Be vigilant in your awareness, look for the signs you can see, the ones which they are outwardly projecting whilst preparing themselves for battle, or sneakily using in the hope of concealing their intent whilst preparing to deliver a stealth attack.

The Ignition
In most cases of a violent attack, it starts here. Both on the streets and in domestic violence, these are often the first indicators to look for on your radar. Spot these signs early, recognise them for what they are and leave, or if safe for you to do so, try to deescalate the situation before it elevates further and erupts:

- *Raising the sound level of the voice* when talking or beginning to shout. They're getting frustrated and showing anger, which is good for you if you can bypass the intimidation they are trying to create. The shouting is good news, as it immediately highlights danger, even the most unaware person will struggle to miss this indicator. If oxygen is coming out of their mouth, they aren't storing it in the muscles to hit you. As soon as they go quiet, duck!

- *Pointing or jabbing with a finger* is symbolic of hitting you with a club, and you should recognise it as a sign of aggression. Don't stand still and let someone point their finger at you. Disempower the symbolism of this by moving away and taking control of the situation. As a side note, if you get frustrated with children and start yelling and pointing your finger at them, it will start the process of teaching them to be submissive when someone is angry. You will start building a conditioned freeze response which will not serve them well, because when faced with over assertive or dominating personalities they will become submissive, believing that dominating behaviour is acceptable in a personal/work/social relationship. Instilling a belief it's okay for them to be bullied and manipulated, and if ever faced with violence they will revert to type, they'll stand still and submit/posture.

- *Swearing/verbal abuse being directed at you,* is again about self-triggering and them causing mental disruption of you and your thoughts. Swearing and saying inflammatory remarks to engage you in the verbal conflict, trying to get you to submit, or even providing their self-justification to attack. Convincing themselves you deserve it.

- *Over-sensitivity to what is said.* Taking what you've said and twisting it to their own means, manufacturing an excuse for their anger, or an excuse for them to play the victim in a battle they've initiated. It's very devious, do not respond, don't play the game and give anything as ammunition which can be recycled and used against you.

- *Standing too close, invading your space,* and trying to intimidate you whilst positioning themselves in the ideal spot to launch their attack. Move off the spot, don't let them into your Intimate Zone.

- *The tone of their voice will change* as they start to get angrier, due to their throat tightening when they tense the muscles in their neck and shoulders in preparation for conflict.

- *Problems with concentration,* whatever anyone says to them doesn't seem to register. A clear indication they're shutting down the link to the analytical, negotiating Cerebral Cortex Left Hemisphere. They are beginning to self-initiate the fight aspect of the fight or flight response.

- *Stamping the feet* is a sure sign they're producing Adrenaline, Noradrenaline, Testosterone and Cortisol, but not using the fuel yet. It's also a noise generating action to stimulate a panic response from you.
- *Banging/kicking* things is the visual display of aggression, testing to see if you crumble and submit.
- *Walking away* showing they're leaving but then turning around and coming back at you quickly. A deception to cause you to drop your guard and discard the hormones in your body, having a relax response of 'it's all over'. You're now unprepared hormonally when they re-enter your personal space. <u>Never think it's over.</u>

The Revving

Hormones are starting to flood their system, creating external signals which give you a glimpse of the effects of their internal fight activation system shifting up a gear. Witnessing the HPAC Axis and the Cortisol Revving in action:

- *Sweating*, preparing their own body for battle, they don't want to be easy to grab, so the body starts to produce oily sweat, also using it as a cooling system.
- *Shaking*, just like a space shuttle with full thrusters on before the clamps are released. The chemicals are quickly building up in their system.
- *Muscle tension and clenched fists*, getting as much blood into the muscles as possible, feeding the troops before the attack.
- *Rapid breathing* as the body tries to get more oxygen into the system to prime the muscles for some serious work. They're preparing to pound you into oblivion.
- *Staring eyes*, making sure they're challenging you for the alpha status. Will you posture and submit, if you do, will this prevent the attack or encourage the attack?
- *Restlessness and fidgeting*, the hormone accumulation is causing involuntary movement.

The Full Throttle
The final stage, and the more physically noticeable signs of impending aggression. There's no more build up going on in their mind or body, no more psyching themselves up. They're about to launch the missiles whilst trying to intimidate you along the way. Some people do the previous stages internally or out of sight from you, if this is the case, all you will see are these final signals as your initial warning signs:

- *Widening of the eyes and searching for eye contact*, intimidating you, causing you to freeze, making you stand still to strike you easily.
- *Tightening all around the jaw and shoulder muscles* as they protect their jaw and neck area. Knowing they're going into battle and preparing by bracing for impact in case you fight back.
- *Their chin drops and they look upwards under the eyebrows* protecting their throat. The facial area changes, particularly around the eyes, scowling and looking up under their eyebrows at you, like a snarling dog, feeding their anger and allowing it to grow inside.
- *Their movement will change,* a change of direction or a change of pace towards you trying to startle you. The intention is to cause you to panic, freeze and stand still.
- *They shift most of their weight onto one side* whilst standing or walking. Loading the body ready to launch their weight quickly with a punch, head-butt, or stab etc.
- *They stop shouting or arguing* and take a sharp intake of breath as they keep the air in the body for the final oxygen absorption into the muscles before attacking. *(This is a great time to strike the jugular notch).*
- *The chest area will expand,* another piece of acting like a peacock to make themselves look bigger and intimidate you in the attempt to make you freeze and submit, it's pantomime and illusions.
- *The redness leaves the face,* and the voice level drops as the blood rushes into the muscles, then the talking stops. They shift away from the left hemisphere and all verbal communication ends and physical action begins.

The Poodle Loop

The OODA Loop, developed by *Colonel John Boyd* [19] is widely used in military training, particularly in the United States Airforce, to enhance the process of decision making.

OODA stands for: Observe - Orientate - Decide – Act

Military personnel being deployed on active duty are prepared for what they may face, they will be using this OODA process all the time. *Observing* the surroundings, using pre-existing information and real-time data for shaping their perception of what's happening around them. If something changes, they *orientate* themselves, the process of absorbing as much information about the new elements which have come into their world, a multitude of factors possibly influencing their decision making. Then they *decide*, a function which you now understand is done subconsciously, but then becoming consciously aware after the decision has been made. They will implement the decision and they *act*. This is a great explanatory system for decision making and it fits neatly with the *RBM* Loop and the Analytical Doom Spiral Loop which I use to explain brain processing.

Only two things can happen when you're under threat, you can be aware of the threat, or you can be taken by surprise. If aware of a potential threat, you will be starting at *observe*, but if caught by surprise then you aren't even on the chart. If you're standing in the supermarket and somebody inexplicably tries to attack you for whatever reason seemed justifiable to them, they will have a head start, literally a head start as their mindset will be moving from the stage of *act*. You on the other hand will be potentially opening the Big Red Box, moving along the Analytical Doom Spiral Loop.

The reason you aren't going to be in the mental gear of *decide* or *act* is because it's impossible to maintain this state of awareness permanently. Analysing every person at every moment leads to preparing a paranoia driven action plan for all eventualities, all day, every day. Thankfully, you don't need to do this, because your acceptance that violence can happen anytime and anywhere helps greatly, as it keeps your awareness levels out of *Zombie State* so you don't completely switch off.

Don't forget there's the safety net of the flinch, if caught by surprise and they're close enough to strike you, you'll immediately go to *act*, you will bypass O.O.D. and the *act* part will be a Sam Axis Reflex, which is the flinch response. If prior to this attack happening you have effectively loaded personal protection

---

[19] Boyd, John, R., The Essence of Winning and Losing, 28 June 1995 a five-slide set by Boyd

information into the hippocampus, then this flinch action will be followed by a HPAC Axis preconditioned (not a set pattern) response, and you will strike a target. If you do anything which disrupts the aggressor and their plan of attack, then you'll be sending them on a psychological trip to the Orientate phase, whilst you're moving into the Act phase. Good news for you, bad news for them.

I have adapted the OODA Loop and made it more applicable to a non-military function for the general population, and you are now presented with the 'POODLE' Loop. It's a silly name for a good reason, to help you to remember it:

Pre-empt- you aren't being deployed into a war zone and therefore, unlike military personal existing in a state of awareness ready to engage, you'll instead be walking around pre-empting the *potential* for a random attack, rather than expecting an attack. Initially it takes attention to train yourself to maintain this level of awareness without sliding into needless paranoia. A main factor here is the acceptance of a potential for trouble to start right now, even if you can't see a reason why it exists. But not worrying about it or expecting it, just a nod to the fact it can happen at any time. Accept the potential for an attack, but don't expect the attack.

Observe- noticing people moving in and out of your Proxemics Zones, monitoring the mood of your environment and trusting your intuition. The *Drills in Spotting Danger* will help analyse the world around you, listening when your brain spots any abnormalities in normal social behaviour. Being able to flag anything out of the ordinary, even someone attempting to act ordinary because they're shielding their more sinister intent.

Orientate- this is all done subconsciously. Assisted by *RBM* giving information to be attentive, learning to spot weaknesses in aggressors, identifying and disrupting their plan and their feedback loop. Assessing if there is an escape route, and whether you can deescalate or if it's time for you to move onto the last resort.

Disrupt- if attacked and taken by surprise, you'll find yourself being thrown straight into an *engaged mental state* as you're under immediate threat. The previous step of *orientate* is performed subconsciously, and a SAM Axis flinch response will be deployed, with a shift to the HPAC Axis preparation initialised.

It's impossible to guarantee you will move from a surprise attack to a meaningful strike on a target with full conviction and mental clarity without any delay. This would be the equivalent of driving your car and shifting directly from 1st gear to 5th gear. You would be asking an awful lot of your brain and body to do this in a stressful environment, and knowing how the brain functions, it's unrealistic to rely on this happening with total conviction. You might lash out in response, but that isn't the same thing as a targeted meaningful action which will stop the attack.

This factor is the gremlin in the machine of the self-defence systems I've come across, because it's not taken into consideration there will be a moment of uncertainty, a fraction of time where you will want to press pause to give time to consciously cognitively work out what's happening. You won't always launch an immediate, calculated, and measured strike as a first response when ambushed and taken by surprise.

To compensate for this window of uncertainty of what to do, it's crucial you immediately move off the spot when attacked. Your movement will cause some disruption to their plan of attack, which is essential at this point, as the odds are highly in their favour if you don't move. You must move off the spot and do something to drag them out of their decisiveness, you need to unsettle them, and your safety is riding on this. If you start moving forwards and clearing some space, by throwing your hands towards their face, *(an action which doesn't require the brain process which is required to deliberately select a target)* the hands towards the face will be creating the opportunity to orientate yourself, deciding on whether to run away, or to pick a target and engage. At this point you should follow the next two steps in chronological order.

> *Leave* - if there is an opportunity to exit the threat area then take it, if there's the potential to safely leave and to take everyone with you, then grab it every time. But you're leaving to avoid conflict, not because you aren't equipped to deal with it.
>
> *Eliminate* - if there's no other option, then you have no choice but to eliminate the threat, launch the missiles and deploy the HPAC realistic self-defence response, strike the target.

Drills in Spotting Danger & Developing Awareness

Of equal importance to learning how to stop someone from attacking you, is the ability to read the world around you, seeing how people function as a collective society and noticing the little nuances others have when moving through their daily lives. If you can't spot people acting out of the ordinary, or pretending not to act out of the ordinary, you're one step behind in the game of survival. The following observational drills are for you to use whilst out and about in a busy place and will help you to develop your situational awareness.

When working through these, don't engage in any conversation, don't make eye contact, and avoid anybody realising what you're doing. You don't want to scare anyone or make them feel threatened or uncomfortable, you're simply monitoring the movements and behavioural patterns of the people around you to see how they function.

Be the hunter
Sit in a coffee shop or a public place where you can observe people walking around. Watch as they pass by, picking the ones you would eat if you were a hungry lion. Write a little note about why you chose them. Was it an injury? Did they walk as though they were weak, even though their body looked strong? Perhaps they seemed overly confident? Once you have a few things on your list, read them and make a conscious effort to never do those things.

The Walking Dead
Observe how closely people move in relation to each other whilst being totally oblivious to movements and intentions. Notice the proxemic zones around people and see how they walk into each other's zones completely unaware, placing themselves in potentially vulnerable positions. How many people can you spot walking whilst texting and using headphones in public?

Boo!
Watch what people do when caught by surprise. See how they flinch, how they jump out of the way and react to the thing which surprised them. It's very educational to watch as you witness super-fast avoidance movements (SAM Axis) when they flinch, followed by a period of time where they stand still and dither. They have a mental stammer whilst trying to work out what to do socially. (Untrained Hippocampus re-firing of the HPAC Axis = Freeze)

<u>Awareness drills to practice with a training partner.</u>
Move the Bullseye! Stand at opposite ends of a spacious room with a practice partner.
- They walk towards you and when they do this, you move off the spot.
- Sometimes your drill partner will ignore your movement and be a non-threat, continuing towards the space you originally occupied, or they may change direction and walk away from you.
- Other times, they will track your movement, indicating they're coming for you. Basically, the target (you) moved so they must adjust their trajectory to be able to catch the target, revealing they are a threat.
- When you make your move, do it by forming a fairly wide circle around the potential aggressor, this way you create the need for them to deviate from their initial course, and puts you in a position where you're ready to close in, striking a target if necessary.

With a drill partner, replicate the signals of the *Ignition*, the *Revving*, and the *Full Throttle*.

<u>The Ignition</u>
Stand at opposite ends of a room from each other, one person at a time walking towards the other. Whilst doing this, replicate one of the warning signs from the list below:
- Elevating the sound level of the voice when talking or start shouting
- Pointing or jabbing towards the drill partner with a finger
- Swearing/verbal abuse to try to cause intimidation
- Over-sensitivity, trying to pick a fight regardless of what's said
- Standing too close, invading your space
- Changing the tone of voice when talking
- Walking away, but then turning around and coming at you again

<u>Now do the same thing with the Revving the Engine section replicating:</u>
- Muscle tension & clenched fists
- Staring eyes
- Restlessness and fidgeting

(You won't be able to replicate the other revving signals without getting into a rage)

Finally imitate the aspects of the Full Throttle section:
- Widening of the eyes and searching for eye contact
- Tightening all around the jaw and shoulder muscle groups
- The chin drops, looking upwards under the eyebrows
- A change of direction or pace towards you
- Shifting most of their weight onto one side whilst walking, or when standing still
- They position their body ready to strike you
- The chest area will expand
- They stop shouting or arguing and take a sharp intake of breath

Repeat these until familiar with the danger signs and confident in your ability to identify them. Spotting these warnings of an impending attack gives you the potential to leave before the trouble starts, or be ready before it escalates.

Learning to identify potential threats via body language and body movements is extremely beneficial to anyone with Autism Spectrum Disorder (ASD) as there are occasions where this can leave people particularly vulnerable. If you describe how autism effects people, every description would be different, yet it's often associated with ASD that individuals find it harder to read facial cues. This makes it difficult to read emotional changes in others, which leads to scenarios where the individual may struggle to see fast changes in their social environment. When considering how sneaky aggressors can be and combining this with any reduction in facial and emotional recognition, it can lead to key warning signals of a threat being missed. Not being able to identify these signs of danger can be devastating, for example, an aggressive person looking up under their eyebrows and staring threateningly may be completely missed as a warning of danger by the individual with ASD. Another example of how ASD can create complications is the associated trait of not wanting to make eye contact, which can give the indication a person is being submissive and vulnerable.

Regrettably, there have been reported cases of people with ASD being attacked by an aggressor who deliberately targeted the individual due to their vulnerability, and cowardly picked an unprepared, unaware target. There have been instances of situations being misread, where the person with ASD missing facial cues, or language indicators of sarcasm and veiled threats, leading to them giving a response others would usually expect to see or hear. These have been misinterpreted as a challenge or a sign of disrespect, and lit the blue touch paper, only afterwards did the aggressor discover they had misread the situation and the person has ASD.

This is only explaining events which have taken place and is in no way excusing or justifying them. At the root of it all is a lack of knowledge, understanding, and a growing lack of tolerance and compassion in our society. It's shocking for the individual with ASD, as when you combine either a deliberate attack, or a misinterpreted situation which led to an attack, in either situation the person is being caught totally unaware and off guard. A horrendous sucker punch attack on both a neurological and physical level.

To counteract this, if you have ASD, work on your strengths, and spend more time focusing on body postural changes which are displayed by aggressors, such as the change in bodyweight and the change of pace as they walk towards you, rather than more subtle cues of language and facial expressions. By highlighting a chink in your armour you can reinforce it, strengthening your defences. Having this condition doesn't make you weak or vulnerable, because you can learn how to shore up your specific defence needs. Knowledge and awareness will help you.

RBM Development

- **Internal Proxemics**
  Stage 1 - Identify your location
  Stage 2 - Pinpoint the location of the threat:
      Is the threat real or illusionary?
      Think Tank - The Mental Spring Clean
  Stage 3 - Move to a new location
- **Target Attractiveness -** *Why does this keep happening to me?*
- **Are you living in 'OO' Land?**

Self-awareness is the key. Becoming aware of your conditioned responses, your triggers. Observing how you respond in situations which cause you to react in ways which you would like to alter. Spotting the seeds of doubt and worry which often trigger stressful rumination is a big part of this section, identifying whether the thing causing stress is a reality, or something you think 'may' happen.

Internal Proxemics

Proxemics Stage 1 - You identify your location

A lack of awareness of your surroundings will drastically reduce the chances of your success if faced with the threat of physical assault. Awareness of your environment, combined with realistic self-defence skills change these odds, by providing early detection of a threat and being able to create a solution to any external danger.

Development of awareness is also needed for your everyday life away from what you consider to be self-defence, switching your thoughts away from the topic of someone trying to harm you and moving instead to thinking how you react to things which cause you stress. Learn to identify your emotional baseline and assess your ability to be in control of your actions, by observing how changes in your internal environment affect you. When I say internal environment, I'm referring to your thought processes and your stimulus response behaviour patterns, the way you react to the difficult situations and demands life places on you. Observing your reactions and highlighting the 'buttons people press' makes you aware of your triggers, and changing how you respond will have a positive outcome for your health. Developing skills to neutralise negative reactions will lower your stress and anxiety levels, limiting the inappropriate use of the stress response system. An increased level of self-awareness and self-observation will enable you to notice fluctuations in your stress levels earlier, giving you a more efficient internal stress detection system. One which you can take control of and reduce the detrimental high/repetitive impact stress has on the human body.

This all sounds very simple on a theoretical level, but it's not easy to apply all day every day, because you will probably forget to monitor yourself, and of course anything which is limited to being a theoretical understanding will have shortcomings in its success rate, as it's unlikely you will remember to apply the principles often enough. It's a big ask to be able to sustain such a level of self-observance in the long term, just as you can't maintain a mental state of always being ready for an attack.

I have found a far more reliable and effective approach is to change your automatic response habits, change your whole mindset and how you react when difficult situations arise. The *RBM* approach to achieving this is using physical movements combined with focusing on solutions and reacting positively. This is what Phase 3 will help you to achieve, changing your operating system and instilling in you the thought loop of focusing on targets, putting all your energy into solutions rather than spending time and effort focusing on problems.

Signs it's time to take time out!
I like to keep things simple. You have one thing to do to help establish a positive change in your response to stressors, you need to stop! Stop what you're doing and adjust any negative thinking as soon as possible, stop the thoughts in your head which are negative remarks about yourself, or others. You stop!

Take time out of a situation if you feel the need to reset your thinking, and take the chance to replace these thoughts with more constructive ones which move you closer to a positive outcome. Stop immediately if you find yourself doing any of the following things to yourself, another person, or an inanimate object:

The Ignition:
- Elevating the sound level of your voice when frustrated, or you begin shouting.
- Pointing or jabbing with your finger
- Swearing/verbal abuse towards other people or yourself
- Over-sensitivity to what is said, or is happening to you
- Standing too close to people, invading another person's space in frustration.

- Your tone of voice changes and you can hear the verbalisation of anger.
- Walking away from an argument, but then turning around re-entering the argument

Revving the Engine:
- You feel yourself sweating with anxiety
- Shaking in the muscles, building of pressure in your body
- You have muscle tension and clenched fists
- Your breathing has become rapid
- Too much intensity for the situation
- Restlessness, fidgeting as your stress levels rise
- You can feel yourself getting a flushed face

Full Throttle:
- Tightening of your jaw and shoulders
- Your chin has dropped, and you are looking upwards under your eyebrows

The sooner you recognise these indicators of an external threat as also being the warning lights of rising internal stress levels and stop doing whatever is causing them, the better for your health and the health of those around you. In turn improving your home environment, your relationships, work environment and any place you find yourself.

Proxemics Stage 2 - Pinpoint the location of the threat

If under physical attack, you'll need to determine which are imminent threats to your life, and which are immediate threats to your life. A person crossing a road walking towards you with a baseball bat is the immediate threat, unless you are suddenly grabbed by someone else with a knife. This new threat downgrades the baseball bat attacker to an imminent threat level, and replaces the immediate threat level with the knife attacker.

The same approach applies to being attacked by one individual, if grabbed by the throat the hand around your windpipe is the immediate threat. If the person produces a gun, the hand on the throat is downgraded to an imminent threat level, and the gun becomes the immediate threat. The ultimate threat is always the driving force behind the problem, and in the case of a human aggressor, this is their brain. Their brain is the power of creativity, constructing and implementing the battle plan, which is exactly why it's the ultimate target, if you stop the brain you stop everything. If faced with an imminent, or an immediate physical threat, standing still and waiting for the attack is not beneficial. Get yourself moving away from the ultimate threat and out of reach of the plan they've created, or get close enough to strike them and end their plan of attack.

This is more relevant to your daily thought processes than most people realise because the same principle applies to non-violent stressors/threats. Why wait for the attack, in this case waiting for something to become stressful? People always avoid the conversations and situations they don't want to face, but if you see a problem coming in the future, why wait for it to arrive in the immediate stress level zone, instead of you choosing to face it on your terms. Why wait until it's more amplified, with more worry and a larger emotional response, bringing with it a larger stress response? Deal with it as soon as you see the issue on the horizon, be compassionate to yourself and others in how you deal with it but act immediately. Not with any fear, anger, or resentment, but with a tenacity to find a positive solution, an empowered outcome. It's the same as if a person is about to harm you, don't wait, find the solution, and move, move now!

Is the threat real or illusionary?
Here we are! We have arrived at a big question which causes many people to have a huge amount of unnecessary stress in their life. *Are you worrying about things which haven't even become a reality yet?* Your long-term survival needs a healthy level of risk assessment in life; a reasonable level of worry, a small amount of fear of death, and the motivation to stay alive keeps you safe, it's a positive balance. The problems begin when one little seed of doubt, watered and fed by a thought process called negative rumination, starts to grow, branching out into the never-ending list of potential *'what if's'*.

Rumination of thoughts is a mental imprisonment, constantly recycling loops of negative ideas in your mind, chasing answers to the things which have the potential to happen, but presently are non-existent problems. This is exhausting, as navigating through one life is hard enough, yet when worried about something, your brain will create multitudes of possible realities, resulting in you seeking solutions to endless illusionary problems and having elevated stress levels about possible eventualities which haven't even occurred, and may never happen. Playing these ruminations out in your mind will overload your senses, creating a feeling of directionless and making you afraid to make any decision in case it's the wrong one. You lose sight of the real issue and end up feeling overwhelmed, becoming lost in a fog of fictional potentials. You can call these thought originated spirals of worry by different names, such as challenges, obstacles, or whatever you like when trying to convince yourself you're in control, but if your mindset doesn't change in relation to how you treat them, then it's simply semantics and positive thinking, rather than a solution focused approach.

RBM offers a different option, conditioning yourself to think differently through dealing with a simulated, but tangible physical attack scenarios to learn how to identify what is a real threat and to ignore the illusionary *what if* outcomes. Pick a target, find a solution then repeat, repeat, repeat, select an outcome and focus on it, rather than on fictitious worries. In terms of a physical threat, the person who worries about getting punched will get punched, but the person who moves off the spot to chase a solution doesn't get punched. Transfer this to non-physical threat situations and you'll see that if you focus on the problem you'll get hit by the problem, ruminate and you will face the onslaught of the stress response as a reaction to the potential outcomes you've imagined.

Don't focus on the problem and what it *may* create, switch your thinking to the solution and whether you can move straight to this point. If not, how are you going to take a small step in a positive direction? The solution is the only thought you should allow to occupy your mind space when a stressor appears, because as soon as you start to drift towards the negative and repetitive worries, you become inefficient. When you feel yourself drifting towards ineffective worrying, stop what you're doing and stop what you're thinking. Break the negative feedback process, *identify what is tangible and real and expose the fictional potential outcomes not worth focusing on.* This is a core principle and one of the biggest challenges you will face in applying the concepts of *RBM* beyond self-defence and into other areas of your life. This is a far greater achievement than learning to stamp on someone's ankle.

Think Tank - The Mental Spring Clean
At the end of each day, having a de-clutter and a reset so as not to carry today's worries into tomorrow's fresh start is a great idea. Anything breaking the pattern of accumulative stress is beneficial and the Think Tank exercise helps you achieve this. Will something as simple as Think Tank work? The top end military teach something similar to journalists in preparation for placement into war zones as a tool to help survive if captured and held hostage. Whilst you hopefully never find yourself in this situation, it's still a valuable tool to be used daily.

People have anxiety about different things at different levels and it's important not to disregard how you or others feel about worries or to trivialise them. To say they aren't serious is incorrect, because sometimes you may feel as though you're a hostage, trapped by worries and unable to see a way out. *RBM* is focused on providing tools to help you lower stress and to take control of your thoughts and as soon as you take control of your actions and thought processes, your mindset changes, then positive actions follow and you reap the rewards, you will see light at the end of the tunnel.

A large proportion of people's problems are made in the mind, and the process of solving them can also start here with a daily declutter, helping to break the constant presence of stress, sleepless nights, and residual muscle tension. You require a method to do it and *Think Tank* is a huge part of this. I suggest you record yourself verbalising the instructions detailed below, then listen to the audio of your own voice. A good time to use the think tank is before you go to sleep each night. Be assured you won't have to find unrealistic levels of time each day to complete the tasks, I have made sure everything is achievable and within realistic time demands.

- Sit or lay comfortably somewhere quiet
- Start to count down from five to one, feeling calmer as you get closer to one. The muscles start to relax and the body starts to feel as though it's sinking into the mattress
- When you reach the count of one, you'll be in a place of your choosing. It can be on the moon, in a garden, on a beach, anywhere which feels quiet, safe and comforting to you. Your safe space
- Focus on the fact you feel calm. Go for a stroll in your safe place, do whatever you feel will help lower your anxieties
- Every few minutes, move your fingers or toes as you don't want to feel detached from your body
- Focus on the breathing (outlined in phase 2), feel as though you are relaxing in a bath and feel your muscles lose all tension
- Start to move your arms and legs, feel more connected to the weight of the body but without any tension.
- Now you can go to sleep.

With Think Tank, most people report they fall asleep before completing their mental spring clean, but it's not an issue because you will sleep well without spending hours with your head on the pillow ruminating. By investing time doing this, you will be clearing your mind rather than entering broken sleep with disruptive, worrying thought patterns whizzing around in your head.

Proxemics Stage 3 - Move to a new location.

Move Now!
'Awareness is key, it's missile avoidance', covered the process of working out what's important to you. Focusing on getting those things right and dropping the self-loaded worry about everything else, lightening the load of pressure which people place on themselves. It's about altering your thought process and focusing on what matters. In my home we have a simple question – *do we need to go to hospital right now?* If it's a family health issue, there will be a level of stress attached to it. This is natural, obviously we will be concerned and it's all hands on deck to get it sorted out. Anything else, no problem, there will always be time to fix it, or there will be a chance to try again if things didn't work out as planned, or another opportunity will come along.

Whatever happens in life, do whatever you can to pick the target which brings the solution to your stress trigger. Strive for the answer which keeps you and the people around you safe, happy, and content. Get the job done, no matter how hard it is to motivate yourself. If the effects of stress have left you feeling empty, then dig deep and drag yourself up off the metaphorical ground and hit the thing metaphorically kicking you in your metaphorical head. Never give up, start the positive snowball effect.

Target Attractiveness

Why does this keep happening to me?
If a person tries to attack you, it's not your fault and their behaviour can never be excused. However, if you walk through life causing trouble, trouble will be drawn towards you and if constantly finding yourself in these tricky situations, it should make you question your approach, and ask yourself are you doing the right thing?

This is mirrored in life, are your decisions and actions allowing problems to keep occurring, are you the enabler to the issues? Repeating the same thing gets you the same result, so instead of defaulting to an inefficient pattern, shift your focus towards how you are going to solve the problem. Don't make excuses, and don't blame the external factors.

If being kicked in the face whilst on the ground, why it's you, how you got there, the decisions you made in the past, all count for nothing at that moment in time and the sole focus is to move, move until you can reach a target to change the situation to your advantage. See the correlation in non-physical threat situations, rather than sit and ruminate about how you got into a stressful situation, seek out what's significant at that moment, determining the actions you're going to take to change your position.

You can reflect on the past as an information board, using the experience of historical decisions to help you avoid making inefficient decisions again, but this is the only reason to look back. Not to judge yourself, not to criticise yourself and not to give yourself a hard time about what went wrong. You are where you are, accept it, and move. Pick a positive goal and start the route to get there immediately.

Ready! Focus your thoughts.

Breathe! Relax, you are still alive, so use the breathing exercise to calm the mind.

Move! Act, right now to improve the situation, no matter how small an improvement, it's still an improvement. Make the phone call, draw up a budget, whatever you need to do.

Apply this to everything in life, regardless of your starting point and whatever is causing you worry, seek the solution, seek the way to eliminate the stress. If you feel you need to improve your health, work on relationships, or further your career, then find the target, seek a solution. Move forwards and re-assess from where your new position takes you, re-focus your mind and use your tenacity to chase the next step towards the solution, towards the next target, keep going.

The answer in life normally comes down to one thing, change, change what you're thinking, and you'll change what you're doing, a change in thought which influences the direction your life is heading in. A life Sat-nav would be useful to indicate which direction you should head towards and whether you're making the right decisions. Thankfully, you have one, using positive results as your compass and the measure of success.

How you're feeling on the journey to the target is the best feedback as to whether it's the right thing for you to do. Are you happy, what are your stress levels like, are the people around you also enjoying the trip? If the feedback says you're getting closer to the target and everyone involved feels good, carry on what you are doing, if not, change tactics. Are the decisions you're making in your personal life, family life and health working for you? If the feeling is no, then despite what you think, your current belief system and approach to life isn't working for you.

Keep your targets in perspective, I have one job in life, and this is something I work hard at to instil in my children so they also have the chance to choose this mindset to apply to life. What is the one job? Well, we may have many career paths, dreams, experiences, educational paths to follow, and relationships to navigate, but the one single job to focus attention on is:

Live for as long as possible in good health, be as happy as you can be, and treat people kindly along the way.

This is what I see as my one job and everything I do works towards this and all decisions are made to contribute to this singular goal. Just ask yourself, will this decision be good for my health, be fun and lead to happiness, and is this kind to myself and others? It sounds like teaching grandma to suck eggs, but people lose sight of this, their focus switches to the wrong elements of life and they make simple things unnecessarily complicated.

Are you Living in 'OO' land?

Repeating the same action will only achieve the same results, and it's obvious a change in decision making and action is necessary for a change in results, so why won't people make the change?

If constantly running around like a headless chicken and having a sense of full-time fire fighting in life, you're living in 'OO' land, stuck in the *observe* and *orientate* stages of the POODLE Loop. Struggling to hold focus on any one task and having your attention dragged to other problems before any solution was found for answering the previous issue. Finding it impossible to have enough hours in the day to get everything done. Then throw in a dash of worry and rumination and you have a chaotic life, never making any clear minded decisions nor implementing any actions to improve a situation. Instead, barely getting through the day and treading water without any real progress.

Day after day spent jumping through hoops due to your conditioned responses, rather than making positive changes, and before you know it another year has passed without you realising and nothing has changed. You're stuck in a cycle of stunned responses, drifting, and not fully engaging with the life you could have. If stuck in a stagnant, permanent freeze loop you will be missing the fantastic opportunities passing you by because you're blinkered by tiredness. Being in this 'OO' mini loop is living with the constant feeling of a daze, confusion, and a sprinkle of Déjà vu, but just because things have always been a certain way, it doesn't mean they have to continue this way. You have the power to break the cycle, changing how you think and respond when facing an internal or external stress trigger is a huge factor in this.

- Make positive decisions, Ready!
- Limit the tension, stress, and apprehension you feel, Breathe!
- Act on these decisions and reap the rewards, Move!

These positive steps will help limit the damage of low-level stress caused by feeling trapped, feeling disempowered and having a lack of control over your own destiny and happiness. Use these steps to reduce, as Selye calls them, *"the indelible scars"* which damage health.

Something I was once told is: *"Everyone has a terminal illness, it's called death, the process starts as soon as you are born. Think of it like this, when you're born there is a rope tied around your waist and death is on the other end of the very long rope. When you become stagnant in life or you start to stress, the rope becomes slack as you aren't driving forwards and living life to the full. Death takes up the slack, moving a little bit closer. Always keep the rope tight!"*

How do you keep the rope tight is the obvious question here? You keep moving forwards, you keep setting yourself targets, making decisions and putting them into action, for me it's hitting the targets of:

- Live as long as possible by protecting physical and mental health.
- Be happy, enjoying time here as much as possible in my own company and the company of others.
- Being kind to others, not contributing to their demise, not assisting in creating these 'scars' for them.

Spend time doing things you enjoy, rather than being pushed along by life, but avoid the things people often choose to do in an attempt to lower stress, things which dull the brain and numbs the senses. Alcohol, rubbish TV, drugs, all have the end product of escaping rather than engaging. Instead, spend time doing things which will have a positive impact:

- Each night take time for the *Think Tank* method. Be creative in your space, reconnect with your childlike imagination. A creative, expansive thought process is a powerful weapon, and it can be developed here. Imagination is an underrated ability of the human mind and is often discouraged in youngsters, your imagination is the problem solver in your mind, start to develop this ability once more.
- Start to look for the aspects of your life you can change for the better, no matter how small, and stay motivated to make these positives changes, even when stepping into the unknown.
- Small steps are still a positive movement, you won't need to cause upheaval by making wholesale changes in one day! Don't be reckless in your decision making but be committed to making the positive changes you've identified and stay passionate about your goals, but also be patient.

Building a Bodyguard
Human Demolition Services Ltd.
- Don't feel guilty about learning how to injure someone!
- Your two Crisis Responders
- Meet the 'Thumping Thunder Fist Demolition Monkey'
- Tools of the Trade, The armoury of your *'Demolition Monkey'*
- The Rice Crispy Principle - Snap, Crack or Pop!

RBM will teach you what to do if someone tries to harm you, because all people have a base need to feel safe, but this isn't the big picture. I keep reiterating this because it's very important to me you do not lose sight of this. I hear people telling me how attending *RBM* courses changed how they felt about themselves and positively altered their lives, and I want you to grab hold of this. So, as you start to progress through the section of text talking about the need to cause harm to another human being, please don't lose sight of the fact this isn't the whole story, it reaches far beyond the physical.

Don't feel guilty about learning how to injure someone!

Understandably and quite rightly, people feel uncomfortable with the reality of having to injure an aggressor to prevent themselves from being hurt. It should feel alien to you, and it should sound abhorrent if you are a well-rounded functioning human being, because nice people feel guilty about hurting another person. The following information gives a clear sense of what to do, if doing nothing will cost you your life, or will cause mental scarring which will negatively alter your life. Knowing how to injure someone doesn't make you a bad person, what you do with the information will determine this. If by hurting an aggressor you stop the attack, it doesn't make you a monster, it makes you someone who is glad to be alive.

A person attacking you will be using the HPAC Axis Circuit, as it exists in them too, in this situation they aren't operating from the logical Left Hemisphere Cerebral Cortex section of the brain. There is a line in the Kung Fu TV series, 'Monkey Magic' [20], *"You can't convince a deaf man by talking",* which is very apt in this situation as there will come a point in the confrontation when they shut down audible and verbal communication and it will be like talking to a deaf person, you'll be unable to reason with them as they won't be listening. Accept this as a sign a critical point has been reached, and prepare for what's about to happen, somebody is going to be injured, but it doesn't have to be you.

---

[20] *Monkey*: 1980 Nippon Television Network System

You can't escape reality, and if you're unable to leave a dangerous environment and you feel under threat, it's imperative you accept what's happening and give yourself the permission to do what it takes to survive. Realise in advance of a situation you might have to harm another person and be willing to do so if absolutely necessary.

Why is *acceptance* such a big topic and why has this word already made numerous appearances in the text?

> *"Individual differences in psychological dispositions, including defensiveness, are also likely to contribute to Cardio-Vascular reactivity. Thus, individuals characterised by dispositional defensiveness involving suppression, distancing, emotional inhibition, repressiveness and denial have all been found to show a greater increase in Blood Pressure (both Systolic Blood Pressure and Diastolic Blood Pressure) in reaction to stress situations than that found in their less defensive counterparts".*

Phebe Cranmer [21]

This relays how significant it is to accept the realism of potential violence in our modern-day world. If you stick your head in the ground with the opinion of *"it won't happen to me"*, it can damage your health. Referring to Phebe Cranmer's work, it's clear that a lack of acceptance of the fact you may be attacked, or are about to be attacked, in addition to the anxiety caused by the feelings of the fight or flight system if you're unfamiliar with them, all combined with trying to distance yourself from the reality of the situation, causes elevations of Systolic and Diastolic Blood Pressure.

The consequences of avoidance and/or suppression are detrimental to your survival performance, and your long-term health. A lack of realism adopted by a person towards the facts of what's about to take place in a violent encounter intensifies the stress response, opening the Big Red Box by way of elevating activation levels of the Pons, in turn causing further stimulation and revving of the Cortisol mechanism. The overstimulation of Cortisol revving brings with it the negative effects on survival performance, as earlier discussed via the Grossman & Siddle scale, due to higher heart rate and blood pressure elevation.

Socially adhering members of society will attempt to do everything they can other than hurt another person, which is commendable, until it reaches a point where the denial of what's needed to be done results in them being hurt, then it's a whimsically unrealistic and dangerous belief system. People struggle with this reality and ask, *'why do I have to injure them, why can't I put them into an arm lock*

---

[21] Phebe Cranmer 1991: Defensive Behaviour and Autonomic Reaction to Stress CV Reactivity, *The Development of Defense Mechanisms: Theory, Research and Assessment*. (1991) New York: Springer-Verlag

or something?' Turning away from the unpalatable truth, they must cause the aggressor to mentally or physically fold in a serious violent threat situation. People always try to avoid accepting this, but on a physical ability perspective it's foolishness to consider restraining a person on your own, devoid of some major strength or seriously good skillset.

When observing the police attempting to arrest an offender (and you can find footage of police arrests with a simple internet search), if the person is compliant then one police officer can cuff them standing up and place them in the back of the police car, no problem, and an easy day at the office. If on the other hand, the offender is noncompliant, possibly under the effects of drugs, or maybe they have an antisocial personality disorder, it can take upwards of five police officers to arrest one person. Hence the need to use pepper spray, tasers *(recent research indicates tasers fail to achieve the desired result up to 40% of the time)*, batons and the like. It's clear from this reality, without you causing an injury, it's a big ask to stop them with limb-locks and restraints, which is why it takes so many police to make one arrest. Without the numbers as back up, or the skill level needed to use arm locks, it isn't a reliable plan of action for you to ensure your safety. Factor into the equation that if you're restraining a person you aren't moving, this means you aren't burning off the hormone induced fuel being released into your system and this leaves you more susceptible to a freeze if they escape the hold. You're also vulnerable if another person attacks you while holding someone in an arm lock or a choke hold, because you are standing still and an easy target.

When thinking about conflict avoidance, it's hard to calm a person down if they're fired up and already approaching you, so verbal de-escalation techniques are not adequate in all situations. Sadly, if you can't remove yourself from the danger then only one option remains, you must remove the danger from you, by means of stopping them with a physical action. If they're intent on causing serious harm, or taking your life, or engaging in a sexual assault, only a significant amount of damage will guarantee you stop them, you must hurt the aggressor.

If you're grabbed by the throat with a knife forced against your body, no amount of wishing you were somewhere else is going to make the situation go away, no amount of fear suppression, or denial, is going to change anything. It isn't ideal, it's not a great starting position but it's where you are, so remove the denial and admit to what's happening, embrace your emotions in the circumstances and deal with it. You have too, it's your only choice, otherwise the aggressor is left to implement their plan, a plan constructed by their state of mind and their moral rules. They will be able to put this plan into action unchallenged, and you have no idea how far that plan extends in terms of the harm they are willing to cause, it could reach as far as taking your life.

To prevent this, an obstacle to overcome is giving yourself permission to cause injury, which is why there's a need to train yourself in preparation to injure another person to protect yourself. This obstacle starts to come into existence for you during childhood, when parents introduce behavioural conditioning for the little ones to try to set some personal interaction rules. Teaching them the expectations of behaviour our society deems as right and wrong, and the youngsters start to function nicely within society. A prime example of this is the 'no hitting rule', since you were young you've probably been told it's wrong to hit anybody else. Walking around hitting people if they do not agree with your viewpoint isn't conductive to social progress, and for the most part of life, this rule is correct, but there's a flip side. You end up with the blanket approach of 'don't hit people' being carried through from childhood into adulthood.

Of course, it's correct teaching children to be civilised in their approach to the resolution of disagreements, they learn to talk things through rather than just go straight to bash mode. It's when we leave the toddler age it becomes more complicated with more conditions put in place which linger later in life in a troublesome way. If somebody hits you tell the teacher, if in trouble tell an adult, if threatened you call the police, leaving you holding the belief you should always look towards someone else for a resolution and a solution. If not addressed this is reinforced all the way through your life leaving you vulnerable if ever faced with a genuine threat and physically attacked, because you would revert to looking for someone else to make it stop. Standing still because in your mind you aren't allowed to hit them, and you look for someone else to come and remove the threat on your behalf.

In a violent situation, only you can be counted on to do something about it, but you need to allow yourself to *step forwards and protect you*. Giving yourself the permission to harm another person, if necessary. This 'permission' is an obstacle the Antisocial Personality Disorder individual doesn't have to overcome, because they simply don't have the capacity to care. You must not allow them to have the upper hand, tipping the scales in their favour because of a different neurological and moral standpoint.

Often, a worry people hold is that if you retaliate and get caught you will get into trouble, I imagine this sounds familiar to most and is the reason I included the law on self-defence right at the beginning of this book. Without removing this fear of getting into trouble if attacked, potentially you won't hit back. Since infancy you've been told you are not allowed to, and with this belief comes the worry about authoritarian consequences. I was once delivering a course to a group, working through a requested scenario of a knife attack, and after discussing this scenario and covering the potential solutions, one of the people in attendance said, "but I will get arrested if I hurt him". In this scenario there are far more pressing issues, and I really do believe this mindset stems from the 'if you hit them, you will get into trouble' conditioning people carry around from their youth. It's restrictive to your survival chances and it must be changed, because in a situation where the Hippocampus is called upon to give a solution, it can be sabotaged by this negative belief, because your moral code influences your decision making in the selection of an appropriate response. Possibly dismissing a perfectly suitable solution to a dangerous threat because you're anxious about finding yourself being on trial, even though they grabbed you by the throat and pressed a knife against you. Indecision leads to doubt, causing yet another HPAC Axis Cortisol spike, pushing you further along the negative scale and towards potentially freezing, which is why it's important to address this.

To prevent barriers being put in place at an early age, instruct children "it's wrong to hit somebody - unless you have to, and there is no other choice". Finish the statement with the remit unless they have to. Don't tell young people they need someone else to protect them, empower them at a young age to feel safe with their own abilities, tell them they need to be smart, not big to succeed and be safe. A vast amount of my time is spent helping adults remove this corrupt data of you mustn't hit and go and ask someone for help, previously loaded onto their internal hard drive. Break the loop with your children and save them from this process later in life.

You can use appropriate force to ensure your safety, the law states this. Decide when it comes down to you needing to cause physical damage to an aggressor to prevent them from harming you, whether you're prepared to do it. Phase 3 will use physical movements to change your thoughts and alter your mental position to one of: *it's okay to strike when needed and I will strike as hard as I can.* The mental strength you need to move forwards and strike the target is found when you tap into the survival instinct inside of you.

Your two Crisis Responders

Envisage for a moment that unfortunately, you've been caught up in a situation where your instincts are screaming at you, hitting the warning alarm, and signalling things are likely to become violent. You've tried everything possible to leave, attempting to diffuse and calm the situation but to no avail, they're not listening to you, not responding to your de-escalation and avoidance skills. Their desire to attack you remains and violence now seems to be unavoidable, you're becoming aware de-escalation techniques aren't working and your safety is potentially on the line. If I presented you with the choice of picking one avatar to face the aggressor in your place, which one would you choose to face the threat?

>Avatar Option One:
>The *Negotiator Avatar*; a very clever and intelligent negotiator, utilising the tactics of diplomatic reasoning. Opening discussions on why engaging in conflict is a bad idea for everyone involved: the injuries, the life threat and legal consequences. Delivering a peace presentation NATO would be proud of. Perhaps even extending the hand of friendship in the hope it takes the heat out of the situation.

As a sensible, functioning member of society, this sounds like a good option, as you would ideally like to talk the person around, making them see sense. Perhaps have a coffee together afterwards and everyone can get on with their lives, all happy, fine, and dandy and this avatar seems to match that ideal. However, this idealism is sometimes a hindrance, once again displaying a lack of acceptance, because the reality about a violent attack is far removed and the truth resides in a different realm.

The problem with this *Negotiator Avatar* option, is in situations where discussions aren't going well, the Pons will over stimulate because you're feeling under threat. Anxiety and stress responses will become amplified by the uncertainty and doubt of what's about to happen, and your mental defence mechanisms will be screaming, because this negotiator is failing, and the threat level is escalating. You're neither running away, nor hitting the threat, instead you're caught in indecision. Insisting on retrying a previously failed, and currently failing verbal approach because you're stuck in a loop which is having no benefit and you have no other option. This anxiety, uncertainty and doubt can cause your negotiator to morph into a new avatar version to be known as *Confused Rabbit*, and just like a rabbit caught in headlights, it will freeze. Submitting and moving to the psychological Blank Zone immediately, rendering itself numb to the pain of being killed.

If you respond to stress and threats from the perspective of the *Confused Rabbit* avatar you will be operating from a negative emotional basis, amplifying your stress response. You won't feel in command of your emotions or your actions and instead you'll be starting any movements from the position of anger, panic, or anxiety. *Confused Rabbit* emerges when you have doubt and also appearing when faced with an overwhelming situation in which you're afraid of failing. Don't underestimate the power fear of failure holds, under threat people often submit and take being hit rather than fight back, as to fight back and fail can be perceived as more damaging than the physical consequences of the punches. It sounds crazy but it can happen, fear of failure is debilitating, and it even comes into play when your life is at risk.

If taken by surprise the brain has no time to send the *Negotiator Avatar* forwards to plea bargain for you, because the threat signal of danger bypasses this negotiator and instead initiates the SAM Axis evasive reflex. Once this SAM Axis evading manoeuvre has been completed, it's here the potential window exists for the skilled negotiator to morph into *Confused Rabbit*, entering the chaos and getting involved. When under attack, the stress and the uncertainty can cause you to pause, to hesitate, and this is where this hole burrowing, carrot munching avatar finds itself in a world it's not designed for, opening the Big Red Box, with the feelings of doubt beginning the Doom Spiral feedback loop. *Rabbit* is the little blighter who causes the problems in stress response decision making by clouding the fight or flight process, breaking the efficient *RBM* feedback loop.

The space between the subconscious and conscious function of the mind is the realm of brain processing I call the 'Mental Flatline Zone'. A space where you can interrupt the survival process by interjecting with conscious analysis at a time where you have no time, where panic and over stimulus can cause you to freeze. This is the *Rabbits* domain, filled with headlights beaming in from every angle in the form of constant fear, rumination, and doubt and indecision about what to do. This Mental Flatline Zone is the domain where you will find all the obstacles you need to overcome in order to move and survive. It's where inappropriate analytical thought responses thrive.

Fortuitously for you, there is another option, a different avatar who epitomises a different way of thinking, and represents a different feedback loop in the brain, and with it bringing new choices for you when faced with conflict. A character who can reach in whilst you are drowning in the pool of self-doubt, fear, rumination, and analytical indecision, and pull you out, dragging you to safety, back into the space of perfect survival functionality. Releasing you from the Mental Flatline Zone and slamming the door shut on the Doom Spiral Loop.

Step forwards the avatar who moves from a place of confidence, self-belief, and self-worth. An Avatar who doesn't need to be forced to take a move forward to protect you, but instead must be told to hold fire and stay back until needed. This is your inbuilt personal conflict survival specialist, always standing by whilst you are negotiating, ready in case things go wrong.

Avatar Option Two.

In a threat environment, instead of using the negotiator once the point of de-escalation has passed, you can select the other option, calling forwards the avatar who represents a mindset akin to a ten-foot-tall giant with huge fists to symbolically smash the aggressor on the top of the head, making the problem go away. Initially stopping you from free falling into a place of uncertainty and anxiety by dealing with the threat immediately. Or if necessary, pulling you out of the *Rabbit* mess and preventing mental capitulation, freeing you to find possible solutions.

People often elect for option one, continuing to try and fix the situation in a socially acceptable way, but still being in danger indicates clearly this hasn't worked out as you had hoped. Maybe there wasn't time to try to deescalate, as the attack is already upon you. It's during times like these you let your protective survival specialist move forwards and do its job. Who exactly is this survival driven, protection specialist?

Meet the 'Thumping Thunder Fist Demolition Monkey'

Visualise yourself transforming into an enormous, boulder smashing primate with the feelings of superior power, increased agility, and heightened awareness. This *Thumping Thunder Fist Demolition Monkey* avatar is a pictorial embodiment of the fight or flight hormones kicking in when released into the bloodstream. This human demolition specialist stands tall, free from intimidation and with the courage to face any challenge. It's optimised to keep you safe, a huge protective avatar of a mindset, armed with the very best *RBM* self-defence information and a potent cocktail of hormones at its disposal.

Embrace the confidence gained from having a *Thumping Thunder Fist Demolition Monkey* avatar standing alongside you, ready to mentally push aside the negotiator as soon as it begins to morph into the *Confused Rabbit* if things aren't going well.

Stepping forwards to offer protection from death, and until death. Always think of this inbuilt bodyguard whenever you feel under threat, or under stress and you will be free from any doubt in your ability to protect yourself. Forged deep inside your psyche, in parts of the brain given to you through human evolution, is where this tenacious, survival orientated, hunter lurks. Born from the strong desire to survive, and driven by the will to live, it's a very animalistic facet to your personality, this is the *Demolition Monkey*.

If you face a monster from the abyss, the situation dictates you step up and match it. If they release their inner beast on you, then you do the same to survive, only controlling and directing it rather than letting it run wild and loose. Most of the population want to deny this facet of their personality exists within them, they shy away from acknowledging it, until of course you ask what they would do if someone was harming the people they cared about. Their reply is immediate, unmonitored, and unrefined, and often carrying the threat of death with no remorse, compassion, or hesitation in their voice. This is the *Demolition Monkey* growling, flexing its muscles at the thought of being set free, released to carry out its primal protective duty. However, you must be able to steer your fight or flight response in a focused direction, being in control and instructing your Demolition Monkey when to move, where to move, and how to move.

Directing your protective avatar with instructions of where to go is achieved via pre-loading the internal hard drive Hippocampus with historical, positive result based actions otherwise known as memories. Memories gained through a high repetition of you and a training partner, with you hitting targets located on your training partners body. Even though in the learning environment you will be moving slowly and safely, your intent will be as though you are striking the aggressor with those big thumping fists, honing that raw aggression and intent, and practicing inflicting physical damage until you achieve the demolition of the aggressor, striking until the threat is removed, no more, no less.

The key to success is owning instant recognition of what to do, what target to hit, and having the motivation to get to the target. To achieve this, you will incorporate two different methods of data loading/conditioning to ensure you get results, giving clarity to the *Demolition Monkey* of a target range so that if called upon, it knows where to deploy these hormone fuelled power bombs, but also when hit the brakes, knowing when to stop!

How you train the Demolition Monkey

Classical Conditioning is a method used as a way of programming new responses into the mind, working via a stimulus response method, with the most well-known illustration of this being Pavlov's' Dogs. This experiment found ringing a bell prior to feeding dogs would over time, cause a conditioned response of the dogs salivating in anticipation of the food upon hearing the bell, even without the presence of any food. A conditioned, learnt response to the bell with the response of the dog having an involuntary reaction to the trigger of the bell. Classical Conditioning occurs without the need of the individual's active emotional participation, making it easy to implement in your learning process, via a trigger and response repetition method.

Operant Conditioning is another approach of data loading and a means of changing current responses, but this behavioural response reprogramming is slightly different to the way Classical Conditioning works. With Operant Conditioning, the response is not involuntary as in Classical conditioning, but instead is based on deliberate action and consequence. By employing a reward/reinforcement or punishment system it's emotionally driven, unlike Classical Conditioning. As I kicked off with the dog example, I may as well continue with the same theme, an Operant Conditioning example would be rewarding your canine friend with positive attention when correctly following the instruction to sit, but withholding the attention when pooch fails to follow the instruction. Through this feedback, the dog will form a link between the 'sit when told' (stimulus) and the positive attention (reward), motivating it to respond with the required action, it follows the instruction as it wants the positive effect the attention creates in the brain, the reward.

This method of conditioning requires the participants' decision to act being motivated by previous reward outcomes. In a learning environment the 'reward' in humans is the feelgood factor, the incentive to comply to instructions given can range from having the feeling of accomplishment, to the sense of relief from dealing with a simulated threat. This feeling of success is a Dopamine release in the brain, which is basically your internal Cocaine store. Dopamine is addictive, as we know from people who find exercise becoming a compulsion, with the physical action and intensity creating an Endorphin release, and the success of completing the physical goals creating the Dopamine release. This method can be used to positively manipulate the learning process of self-defence.

Being successful in the self-defence practice environment, and the feel-good sensation achieved, stimulates the willingness to repeat the action on cue of seeing the stimulus or the trigger in the future in a real threat, because you enjoy the Dopamine hit from using positive reward training. You can programme the mind to respond to a threat stimulus with a positive action of moving forwards towards the threat, using the knowledge the person will have a desire to receive a Dopamine release at the end of this action. Positive data loading where you move forwards and strike a threat to stay safe limits your resistance to moving forward to strike any threat, as this movement is associated with previous success in the training room.

Both Classical and Operant conditioning, when used positively, are necessary in your leaning journey if you want to be successful. Whether your self-defence protocol is a martial art or the other end of the scale relying on a firearm, if your strategy does not integrate both learning methods into the process, then you're on a very risky path for numerous reasons. One of these, is that when learning a self-defence system people have the idea the more things they learn in each session, the better. They think having lots of options is a good thing. Conversely, I believe this is false, as I realised the way for people to leave the room with nothing is to show them everything, and if I demonstrated 25 techniques in a one-hour session, the people attending will replicate them all and think it's great. Yet in reality they've seen a lot but learnt very little because there's been a low level of repetition, not enough to stimulate the data being loaded into the Hippocampus. Not enough Classical Conditioning stimulus response repetition to ensure the information is being stored in a manner which will provide instant recall under stress.

If you repeated only two or three short sequences per session and practiced hitting the same targets in high repetition, the memory load is far greater than a session consisting of low repetition of different sequences and a larger selection of different targets. The truth is the more you think you are getting, the less you are retaining, and it reduces the likelihood of the data making an appearance when needed in a real threat under stress, because it's not becoming deeply embedded with positive memories.

Another important reason for including both conditioning methods is because of distance. *RBM* uses both Classical and Operant conditioning methods via a variety of stimulus and response triggers in the learning format, because you absolutely require both. If an aggressor is close to you, the threat is now, there is no time to think. In a situation like this a self-defence method which uses Classical Conditioning comes into its own. When immersed in the learning environment, a person simulating the role of the aggressor grabs you by the throat (trigger), and you immediately deliver a positive action of moving off the spot and striking a target (response), it's a success! The simulated attack of 'the grab to the throat' provides numerous triggers; the kinaesthetic feedback of touch as they grab you is a trigger, the visual recognition of them moving towards you is also a trigger and your response to the aggressors' attack is to strike with an action you have learnt through repetition. A movement where no conscious thought or deliberate memory recall is necessary. This is a Classical Conditioned stimulus and response solution. But the conditioned learning does not stop there.

The *RBM* learning method requires your drill partner to simulate the role of grabbing you by the throat. They will also act accordingly by incorporating relevant and appropriate reactions in accordance with your movements. For example, after you moved to simulate pushing your thumb into their eye, they'll release the grip on your throat and instead hold their face as a response to your thumb being embedded in it, because this tends to happen when you're treating their face like you're holding a bowling bowl. Their movement will simulate shielding the damaged eye or recoiling to prevent further damage and pain to this area. Or they may instead flinch away before the thumb strikes the intended target of the eye to avoid the damage.

Their movements will be due to one of two things, you're attempt to put your thumb into their eye, but they see it and jump away because of their SAM Axis Flinch Response (Polysynaptic Reflex, or a Withdrawal Reflex), or alternatively you manage to get your thumb into their eye, causing them to retreat away from the point of injury. Their response is your feedback of what's happening, you're learning from what you're seeing and feeling and adapting to the situation in front of you as it pans out, and not sticking to a predictable pattern of movement. All this data contained in the learning environment is being recorded, all absorbed into the memory bank of the internal hard drive of the Hippocampus.

Closely attached to this information is the huge feeling of success as you have achieved what you set out to do, which is to eliminate the threat. The empowering, confidence elevating feelings of you successfully protecting yourself are enhancing your self-belief and your self-worth. The sense of touch on your drill partner as you strike the target is cultivating the positive reward feedback, taking in the sight of seeing them moving backwards away from you after the target is struck is a positive reward feedback. Operant conditioning is now taking shape in your mind.

Even in this close-range attack situation following the initial Classical response there is an element of Operant conditioning, because the sight of their body moving away from you is registered as a great feeling of success, the newly exposed targets and weaknesses you spot as they move is another feel good factor, their physical and mental retreating being programmed into you as a positive result, a triumph. What happens when you have these feelings of success? You get the massive shot of Dopamine you were seeking, and this Dopamine loaded positive outcome creates positive actions and movements, which you will recall and repeat when under the stress of a real attack.

If attacked at close range, if you responded with a strike to the aggressor's eye then your movement was a 'classical conditioned response'. They were close to you and with no thought, and no time to think due to their proximity you responded immediately. Striking the first target the spatial aspect of your brain zoomed in on. The reason it focused here was the Hippocampus recognising it as a viable target, one which was learnt through the repetitive training of 'hit this target and the problem goes away'. Amazingly simple, and fast to programme, becoming ingrained in your mind as a valid and positive response which also highlights the importance of a drill partner and not only moving up and down a sports hall in lines hitting empty air in front of you.

The Classical Conditioned response is perfect, the hormonal and physiological response all coming from the Amygdala/Hippocampus dream team. This learning process also gives your *Demolition Monkey* the permission to move and strike a target on another human being. If you recall, the child who was told not to hit people still lives inside of you. This new stimulus and response positive conditioning is overwriting the negative, limited thought that it's wrong to hit people.

Classical conditioning is used as a learning tool for when someone has grabbed you or is close enough to trigger an immediate response, but what happens if the person is walking towards you from a distance with a clenched fist? Maybe they are shouting threats towards you which is a frightening thing, and they're getting closer and closer to you, and you have no way out. This is where Operant Conditioning comes into play, because of the stimulus of a threat being registered but it's not in proximity to you, not close enough to trigger an immediate classical response.

In this situation, upon identifying the threat of their clenched fist closing in, or the person shouting threats at you, the Amygdala/Hippocampus dream team will have already brought forward an action plan, move away quickly or alternatively move in to nullify the threat, but in this case the threat is too far away for you to be able to reach them. Whilst the intent and mental conviction of the *Demolition Monkey* is driven by the will to live, there is a restriction of the ability to put this into action determined by the limitations and dimensions of your physical body. Your arm length, leg length and stride length, makes the distance between you and the threat an issue because the *Demolition Monkey* cannot yet reach the target.

Distance provides time, time to think while the threat closes the gap, but time is an opportunity for you to mess thing up with the *Rabbit* bursting open the big red box and analysing the hell out of the situation, creating indecision, doubt, or even hypothesising with too many choices, leading to left hemisphere analysis blocking the intuitive movement of the *Demolition Monkey*. All done standing still on the spot, whilst the danger closes in on you.

This little mental stammer created within the Left Hemisphere can take a perfect plan of which target to strike, and 'jam it' causing you to freeze. So how do you avoid this stammer turning into a freeze, stopping the *Confused Rabbit* trying to get its analytical boot in the door? You step forward and close the gap, remove the time, and remove the distance, restricting your freeze inducing thinking time and simultaneously disrupting the aggressors plan of attack. You have progressed through your POODLE strategy, and concluded that leaving is not an option, *(which should always be the first choice)* and through no fault of your own, this means you have been forced to step forward and eliminate the threat.

'Whoa there, hang on a minute! Step towards the danger, are you nuts?'

I know it's counter-intuitive, but yes! If you can't get away, if you can't talk the situation down and you know there is going to be a physical altercation, then close the gap. You probably feel it's crazy to step forwards, as moving towards the attack is frightening to the extreme, but the benefits of this action are monumental. Thinking time is the most disrupting factor for you at this moment. The most dangerous thing about them is their brain, but until they can reach you the biggest threat is your own brain, because you have time to overthink, to overstimulate and freeze.

Moving towards them, or alternatively moving in an arc around them, will result in your GPS location changing, causing a change to the aggressor's plan of attack. Consequently, due to this movement, the landscape of the attack changes micro-second by micro-second, creating more triggers and more solutions to fire in your subconscious mind, all encouraging the flow of intuitive *RBM* conditioned responses ready to launch, the opposite of freezing because you're processing while on the move.

They will predict you will be intimidated and either retreat, or stand still and try to negotiate, both of which are perfect scenarios for them to deliver blows with or without a weapon. But by moving, you change their plan and cause some disruption. Your movement will change the starting position, and the new direction of your movement creates a glitch for the aggressor. Not staying stationary restricts the chance of being hit, and moving towards the aggressor and creating an element of concern for their own safety rather than the singular focus on destroying you, you've now split their focus. You have become the decisive factor of the situation, because to hit you they must track you and your movements, you've seized control over the one variable you can influence, which is moving.

Moving off the spot and in an arc around them may have made the *Leave* aspect of the *POODLE Loop* a new option to take. If this option isn't on the table, you will have to launch the last resort, the final stage of the *POODLE Loop*, which is *Eliminate,* which is basically your body having a collision with their body, and to achieve this your body must move to meet theirs. The principles of movement outlined in Phase 3 will instruct you on how to use the strongest parts of your body, to target the weaker areas of their body to end the threat. But how do you train yourself to move forwards and attack the threat without any hesitation, to do something so against the grain of what makes sense?

It's achieved using Operant Conditioning, by simulating realistic attacks in your training, *(they don't have to be fast, they should however be truthful and representative of what you will see and feel in an attack),* you teach yourself to recognise threats by the posturing and aggressive movements shown by a drill partner simulating aggressive behaviour and attacks. Then you respond, you act, learning how to be successful when dealing with these attacks, creating the positive reward chemicals in the brain. The end result, you will be motivated and conditioned to step towards a real threat if necessary, with those Dopamine releases working like a Scooby Snack reward for your brain.

Reward after reward handed to the *Demolition Monkey* in a practice environment is a neurological pat on the back for bashing the threat. The Dopamine release in the Cerebral Lobes harnessing a strong recognition the movement of going forwards is a positive action for the Hippocampus, registering this option on the internal hard drive as a good choice to use in the future if facing a real threat. The importance of this feel-good factor of the training process must not be overlooked nor undervalued.

In my opinion it's imperative when instructing people in a self-defence method and developing their sense of personal empowerment that you do not enhance a fear of failure through unnecessary micro-management. If you are taking part in a self-defence class or a martial art class and the person instructing you corrects you by saying you've moved the wrong leg, or used the wrong arm, or perhaps used the wrong response to a threat, I suggest you spend time considering if this approach really is the best thing for you, because this will enhance the fear of failure.

Based on what I have researched and experienced, my opinion is any tuition which says wrong leg or wrong height of a punch to the sternum on a fictitious attacker, is harmful for your chances of survival if ever faced with physical danger. Conversely, if you stepped in any direction by moving off the spot, and struck the aggressor, who cares which leg you moved? You seized control of variables you could change by moving to influence their plan, causing the *Disruption* part of the *POODLE Loop*. Which is why I believe there's not 'a wrong leg or wrong arm'.

I will never say a person has made a mistake in performing a movement or did it wrong when learning *RBM*, because this erodes their confidence, inhibiting the progress of building of a positive *RBM* Loop. Even if a person does something different to the instruction I have given, they were still moving and influencing things, for this reason I always say it was a good building block, because they moved. Then taking that courage and doing it again, this time making it even more efficient by using better principles of movement. Using the raw tenacity and will to live they displayed, and channelling this into an effective and efficient physical action to maximise their chances of success. Not saying to someone, *'that was wrong'*, because they moved their left foot instead of their right. That is ignoring the courage it takes to step forwards towards a threat, taking a chance and moving off the spot, you know, the important bit. The psychological aspect is far more important than the physical in self-defence.

If the self-defence method you're learning requires the perfect replication of patterns and being able to recall every detail you've been shown for it to be a success, this highlights the limitations and failings of the system, not the person doing it. A self-defence system should not fail if a person moves a different arm or leg when under the stress of a physical attack. The self-defence method should make you be able to operate from any position, regardless of where you find yourself and regardless of which limb you move first. If the system fails because you moved your left foot with the left arm instead of right foot with left arm, you need to seriously question just how effective that system is under stress, at a time when things don't go according to plan. Don't take ownership of the inadequacies of a system, don't adopt them as your own personal failings, thinking it might be your fault for not being proficient at it.

I wholeheartedly believe self-defence should be built around an exceptional system, and not requiring people to be exceptional at using that system. The principles, the information and applications contained in a system should remove the need for you to be an exceptional martial artist or athlete, the system itself should be doing the hard work.

Question the self-defence functionality of any system expecting you move up and down an empty space performing movements without a drill partner providing realistic attack simulation, because in cases where self-defence is taught in this way, it will take a vast amount of time to program the information into the brain to the level required for it to become a trusted source of data under stress. Learning in this way is also missing the kinaesthetic sense of the other person's body weight pressing on you, vectors of force, etc.

<u>Keep the monkey on a leash</u>
RBM gives you a stimulus–response method for self-protection, one designed to prevent you from spiralling out of control and using excessive force, which is reassuring for those with morals and living within a society which punishes unjustified violence. When the aggressor's movements stop and they're in a position which is submissive, the stimulus for you to move stops. When you recognise they're recoiling into a protective position to nurse a damaged part of their body and are incapacitated, you will stop striking them, because there are no movements to trigger any further action from you, no ducks popping up for you to shoot.

The pre-frontal lobe acts as a handbrake to prevent us from killing each other, what you're learning to do is control this handbrake, to have command over the leash and shackles on the *Demolition Monkey*. Loosening the handbrake to step forwards, doing what you need to ensure your safety, then pulling on the leash and putting that brake back on, returning to the para-sympathetic, compassionate aspect of yourself. The ability to control this handbrake helps prevent movement in the wrong direction along the Grossman & Siddle sliding scale. When you stay in a positive and efficient feedback circuit, you have total control. Stand still and let the stress response run wild and you will panic and let go of the leash, and before you know it, it's red mist time. This needs consideration, and your method of personal protection should have plans in place to prevent this one-way ticket to overkill city. Stopping yourself is of equal importance as knowing how to get moving, both are protecting yourself, one is getting off the spot and defending yourself, the other is stopping when the threat is over and safeguarding yourself morally and legally.

Again, it's acceptance of the reality of violence which helps to prevent this loss of control. This stop/start control is established through the simulation of an attack in a practice environment, giving the brain the opportunity to learn to respond to the threat of an aggressor with the movements of delivering blows to vulnerable areas. This process develops the desire to cause an injury (when necessary) to stop an aggressor from causing you any harm, resulting in positive cognitive desensitisation.

Some people have a short, fixed leash, and this can break with the pressure and stress of life and they 'just lose it', other people have no leash at all causing chaos everywhere they go. You, well you will be different, because you're learning to have a lead which you can loosen and tighten at will, complete control. The external stimulus-response based method of *RBM* helps you to move and operate from a place of decisive action and acceptance that you need to injure a person. This mindset takes the emotion out of the task in hand, it's a thought process void of anger or rage, which is important because if these emotions take over you will lose control. You will go to town on them and become a distributor of justice, finding you still get hit at a later date. Although it won't be from the bat of a thug, it will be a psychological blow which hits you, having to come to terms with what you've done if you can't justify your actions to yourself when you have needlessly killed someone. Followed swiftly by justifying your actions in court. Stay in control of your emotions, stay in control of your actions, then everything will work as it should.

When progressing through PHASE 3 and going through the movements, never finish a practice session on uncertainty. Remember it's the confidence being built and the removal of the feeling of helplessness which is attained through learning the self-defence skills which motivates you to take that first step towards the aggressor (when running away is not a viable option). Anything which goes against this positive programming will contribute to a freeze response. Any doubt, or a lack of belief in yourself will hamper you. Always finish a practice session on a high.

Familiar with the roles of *Negotiator, Confused Rabbit* and the *Thumping Thunder Fist Demolition Monkey* and being equipped with an understanding of how and why you may sometimes need to loosen the shackles, the next stage is to arm the *Demolition Monkey* with weapons and train it like a soldier. Identifying your body weapons and the targets on the aggressor you intend to unleash these weapons on if ever under threat. Get ready to kick start the Classical and Operant conditioning upload, connecting with your inner self and acknowledging the existence of your sleeping giant, one the predators in society would not want to meet.

Tools of the Trade - The armoury of Demolition Monkey!

Important note: *It's advisable to consider your relationship with alcohol, or any other drug or stimulant intake you have. Anything which will compromise control, including steroids/HGH which increases aggression levels, a few beers in the pub, all the way along the scale to recreational drugs on the weekend. As soon as you own the information and ability to injure another person, you should also own the responsibility to be in control of yourself, always.*

If you are under the influence of any drug, either liquid or chemical, the feedback in the brain is altered, emotions towards others numbed, and the brake system is loosened and weakened. The evidence of this is in A&E departments across the UK during the early hours of Sunday morning after a Saturday night out. When your brain chemistry is affected, you will not interpret situations as clearly, but most notable and of a massive consequence, you will not be able to stop yourself as quickly.

The implications of this are serious, as it's bad enough if you don't put the brakes on when the threat is eradicated and tip into overkill, but even worse, if due to stimulants you read a situation incorrectly and strike an innocent person, meaning you have now become the violent, unprovoked, sociopathic attacker which society despises.

Criminals will get 'tooled up' when going into a fight. Knives, bats, guns, and other creative implements are used because they can make a big mess of a person and sometimes make it happen faster than with bare hands, and from a further distance. But never assume a weapon is more dangerous than a punch, because I have read plenty of news reports of people being killed with one punch.

There are places on the planet where the number of criminals carrying firearms is higher than others and the usual retort is *'I will get a gun to protect myself from them'*. But having a weapon will make no difference if the aggressor is at close quarters and they've caught you by surprise, or if you haven't prepared for the SAM Axis & HPAC Axis. Because the time needed for you to draw your weapon and shoot will far exceed the time it would take for you to move off the spot, secure their weapon and strike a target. Alarms and pepper sprays are available to buy, but you will discover later when reading about *Tueller* [22], that just like a concealed weapon, these are not the most reliable of devices for your safety. Consider how taking a weapon into a fight means you must make sure you don't drop it or have it taken off you and used against you.

For you, it's not about making the biggest mess, or doing the worst thing you can to an aggressor, it's about protecting yourself by doing what the situation requires. It's extremely difficult to prevent yourself taking that trip to

---

[22] Dennis Tueller, 1983 How Close is Too Close? *SWAT Magazine*

Overkill City if you rely on using a weapon, as you can't half stab, or half shoot someone, so learn to be able to survive without these things.

'If it's not about doing the worst thing possible, why learn how to attack an aggressors' eye, resulting in an injury so horrible it makes you feel sick?'

This is a question I am often asked, and the reason for teaching the movement of placing a thumb into their eye socket, is because it's the hardest of all the targets for people to achieve psychologically. The eye is the part of the body structure which humanises people the most. If you can remove psychological barriers to this target area, and remove all resistance about deliberately damaging their eye, then you will be able to strike all the other targets on the list.

Does it mean you should always go for their eye? No, just because you can doesn't mean you have too. Will you start to carry yourself a little more confidently when knowing how easy it is to damage an aggressor's eye? Yes, and as you know from the previous information, it's important to alter your target attractiveness by building a real confidence within yourself.

The Weapons

Your inbuilt, organic tools of human demolition are your safety net, and unlike projectile weapons, your arms and legs do not need reloading after use and they cannot be dropped on the ground and used by others. You have an expansive box of tools from which you can select a weapon, and many ways of using them to avoid being the recipient of a violent attack. To keep things simple, I have only included the big guns here, the easiest body weapons to use and master without specialist face to face instruction.

The pictures used to depict what is happening during the various stages of a physical assault and the response options available to you, will focus on the blue character being the selected target, and the grey character being the aggressor. The detail of the blue character is more visible in the pictures, so this is the better option.

Fingers & Thumbs
Go into the aggressor's eyes as though picking up a bowling ball. All rather unpleasant, but there may be a day when it's appropriate and necessary.

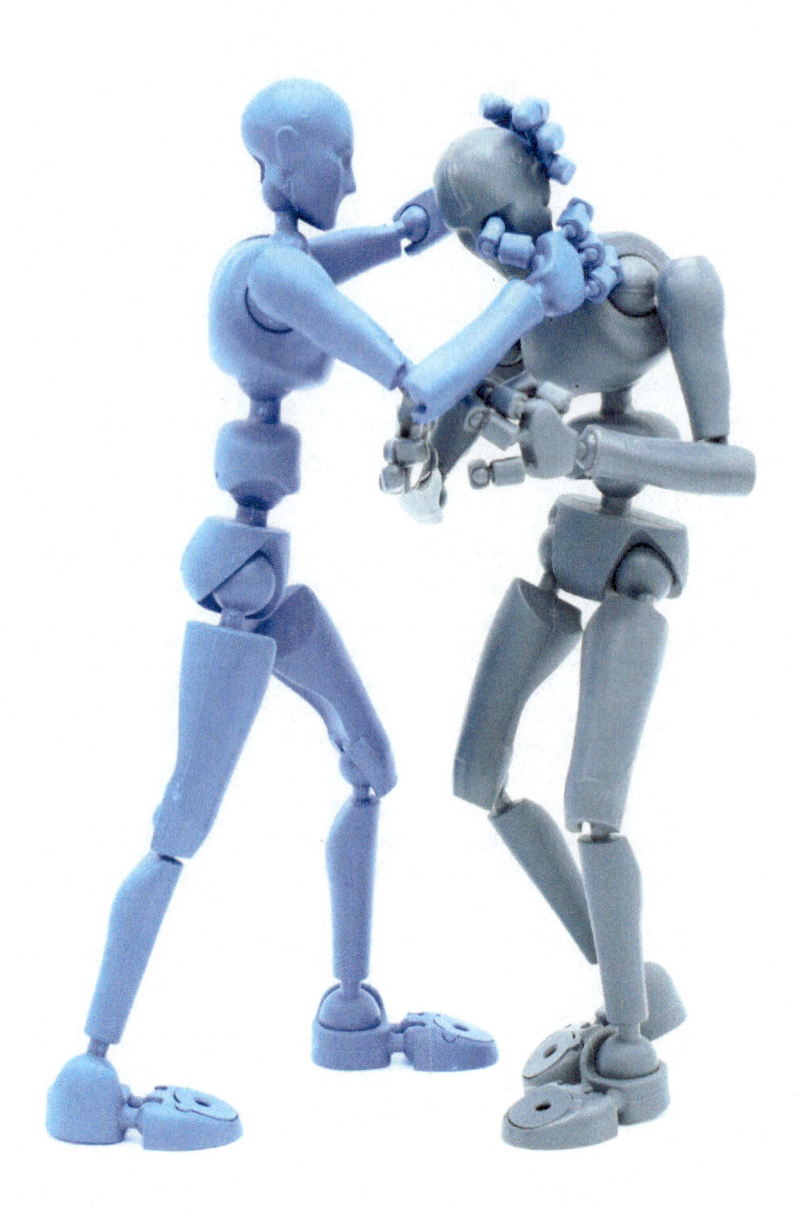

Hammer fist & Forearm Strike
Once you have made a fist, the forearm is a large surface area ready to crash down on the vulnerable areas of a human body to cause damage.

Elbow
The elbow is a powerful tool, it's a joust which can be used to drive into the aggressor's bone structure and muscle mass.

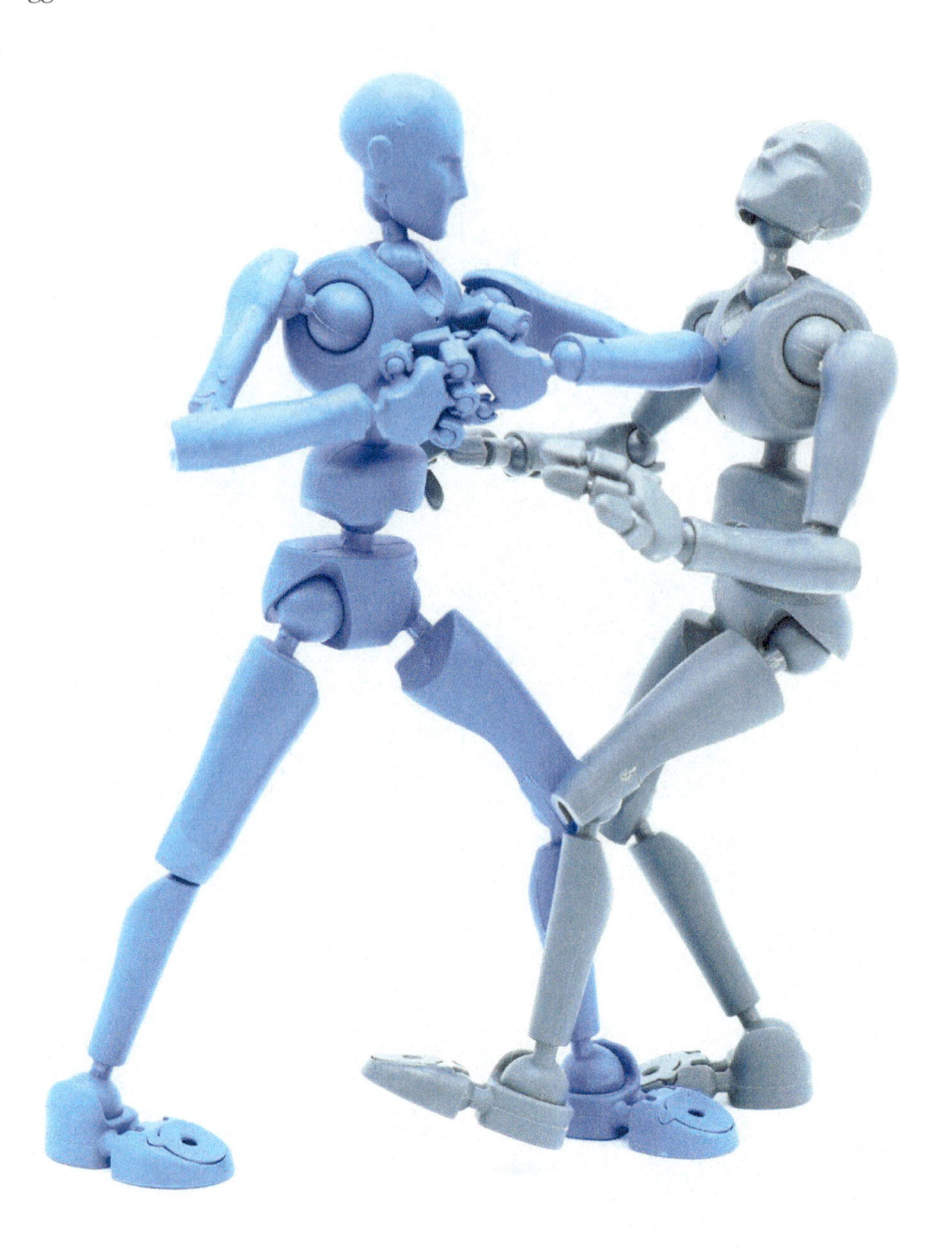

Knee Strike

The knee is a valuable weapon for when the space is too tight for you to swing your leg. It also allows the opportunity to strike the aggressor whilst creating torque in your body in preparation for a throw which is completed upon your foot landing on the ground. You can use the knee to drive though elbow joints, or to strike the Vagus nerve. It's not limited to only striking the groin.

Shin Kick

The shin kick is not a front kick as in martial arts, but more of a straight leg swing. Usually deployed with the intent of driving though any testicles which may be present and continuing this movement to infinity and beyond, causing structural damage of the pubic bone and pelvis.

A traditional front kick to the groin may not stop an aggressor, who for want of a better term, is off their nut on drugs. However, smash through the pubic bone and you have a whimpering mess of an aggressor to contend with.

Heel Stamp

Use your heel to stamp down on the main bones in their foot structure and remove their ability to put weight on the foot, preventing them chasing you when you proceed to run like the wind. The heel stamp can also be used onto the knees to cause structural damage. If the aggressor is on the ground the heel can be used anywhere to cause damage.

"What about punching"

After many years of teaching self-defence, I can say punching takes specialist training, obviously, otherwise we would all be top-level boxers, so punching isn't included here. Most people hurt their wrist when attempting to punch if untrained in the mechanics of the movement. In comparison to the other weapons available, punching takes a lot longer to get to grips with. You want something you can use right now if needed under stress, which will be more of a clubbing movement than a punch anyway, so for the information presented here, the five-knuckle face buster is out!

The Rice Crispy Principle - Snap, Crack or Pop!

Familiar with your body weapon options, it's time to learn how to use them effectively and efficiently, and to succeed in this you will have to change your view away from that of the norm when it comes to the prospect of a threat of violence, altering your perspective of what needs to be done.

Watching boxing or rugby, you will see a broken nose doesn't stop the boxer continuing the bout, or stop the rugby player from completing the game. The single motivating factor for the sports person is the desire to win and compete, it's only a contest, yet with the injury of a broken nose they can still carry on. This shows you there's no way you can count on an injury like this to stop an aggressor who is determined to cause you harm, not if it doesn't stop someone competing in sport. When a person is totally committed to causing harm, you must replicate the things that end the boxing match immediately or stop the rugby player from continuing the contest. The injuries that would halt the athletes return to action for several months is what you prepare yourself to replicate to ensure your success in ending a threat.

Yet when people embark on learning a self-defence system one of the first moves taught in many systems is palm striking the attacker to the nose, with the information passed off as an efficient way to stop an attacker. It's dangerous to present information like this, because if the aggressor is committed and possibly one who has taken stimulants, they will respond to a palm to the face by repeatedly punching you in yours. Instead of palming them, use your heel to break their ankle, that will stop them, just as it would stop the boxer or the rugby player. It's unpleasant to think about, and hopefully this will help reinforce the only time it's applicable to use this for injuring somebody, is when you think you aren't going to make it home if you do nothing. The principles of *RBM* applied in helping to be a confident, solution based, positive focused human being, comes into play every day, but causing a serious injury to another person, is only for when you think the worst is going to happen to you.

Whatever their reasons for attacking you, or threatening your loved ones, they are still a human being, you just don't know their story. It's this compassion and understanding which will help to stop you entering overkill, stopping the red mist consuming you. Reminding you to avoid having to strike another person until you deem it the only option, then you do what you need to do to end the threat, don't act as judge and jury, dishing out your own physical sentencing. Keep your emotions and sense of injustice out of it. Stop the aggressor from being a danger to you but what they may or may not do in the future is not your responsibility. You do not *'stop them from attacking someone else in the future, by paralysing them today!'* That's not your call to make.

Where do you drop the Thunder Fist bombs?

- **The Hot Zones**
- **Test Drive the Weapons Systems**
- **De-escalation and Breakaways**

Once a person has started racing towards you with a knife, or perhaps pinned you on the ground and started screaming that 'they'll kill you if you move' before trying to rape you, it's at this moment people realise talking is futile and they wish they had a different option available to them.

RBM is having that backup plan for when the poo hits the fan. At times like these it's best to avoid anything which asks you to attempt to hit a precision spot the size of your little finger. Pressure point fighting for the average person, in my opinion, is useless under the stress of a violent attack and I wouldn't trust my life on small precision targets, others might, I won't. It's more reliable to have large, visible targets to aim for, targets which require very little skill to hit, and targets which prevent the attacker from harming you. Big targets for big bombs, perfect!

The Hot Zones

The targets you will aim for and the damage you are trying to cause when struck with the full intent of the *Demolition Monkey* is outlined next. The targets are catagorised into primary targets highlighted in red, and the secondary targets highlighted in black. Red targets are the ones you can open with, reachable and achievable once you have navigated around the aggressors defences. The targets in black are ones which you will not be able to open with, unless they have grabbed you, or you have grabbed them. If contact has been made, then the targets of the wrists and elbow becomes upgraded immediately to red primary targets.

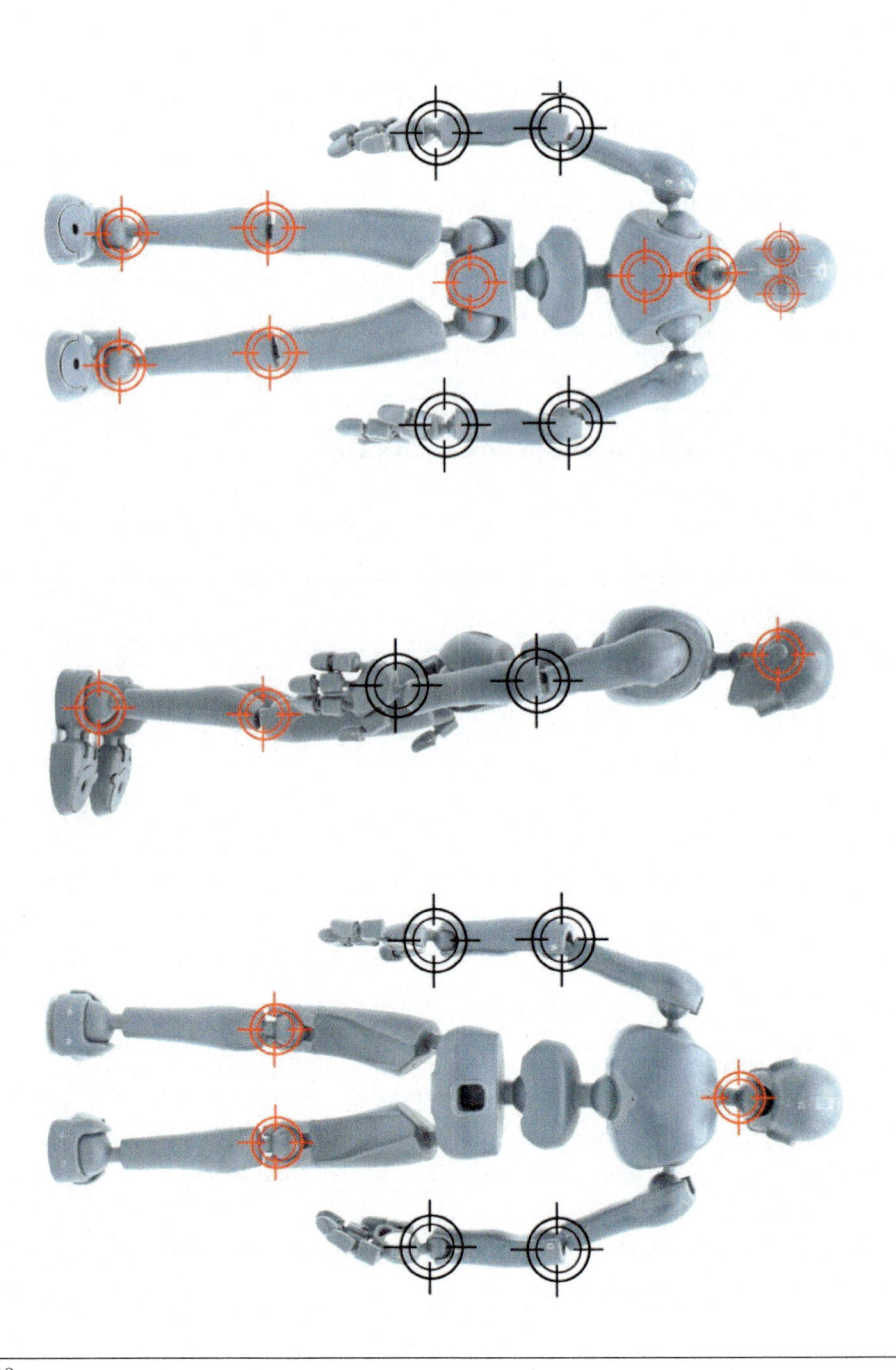

The areas you aim your strikes at give numerous options for you, which on the surface, seems a good thing, but too much choice can cause target confusion and create a delay in your response. Before I go on to outline the concept of Target Hot Zones, I need to explain why you need them and what I mean by too much choice, and the confusion caused by this, as it's a hugely important piece of information in terms of self-defence.

<u>*Will I be fast enough, will I react in time, will I remember what to do, or will I freeze?*</u>
These are the main doubts people have when learning self-defence. Hopefully the brain schematics of the SAM Axis and HPAC Axis, with the explanation of the two avatars representative of the two different feedback loops in the brain and how they function, have helped to alleviate these concerns. But there's a need to hone-in further, specifically on decision making under stress, and how to shape your realistic self-defence method around this information to further remove doubts. Doubt is the performance killer, not fear, which is why the information I am presenting must be detailed, to answer your questions, because questions are essentially little seeds of doubt. Remember, a bit of fear will activate the fight or flight system, putting you in charge of a rocket power fuelled body capable of amazing things, but doubt is linked to either a lack of faith in the success rate of your self-defence system, or a lack of belief in your own ability to deliver it when needed. To overcome this hurdle, further information explaining how fantastic your performance capabilities are when your life is on the line will be a big help.

<u>Will I be able to remember what to do, and will I do the right thing?</u>
The relationships and influences between choice, the number of options available and the time taken to make decisions has relevance to self-defence. The main reference points used to explain this subject matter being Hick's Law[23] and many self-defence systems use this in the structure of their methods.

Hicks-Hyman Law is founded on the work of British psychologist William Hick, and American psychologist Ray Hyman[24], stating the higher the number of choices available, the longer it will take to make any decisions, thus hindering the speed of selecting the most applicable solution. They experimented with the variances of a person's reactions when asked to activate a switch in response to a corresponding light being illuminated. The number of lights would range

---

[23] Hick, W. E. 1952: On the rate of gain of information, *Quarterly Journal of Experimental Psychology*

[24] Hyman, R (March 1953). "Stimulus information as a determinant of reaction time". *Journal of Experimental Psychology*

between two and ten throughout different phases of the experiment. The results were conclusive, showing the 'more choice' you have in your decision making, the longer the response time will be. This has been picked up by the self-defence world and used as a model to explain choice, reaction time and response time if attacked.

Done deal, fantastic, because this clearly states the more options you have, the longer it will take to make a choice, so all you need to do in your self-defence practice is limit the options and you will react faster, right? But by doing this you will be restricting your options, therefore limiting your potential, and possibly lowering your chances of survival.

The issue I see with using Hick's Law in relation to a threat on your life is that the experiment wasn't carried out with the participants placed under any stress conditions, there's no data to suggest how this law applies when the participants stress response kicks in. What is known, is that under stress cognitive function is negatively affected and too much conscious thought, (i.e. trying to think of the right thing to do whilst under threat), will overstimulate the use of the revving of the fight or flight response, likely causing you to freeze. Yet when under stress you will switch to the fastest of the brain schematics, the processing loop of 12 milliseconds, moving away from the conscious cognitive thought process which takes 25 milliseconds. To suggest option selection performance under stress would be negatively affected by more choice does not fit with what we know about brain schematics, so to follow Hicks Law could result in unnecessarily removing options. When placed under stress, you are subconsciously operating at your most efficient output, as your natural self-preservation system kicks in, your hippocampus will be reeling off hundreds of potential answers all whittled down to one solution, one decision for you to subconsciously deliver, in only 12 milliseconds!

I believe it's not the number of choices on the list which is the issue, but how the choices are made and executed.

If using a self-defence system which is based on matching an exact response to a specific attack, such as in a block and counter method, you'll be overthinking at a time when your brain is not set up to think. You will be waiting for their attack so you can identify it in order to block and counter, using a deliberate and calculated thought for matching up the correct routine is too much for your brain in a threat situation, the freeze fuse will blow, and you stand still, or you abandon all you have learnt. Finding yourself discarding the self-defence and martial arts skills and trying to brawl with the person attacking you. I've found this to be a common occurrence, talking to ex-martial artists, they relayed the stories of being attacked and fighting back, yet not using any of the skills they were taught in the dojo.

To reiterate, I believe it's <u>not the number of choices you are taught</u>, <u>but how you are taught to implement them</u> which is important. Do you need conscious and deliberate thought about which choice to make, such as block and counter? Or is it a method based on 'if they attack with their left hand you do this, if they attack with their right hand you do something else'? Without intending to criticise anyone or any system, it's necessary to question the application of some methods. As previously written, everything has its use and place in the world, yet questions need to be asked and answered to transmit why *RBM* is taught in a very specific format, and to help you appreciate the value in this.

Rather than limiting choice, perhaps the solution is changing the self-defence system so it doesn't rely on conscious decision making under stress. Remove the things which require you to perform unnatural actions under stress, which is exactly where things start to go wrong. Things like intricate moves, or attempting to remember a pattern, or a set drill which forces your left hemisphere into action using a cognitive heavy-laden method of *'if they do this then I do that'*.

Hick's law should not be discarded because it does have value in that it highlights *how* you should be taught, but not necessarily *what* you are taught, let me expand on this. I don't believe Hicks law and the number of target choices in a self-defence system is relevant in decision making when under stress, *unless you have set patterns or drills which you must remember to apply*. I expect a lot of people to disagree with this, which is why I need to come up with something solid to support my opinion, otherwise it's just my theory. Step forward the big brains from Tel-Aviv University, *Eran Chajut and Daniel Algom* who, in their work, *Selective Attention Improves Under Stress: Implications for Theories of Social Cognition 2003 Journal of Personality and Social Psychology, Copyright 2003, American Psychological Association, Inc.Vol. 85, No. 2, 231–248*,[25] concentrate on three elements: The Attention Approach, Capacity-Resource Theory, and Thought Suppression Approach, all three elements explaining choice selection when placed under stress, and this information can be applied to self-defence decision making when the brain is launching the fight or flight system.

Hicks Law didn't record responses when individuals were placed under stress, but the work of *Eran Chajut and Daniel Algom* was based on decision making in experiments where participants were placed under stress conditions,

---

[25] Eran Chajut and Daniel Algom 2003: Selective Attention Improves Under Stress: Implications for Theories of Social Cognition 2003 *Journal of Personality and Social Psychology*, Copyright 2003, American Psychological Association, Inc.Vol. 85, No. 2, 231–248

not stress of physical harm or a threat to life, but measurable stress climates, and observing what happens in relation to decision making and choice when the stress response kicks in. The three sections of work help support the reasons why the self-defence movements in RBM Phase 3 are so different in their methods and application to anything else I have seen. You may be taught to hit the same targets, and the way you hit them may be similar too other things out there, but how the information is loaded into the brain and the format of the approach to striking them is unique. The most important part of the self-defence system is different.

The Attention Approach

Kicking off with the first section of their research on choice under stress, they state:

> *"The logic of the attention approach is simple and compelling. Stress depletes one's available attentional resources. The scarce resources left are necessarily committed to processing the task relevant dimension at hand. The paradoxical result is that the deficits on the task-irrelevant dimensions render the processing of the relevant dimension intrusion free"*
>
> *Eran Chajut and Daniel Algom*[26]

The statement *'stress depletes one's available attentional resources'*, and *'the deficits on the task-irrelevant dimensions render the processing of the relevant dimension intrusion free'* supports the need for a self-defence method which doesn't require any deliberate, focused and conscious thought, because any system based on matching a specific block and counter to an exact attack will not have the necessary brain processing resources allocated from which to draw from under stress. If your method demands conscious processing power of analytically recalling and selecting a set routine to match a specific type of attack, you will be unable to do this while the attentional resource is being narrowed. You will be losing the ability of deliberate and measured conscious thought and because the things you learnt aren't being recalled quickly enough, you'll start to act irrationally, freeze, or even break into sporadic fight or flight.

The *Attention Approach* supports the explanations I have given about the *RBM Loop and the Doom Spiral Loop* when describing the brain processes and also how the Amygdala overrides the left brain thinking. The brain moves away from conscious deliberate thought towards a fast-track process of auto-pilot responses when under stress. It acts instinctively and automatically, rather than relying on consciously made solutions. The benefits come when you replace and upgrade the autopilot, providing new information which can be sourced as

---

[26] Eran Chajut and Daniel Algom 2003: Selective Attention Improves Under Stress: Implications for Theories of Social Cognition 2003 *Journal of Personality and Social Psychology*, Copyright 2003, American Psychological Association, Inc.Vol. 85, No. 2, 231–248

instinctive, automatic responses. This new data needs to be drilled into the memory banks of the Hippocampus, becoming hardwired options to be used without deliberate conscious thought and is achieved by using repetition, so that under stress, or threat to your life, you recall these options and use them. Implementing this through Classical and Operant Conditioning.

If you don't use repetition, the memories won't be strong enough, they will not be hardwired and when the available attentional resources are narrowed, *you will revert to type*. You will start brawling and all your self-defence skills learnt in the training room will abandon you when you need them the most. If the data isn't drilled into the subconscious in a format which demands no deliberate thought, you won't do it under stress.

The upside of the *Attention Approach* is the paradox of losing conscious processing speed when under threat meaning you will ignore consciously held data and switch to instinctive, automatic responses. This sounds terrible, but it's beneficial for you because the closing down of the wider thought-based options will improve your functionality of instinctively selecting which action to take from your *RBM* options, hard-wired through repetition, and learnt through specific conditioning methods, these new solutions require no thought to put into action. No blocks or counters, not waiting to see the attack and trying match it with a set answer, simply hitting the first target available. This is the fastest option.

Eran Chajut and Daniel Algom continue this explanation of the Attention Approach by expanding with:

> *"The diminished resources available are fully engaged by the former with the net result of better selectivity in responding. This differential deployment of attention occurs regardless of the composition of the two classes of dimensions. The to-be-responded-to dimension always commands priority, if not exclusivity, in attentional processing".*

Eran Chajut and Daniel Algom[27]

This tells us 'strike the target now', will always take precedence over a 'think what to do and then strike' option. Under stress automatic wins every time and if your self-defence data hasn't been put into the Hippocampus in the correct way, via the use of simplistic moves with a high repetition of striking targets to imprint them, then there won't be a viable instinctive option to call on.

If there is no option available, you will start to revert to type, which is unpredictable and often irrational, opening the door for *Confused Rabbit* to step

---

[27] Eran Chajut and Daniel Algom 2003: Selective Attention Improves Under Stress: Implications for Theories of Social Cognition 2003 *Journal of Personality and Social Psychology*, Copyright 2003, American Psychological Association, Inc.Vol. 85, No. 2, 231–248

in, bringing doubt and uncertainty which interrupts the effective and natural *Attention Approach*, causing the Doom Spiral to begin and guess what, you freeze. Because of this, *RBM* is designed around the natural functioning of the *Attention Approach*, enabling the natural dominance of the *Demolition Monkey* to step forward under threat, by subconsciously selecting targets made available via correctly loading the data in a way which requires no conscious thought.

How you select the target falls under the next section of *Capacity Resource Theory* which is the reason why I made huge adjustments from the early days of *RBM* in how you move to strike a target.

Capacity-Resource Theory
Several years ago, I noticed when instructing people in *RBM* their knowledge of different targets left them spoilt for choice, sometimes this extended menu of options created a stutter in their physical movements, a mini-freeze. As though something made them pause momentarily, and they were having target confusion. They knew a wide range of targets, but they were stopping and making deliberate, thought out decisions in the choice of which one to strike, and this decision making was visible. I didn't know anything about Hick's Law until I started my own research into why this mini pause was occurring. The element of too much choice of Hick's Law was creeping in, because the menu of target choice was extensive and at this juncture, I did consider reducing the targets I was including in the system and reducing the ways of hitting the targets. This would have resulted in detrimentally limiting the ability of *RBM* to succeed in a self-defence situation, because it would limit options. This created a problem and is exactly why I said Hicks Law shouldn't be binned completely as it's very relevant to what and how you are taught.

Thankfully, I didn't stop my research at Hicks Law, as what I found within the research of *Eran Chajut and Daniel Algom* and in particular their *Capacity-Resource Theory* led me to completely revamp and restructure *RBM* in every aspect of how it's taught. Evolving to become a self-defence method not only with an understanding of the fight or flight system, but instead becoming a method of self-defence with its whole ethos **based around the fight or flight system.** This is why it's called realistic self-defence, the reality is not just about how real the attack looks and whether it appears like street violence, but more importantly, how realistic the method is in terms of you being able to perform the task of striking a target when the stress response has started within you.

Many people talk about the fight, flight, and freeze response, yet proceed to show movements and principles of self-defence which do not work in tandem with the stress response system they have just explained. The knowledge of the system and the physical self-defence movements *must work in unison*. This is an obstacle I have had to overcome in developing what I consider to be a functional approach to self-defence. Previously a sequence used in *RBM* would have been along the lines of:

> The aggressor grabs you and you respond by driving your thumb into their eye. Follow this with a stamp to the ankle, then strike the sternum with your elbow. Finish with a shin to the groin.

Four moves, four targets, this wasn't a set pattern and the targets could be selected in any order and could be changed as the person saw fit, they could have opened with the stamp to the ankle and then hit the sternum, so it wasn't a set drill to be remembered, just a collection of targets.

In terms of principles this was correct at the time, because you're moving off the spot towards a target and causing disruption to the aggressor, and as soon as a target is struck with a meaningful blow the threat is removed. Yet upon learning about the *Attention Approach* and *Capacity Resource Theory*, this sequence, and all others like it had to be discarded, and it was back to the drawing board to construct something different.

Why? Because if you are taught to strike all over the body, hitting the ear, then the foot, then the eye, consciously picking places to hit all over the body to cause carnage, then you're thinking about which target to strike, you're deliberately and consciously selecting targets. This hitting all over the body won't happen under stress as it's outside of your brain operations because if you are looking at the eye as a target, at that very moment due to the natural and efficient *Attention Approach* all other targets which are out of your field of vision in that isolated timeframe cease to exist to you.

It takes only a very basic level of anatomy to know the person attacking you will in all probability have feet, but under stress and looking towards their face, the option of stamping on their ankle will not exist, unless you stand still and think about it, which is why in the past people learning *RBM* had a slight pause in their movements. Remember you revert to type under stress and what you train is what you will do, indicating if in learning self-defence you stop and think which target to pick, this is what you will want to do in conflict. Now your self-defence system may fail you when you need it the most, because standing still and refraining from letting yourself act instinctively is the polar opposite of the *Attention Approach*, you will break the system, you will freeze and this is why I believe people who learn martial arts or set pattern self-defence often end up on the wrong end of violence.

I had to alter how I was teaching self-defence. The dilemma is removing the problems which come with choice and the need to stop using conscious thought, but without the restriction created by taking targets away from the list. Options without conscious decisions is what you are seeking, that's the holy grail of self-defence. Choices aren't limited under stress, the problem is thought intrusion about these choices, so how do we keep the versatility without compromising on efficiency? Once again thank you Chajut and Algom:

> *"Attention narrows under stress. However, the narrowing is directional, with efficient processing confined to chronically accessible, automatically activated dimensions".*
>
> Eran Chajut and Daniel Algom[28]

Your operating system changes to emergency protocol when the *Attention Approach* kicks in, and the *Capacity Resource Theory* means you need to ensure data is stored and used in a way which is simplistic in its execution. This *chronically accessible, automatically activated dimensions* gave me the answer, not restricting options but instead creating folders to neatly store the information to make it *more accessible in stressful situations* and having a method which works on the principle of hitting one target at a time as they appear to you. Not searching for them outside of the parameters of what's possible under stress, not remembering sequences, just one target at a time.

When they approach you, or grab you, the physical structure of an aggressor will draw your focus towards a target, the most viable target, and you will only see that one target at that point. Then the conditioned response, the chronically accessible automatically activated response (hard wired option) for that target is pulled out of the memory banks, an instinctive option due to what you have learnt. Then you will strike other targets in your current field of vision because they exist without you having to think about them or search for them, they are already in your capacity, already in your field of vision.

It took a lot of research time, testing, and as always, using my test group to turn the theory into a practical principle, I found the way of operating within the understating of the *Attention Approach* and the *Capacity-Resource Theory* without restricting target options was to introduce the concept of what will be referred to as Hot Zones. I found grouping targets located within close proximity of each other on the human body into visual clusters to be a very effective approach. This made only four folders to access, four places to initially look towards as a first option to strike, rather than trying to pick somewhere from a list of targets scattered all over the body. The benefit of the folders is

---

[28] Eran Chajut and Daniel Algom 2003: Selective Attention Improves Under Stress: Implications for Theories of Social Cognition 2003 *Journal of Personality and Social Psychology*, Copyright 2003, American Psychological Association, Inc. Vol. 85, No. 2, 231–248

having four options to focus on, four Hot Zones in the brain containing the target information, making it more *'chronically accessible'*. As the explanation of the *Attention Approach* identifies, you will only register what's in your field of vision at any one moment, therefore it makes sense to stay within the initial Hot Zone chosen as a response to being attacked, and keep striking that target area, keep hitting it until it disappears. Not stopping and looking for somewhere else on the body to strike.

Put into a more tangible description, they run towards you and start threatening you, your thoughts and ability to think clearly, logically, and analytically are restricted due to the stress and severity of the threat situation *(Attention Approach)*. You feel the butterflies in your stomach etc. *(HPAC Axis activation)* and you find yourself visually zooming in on the Vagus nerve on the side of the neck without any deliberate thought because of the data loading in Phase 3 *(intuitively choosing an option from the hard-wired data)* and you step forwards to strike the target *(Classical and Operant conditioning)*. Now the hot zone folder opens, and you see the next target in the vicinity, it may be a decision to strike the Vagus nerve again or this time you may go for the ear, stepping forwards and striking the target. Without any pause, hesitation, or deliberate thought you move again, this time aiming for the eye, as again it's in the same visual targeting area for you as the ear and Vagus Nerve. This is the data being stored in an accessible way *(Capacity-Resource Theory)*. Preventing you from pausing and preventing you needing deliberate cognitive intent to look for other targets in different areas of the aggressor's body, such as trying to hit the groin after the eye. This is necessary because:

> *"Attention fails for all of the other dimensions, regardless of the task demands"*
> *Eran Chajut and Daniel Algom*[29]

If you're looking at a zonal area of an aggressor containing their eye, ear and neck, your attention for other areas will fail and it would take a deliberate thought action to switch your focus away from what you are looking at when taking into consideration the *Attention Approach* and the *Capacity Resource Theory*.

To reiterate, if you're looking at the zone consisting of the eye, ear and neck, at that moment under stress their knee does not exist to you, so you won't be able to hit it, because mentally it doesn't exist until you see it, and you will only see it if you stop and allow yourself the time to seek it out. Which is exactly the process you want to prevent from creeping in, as it's the most inefficient way

---

[29] Eran Chajut and Daniel Algom 2003: Selective Attention Improves Under Stress: Implications for Theories of Social Cognition 2003 *Journal of Personality and Social Psychology*, Copyright 2003, American Psychological Association, Inc.Vol. 85, No. 2, 231–248

for you to operate and it allows a chance for the gremlins to get into the machine, causing you to freeze. You will only hit what you can see, or what you can feel if they grab you, and any system which draws you away from this natural way of functioning will enhance the potential for you to break away from how your system has evolved to function under stress, resulting in over-stimulating it and freezing.

The Hot Zones give you multiple target choice, multiple ways of striking, but within a narrow field of selection choice, because the neat structure holding the data in the Hippocampus is found in only four folders. This prevents target selection issues from having a negative effect, and means you don't have to limit your options, it's a perfect solution! You now have a self-defence system built on how you truly function under stress, making intuitive decisions without conscious thought, no pausing between targets, and no left hemisphere interruption caused by trying to remember a pattern or set drill.

After introducing this zonal targeting into *RBM,* I noticed an immediate change in the output of the test group after only a few hours of adopting and applying target zones. It simplified everything. You may not be able to see an aggressor's ankle or knees when they are wearing clothes, but their physical movement will give you a structural outline so you can still locate the targets of knees and ankles by the aggressors body shape, whereas the internal organs are hidden and because of this, they won't register as viable targets without a deliberate conscious thought of striking them, and remember a deliberate conscious thought means you have paused to think.

The Thought Suppression Approach

> *"Selective attention is bound to fail, but it is most apt to do so under stress. Stress depletes attentional resources. Because the act of focusing draws heavily on such resources, stress exacts a toll on the quality of selective attention. Because automatic processes do not require attention, stress exerts little effect on the monitoring of the to-be ignored dimension. Selectivity thus is disrupted under stress, with performance fraught by numerous intrusions from the task irrelevant dimension".*
>
> *Eran Chajut and Daniel Algom*[30]

It's important each *RBM* session has a slow-paced, low intensity section for data loading of the movements of striking targets. It's also important each session includes a section where there is a significant increase in the level of stress you are asked to perform under.

This is where people think about grabbing the pads and doing intensive sparring, or beating the innards out of each other, but it's not about physical stress. Self-defence effectiveness is about the mind, and using ways of training to help cause the onset of the *Attention Approach*, so that you get to feel and experience moving off the spot when you see an attack, and to do so without any preconceived idea about what you are going to do. Finding solutions to the problem of the attack on the fly and continuing to hit targets, without stopping and without any thought as to what you are doing. Its intuitive, bespoke to that situation, and effective. Giving yourself the tools to be able to 'wing it!'

Because automatic processes do not require attention, there is a need to prepare yourself to be comfortable operating from a state of mind which is void of the luxury of time for conscious decision making, this is the stress element to include but it doesn't necessarily mean an increase in speed, it can mean a change in comfort zone. People learn self-defence because they are seeking comfort, comfort in the knowledge they can protect themselves and be safe, allowing a sense of control over situations which could be dangerous and harmful. This means the big challenge is to 'give up' this sense of control and be happy to hand over responsibility to the autopilot, which is why you must be given the opportunity to see how this new data will come out under simulated stress, because the autopilot is the best person for the job and you need to see this in action.

It's a massive confidence boost to see how you respond when caught by surprise or distracted by mental confusion, it shows you can function effectively

---

[30] Eran Chajut and Daniel Algom 2003: Selective Attention Improves Under Stress: Implications for Theories of Social Cognition 2003 *Journal of Personality and Social Psychology*, Copyright 2003, American Psychological Association, Inc.Vol. 85, No. 2, 231–248

when experiencing this *Thought Suppression*. You will gain confidence in being able to succeed and being able to create 'live' solutions which are orchestrated around the attack as it unfolds and not having a set pattern to remember.

When asked what would you do if a person grabbed you? People learning self-defence want to be able to give a definitive answer, step one, step two, and step three in a structured format. Yet this doesn't work under stress, the answer must be you have no preconceived ideas, you only know you will hit the first target you see. This is achieved by creating an environment where mental stress exists and then observing and monitoring the revert to type responses, clearly identifying what your base level functions are when you haven't got a clue what's going on, with no time to think, at a time when you must act to stay alive.

Accepting you will need to give up the Left Hemisphere logical analytical driven thoughts and leave it in the hands of the instinctive, intuitive operator is no easy step. Accepting you have to give up the illusion of control, not seeking the comfort of an *'if they do this, I will do that'* system, but instead being happy to make it up as you go along, finding a sense of normality in the chaos of unpredictability is a challenge. But in releasing yourself from the need of this control you hand over the reins to the most suitable and capable part of your brain for the situation, the expert not the ex-spurt.

<u>HOT ZONES</u>

Having explained why the targets need to be placed into folders which you're now referring to as Hot Zones, it's time to identify the clusters of targets where you can focus your strikes.

Zone 1 Targets: Eye, Ear & Vagus Nerve

Target – *Eye*
Tools for the job – *Fingers & thumbs*
Injury - *Severe injury, may result in permanent loss of sight in the targeted eye.*

Target – *Ear*
Tools for the job – *Open hand strike, like a one-handed clap.*
Injury - *Perforation of the eardrum. Will cause the aggressor to fall to the ground as their balance mechanism will be compromised.*

Target – *Vagus nerve / Pneumogastric nerve*
Tools for the job – *Forearm, elbow, knee, heel*
Injury - *Also known as the Pneumogastric nerve, this controls the autonomic functions of the body. A blow to this target will cause unconsciousness.*

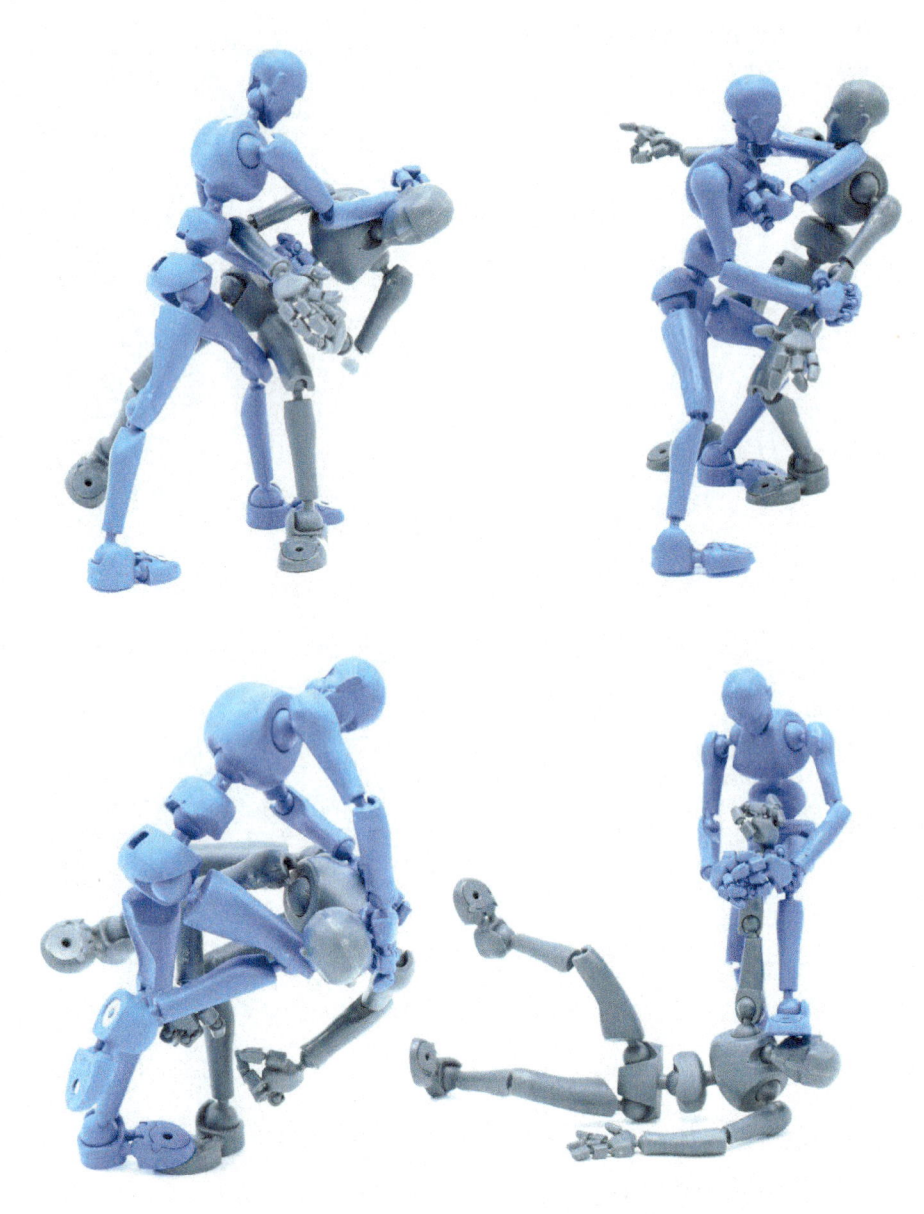

*Zone 2 Targets: These are the same as illustrated in Zone 1, but on the opposite side of the head

Zone 3 Targets: Jugular notch & the Sternum

Target – *Jugular notch*
Tools for the job – *Fingers*
Injury - *Striking this target will restrict airflow, affecting the anxiety levels of the aggressor. Also, lowering the amount of oxygen intake to be used as muscle fuel.*

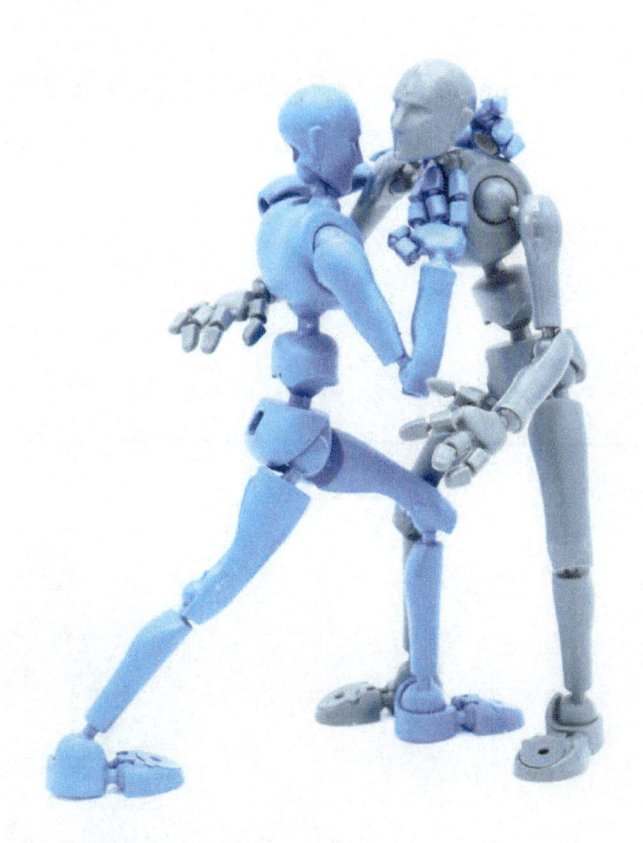

Target – *Sternum*
Tools for the job – *Elbow, knee, heel*
Injury - *On impact the cartilage fixing the ribs to the sternum will be compromised causing structural damage.*

⊕ Zone 4 Targets: Groin, Knees, Ankles & Feet
*Plus, nerves on the back of the neck

Target – *Groin*
Tools for the job – *Shin, knee, or heel*
Injury - *Smashing the pubic bone will affect the operational ability of the hips. The aggressor will be unable to stand*

Target – *Knee*
Tools for the job – *Heel*
Injury - *Stamping to either the outside or inside of the knee joint to cause dislocation. To damage the patella, stamp through the back of the knee, driving the knee downwards into the ground.*

Target – *Ankle & Feet*
Tools for the job – *Heel*
Injury - *Stamping to either the outside or inside of the ankle to break the joint and hitting the main bones at the top of the foot.*

Target – *Back of the neck*
Tools for the job – *Knee, forearm, elbow*
Injury - *Causing trauma to the spinal cord and directly attacking the feedback between the brain and body, this will render them unconscious.*

*This target is included in Zone 4 because once you strike any other targets in this zone, the aggressor will bend forwards, presenting the back of the neck into your zonal awareness.

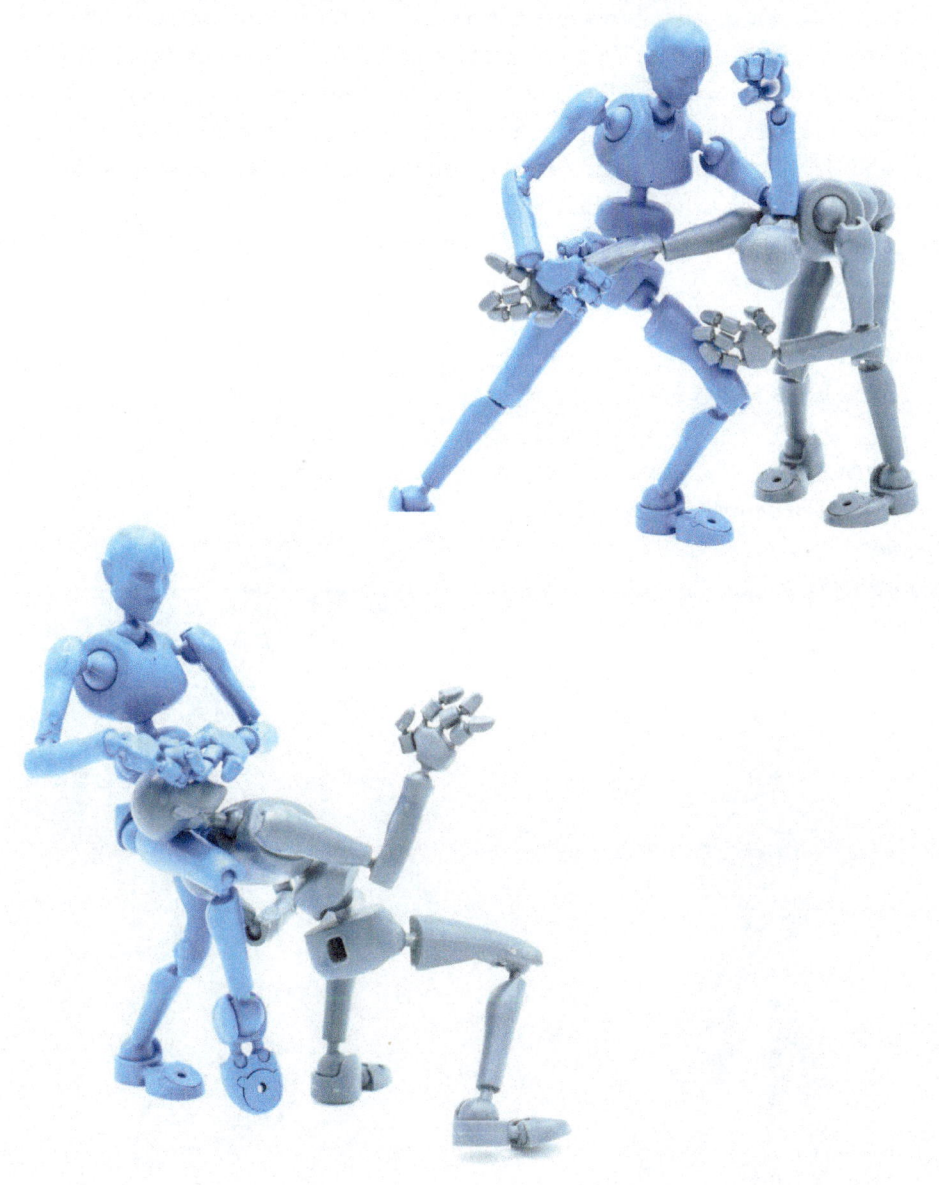

Reserve Zone Targets: Wrists & Elbows

These are targets which are difficult to achieve as a primary target, due to the aggressor's ability to remain mobile or to put up resistance. For example, it's difficult to achieve an elbow dislocation as an initial movement whilst the aggressor still holds the ability to resist. Yet stamp on their ankle first and they will be structurally weakened, enabling the elbow dislocation. It's also tricky to start with a throw but perforate the eardrum and it's a lot simpler and requires less skill. If they've already grabbed you, there'll be the potential to dislocate a wrist, if they haven't then it's difficult to achieve and therefore does not fit into a primary zone.

Target – *Elbow*

Tools for the job – *The aim is to finish with the aggressor's elbow bending the way it's not designed to. You can use your shoulder, or stamp through the elbow joint, or use your forearm or knee to create leverage to overload the joint.*

Injury - *Painful and it removes one of their primary weapons from their armoury*

Target – *Wrist*

Tools for the job – *Grab hold and twist! There isn't an associated body weapon for the dislocation of the wrist. It's achieved when a person grabs hold of you in some way and you seize the hand, keeping it on your body, then moving your torso. Causing a leverage which is greater than the load bearing weight of the wrist joint and it becomes structurally compromised.*

Injury – *Painful, and it removes one of their primary weapons*

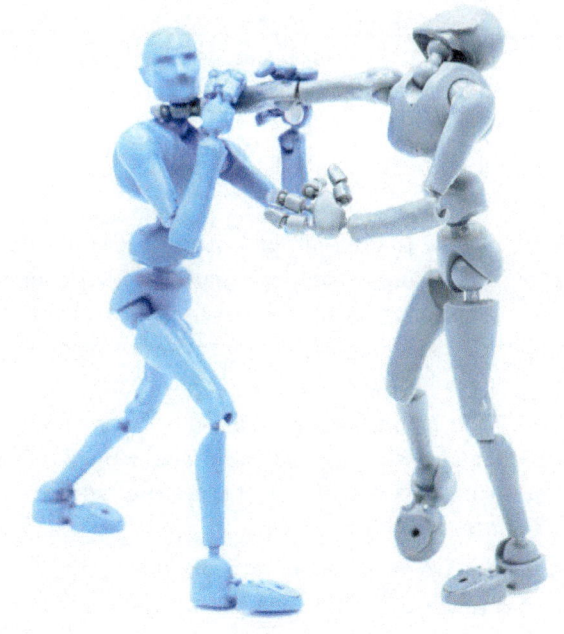

Test Drive the Weapons Systems

With targets bunched into zones to avoid thought confusion and to restrict the potential of freezing, the next stage is taking this information and loading it into the memory banks, so you don't ever need to think about it on a conscious level. For this to happen you will use physical movements, and the most efficient way to achieve this is with a drill partner, because there is no real substitute for physically moving another person around to load the data into your memory. You will move slowly throughout all of this. Phase 3 will put the hot zones into the context of working in relation to a variety of attacks, such as a grab or a punch, but prior to this comes individual target data loading.

Using your drill partner as a visual and kinaesthetic aid, you move to simulate how you would strike the target with the weapons available in your armoury. MOVE SLOWLY, as if performed at speed you will seriously injure your drill partner. Follow this procedure:

- Timing is everything, move slowly and ensure the foot you're stepping with lands on the ground when you make contact with a target. Not before or after, but at the same time. If your foot is off the ground, you have no structure to cope with the collision. If you hit the target after the foot lands, you lose the body weight from your strike.
- Don't overreach and lift the back heel up off the ground, it compromises your structure and ability to cope with the impact. If you find your back heel is off the ground quite often, your timing is out. Move off the spot earlier, and get closer before you launch into an attack.
- Don't bend forwards or lean towards the person, it compromises your balance.
- For the first target, pick Zone 1 and use the eye as the initial data load. Start from a front facing position to your partner and move forwards to practice striking the eye. Return to the start position and repeat the process again to the same eye only, stick to the initial zone and the initial target.
- Next begin from a position as if you are facing the side of their body, practice striking the same eye. You won't be able to attack from the back as you can't see the eye. Remember, under stress if you can't see it then it doesn't exist.
- When you simulate striking the target, your drill partner will react as though the target has been hit and injured. This is easy, for all targets they simply need to move the area which has been struck away from the attack and hold it to protect and shield it from further injury.

- Run through this process and allow at least 10 minutes each for the front, the side, and the back for this target. You may want to take it in turns and do three practice strikes and then change, so the other person is engaged in the data load and not getting bored.

When the time is up, you move onto the next target in *THE SAME FOLDER, the same Hot Zone.* This would be the ear, located on the same side of their face as the eye you just practiced hitting. Repeat the process of striking from the front and then the side, but with the target of the ear, you can also begin from a position where you are behind the drill partner, because you can see the target from this position. Then you move onto the Vagus Nerve, be gentle and push slowly through the targets. No clunking or bashing of your practice partner.

Once you have completed all the targets in one zone, you then begin the process of pick and mix *within the zone*. Again, moving slowly you can for example, strike the eye, then the Vagus nerve, then the ear. Or start with the ear, then the eye and the eye again. Run through as many combinations as you can within that one specific zone, punches in bunches!

Continue this process for all 4 zones. It's impossible for you to spend too much time on this, the more familiarity with the targets and the zones the better. *You can ignore the Reserve Zone for the time being.* To help you with this I have listed the targets and their accessibility:

Target	Angle of Approach		
	Front	Side	Back
Zone 1 Eye	✓	✓	✗
Zone 1 Ear	✓	✓	✓
Zone 1 Vagus Nerve	✓	✓	✓
Zone 2 Eye	✓	✓	✗
Zone 2 Ear	✓	✓	✓
Zone 2 Vagus Nerve	✓	✓	✓
Zone 3 Jugular Notch	✓	✓	✗
Zone 3 Sternum	✓	✓	✗
Zone 4 Groin	✓	✗	✓
Zone 4 Knees	✓	✓	✓
Zone 4 Ankles	✓	✓	✓
Zone 4 Foot	✓	✓	✗
Zone 4 Back of the neck	✗	✓	✓

De-escalation and Breakaways

Alongside developing the Thumping Thunder Fist Demolition Monkey, it's beneficial to ensure your negotiator is deployed as efficiently as possible for conflict calming measures, as this is the area it specialises and excels at. Not the *Rabbit* headed version, where the situation has caused it to morph into characteristics with no use to anyone, and acting in ways which are to your detriment.

RBM sets out to help you achieve a balance of seizing the opportunity to use the analytical left brain for all its worth, right up until the point a situation changes and shifts to a place where it would be best if the left brain led diplomat moved aside and didn't intrude in the *Demolition Monkey* domain. But until that point is reached, conflict avoidance is always preferable, and deploying the negotiators skills to avoid conflict is always a preferred tactic. The negotiator avatar will be far more proficient with the *Demolition Monkey* standing behind it, peering over the shoulder in case things escalate and turn out differently. With the backup plan of human demolition breeding confidence within you, this safety net enables the Left Hemisphere to accomplish more, using diplomacy and negotiation to evade conflict. Without this safety net there is a far greater chance of spinning out of control, morphing into the *Rabbit* in a panic and entering the Doom Spiral loop.

This is the surrealism of *RBM*, the more adept you are at dealing with violence, the more accomplished you become at avoiding it, because with anxiety and uncertainty contained to the lowest possible level, there is lower stimulation of the neurotransmitters for fight or flight activation, meaning less fluster, less panic and a lower freeze potential. You will operate in negotiations as if accompanied by a bodyguard, it just happens this bodyguard is on the inside of you in the form of brain schematics.

The *Demolition Monkey* doesn't talk, it bashes, so it's not the best option to turn to as a communicator to open a debate, for this reason the negotiators time in the spotlight is here, the auditorium of de-escalation.

Let's cool it!
Verbal communication skills added to a pinch of knowledge about how to get another person's hands off you, creates a very lucrative business in the field of conflict management training. These methods are mostly successful when applied in a workplace environment, and it's important to have non-aggressive communication reaching as far across society as possible. For people who work in schools, care workers and the medical profession just to name a few, these verbal skills and break away techniques are appropriate as they cause no injury.

Which raises the question, why didn't I start with this at the beginning, so nobody ever gets hurt?

De-escalation and breakaways are important and are very valuable when used in the appropriate situations, the issue to be addressed is courses often neglect to include efficient fail safes, in case these tactics do not succeed, or the situation doesn't play out as you would have hoped. Any conflict can elevate in threat level faster and higher than you've been told it would or expected it could, and people in the self-defence and conflict management world tend to skirt around the reality it could all go downhill rapidly. Often, courses are disassociated with the reality of violence, only covering what to do if you are shoved, or grabbed. Rarely touching on the topic of what to do if when attempting to de-escalate you are punched, kicked, or a knife suddenly appears. That falls outside of the remit of the course and for that you would need to seek additional training.

As previously stated, it's easier to use de-escalation strategies with an aggressive person when you don't have overwhelming, distracting and worrying thoughts about what might happen if they grab you, or try to strike you. You achieve mental clarity from being confident in your ability to protect yourself if things take a turn for the worse, and this is the reason not to begin with de-escalation techniques, and why it isn't on page one. You must learn what to do if it all goes wrong as your first step of your self-defence, not de-escalation.

De-escalation is not the foundation of your realistic self-defence strategy, because the skills are not transferable to all threat levels, and they can leave you with a big gap in your safety strategy. In a situation where communication can calm a situation, then of course you should take this path, but if this doesn't have the desired outcome and the person grabs hold of you, then depending on the circumstances it's a good idea to use a breakaway technique rather than go straight to destruction. Breakaway techniques are designed to create an opportunity for you to leave the area and put distance between you and the threat. At this stage, having tried talking and putting distance between you and the potential threat, you have done all you can for them, if it escalates further then you have your safety net, the *Demolition Monkey* and knowledge of body weapons and targets. You need to have the choice to decide what the situation needs and to be equipped to deal with it in a multitude of ways. I hope this clarifies why de-escalation is not found in Chapter 1.

When I teach de-escalation principles, the emphasis is placed on you're doing it for the benefit of the aggressor and not from a place of panic, or the need to get them away from you, or the need to try and make the situation go away. You're not using de-escalation techniques to keep you safe from them, it's the flip side, it's to keep them safe from you. *This changes your perception, doesn't it?*

De-escalation is all about situational management!
The four W's and the H.

Who are you talking too, and do they know you? Have you asked their name, and have you given the person your name? (Or a different name if not wanting to disclose personal information) Humanising yourself by putting yourself firmly in their thoughts as an existence as a person, not an object or a symbol of something which is causing them to be agitated. Build up a threat profile of the person/people involved. A threat profile is based on displayed behaviour, not stereotypes. Listen to your intuition and at any time, if the situation elevates beyond what you feel is comfortable, then leave, if you can't leave, act.

What are they asking for, what do they want out of this situation, and what are your objectives in the situation? Focus on outcomes rather than the problem, not asking "what is wrong or what happened?" Be solution focused, let them see a positive way out and see a resolution. Start with *"is there anything I can do?"* Determine what you're trying to achieve, are you seeking a resolution, or distracting and stalling for time so others can leave, or others can arrive?

Why is this situation occurring? Why is this person in need of deescalating, is it personal and relating to you, or did you just happen to be there?

When is your deadline, when do you foresee this coming to an end? Are they showing signs of the *Ignition*, *Revving* or the *Full Throttle*? How long do you think you have to calm this situation or leave? Are all parties involved maintaining a constant emotional state, or is the situation escalating? Is any help/support available to you right now if you need to try to end this without the use of violence?

How do you maintain your safety, whilst operating as a conflict negotiator? Keep your distance, monitor their behaviour, look for the signs of increased fight or flight activity. Are you going around in circles with dialogue, or have you made process? Ensure you have an immediate escape route option and accept you might not be able to find a resolution and stick to your cut off point and walk away. Know what to do if they make physical contact with you, know how to put distance between you both to give them the chance to avoid injury. Know what to do if the situation changes and you need to remove the distance and strike the person to ensure your safety.

Some key points:
- The transfer of communication data between you and the other person (potentially a group) will be both verbal and non-verbal, the non-verbal being physical cues happening both unintentionally and intentionally. The priority is always ensuring your safety, so your body positioning must be considered to prevent accidently escalating a situation and placing yourself in danger.
- Stay out of their personal space! Aim to be in the social space zone of 4 to 12 metres away from them and always assume they have a projectile weapon so you may need to expand this space quickly or reduce the space quickly. Do not get caught off guard.
- Avoid standing square on to the person, stand slightly at a side on angle, it's less confrontational, and less vulnerable for you.
- If water is available give them some but place it somewhere for them to take themselves unless you are confident the situation dictates you are safe to close the gap to hand it to them. The process of them accepting water from you or taking a seat when offered by you creates the enforced teaming, which you can use to your advantage.
- Do not force eye contact, remember the eye connection from earlier.

Remember, this isn't done in a stressful situation where the *Rabbit* is running around, this is done when you feel confident in letting the negotiator handle things. If this changes and your stress levels start to rise, then push the negotiator aside and either run as fast as you can or pick a target. Am I safe? Is the main question you should be asking when negotiating/de-escalating, as this supersedes everything else, and will rule your decision making.

There are options available to you if the person makes physical contact and you want to make a fast exit. These will not end the conflict and will not neutralise the threat, but they will create a window of opportunity for you to leave. These are excellent things to teach teenage children, as it gives a way of removing someone else's hands off their body but with a minimum chance of causing long term damage.

Breakaway 1, the face palm push.

If the situation requires creating some space to quickly leave, thrusting your palm towards the persons face can create the opportunity for you to make a quick exit.

Please note, this will not end any conflict and will not guarantee safety, this is only a breakaway technique regardless of what other self-defence and martial arts teach you.

Breakaway 2, the forearm press

If grabbed, and you need to manoeuvre the person so you can get yourself closer to an exit, a method you can use is the forearm press. One hand reaches around the back of their head, whilst the other forearm presses upwards against the underneath of their nose. You drive forwards, moving them with you and positioning yourself ready to run as soon as the space opens up for you.

<u>*Breakaway 3, the circle of power.*</u>
If grabbed, by the wrist, hand, or arm, bring both of your hands close together and make a large circular motion. To ensure your success in removing their hold, you must move forwards whilst circling your arms.

*Remember, these breakaways are to buy time and space and not to end a physical conflict.

* * *

Returning once again to the point, "why didn't I start with this at the beginning, so nobody gets hurt?" In addition to the deliberate verbal and no-verbal communication existing between you and the person/people you're trying to pacify, there will be subconscious communication. This will be in the form of your emotions betraying you, giving out subtle cues of how you're feeling, regardless of what you're saying, and how you're 'acting'. You can stand in front of a person acting confidently and as if in control of the situation, saying all the right things in the perfect tone, but if underneath all of this you are anxious and trying to hide it, then the fight or flight system inside will start to fire due to the increased activity of the Pons in the brain. The other person/people will pick up on this, which is why it's essential you have a real confidence and not false confidence.

How do you get this? By learning how to stop an aggressor in their tracks, and from this place of security, calmness and clear thinking, everything else is easier!

If the breakaways gain you the opportunity to escape, leg it before the person who became a physical aggressor can re-orientate themselves and proceed with a follow up plan of attack. As soon as a physical threat becomes likely, discussion time is over, but you have your safety net of knowing how to stop the aggressor. If the de-escalation techniques, or the breakaway and leave choice didn't get the desired result, then be generous and let them have all of you. All of you, right now, onto one target. The failsafe!

The Mental & Physical Obstacle Course

- Be generous, and if they want a piece of you let them have all of you.
- The Moral Freeze
- Surprise! Flinch response.
- Colour codes of Scaling Flinch Response Recovery
- There are No Blocks!!!

With a fully loaded and primed Thumping Thunder Fist Demolition Monkey at your disposal, this next section will cover the things which may get in the way of the *Demolition Monkey* getting the strikes onto the targets and stopping an attack. Equipped with the data of where the appropriate targets are, and how to bash them, the next step is navigating the psychological stumbling blocks and the moral and socially conditioned tripwires which can get in the way of your success in dealing with a threat, when everything is trying to stop you, including yourself via incorrect beliefs.

Be generous, if they want a piece of you let them have all of you

A friend told me how he'd once been pinned to the wall with an aggressor's hand around his neck and was about to be punched. He told me *"I said to the guy I don't want to fight"*. My take on the situation and my response was 'it wasn't your decision to make at that point'.

If you were to find yourself in this same position, but rather than using the negotiator in a situation which is too risky for that tactic, and you instead used the *Demolition Monkey* and moved, proceeding to stamp on the aggressor's ankle causing it to break, then at this point you could hold the conversation about not wanting to fight and choose not to cause any further damage. But by not moving and failing to influence the situation you wouldn't have the luxury of being able to determine whether you were going to be drawn into a fight, it would have had nothing to do with you.

Submitting and being bashed on the head is still being in a fight, only one you aren't doing very well at it. If de-escalation or breakaway techniques are not going to do the job, sadly you must commit to the decision of striking a Target Zone with a pro-active movement, with the intent that nothing in the world is going to stop you getting to your target. Avoid violence at all costs, but if this is not possible, there is only one way to hit an aggressor, which is as hard as you can. All your weight in one movement onto one target, causing the area you hit to explode in the seismic manner you're aiming for.

Stopping them from attacking you requires mass and velocity. Even though physics explains this, most methods of self-defence focus on teaching you to move quickly in reaction to being attacked and to deliver fast strikes to the aggressor, they develop the speed but not enough shift in mass and I believe this is concentrating on the least important aspect to be developed. Think about a time you were crossing a road and a car suddenly appeared, almost on top of you, *did you jump away slowly*? Perhaps think of the time you dropped something heavy, and it fell straight towards you, *did you slowly step to the side*? How about walking with the children and one almost falls into a pond, *did you move slowly to catch their arm to keep them safe*? No, you absolutely have never moved slowly when you saw danger, it may have seemed as though time itself was moving at a snail's pace due to Tachypsychia, which is the distortion of the sense of time under stress, but physically you move quickly.

Under threat of a physical attack, you'll have plenty of motivation to move fast and have all the required hormones available to move at speed, and you will. The only people who don't move quickly are those who freeze, but you have this covered by loading information into the Hippocampus memory vault, the solution hard drive. I have previously taught *RBM* to a person who works in the probation services, being a part of the process for seeing people prior to their trial and assessing them during their sentence. The information I have from them is those arrested after carrying out sexual assaults have wounds, primarily scratch marks on their faces, which were inflicted by the person they chose to attack. This reinforces you'll be fast enough to get to a target, knowing how to create the necessary damage when you get there is where to focus your learning. Moving the mass of your body is of higher importance than focusing on speed. The best approach to achieving the most efficient results when learning *RBM* is to move slowly. This way the body will develop the motor skills and memory load in a shorter amount of time by moving at low speed, due to the activation of the kinaesthetic senses for a longer period with a drill partner. The brain to body link is being engaged for a longer period of time.

Mass/bodyweight is key to the destruction of the target area you are aiming for. I know the terminology of destruction sounds over the top and horrendous, but you must understand, this is the last chance saloon for you and the only thing standing between you and physical harm is causing a bit of them to break, to keep all the bits of you intact and safe. If they grab you, or select you for an attack, and if leaving isn't an option, then club them with every fibre of your body, and every ounce of desire to live you can muster. It's not pleasant for anyone involved but it's the reality people try to avoid accepting.

To create damage to an aggressor you will need your mass to move through their body, so this is what you practice when learning your chosen self-defence method, or you should, because what you practice is what you will do when under stress, it's called your revert to type. Practice perfectly and don't include anything in your learning process you don't intend on making an appearance when under stress. If you practice sparring and tapping targets by moving quickly when learning, this is what you will do under stress. If you practice driving through targets using your body weight, this is what you will do under stress, you will replicate these movements but faster due to the stress and intensity of the situation.

When working through the information in Phase 3, GO SLOWLY! Slower than you think you should, and really learn to move your weight through the drill partner. Be mindful that if you move too fast, it's your drill partner you will feel obliged to take grapes to in hospital during visiting hours, *because you will injure them*. In a real threat, your force drives through the person attacking you further and faster than they can move to avoid it, moving right through their structure and overloading the bodies structural shock absorbers. With the aggressor unable to let the force dissipate by using an avoidance movement, something must give and that something is the target zone.

When learning and working through the drills, you can check if you're doing things effectively by the physical feedback from your partner. Moving your body weight slowly and moving through the target, your movement will cause your drill partner to move their feet, because of the force felt on their body, but not yelp or lose consciousness. If your drill partner didn't have to move their feet when you moved, then you need to get closer and move right through them next time. If you're ever attacked, this body mass shift combined with the speed created by the urgency of wanting to live, will cause the area hit to have what we will call, *an event*.

The targets you are learning to hit will break with body mass, and they do not require you to be big, strong, or very skilful to get results. The force needed to break a Femur/Thigh bone for example is beyond most people, it has so much muscular protection and is a main bone in the body, which is why it's not a viable target and not included on the list. The target areas you're aiming for will:

- hit nerves for incapacitating the movement of a limb, or nerves effecting the functionality of the brain
- effect the intake of oxygen into the body
- disrupt the flow of oxygenated blood

- tear joint ligaments with mass movements resulting in dislocations
- damage the sensory organs of the body such as the ears and interrupt brain function with damage to the sensory nerves causing chaos to the brain lobes

Contained within the target list, which can all be damaged without relying on size and strength, there are some Break Something in case of Emergency Escape Targets available. It's always best to use movements to shift your bodyweight if you can, but if you are ever stuck for movement, then attack these targets with the force you can generate by moving a limb to cause them to explode. The *Break-Something-in-case-of-Emergency-Escape-Targets-*are: Eyes, Ears, Vagus Nerve, Jugular Notch, and the Groin

The Moral Freeze

Not all obstacles for you to overcome are physical, as mentioned previously you need to remove the belief of *it's wrong to strike another person*, and this will be one of your major obstacles. I often hear people say that if attacked, they would break this or kill that, well if you are a normal functioning member of society, I can tell you that without training this isn't guaranteed. There's a reason the military train people in the manner they do, it's to ensure the soldier can shoot, is able to strike, and is able to kill, they manipulate the switch which says 'no' to all of the above, because they need to guarantee these outcomes and not leave it to chance.

You may think it's easy to put your thumb into an eyeball, and yes, the physical action is simple but the mental capability to do it is harder than the physical action. The willingness to cause deliberate harm to another person is something which needs to be developed and you must learn to remove the barriers to striking the targets that could save your life. Another obstacle to overcome is that it's okay for you to strike them first, when appropriate and necessary, and for many people this is a huge stumbling block, because they need to change the perception that whoever throws the first punch is causing the trouble. This is a false view if you're only striking first to stop the danger, to end it quickly and efficiently if you see no other option. Retaliating first is still self-defence.

These are two mental barriers to overcome when under threat, and you get around these by completing the Hot Zone drills from the earlier section, walking towards your drill partner to strike the hot zones. Slowly, doing it from a position of you striking first and wanting to end the conflict by causing injury. This does sound as though you are starting the attack, which is correct, but there's a huge difference in starting the attack and being the cause of the problem. For example, if at home and you find yourself behind an intruder with a knife walking towards a family member, in this instance you need to move right now and strike them, not wait for them to see you, and plan their attack. It sounds obvious, but people often wait until they are face-to-face with the threat, they think you must *'fight fair'*. It's the negative conditioning and the self-justification aspect getting in the way again, people worry about getting into legal trouble if they strike first, but you know this isn't the case, justified force applies when feeling threatened, not only if you are being hit.

Another example of retaliate first would be if walking home one night you see someone rushing towards you, you move off the spot and they track your movements, you know they're coming for you. Are you going to wait to let them get into their stride and see what the attack is, or step forwards and kick their patella so hard their ancient ancestors feel it? Standing still and waiting to see what they're going to do is only going to give you the chance to slip into the freeze loop, so if under threat, don't stand still and wait to see what they are planning to do to you. Create disruption by moving straight away, now, towards the targets you can see on their body, or leave, now, as quickly as you can.

Surprise! The Flinch Response

Not being ready, not knowing you're about to be attacked is a danger to your safety in a violent attack, but being caught by surprise is the most likely reality and an enormous psychological obstacle to overcome. Despite this, the self-defence methods I have seen train you for when you're aware of an attack and ready for conflict, even having the time to get into your fighting stance. Some do include a small flinch aspect, but even then, they appear to be a flinch where your mental starting position is one of knowing the attack is likely to happen. Some tell you to always be ready, always switched on.

The elite soldier is fully briefed, fully prepared, and battle ready in their mindset when entering the theatre of war. They've been trained, prepared, and are switched on and ready when deployed. There's a reason the military have a rotational format whereby soldiers will be taken off active duty for rest time, letting them switch down their level of alert, and return to active duty where it all steps up again. If they didn't do this, behavioural changes start to creep in and stress levels rise, which can cause group fragmentation and the constant high intensity level can lead to post-traumatic stress disorder. All caused by the anxiety of remaining in a *'ready'* stress response for a prolonged period.

Knowing that maintaining a high level of alert for a long period of time creates detrimental effects in well drilled soldiers, it's reasonable to suggest it's not a great idea to think you can spend all your life in a *ready mindset* and not damage your health. Self-defence systems based around maintaining this high level of awareness at all times, are rooting their principles in a fantasy land. Even if you've accepted the potential for violence in our society, and you've prepared for it by learning self-defence information, if attacked you're likely to be caught mentally and physically off guard because walking around in a permanent state of battle-ready awareness is unattainable.

One aspect I created for *RBM* is the *Scaling Flinch Response*, factoring in the likelihood of a flinch making an appearance. I believe it's essential to have a flinch aspect integrated into your self-defence system and replicated as a part of any solutions to an attack, this way you're being taught to see these avoidance responses as positive, rather than a failure or a weakness. Getting used to fighting for your life from these seemingly irrational positions which you may find yourself in affords you the opportunity to prepare for the eventuality of a flinch, and enables you to start the process of mentally recovering from any physical or mental flinch positions you may find yourself in.

If caught completely by surprise the SAM Axis issues an evasive movement before the Hippocampus memories have even been consulted, and no matter how well drilled you are, when there's no precursor to trouble and caught by surprise you will not immediately perform a measured meaningful strike as an opening move, the flinch will override this. Because without the luxury of time and distance allowing the opportunity for the Amygdala/Hippocampus consultation to take place and make a plan of defence, you'll always try to evade the threat first when caught by surprise. After this initial shock, if the Hippocampus hasn't had any self-defence data telling it how to continue positively from these evasive flinch positions, then you're likely to freeze or panic. These flinch reflexes leave you on the back foot structurally, or in awkward positions which you must be able to move from, so a self-defence method considering this factor and building familiarity around these flinches is beneficial.

Considering the reality that if attacked, the aggressor will be using the element of surprise, you should avoid adopting a fighting stance in your self-defence because when caught by surprise you won't be in one, you'll be in a flat footed, contorted, punch dodging, knife evading flinch starting position. Learn to move from these positions rather than the *'everything's under control and going exactly as planned'* posture.

There are times when a more assertive reflex flinch, such as a fast jab would be available as an option, but only when your mind is in already in the gear of *ready*, and you're aware of the attack before it happens. An example of this would be if an aggressor who you've already identified as a threat, suddenly leapt towards you, and as a response you thrust your arm straight out towards them, introducing your fingers to their eyes.

Colour codes of Scaling Flinch Response Recovery

Studying the flinch reflex, I have noticed there are five main postural responses to different attacks based on different mindset, threat level, distance, and type of attack.

1. In the mental gear of *Ready*, switched and in fight/combat mode, you're aware of a threat and will have picked the target you want to strike on the aggressor. Your *Demolition Monkey* is already on the move with the shackles loosened. On the way to striking the aggressor, a missile comes towards you (punch/kick/grab/knife/bat etc.) and you pounce on it, striking their attack like you are swinging an axe, hammering down at their attempt to harm you. You have the intent to strike them, the *Demolition Monkey* is on route to destruction! This is going to be classed as **The Green Response**. Opportunistically whacking whatever comes your way.

The following Postural Flinch Reflexes happen when caught by surprise and the SAM Axis response has been fired, with you taking immediate evasive action, or you instead try grab the thing coming at you to stop it. These are not instinctive strikes, not the same as in the Green Response, where you were already mentally alert to the danger and intent on hitting whatever moved towards you as you approached the threat. These are the 'caught by surprise' evasive postures.

2. You sense the attack at the last moment because it's very close, from a subconscious action you quickly move backwards or sidestep, bringing your hands up and forming a shield to stop the thing hitting you. Sacrificing the limbs to protect the more essential parts of you, such as the heart, the throat, the neck, and the eyes. It's not a starting position you'd have chosen if you could have picked one, but at least you didn't get punched or stabbed in the face. Comfort yourself with the knowledge this is your missile avoidance system, it doesn't mean you're losing. I must keep repeating this, as people find it hard to adjust their perceptions of flinching. The people who capitulate at this point are the ones who haven't prepared to start from this mental and physical position. You will class this postural reflex as *The Yellow Flinch*.

3 If a person throws a punch at you from close range, or you turn around and see a knife pointing at you, the yellow flinch may come into play, or you may even deploy a different postural reflex which you will label as **The Orange Flinch**. This is where you grab the arm which is coming towards you as you try and stop it dead in its tracks. Throwing your feet backwards away from the threat so you can arch your body to move the torso away from the threat. Again, not what you would pick given the choice, as grabbing anything which is moving quickly has a chance you may dislocate your own thumb. But this wasn't a conscious decision, it's above and beyond choice, it was an override action which you need to be prepared to start from.

4. **The Red Flinch** is where you try to stop their body moving towards you so you can get some orientation time, hoping to work out what the hell is going on. You grab their arms in a clinch to try and work out a plan. 'Stand still while I work out why this is happening and how I am going to hit you' is the process trying to force its way into your head. If you fail to turn this around quickly you may freeze.

Postural Flinch Reflex's yellow, orange, and red are avoidance actions as a response to the attack coming at you, or attempting to stop the attack by grabbing the thing coming at you. If you include these reflex postures in your self-defence training and make sure you are using them as a starting position as a response to an attack, you will develop familiarity with them and program muscle memory of what to do from these positions. You don't need to start from one of these postures all the time, just ensure they are included.

Uncertainty of what to do from these postural flinch reflexes can open the door to a freeze response and if you try to remember a sequence or a complicated or high skilled response you will struggle. Attempting to formulate a thought-based solution from the Left Hemisphere Cerebral Cortex whilst standing still will lead to you slipping into freeze. The alternative option, and a preferable one, is having your memory banks loaded with information on how to recover quickly from a flinch and to get moving without standing still, without having to think. Information drilled into the brain to instinctively get you moving forwards from these positions, immediately influencing the situation. Using the flinch positions as a physical and mental springboard. This will be covered fully in Phase 3.

There is another type of postural flinch reflex, the 'The Black Flinch', the position of submit, and heading towards the high hormone elevated heart rate phase out zone where you shut down mentally.

5 **The Black Flinch**, is a state of psychological chaos. Covering up and taking the blows, hoping it all stops and goes away, total submission. You may even drop to the ground and go fetal, trying to avoid the confrontation. All is not lost, there's still a way back, if you can see their ankle, or maybe see their arm, getting a glimpse of a potential target, you can still drag yourself out of this position.

The postural flinching scale has outlined how an attack can trigger you to physically flinch, moving away from the attack or try and cover up and often people follow this by standing motionless. But there's also another type of reaction which may happen, you may psychologically flinch at any point of the attack, and this psychological flinch/mini freeze needs to be considered.

The *Mind Gears* are how these internal flinches and the varying internal states of mind you may find yourself in are described, these mind gears will influence how you are operating at any given moment. I have used the same colour coding as the postural flinch reflex to explain the different stages of you mentally sliding along this scale of anxiety, causing disruption and doubt which will trigger repeated hormone release until you submit. You can slide from a ready mindset to a freeze mindset in a heartbeat, influenced by what you are faced with in your environment:

> *'You return home and find the door has been kicked open, rather than wait outside and call the police, you enter because you think the house is empty. You switch into your Demolition Monkey mode as you enter the house, ready, in case there's a need for you to protect yourself. You hear a noise in one of the rooms and you rush in, you see the intruder and you've picked your Hot Zone Target. You're now focused and ready to strike, but as they enter your personal zone, you see a machete dripping with blood, and they start screaming at you and rushing towards you.'*

If you tell me this wouldn't cause any psychological effect within you, then perhaps you aren't grasping the realism of the situation or not accepting how you would function psychologically in this situation. You would have a mental flinch, so prepare for this psychological flinching, which is like a feedback stammer. It's a glitch in the machine as your Left Hemisphere Cerebral Cortex tries to interfere to make sense of the situation, but there's no logic in violence and the Left Hemisphere has no place here trying to find any. This feedback stammer needs to be kept to a minimum, and you must learn to recognise what this brain freeze feels like during your self-defence training, and teach yourself to instinctively always move off the spot whenever you feel it happening.

Through the carefully constructed training methods used in *RBM,* you will be placed into situations where you can feel this mental stammer, it's very odd when you first become aware of it and you can feel the moment you almost press pause on your instincts and attempt to have a Left Hemisphere think as you mentally stand still, as well as physically. The *RBM* training methods create an understanding of this sensation and use this as a trigger itself to launch a movement from you as a response to this feeling of stuttering to get you off the spot.

Hopefully, you now see flinching as a positive, and a potential starting position rather than the end of all hope. It's a highly sophisticated autonomic system you have inbuilt and it's the fastest thing for avoiding a missile directed at you, so embrace it and prepare for a flinch to happen.

There Are No Blocks in RBM

There can be a defensive guard, shielding movements with your arms, but there are no blocks, and for good reason. I started in Karate, learning the cornerstones of defence through block the punch, block the kick, block, and counter. After this was Tai Chi and Kung Fu, the same concept but with different words, parry the punch, deflect the attack. It was challenging, even when I knew the drill sequences of attacks in advance, it still didn't help and I always felt as though I was second best, I was getting there just in time to block the attack or getting there too late. When moving into a stance and performing a big blocking movement in Karate, I always felt like I was on the back foot mentally as well as physically. In Tai Chi & Kung Fu I felt parrying and slipping past the attack just put me into a different position of vulnerability. There was also the feeling of it not being a true reflection of a real attack, and this itch in my brain took a long time to scratch. Violent attackers don't use front kicks and roundhouse kicks, they don't throw a punch and stop, they grab you and beat you to the ground. They just keep coming until they pulverise you.

If you found yourself under an onslaught of an attack, and you started to move backwards with a natural foot movement whilst blocking, you will be covering around half a metre of ground each time you step. If you land backwards in a stance, longer than half a metre to create a better structure then you will be flat footed, rooted to the ground, and be like a sitting duck.

If they are committed to hitting you, they will be stepping forwards and covering a distance of around one metre each time they step with a normal movement pattern. I'm not renowned for my ability in mathematics, but I can see problems are starting to begin here, because if a person is coming forwards with their mass at a ground coverage of one metre per step, and you're going backwards half a metre per step, then at some point you will be overrun. Overrun meaning knocked back off your feet to the ground, being overpowered and smashed to bits.

This is only discussing the aspect of them physically moving forwards towards you, there's still no demand placed on you at this point to determine the type of threat. I haven't even mentioned whether it's a kick, a punch, knife, bat or gun and there are already problems to deal with by the backwards step.

When the type of attack has been identified, *which is something you need to do to be able to block it*, you will need to perfectly coordinate your blocking movement to coincide with their attack, and time it so it will arrive at an exact time and in a precise place and judge the force behind the attack to be able to intercept it. Timing these elements to sync together is a challenge within itself.

Bring the stress element in, and consider that during an attack there will be disruption to your performance levels due to the psychological chaos bombs detonating in various parts of your brain, and the odds of this block and counter approach being successful are greatly reduced. Especially when your hormone induced heart rate elevation is kicking in, affecting depth perception, speed recognition etc. all at a time when you are trying to match your movements with the aggressor's attacks.

Disregard the concept of block, and instead moving your arms with the intent of smashing their attack, rather than intercepting and deflecting. This takes very little coordination in comparison to a block and is faster in terms of brain processing.

Proxemics will come into play again here and it's of value to bring in the work of *Dennis Tueller*,[31] who wrote an article published in *SWAT Magazine in 1983 entitled How Close is Too Close?* The findings have been used in armed response units ever since. Tueller discovered if an aggressor armed with a knife ran at a police officer from a distance of 21 feet or less, the aggressor would reach the intended target either prior to the officer being able to draw their weapon and shoot, or it would be too late for the impact of the bullets hitting the aggressor to halt the momentum of the knife from reaching the officer. This test was completed under conditions whereby the officer was consciously aware of the simulated attack drill they were about to perform, and yet were still unable to react quickly enough. There wasn't even a surprise element involved.

Something I find mind-scrambling is the Tueller information is often taught in self-defence methods to explain an individual cannot rely on pepper spray or a firearm, and in the same system they *'still insist'* on teaching you to block, even though the Tueller concept they are using highlights you won't have time to block. It isn't going to work but they do it anyway, it's beyond logical belief.

The Tueller drill has relevance to the topic of blocking and countering, because of how fast a person can close the distance between you. Within this short time frame, would you rather use the 25-millisecond speed processor, attempting to think which blocking option is the best for a type of attack you may not have even identified yet. Or call on a single option, a simple movement you can decide on which is to move and strike them, a decisive process taking

---

[31] Dennis Tueller, 1983 How Close is Too Close? *SWAT Magazine*

only 12 milliseconds? Blocking is reactive, it's complicated and it's clumsy under stress, trying to assess the situation, and waiting to see what their attack will be encourages you to stand still, routed to the spot and trying to pick the relevant matching block for the attack. It's too complex and has numerous unpredictable variables to try and manage under time limited pressure. If on the other hand, you instead focus on yourself and what you can do rather than being reactive, it suddenly becomes easier. You see them coming towards you, you select a Hot Zone, step forward and smash it, subconscious decision making to select the fastest execution of a positive response. If you rely on a thought-based block action, as appose to an intuitive response to eliminate the threat, you will always be on the back foot.

In case you're still not convinced and are hanging onto the belief blocking will work, *(because you spent lots of time, money and effort learning blocking and put your faith in it, which I understand as I found that to be a bitter pill to swallow as well)* here is an exercise for you. It will help debunk the myth of the block and counter principle under stress and attack.

With a drill partner ask them to stand facing you, both standing side on to a wall at arm's reach. Facing your drill partner:

- They will have their left shoulder closest to the wall, you have your right shoulder closest. You can switch sides later, the specific action of how you are standing is only important in the explanation of the drill
- Your partner has their right hand six inches away from your left shoulder
- you have your right arm straight out to the side with fingers touching the wall
- They are looking at your hand on the wall at all times
- When you move your hand off the wall, they will try and touch you on the shoulder
- You will move you hand across in front of your body, pushing away their attempt to touch you on the shoulder. Your right hand coming across the body as quickly as you can, knocking their hand away before it can touch your shoulder

You have more than a metre to cover, yet they will only have a few inches. They will win right? Try it! No cheating. Ensure they watch the hand on the wall and they only move when you move. No jumping the gun.

Once you've completed the exercise, and if as I expect the person with their hand on the wall won every time, do you still seriously want to rely on a block, when under stress? If you are still unconvinced, try this one:

- Your drill partner is facing you, with their index finger of one hand pointing towards to you
- Point your finger at their finger, so your index/forefingers are almost touching
- Okay, now here is the drill, they move their index/forefinger as fast as they like in any random pattern of movement, and you must try to keep up with it. Good luck.

It's impossible to keep up with their finger so if you think you are going to be fast enough to block and counter, think again unless you are very highly skilled, and this is why there are no blocks in RBM.

RBM Development

- Finding yourself in a psychological avalanche
- The bucket of self-worth & the shield of confidence
- Why taking time for you & learning new things, matters
- The importance of self-reliance
- De-escalation - *take the power away from the doubt*
- Pick a target

This section is getting the knowledge of the topic of self-defence into the stress defence of your daily life. Repeating this point again, you're most likely to be at risk of stress in your daily life far more often than the threat of physical violence, and this applies to most of the population.

If you can take the confidence gained from feeling safe and secure in your life, and extract the self-defence principles from the training room and use these on a day-to-day basis to alter your reactions to stressful situations, then you've grasped the essence of *RBM*.

Finding yourself in a psychological avalanche

If ever in danger from a physical threat, there will be a time element involved, a timeframe and a time limitation of when you must act to eradicate the danger. This restriction of time increases the urgency of a situation, triggering the *Attention Approach*, where you will focus on one thing, the *Capacity Resource* will hone-in on what you know from loaded information, and the *Thought Suppression* will stop the mind from becoming distracted.

Yet in your normal average day, in non-physical threat situations, the stress response is activated due to anxiety levels being triggered by something which has worried you, and this is where you find yourself sitting precariously on the verge of triggering a huge psychological avalanche. This all sounds a bit dramatic but it's not an overstatement, because this is where a lot of people's health takes a battering. Having an abundance of time to worry about things causes confusion and clouds decision making, and it's often within an unrestricted timeframe which allows you to be able to run through an extensive list of possible outcomes and variables. These are the dreaded *what if's*, associated with anxieties, and when these trigger the stress response the *Attentional Approach* is initiated, but instead of having a physical cue to act on such as a punch, it will instead latch onto the thought at the forefront of your mind. If it's an anxiety rooted thought, then the trouble grows, with you focusing on this one problem obsessively. *Capacity Resource* will now start to act on this worry, but from a negative mindset and it will draw on what it knows, which is what you have done in the past, your learned conditioned behaviour. Hence why people keep making the same mistakes repeatedly, putting off doing the things they logically know would help, attempting to push the issue away rather than solve it. Partly because the *Thought Suppression* has kicked in, reducing your ability to look outside of the problem and outside of revert to type responses.

Positive response action has diminished, because the corruption of clear thought has occurred due to the rumination spreading, causing the stress response to fire at an inappropriate time and level. You're now stuck in a rut, frozen in life and unable to see a way out, with all your ideas stemming from a place of limited thinking which won't solve the issue. This is when people feel under pressure and driven into making decisions which have a lasting negative impact on themselves and those around them.

It doesn't have to play out this way, you can prevent your thoughts spiralling out of control by breaking the negative thought circuit, and it's the skills and drills of *RBM* which will arm you with the tools to achieve this. The breathing techniques in Phase 2 will be an effective way to put a halt on the over stimulus of the Pons, stopping the anxiety running away from you and consequentially reducing the stress response activation. The skills in Phase 3 will develop your positive responses to any problem which require a solution, not just violent encounters. You'll learn to trust your instincts, focus on solution seeking, and be decisive in your decision making, leaving less time for self-sabotage through indecision and doubt.

The bucket of self-worth & the shield of confidence

Here is an exercise for you to complete:

Either in your mind, in the space below, or on a piece of paper, make a list of 4 people you really care about. Four people who are of upmost importance to you, and you would do anything for:

1.

2.

3.

4.

Once you have completed the task, look at the names you have written down.

*Now look at the footnote at the bottom of this page! [32]

One of the major goals of the *RBM* program is changing your perceptions of yourself to the highest positive view it can be. Holding yourself in high esteem and to value yourself, and everything you are. This positive change to embracing the magnificent person inside of you starts with accepting it's okay to see yourself as equally valued to those you hold in high importance in life, helping you get yourself onto that list.

Using realistic self-defence to injure another person to protect yourself doesn't make you a bad person, and another false perception people hold is looking after yourself makes you selfish, it simply isn't true. It makes sense to put yourself in charge of making sure you're happy because you're the best person qualified to do the job of looking after you. You may need to ask for help and support along the way, but you're the one project managing your mental health. It helps to limit the feeling of selfishness and the guilt of doing something for yourself if you realise you can't efficiently care for those around you if you fail to look after you.

Value yourself, and your life, as much as those who you love, it's not rocket science, it's not a ground-breaking revelation, or an ancient secret, but you would be staggered to know how many people fail to implement this basic, but vastly important level of self-worth into their lives. Self-worth is pivotal for you to be the best you can be, and the happiest you can be, and it cannot be achieved until you see yourself as equally important as everyone else you value in your life, you must be on the list.

<u>The abusive, aggressive attacker who lives in the shadows</u>
I previously said there aren't monsters out there waiting to attack you, there aren't people watching you, waiting for their chance to strike. There is however an exception to the rule, there is a vicious, cruel, and dark figure observing every move you make, moving in the shadows, whispering, and plotting your demise and is the deadliest opponent of all. One you must spot and identify as the biggest threat to your happiness and health. Who is this? It's the voice of how you see yourself and how you talk to yourself.

If the average person in our modern-day world counted the number of times in one day they told themselves they looked scrawny, fat, ugly, called themselves stupid or an idiot for making a mistake, or spoke to themselves void of all love and compassion when comparing themselves to the images projected by

---

[32] Footnote: I'm guessing you aren't on the list, and you forgot all about you. If you happened to be one of the rare people who included themselves, then fantastic, you're already at the target destination for self-worth.

'celebrities and influencers', the numbers would be astonishing. The cutting remarks people say to themselves are worse than anything other people would ever say because they are as personalised as anything can be. Other people try and push your buttons, your inner voice ruthlessly stamps all over them. Change this by taking all the hurtful things you wouldn't dream of saying to anyone else and stop saying them to yourself.

On top of this self-criticism and constant self-loathing, the nasty little self-worth saboteur will welcome with open arms all the negative remarks others have said to you. Storing these to a playlist and regurgitating them at will on repeat as an internal voice until you adopt them as your own view of yourself. If you hear something often enough, you believe it, letting it becoming your vision of yourself, it becomes who you are. This internal voice is the master of the dark arts and is the biggest blockade to stand between you and your happiness. Stress is one of the biggest threats to your life through compromising your physical health and mental wellness, low self-worth is as closely connected to unhappiness as a bullet is linked to a gun. You can't lower anxiety, reduce stress, and elevate your happiness and levels of fun, without elevating your self-worth. They are mutually exclusive.

Just as Classical and Operant conditioning are tools used for loading information into the brain, if you constantly criticise yourself, you're using these same methods powered by a negatively loaded emotional charge to drive a low self-value into your brain, which becomes the revert to type view of yourself. Thankfully, this can change, starting by positively loading a new way of how you see and value yourself and making sure your thoughts about you are filled with compassion, understanding and tolerance. If you drop something on the floor, rather than telling yourself you're an idiot, smile, you're human, it's not just positive thinking, it's positive programming. Start by changing how you see yourself, keep your self-worth overflowing and as a result create an impenetrable shield around you. If you're happy with yourself, outside opinions can't penetrate this protective dense layer of self-worth and confidence and you starve the negative voice inside of you of fuel, just like starving the aggressor of oxygen by striking the jugular notch.

In life, don't give away your personal power, I frequently hear people opt out of personal responsibility by saying; "they made me so mad". Well, unless another person can put their fingers into your brain and have a twiddle about causing the emotional response of their choosing, this just isn't true. Another person cannot *'make you'* anything, it's all on you, it always has been, and it always will be, you have the choice in how to act in all situations. They may be the potential trigger, but you're always in charge of the reaction. With confidence in your ability to protect yourself and with a high level of self-worth, you can take charge of your life by selecting how to react or not react to things which are said and situations you find yourself in. There is always the option to continue to absolve yourself from taking responsibility for your own life, blaming other people for causing you to react, but that doesn't usually bring the best results.

The things which people say only become an issue if the remarks reflect how you see yourself, the remark is never the issue, it's your self-worth. If you find yourself on the receiving end of a cutting remark, learn to realise the remark has nothing to do with you, it's not personal unless you choose to allow it to become personal and seeing it as your truth. Don't allow yourself to have reactions driven by other people. To prevent this, plug any gaps in your shield by increasing self-worth and confidence, the powerful weapons for the peaceful warrior. You aren't anxious or intimidated by anything they may try to do physically to harm you and you have no interest in anything they may say to verbally attack you.

Take control! Control how you respond, control how you act and interact with others. You cannot control life, but you can control how you act and react to it and achieve a simpler, quieter life as a result. Sounds like bliss, and you can obtain this by accepting you're always in control of how you feel, by taking responsibility for your actions, and not handing your power to others.

I think it's important to impart this knowledge to children, helping them at a young age to avoid the misery which travels hand in hand with the over critical, damaging judgement of oneself, and to stop letting other people drive their emotions. I realised when I became a parent an important role was to help fill up my children's buckets of self-worth, because as they journey through life, they'll inevitably meet insecure people who find comfort in psychologically attacking others. Those willing to make holes in other people's confidence and self-belief, to elevate themselves above their own insecurities at the expense of others. It's the psychological version of climbing over others to get into the lifeboat and it happens right through life if you allow it. If positive, confident thinking isn't instilled in children at a young age, they will likely find themselves on route to joining the masses of adults in the lifelong battle against their whispering internal nemesis, the destroyer of self-esteem.

Increasing self-worth, and achieving and maintaining high levels of happiness, is probably the biggest and most important challenge people face in their lifetime, because without self-belief people are unable to motivate themselves to reach their goals. No longer feeling as though they deserve meaningful and equal relationships, losing their aspirations and seeing all their dreams evaporate. It could be said this is a far more deadly and commonly occurring attack than physical violence, and in that sense, the self-defence systems which only teach people what to do if grabbed are focusing on the wrong assailant.

Never hold someone else's emotional hand grenade

Never take ownership of someone else's failings, picking up other people's bombs of misery and claiming them as your own. If a person is treating you badly, don't allow your own thoughts to say you are at fault and you deserve it, see it at face value, for what it really is, they are treating you badly. It's their issue, their bomb to diffuse, it's not about you, just as it's never your fault if someone attacks you.

Someone else's personal issues can only hold any bearing on your life if you're close enough to them to be caught up in the carnage. When facing a physical threat, you have two options, get away as soon as possible from the danger, or go close and eliminate the danger, and the same rule applies in your interactions with the people in your life. You need to put distance between you and the dangerous person, in this case they aren't a physical threat but instead an emotional and psychological danger. If your own self-worth is being attacked, and the value you place on yourself isn't high enough to protect you from their behaviour, you need to go.

You can be compassionate by helping the person seek external support to solve their issues, if they are willing to acknowledge and recognise what's happening. At that point you go closer to eliminate the threat, not striking them in the eye but working together to hit a target, to find a solution. But this should never be done at your expense, not if staying in their presence means you lose value in how you see yourself, not if it will puncture a new hole in your self-worth bucket, you must not accept a toxic environment.

Hold a high value of how you see yourself, don't allow others to deplete your view of what you are worth. You must put yourself first, it isn't selfish, it's not arrogance or being self-absorbed, it's self-preservation.

Keep the *Demolition Monkey* on a leash - Injuries hurt, and so do words.

'Sticks and stones may break my bones, but names will never hurt me'. I remember having this drilled into me as a child, being told to ignore what others say and what they say isn't important. In a sense it's true, but only if you're in a position where you feel safe and secure in your life and have a confidence in yourself where nothing anyone says can rock your self-worth. If this is the case then the phrase is correct, and exactly how I hope you feel. If not, and in most cases people aren't secure enough in themselves, then in fairness it's dangerous to

peddle this nonsense. The number of teens self-harming, people desperately looking for approval on social media, and the rise in numbers of suicides would suggest the power of words does have a significant role to play in society and can harm others just as much as a stick or a stone, perhaps even more because words can travel the globe and damage at a greater distance.

Be careful of your actions towards others, speaking or acting negatively to people may be the tipping point which triggers a person to make the decision to give up the struggle of coping with life and take a one-way ticket out. *RBM* in a self-defence application is only used to cause harm to another person when it's absolutely necessary, so it makes sense you apply this principle across the board. I'm not saying you must fret about every word you say or pander around people, or in any way implying you're responsible for other people's lives, but highlighting there's a need to take ownership of your actions and accept when a word leaves your mouth the influence and impact it can have may be a far bigger than you thought. When protecting yourself from a violent attack, you aim to do so by inflicting the minimum amount of damage needed to ensure your survival. If you can implement this principle day to day by refraining from saying negative, attacking, aggressive remarks to others, which are the psychological equivalent of a kick to the groin, you're being the best version of yourself that you can be, for you and everyone else.

- Never hold anyone else responsible for how you feel. You're in control of your feelings, and you're always in control of yourself, and your decisions.
- Prevent outside influences taking you where you do not want to go, psychologically & emotionally. If you feel as though you're relinquishing your personal power, move away from that way of thinking and the people who contribute to you feeling this way.
- Don't give up your individuality. See yourself as unique, a one off never to be repeated and with a life which is worth fighting for.

Why taking time for you, & learning new things matters

A way to boost your self-worth is by taking time out of life for yourself and learning something new. Doing something which takes you out of your comfort zone comes with a sense of reward in your achievements and accomplishments.

Life moves so fast, it's hectic and if advice telling people to make time for themselves is given, the response is often *'you've got to be joking, I haven't got time for that'*. When you're flat out busy, when you see or hear something *'may do you some good'* it doesn't carry enough weight to motivate change. If you are to embark on the process of learning *RBM* you need some data to convince you it's worth the time and effort to do something for yourself, and not seeing time away from your busy schedule as dead time. To justify finding this time and harness the motivation to engage with a new activity, the question to be addressed is *how does focusing on yourself and valuing yourself improve your health and reduce stress and anxiety?*

The Hawthorne experiments[33], led by sociologist Elton Mayo can help to explain this. In the 1920's and 1930's experiments were carried out at Western Electric's factory in Chicago, the purpose of the tests was to observe what effect, if any, changes made in an environment could have on staff productivity. The most well-known of the Hawthorne tests was that of a factory lighting change, and it further explored the relationship between environment changes and productivity by altering work hours, breaks scheduled etc. In each case, after any adjustment was made it was noticed positive productivity changes occurred, even when a negative environment adjustment was made. When the lighting was restored to the original fittings, and the room was dark in comparison to the first test, productivity was still high.

When the testing period was over, and the factory returned to its normal working environment as it was prior to the test observations, productivity remained high and staff absence levels were low. Mayo concluded the environmental changes had no effect on productivity, proven by an increase in output when light levels were manipulated from low to high and high to low. He noticed productivity increased when any factor was manipulated in any way, and this increase was attributed to be due to the workers being aware they were under observation. Mayo placed a greater level of importance on the workers feeling an increased sense of self-value because they were being focused upon and included as a part of a study, it was the value of oneself, and the increase in self-esteem which caused an increase in productivity. Appreciate the importance

---

[33] Elton Mayo, Hawthorne and the Western Electric Company, *The Social Problems of an Industrial Civilisation, Routledge*, 1949.

of placing greater value on yourself and how taking time for you will have a positive effect on you as a person, in essence creating your own Hawthorne effect, from which the benefits will reach far beyond the activity you are taking part in.

The relatively new concept and understandings of Neurogenesis shows how your super-computer of a brain benefits from time spent on learning new things, and how it keeps the mind healthy. Neurogenesis has brought forward some interesting concepts about the process through which we see the creation of new neurons/new brain cells, and the implications of the theories are wide reaching. It was previously thought the creation of new neurons would slow as a person aged, and eventually stop during their mid-twenties and onwards, yet recent discoveries have found this isn't the case, with new neurons created every day in specific areas of the brain. In the Hippocampus alone, 700 new neurons are created per day when stimulated growth is induced by learning something new, and this is important, because there is a direct correlation between the level of Neurogenesis in the Hippocampus and depression.

The levels of new neuron creation in this area of the brain are greatly reduced with people suffering from depression. The Hippocampus is responsible for memory and mood regulation, which is why if suffering from depression, moods are lower and the ability to remember things and complete everyday tasks is reduced. What scientists do know is stress inhibits the level of Neurogenesis in the Hippocampus, which is how stress causes depression, with these low moods causing less Neurogenesis function in this brain region, resulting in fewer cells being generated here, so a negative self-fueling loop is formed.

The way anti-depressants were thought to work, until very recently, was by using the medication to release 'pick me up' chemicals in the brain, but this idea has now been thrown into doubt with the recent discovery the medication causes a gene expression reaction which promotes Neurogenesis in the Hippocampus, creating more neurons and alleviating the depression. If you're unaware of the term gene expression, an example of this is sitting in the sun and you get a suntan, this is the skin trying to protect itself from further damage, this reaction is a gene expression. Just as it takes time for the skin to tan and lose the tan, anti-depressant medication doesn't have an immediate effect on a person because it takes time for the stimulation of the neurons and gene expression response as a result of the anti-depressants to create neurogenesis cell growth.

If you would like to prevent yourself needing anti-depressants, the answer could be that medication is only one method, another route could be via the creation of new memories, because new memories equate to more Neurogenesis leading to an improvement of mood.

Is it plausible to suggest you can use learning new things as a tool to positively manipulate and affect the mood centre and lower depression? This at present hasn't been clinically assessed, but the evidence seems to strongly suggest it's worth a punt! This book covers as much as I can include on the topic, but there is so much more to neurogenesis and it's a fascinating topic to explore.

The importance of self-reliance

Conquering the battle of anxiety, increasing your feelings of safety, boosting self-worth, having the sense of belonging, and building positive meaningful relationships are all facets contributing towards a calm and peaceful life. Many people reading this will be familiar with Maslow's concepts, and his original works, *A Theory of Human Motivation*[34] and *Motivation and Personality*[35] hold great value as a personal development tool, and whilst his work is by no means perfect it does raise some useful points. Why am I talking about this here? Well, to ensure you don't feel as though there is a tenuous link between self-defence and changing how you feel everyday it's helpful to know a little more about why people react differently to things in their lives, and how *RBM* can help in terms of personal growth, through identifying some of your inner drives and needs.

Physiological needs

Needs which if not met result in death, carrying a critical level of importance to your survival. Individual needs are; air, water, and food, and in addition to this, the provision of shelter as protection from the elements are necessities. Moving away from individual needs and towards those of a species, these are fighting off extinction through reproduction for keeping the numbers up. Incidentally, this is one of the reasons the testicles automatically draw upwards when the fight or flight system kicks in.

Safety needs

Protecting your shelter and continuing to source food and water, in modern times is achieved through employment. This financial safety net, during the recent global upheaval may have seemed a little more threadbare and not as strong as in the past. In years gone by, people would have cured meat, salted

---

[34] A Theory of Human Motivation, A. H. Maslow (1943) Originally Published in *Psychological Review*, 50, 370-396.

[35] *Motivation and Personality* published A. H. Maslow, 1954

cod etc., to preserve it, to see them through, but nowadays it's savings and investments which satisfy the inner calling to squirrel away money, just in case. To further enhance your safety, you choose to live in safer areas, enjoying the comfort of personal security, being locked up safe at night. There's private health care insurance in case of injury, and lovely gyms and spas to visit, helping you increase your longevity.

<u>Love and belonging</u>
Personal needs extend beyond purely physically driven necessities, humans are not solitary beings, and we understand the value of being part of a community. The time a prisoner can be in solitary confinement is restricted because it's a brutal form of punishment, taking human connection away from a person is psychologically damaging over a prolonged period. We are starting to see the mental health effects of this in people who have had to drastically reduce their contact with friends and families during the Covid pandemic. With the population staying at home, the reality of the need for human interaction has been made very apparent. A positive which could come from this is the lack of social interaction could be the catalyst for people to put aside their artificial, false connections via social media and move back towards authentic human connections. Healthier interactions through spending time with people who have mutual appreciation for each other and not constantly seeking approval and 'likes' from those they're unlikely to ever meet.

Humans are not designed for being a lone wolf, on occasion this drive to belong, seeking family, friendship, and intimacy and to feel a sense of worth gained from being in relationships, can exceed and overtake the need of safety. This is where people put themselves at risk due to the desire to belong being such a strong impulse. Abusive relationships are an example of this, not having a sense of belonging is too painful, perhaps more painful than the abuse.

I used to visit a school once a week to deliver sessions for children who had been excluded from mainstream education, and my role was delivering mentorship through Tai Chi, conveying the message to these pupils they were worth more than the value they placed on themselves. Altering their view to one where they believed they could be successful, regardless of what they have been told before. It was a positive and productive time, but one memory I have is where a pupil had a black eye, dished out by their father. The story told by the pupil was they'd deliberately been winding their father up until he snapped. I asked the pupil the reason for doing this and was completely unprepared for the answer given, *'it's better to be hit than completely ignored, it hurts less'*.

Sometimes the holes in the self-esteem bucket are wrenched open by a person who should love you unconditionally, but instead they make you feel as though you are worthless, and the damage this causes is immeasurable. This is called Coercive Control, one person in the relationship/family/friend has manipulated the one receiving the physical and/or emotional abuse to the point where they feel so worthless that they believe they don't deserve to be happy, perhaps due to this. Carrying the belief they don't see themselves as worthy of a healthy relationship.

Esteem

Maslow identified two types of respect sought by an individual to influence their esteem and contributing to the feeling of happiness. These two types of respect are: self-respect, classified as lower esteem *(get yourself onto the list of important people in your life)*, and the respect you receive from those around you, called higher esteem. Higher esteem is closely linked with love and belonging, we need to feel as though we hold value in our pack and seeking approval and respect from our peers is a huge part of life. I suggest it's because when we lived as hunter gatherers, we didn't want to be ostracised, as out of the pack means a higher risk of death. People will even sacrifice their self-esteem and how they perceive themselves to be accepted, risking their safety to be part of a group. Think of the people who take initiations into violent street gangs, risking their lives to be a part of that group. It's safety in numbers, and if you're part of the gang, then you won't get attacked by the gang, most of the time!

Low self-esteem combined with being ostracised from peer groups may drive an individual to seek the respect they crave through fame, by building a legacy worthy of respect, and in conjunction with prefrontal lobe damage through either abuse or developmental damage, this can create the ideal cocktail for a person to seek notoriety, and you get the perfect storm for something like a school shooting. Elevating self-respect by using power and control, whilst simultaneously punishing those who rejected the person, or that which symbolises the ideology they longed to fit into.

When self-esteem is high, self-value is high and you're less likely to place yourself in dangerous relationships, dangerous peer groups, or feel the need to seek approval from others. I previously said when under attack you cannot count on others to come and save you and looking externally for the teacher, the police or some knight to come to your rescue you isn't reliable. The same can be said for seeking happiness and self-worth outside of yourself, it's doomed for failure. Not handing the responsibility of your happiness to others is liberating for all parties involved. Never give away your personal power, stop looking outside of yourself for your personal safety, or your happiness.

<u>Self-actualisation</u>
What's out there, what's beyond the horizon, what's beyond death? Humanity has never been able to stand still, always yearning to move forwards discovering more, growing within ourselves, and enriching our understanding of the universe. Self-actualisation is finding a way of life which is important to the individual, not necessarily becoming spiritual or seeking answers to the meaning of life, but instead finding the purpose of *your* life. This will be very individual and unique to all of us, and self-actualisation is a continual process, evolving and developing as you grow and shape your values.

Maslow's work helped me to shape *RBM* into something beyond self-defence, and into a powerful tool for personal growth, ticking lots of boxes at once. Gardening, walking and sport and recreational activities are all relaxing and of great benefit for reducing stress and bring the benefits of gentle exercise. These activities represent you taking time out for yourself, which improves your self-value, self-worth, and your health, the Hawthorne effect explained this. But you can achieve more, because *RBM* has an additional benefit as the realistic self-defence method elevates your confidence, something you don't get from gardening, walking, cycling etc. You will tick the box of *'safety needs'* by learning the ability to provide physical security for yourself and the people around you if faced with a violent attack. This isn't the same as a feeling of safety achieved through financial stability, but a sense of safety which comes from within, because you will know what to do if things take a sudden turn for the worse.

Implementing the principles of *RBM* into your life will create positive change, as you'll become calmer, less likely to argue and less likely to lose your patience. Managing your stress levels more effectively and not taking what other people say about you personally will help your esteem skyrocket, and your value for life increases. The section *'Looking After Your Organic Motorhome'* will help you to maintain a high level of health and well-being. *RBM* always surprises people, because on the surface it looks as though you are only learning self-defence, yet the process of learning to protect yourself combined with the right mindset will accelerate your personal growth in all areas of life.

De-escalation - take the power away from the enemy known as doubt!

> *On seeing Yoda using the force to levitate the X-Wing out of the bog;*
>
> Luke: *I don't... I don't believe it!*
>
> Yoda: *That is why you fail.*
>
> *Star Wars: Episode IV – A New Hope* [36]

My son would be very disappointed if I didn't grab the opportunity to include a Star Wars quote at some point in the text, and this one, encapsulating doubt, is the one. If we could allocate a different persona to each of your emotions, doubt would be the arsehole of the group, waltzing into your day and ruining everything. The real spoiler in life, the one whispering in your ear telling you that you can't do something, saying you aren't good enough, not capable of success or you aren't worthy of it. The self-sabotaging little git most people aren't even aware of is the trickiest nemesis to beat.

Have no doubt, that having doubt is the main obstacle to you achieving your goals. Anxiety about an issue to resolve may be the *immediate* stressor. The *imminent* stressor may be a big life change ahead, but the *ultimate* stressor and the main obstacle, is the doubt in yourself to succeed in your attempts to move forwards. Doubt creates a fear of failure which prevents you from being who you want to be.

Anticipation and trepidation are opposite sides of the same coin, different perspectives causing different outcomes, and it's you who always has, and always will be, the one who flips the coin and makes the decision of which mindset you have and which side of the coin you face life with. The difference between anxiety and excitement is a simple thought, with the physical sensations of butterflies in your stomach, goosebumps, etc. happening when you're both; (a) excited and anticipating something good is about to happen, and (b) when you're expecting something which makes you nervous. Having doubt in your ability to succeed stacks the odds unfairly against you, it creates a double-sided coin used in the toss, giving you the result of trepidation every time.

Belief in yourself is so pivotal to happiness that I strongly believe it's time to place a higher level of importance on emotional education, starting with children at school and concentrating on this far more than physical education. Teaching children it's okay to make mistakes and that it's how you respond which is key. With this approach you are never failing, you're a dynamic and responsive responder, acting on what you see in front of you and building faith

---

[36] *Star Wars: Episode IV – A New Hope* Lucasfilm 1977

in your ability to succeed in the face of difficulties. This change of mindset takes the pressure off you, preventing rumination and worrying, and directing your focus away from problems onto solutions will reduce the level of doubt in yourself. Allowing you to be unrestrained in your creative thought process, confident and holding a high belief in your ability to overcome obstacles. You'll live knowing that whatever is going on, good or bad, you can cope with it, you will become resilient. Bouncing back from harder times and building up a mental strength to keep going. This is where the *RBM* approach becomes *'life stress de-escalation'*. If you find yourself on the floor being kicked, you fight to get up and get moving. This resilient mindset spreads and picks you up from mental setbacks you may face and drags you towards a positive outcome. This mental resolve and belief in yourself will dissolve doubt, de-escalating the worries of life.

Completing the *RBM* development exercises will establish a connection with your inner will to survive and the drive to succeed. When you feel safe with self-defence skills at your disposal, you're more confident in taking risks in life and more likely to step outside of your comfort zone, because you have a surplus of self-worth and a genuine sense of security. In the same way real confidence helps you to drop the camouflage predators see as a flare, you will drop the wall which restricts your expansion and growth as a person, you start believing you can make changes, you have faith in yourself to be able to hit a target.

Many martial arts and self-defence systems insist you stick to a pattern, you must follow the routine. If the left arm was used to strike instead of the right arm, instructors pounce on this and label it as wrong. I refuse to incorporate that way of thinking into *RBM*, because it causes doubt within the person of their ability to succeed and reinforces looking for an external source to tell them if what they are doing is correct, which doesn't promote self-reliant, confident, positive action. This is relevant, because in your personal life if you make a decision but it's not the best option, don't give yourself a hard time about it. Don't do the equivalent of saying you should have moved your left arm instead of your right, at least you're trying, you're moving and attempting to do the best you can, so these decisions can't be labelled as wrong, they should be seen as being brave because it's easier to curl up in a ball and quit, and you haven't done that. Rather than being critical of yourself, see the courage it takes to keep going when times are tough, you haven't frozen in life, you're still moving!

The next step is to make life more efficient, using the mental resilience you have built up in tough times and thinking how easy it's going to be when you find the most efficient way for you to do things. Remember what is important in your life. For me it's simple:

- *You have one job, be happy, live as long as possible, and be kind along the way.*
- *If we don't have to go to the hospital right now, then I will always have time to fix it, or find another route or opportunity later so don't stress about it.*

Without doubt, life is a lot simpler and easier this way. Obviously not implying everything in the world is super fantastic every day and you'll skip through life without even a hiccup, and certainly not suggesting you adopt positive thinking and live with denial of the reality of difficult situations. But instead, keeping the problems which pop up in life in perspective of how serious they are, this way it all becomes slightly less scary and less stressful.

Pick a Target

The self-defence drills of *RBM* require you to move off the spot, stepping forwards into the unknown to find success, which at first is mentally tough, but logically this is preferable to standing still and taking the hits. You learn that moving and taking a chance will yield results, it becomes ingrained in you to look for a solution and however hard it may be mentally, you must move to make a positive change. This principle is transferable away from self-defence and into decision making in general. A positive mindset will be developed through continuous success when faced with a simulated attack threat, giving you the confidence needed to strive and thrive and change things you don't want to be present in your life anymore.

There are plenty of stories of people, who after attending personal development courses *(most often Yoga and meditation based)*, rushed home from their weekend of enlightenment with a new clarity of what they wanted, proceeding to hand in their notice, put the house on the market and telling their partner they want a divorce. Then proceeding to embark on radical life changes they later regretted. To those on the outside looking in, this was clearly the person slipping into a crisis, because their whole belief system had been monumentally shifted in a weekend and they were essentially acting from panic disguised as a new clarity. They did this all on adrenaline.

This isn't the approach *RBM* recommends, changing various aspects of your life can be overwhelming, so go slowly, moving in a measured way, like picking targets on an aggressor. Clinical decision making, being brave but not reckless, recklessness comes from doubt, anxiety, and an irrational stress response. Make small, measured steps from a place of calm, confident decision making, rather than giant leaps of panic transition.

Make decisions on what you would like to change and break these down into smaller targets, being compassionate to yourself and others in your life by making changes gently. It will be easier to monitor your transition to success and to achieve your targets, without dropping a personal destruction bomb into the epicentre of your life. Focusing on your targets is essential, but resist the urge to change everything at once, don't try and hit every target right now. Rather than rush through your personal life like a someone with a machine gun spraying bullets in the hope something hits, be like a sniper, calmly pick a target and act on what you see. Monitor the results, and if they're positive then repeat and keep moving forwards!

How do you identify your targets and see which ones are the priority? If in a situation where you're under the threat of an attack, you identify the most pressing issue at the time:

- Imminent Threats – Person shows threatening behaviour towards you
- Immediate Threats – A knife is introduced
- Ultimate Threats – The aggressor's brain

Apply this principle of operating to everyday life. Identify which are the most pressing issues which need to be faced first; *immediate, imminent, ultimate*. Place them on a scale of importance, change your problems into targets and put your focus onto how you're going to solve the puzzle, not what may happen if you don't. Always striving for the decisive solution.

<u>Obstacles? I didn't notice any, I was too busy getting on with the solution!</u>

Set your targets to get the ball rolling, and be aware that what's likely to happen now, is obstacles will formulate in your mind placing hurdles of doubt for you to overcome. *How are you going to achieve the goal? Where will you start? What if you make the wrong decision?* An abundance of problem derived questions swirling around in your mind, and you need to hit them head on with a positive mindset. Be generous in a physical conflict, if they want a piece of you let them have all of you, the same principle absolutely applies to daily life. When carefully selected decisions are made, commit with all your effort as best you can, no matter how hard that little voice of doubt tries to hold you back. Don't do something with a half-arsed effort or commitment, do it, or don't!

BREATHE

And Breathe......
- Box Breathing
- The Top Trump Card - Breathe like a Baby
- The back to front-ness of Tai Chi, Yoga and Meditation

Three simple things which make a massive difference to people's lives are:
(1) get enough sleep
(2) drink plenty of water
(3) breathe properly

It's astounding how many people need to be told these three things, especially how to breathe, and it's because people are often disconnected from a relaxed way of living. Their breathing patterns and functions have altered, mainly due to negative thought patterns resulting in stress. So much so, as adults people require exercises and directions on how to breathe efficiently, how to carry out what should be an efficient subconscious operation. Stress effects the breathing mechanism to the point where this autonomic action is so crippled by the residual muscular tension held in the body, its function is compromised in efficiency levels. There's now a need for guidance on how to do this to maximum effect, yet you didn't need an instruction manual as a child, so where do the problems begin?

The conscious mind is linear in its thinking, it can be diverse and expansive when thinking about a topic, but it can only hold attention on any one topic at any one given moment. There are plenty of theories which go against this singular conscious thought concept, but let's challenge the theory of multiple thought focus. You may think you're the best multi-tasker in the universe, so have a go at the following exercise: *count aloud to fifty, whilst simultaneously writing the alphabet on a piece of paper*. You'll be able to do this successfully, so you're doing two things at the same time, right? No, the object of the exercise is to help you identify and feel the mental switching of focus between the two tasks. Noticing a slight slowing of pace whilst you are speaking or writing during the exercise as your focus quickly switches back and forth between the two tasks. The switching of focus is fast and is an incredibly impressive display of the versatility of the human mind, but nevertheless you can only really focus on one task at a time.

People are great at switching focus between a multitude of things within a short window of time, but in any one moment, they'll only be focusing on one thing. Like an air traffic controller, monitoring several planes in their allocated airspace, but only able to talk to one pilot via the radio at any one given time.

This singular thought information can be used and applied to help arrest the slide into rumination and the anxiety which comes with it.

Box Breathing Method

There is a popular method called 'Box Breathing' which is found in many relaxation methods. It has its uses and holds many benefits and is certainly worth implementing into your life. The Box Breathing Method is as follows:

- Either sitting upright, standing, or lying down:
- Breathe in whilst counting to 4
- Hold the breath for a count of 4
- Release the breath to a count of 4
- Pause for a count of 4
- Repeat

Counting to four during the different stages of the breathing exercise ensures you cannot think of anything else, it's a form of brain distraction because you can only really focus on one thing at a time. The challenge is to hold your concentration in one place, and the counting method helps to do this by drawing your mind away from previous anxiety led thoughts with the task of counting.

The old counting to ten method as a mental distraction to keep calm is okay, but it's not the most efficient method as people count to ten really quickly when anxious or angry. It doesn't directly influence the breathing pattern in the way the Box Breathing Method will by calming your emotions and putting the brakes on the stress response, which is important for limiting those indelible scar wounds from the overstimulated stress response activation. The Pons are responsible for monitoring your breathing pattern as well as external stress responses, and relaxed breathing equates to happy Pons. Exhaling is linked to the parasympathetic nervous system, the branch of the ANS responsible for calming the stress response. When you follow this box breathing pattern, you will arrive at a calmer breathing pace due to the mind distraction and the controlled exhale, this slower and calmer breathing rate instructs the Pons that everything in your environment is safe and relaxed, and the stress response level will be influenced by this and lowered. Oxytocin, a hormone produced in the Hypothalamus and often referred to as the cuddle hormone. It's a feel-good hormone usually produced by social contact and interactions, but it will also be produced as a result of calm controlled breathing.

When your emotional state changes, so does the breathing. It changes when you laugh, when you're surprised, when you're angry, anxious, and relaxed. These changes in breathing pattern are registered by the Pons and will determine whether a stress response is fired. When the distraction of the counting is linked to the calm breath control pattern of box breathing, it's a powerful reset button for any stress response triggered, it settles the Pons. Aim to use the Box Breathing for a few minutes each day, or anytime you feel you need to get back in control of the mind and the emotions.

The Top Trump Card - Breathe like a Baby

Skipping between lots of thoughts at once is inefficient and exhausting and exactly why developing a focused mindset is a major goal of *RBM*, becoming more efficient in your decision making with less dithering and procrastinating. Halting the feeling of spending your life like a plate spinner dashing back and forth attempting to keep everything moving at once.

Box breathing is the reset button, stopping the thoughts spiralling out of control, but to take this breathing control further, you need another tool for the job. I have found the Tai Chi & Chi Gung breathing exercises to be the most beneficial for this. By returning to the mindset of a pre-stress era you can unlock the many physical and mental health benefits which natural breathing holds, and to achieve this, the practice called breathing like a baby is the best I know of.

Breathe like a baby
An internet search will give you page after page of breathing secrets, endless information, and courses about breathing to gain the ability to relax. For starters, relaxing isn't an ability, it's your natural state and it should be your default position. As for secrets, there aren't any, it's very simple information and the reason Phase 2 is tiny in comparison to the information contained in Phase 1 and Phase 3.

When young children sleep, they don't hold onto their out breath. They draw a long, but unforced inhalation, the air stays in the lungs for a short while and is followed by the out breath being released in one hit. No holding of the breath, no long out breath, and no forced exhalation. Allowing a complete relaxation of the intercostal muscles in between the ribs and diaphragm, releasing the breath as though making a 'puff' sound.

If you are holding residual tension caused by stress in the muscles, you will probably find letting go of the breath in one go quite challenging. There are two options, the first is keep breathing as you normally do and wait for the stress to pass, waiting for the mind to run out of thoughts on its own accord and bring the breathing into a soft and relaxed manner. This is the process often taught in meditation which can take a very long time and isn't always successful.

Or the second option, and the preferable one, is to concentrate on getting this *Breathe like a Baby Method* correct which will lower stress immediately, the latter is a far more efficient way to achieve the desired result. Using the *Box Breathing* to slow the mind followed by *Breathe like a Baby* is a highly effective formula.

When you learn meditation, yoga, tai chi, or martial arts, they tell you to breathe into your belly, but I've never met anyone who can breathe directly into the intestines, it's impossible to do this. The respiratory system is lung capacity and not belly capacity, but when explained correctly it does make sense, as the phrase breathe into your belly is to encourage you to breathe deeply rather than only using the top third of the lung. Which people visibly do when they're stressed, due to holding residual stress in the body, or from poor breathing habits. This shallow breathing can also be caused by poor posture, restricting the freedom of movement of the diaphragm. The drawback with using the breath into your belly description, is that it's confusing. Inside the human body, when the lungs are inflating, they will spread outwards to the side, and downwards towards the back of the ribcage. They do inflate a little towards the front, but not much because the Liver, Spleen, Stomach, and the Heart are in the way.

How I explain the breathing process to avoid this confusion, is when inhaling, feel as though you're inflating your belly but by doing it backwards not forwards. This is quite tricky to explain if not face to face with a person, so please hang on in there while I do my best:

- Stand up and place your hands on your belly button
- Inhale through your nose so the belly inflates
- Feel this pushing your hands outwards and forwards
- Then exhale and the hands move inwards and back to the starting position

This is an inefficient way to breathe, which is taught to a huge amount of people. Remember how this feels so you don't repeat it, it won't cause any harm but it's not the best way to do it.

The most efficient way is this:

- Start in the same position as above, with hands on your belly button
- Inhale deeply but this time feel as though your belly is inflating backwards away from the hands, not pressing the hands in front but inflating backwards away from the palms
- You will feel your lungs inflate, giving the sensation the abdomen is expanding sideways and out into your back
- Exhale, releasing the breath through the mouth in one go, as though making a 'puff' sound
- Wait a little while, where nothing happens, then repeat

(Your posture will affect your ability to do this, so if you're slouching in a chair, you will find it hard to breathe in this way, but if sitting up straight you will be able to perform this seated)

When inflating a balloon, to stop it from deflating you hold the neck tightly or tie a knot. Unfortunately, a similar thing happens in the body with tension caused by residual stress being held in the intercostal muscles found between the ribs. This is detrimental to health, as it restricts the elasticity of the muscles and prevents full inhalation air flow, and shallow and rapid breathing soon follows and breathing becomes laboured. You now need to breathe more times per minute to get the same oxygen and carbon dioxide levels as found in natural breathing, placing extra strain on the respiratory and cardiac systems. *Why do the muscles tense?* Because the Pons activating the stress response will cause the muscles to lock down, you become stuck in a permanent flinch.

To break this cycle, you reduce anxiety levels by convincing the Pons there's no external threat present and to stop fiddling with the panic button. As explained, control over the breathing is needed to achieve this, as any fluctuations in breathing pattern will rapidly bring activation of the stress response panic button. The breathing like a baby method has this covered, use it and it will keep the brain stem calm and anxiety levels low, finding a calmness in life.

Box Breathing and *Breathing like a Baby* methods are not suppressive, escapism methods. There is growing evidence that meditation and mindfulness used as a means of escapism from reality is damaging to your mental health, yet the mainstream providers of these practices are denial orientated with a stick your head in the sand approach. It's a tricky area to navigate as people are presenting these as acceptance due to the language being used, even though the practise is rooted in denial. I must emphasis this isn't all people, and some are doing it unwittingly.

The more the neuroscientists are learning about the brain, the more evidence stacks up against any avoidance concept, which is why the breathing methods presented here are to help you take momentum away from runaway thoughts and emotions, resetting your mind to start afresh, but not denying they are your thoughts and attributing them to some other entity. I'm not promoting using the breathing methods as a means of meditation to enable you to run away from your emotions, and it's not about detaching from your thoughts, disowning them as a means of escaping your reality. That process if followed can lead to psychosis.

The breathing methods found here will help you to slow down and restrict irrational emotional responses to situations. Enabling you to focus on the facts of what's really in front of you at any moment in life. Letting you efficiently evaluate the situation you're in, and accepting any challenges you face with clearly made solution based decisions. These breathing methods help prevent you from feeding irrational worries, but they aren't for suppressing emotions, detaching from reality, and avoiding the hard times in life. The escapism methodology often found at the root of a lot of meditation based practice and eastern arts, is not a part of *RBM*.

The back to front-ness of Tai Chi, Chi Gong, Yoga and Meditation

How many Yoga, Tai Chi and meditation classes have you attended where you end with the breathing exercises? These popular systems are often taught in ways that are out of touch with our modern understanding of the brain. The session structure is in the wrong order, instead of following the current lesson plans, flip the structure of the session around and start with breathing exercises and you'll maximise your rewards.

Start by standing still or sitting down, and use the methods outlined in *RBM* breathing to relax. When you feel calm, only then do you start the movements of Tai Chi, Chi Gong or Yoga to remove the residual muscle tension. You can't effectively remove the tension if you haven't relaxed first and switched off the low-level firing of the stress response. Once you are relaxed then you start the movements of these Eastern arts to help maintain the relaxed state of mind for as long as possible. Calmness when stationary, followed by calmness in motion, the original intention of the Eastern arts. This teaches you if you're anxious, stop what you are doing, stop what you are thinking, and breathe. From this neutral point you're able to choose how you want to express yourself, you become the emotional gear selector rather than the emotions ruling you. This is what these arts are trying to teach you, not how bendy you are or how slow you can move.

Do you need to fly to a remote monastery and sit on a mountain with your body contorted and chanting to achieve a state of relaxation? Nope, just breathe, learn to control your mind, your thoughts, and your feelings. Not being controlling but being in control. You want to be in your best operating state to deal with any of the things which can pop up in this rather unpredictable and dynamic thing we call life. Concentrating on trying to control all the variables and all the potential outcomes is where you'll get blindsided by something you didn't anticipate, stress. But by being aware of your breathing, and your emotions, you have one thing which you can steer the way you want it to go.

As with everything, the more frequently you practice this, the easier it becomes and the faster you can find this calm baseline. You become the decision maker of how you will act upon situations, rather than situations triggering unwanted reactions from you.

How are you going to integrate this into your day, at the times when you really need it?

It's natural to feel a little self-conscious about what others will think if you start doing breathing exercises, but in truth nobody will notice, it's not as if you are doing some mystical movements. You're either sitting up straight or standing to use these breathing methods, so you'll be able to do it anywhere without anyone even realising.

In scenarios without a physical threat present, you can use the *Box Breathing* or *Breathe like a Baby* methods, and you will notice you stay in an emotionally calm state, making very clear decisions. You won't get frustrated, and you won't get angry because your mind stays clear. A lot of self-help books refer to this state as being in the moment, content or bliss. I call it neutral, as you're in control and ready to move in any direction, mentally and physically. It doesn't mean void or empty, but the mental clutter in the way of you seeing things clearly is pushed aside, and the emotional charge behind any decisions has been removed, leaving you in a position to make better choices. When giving advice to friends, it's often clear to you what the solution is because you don't have the emotional charge they have getting in the way of the decision. If you can achieve the goal of being able to clear the emotional block in the way of giving yourself the best advice, you will be better for it, and breathing is the starting place.

As well as having breathing tools you can use each day, the hands-on self-defence drills will teach you when you feel somebody grabbing you, your response to the pressure on your body is to breathe, relax and move. This has its benefits in daily life, because it trains this conditioned response into you through classical and operant conditioning. In daily life when you feel stressed you will tense up, and this is a similar sensation to pressure on the body, but now your response will be different because you will breathe, relax, and move.

Immediately limiting the level of stress and the negative effects of stress. The self-defence facet of *RBM*, in addition to the feeling of safety and confidence it brings, will program this into your way of operating, making it a natural and instinctive response.

MOVE

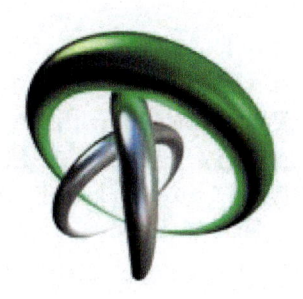

DATA LOADING
The Solutions to Physical Threat Drills

- *Forest Gump It!*
- *Physical Chess, when you move, they must lose a piece.*
- *"But I do Yoga"* - *The movement of joints and how to damage them, even in bendy people!*
- *Identify the target, lock on, and get there, no matter what's in the way*
- *Remember you have work tomorrow - The Safety Guidelines*

Forrest Gump it

The first action to take if threatened with violence is to run like Forrest Gump, take all the self-defence skills you know, pack them away and scarper. It's always a good idea to make yourself lighter and faster by chucking your ego on the floor and happily running towards safety, ready to live another day with a nice cup of tea. Toasting what some people call cowardice and others call common sense.

Sometimes it seems common sense is not very common at all, and even though it's logical to run away from danger every single time, people neglect to choose this action as a first choice, because their ego gets involved and their public image worries come into play. What's important is how you perceive yourself, and if you have enough self-worth you won't give a second thought to what other people think of you for running, and you won't criticise yourself for running either, because you'll know you've done the right thing. The self-defence drills which follow all include tactics to create the opportunity to scarper where possible and also what to do if running isn't a viable choice.

If you engage in a conflict, there will inevitably be time spent filling out a police incident report form, having to make a statement and worrying any error in recounting and recording details of the incident could leave you open to a criminal charge. Adding this to the fact you aren't a superhero and ending up in a hospital bed because the gamble did not pay off is a reality. When considering this, the thought of leaving the danger zone with a hormone driven sprint suddenly becomes more appealing. Swallow your pride and run, it's the easiest thing to do if you can get your ego out of the way.

Running is going to be your go to option as a response to a threat, choosing to leave as quickly as possible, but you can't rely on this as your only option, you need a backup plan, because sometimes a situation doesn't present the option of running, or running by itself doesn't solve the issue. For example, if with your family or friends then running would leave them exposed to the danger, and without you there to help. Perhaps you're in a narrow street with both directions blocked by a gang closing in at the front and rear. Another thing to consider is there are thousands of video clips on the internet showing you how to break away from a grab so you can run, but these fail to provide information on what to do if the person who grabbed you chases you and catches you.

If there's an option of getting out of the danger area, take it every time. If not, act immediately to ensure the safety of yourself and your loved ones. The reality of the situation will now come down to a basic factor, who is the most efficient at stopping the other person.

Physical chess - when you move, they must lose a piece

A threat situation needs to be the equivalent of the most aggressive chess game you've ever played. Every time you make a move with any part of your body, you must attempt to take away one of their major chess pieces. These aren't a knight or bishop, but the essential attributes the aggressor needs to be able to injure you:

- *their ability to hold clear and conscious thought*
- *their ability to move their limbs to put those thoughts into action*
- *their ability to breathe and get oxygen into the muscles to fuel the movements*
- *their ability to maintain physical structure, with their balance and strength being a threat*

Under attack, it's these pieces you aim to remove from the board at every opportunity, the checkmate move is disrupting their brain and making it topple like the defeated king at the earliest opportunity because the brain houses their plan of attack, and the ability to put the plan into action.

If a chess opponent wrote down their planned moves for you to study prior to a chess match you couldn't lose, because you would be able to structure your tactics around knowing what they were going to do. Similarly, in a physical conflict, knowing how things are most likely to play out helps you to avoid the traps being laid for you, and highlights the pitfalls many people stumble into. One of which, are movements which don't have an immediate impact on the person trying to harm you, and is exactly why blocking or attempting arm locks are both off the table. Hurling multiple punches to their face and trying to outbox them is also a weak tactic. This isn't time efficient if there's more than one aggressor, and of course, they may be a better boxer than you. Don't try to compete on their terms.

Having pre-set plans and choreographed patterns of movements to be remembered and rolled out under stress as a response to an attack is a bad idea. *RBM* throws this approach out of the window, actually throwing someone out of a window is a far simpler and better idea than attempting to block and counter or trying to remember complex sequences when under attack. Rather than sticking to set plans and routines which are complicated and difficult to remember and use under stress, you will instead follow bullet point principles:

Get off the spot, now!
Stand still and you will be easy to hit, stab or shoot, stand still and try to wrestle/grapple with them and you will be easy to hit, stab or shoot, but move off the spot and you've immediately changed your GPS location, meaning they need to track you, causing them to initiate a route recalculation. Without doing anything else other than moving off the spot, you've caused a change to their plan of attack, which is disruption of their brain. You haven't stopped their attack yet, but you've made their immediate plans of injuring you harder to implement by not being where you were a moment ago. Get them thinking, slow down their brain speed whilst they move into the mental space of Observe and Orientate of the POODLE Loop by altering their strategy, all whilst you get yourself into the optimum mindset. They move into Observe and Orientate as you move towards the Disrupt, Leave or Eliminate stages, the business ends of things.

The Balancing Act
If attempting to jump upwards off the ground from a standing position, first you would need to have downward pressure through your feet into the floor to generate the force necessary to jump upwards. The downwards pressure is created by dropping your body weight into your feet and loading the tendon and muscle system like a coiled spring, ready to release this force in the direction you choose to move. You can't do this if you're off balance, and this principle applies to the launching of an attack, it's harder to throw a punch or deliver a kick with any meaningful force from a position of imbalance. This tells you to stop them from gaining any downward pressure and the explosive release it generates, which is done by taking away their balance via physically moving them to an imbalanced position. Or you can perforate the eardrum and disrupt the balance mechanism via distorted feedback to the Temporal Lobe. Another option is to disrupt their balance by breaking one of the structures they stand on, the knee joint, ankle joint or major structural bones in the foot will do the job. What else does this tell you? That you must do everything possible to always maintain your own balance and physical structure at all times.

If I had to choose who was attacking me, I'd pick someone who's blind!
Kinaesthetic sense occupies the largest part of the sensory brain, but when conditions for sight are favourable, we rely heavily on vision, and it becomes the more dominant sense. The benefit of taking away the aggressor's vision and removing their ability to visually locate you is obvious, but it's often achieved via a very unpleasant route of gouging their eye *(very unpleasant and not to be taken lightly)*. You can also remove sight temporarily, by causing them to blink as a flinch response reaction to your hand flashing towards their face.

Starve them of oxygen
Creating a spasm of the diaphragm will led to restriction of the oxygen via disruption of the respiratory system, 'winding them', and can be attained by means of; a swift kick to the groin, hitting the diaphragm directly, or throwing them to the ground so they land heavily on their back. Striking the jugular notch is another way to disrupt the breathing, but being aware if you strike the Adams Apple area you may cause the windpipe to collapse, resulting in a fatality, unless you are skilled in performing a tracheotomy. Damaging the lung is another option, but if you're in a position where you can do this, there will be other targets available with lesser long-term health implications and less likelihood of a fatality.

Oxygen can also be stopped in transit via manipulation of the cardiac system, striking the Pneumogastric Nerve/Vagus Nerve will cause overstimulation resulting in vagal syncope, whereby the blood pressure will drop rapidly along with the heart rate, and it's '*have a little lay down time*' for the person attacking you, because oxygenated blood isn't getting to the brain in the quantities needed. Every time you strike another person there's always a risk you may cause an injury beyond what you intended, and with the Vagus nerve the person you strike may end up with a partial dissection *(small tearing)* of the carotid artery caused by the impact of your strike. This tear of the artery can cause a minor, or full-blown aneurysm resulting in a stroke. Falling from an upright position to the ground when unconscious has the possibility of the person cracking their head on the ground, reinforcing the need to be certain striking a person at any time is the only option, before you move.

Take away their ability to stand, or to move their arms or legs
This isn't Texas Chainsaw Massacre style removal of limbs, but emphasising practical thinking is required. Breaking the aggressor's ankle means they're unable to stand on the leg, limiting their ability to move quickly and giving you the chance to leave. Dislocating the aggressor's elbow removes an important weapon from their arsenal, as they're unable to grab or strike you with that

limb. Injuries which don't hold long term health implications can end a threat just as effectively as lethal techniques.

* * *

Any movement which doesn't remove any of these pieces from the physical attack chess board signals an inefficient action or non-action on your part. One or more of these pieces should be captured every time you move, otherwise the movement was empty, not affecting the aggressor, not disrupting their plan, and not stopping them putting their plan into action. In a life or death encounter your mantra is *every move counts*. Sometimes things don't work out as planned and you might end up making a move which is ineffective, and that's okay, as long as your self-defence method isn't based on inefficient movements, and you're able to recover from a mistake and strive towards taking one of their pieces with the next move.

"But I do Yoga" – The movements of joints and how to damage them, even in bendy people!

Quite often, someone who would win the world flexibility championships will attend an *RBM* course, and when talking about joint dislocation they remark, *'but I do Yoga, my joints will bend further than other peoples'*. Being able to scratch your head with your foot doesn't mean you are exempt from joint dislocations, flexible people still have an anatomical limit of joint movement, regardless of how bendy they may be. Without a range of motion limit, the joint wouldn't be able to function, and the body would resemble a jellyfish. A limit to a movement of a joint will by its nature, set a range which can be exceeded, and when a joint is taken past its movement limitations, irrespective of flexibility, it will break just like everyone else's.

Spending time and effort learning about different joint types and the range of motion for each joint will certainly inform you how to manipulate a joint to break it. I personally don't see this as a necessity for those starting out in self-defence, because if it's necessary to retain information about leverages, fulcrums, required forces, and various ranges of motion required to pop joints there's too much theory involved, and you can get bogged down in the detail. As you're aware, too much thought leads to freeze potential. Instead, I suggest you follow the *SOUP* approach, **s**imple, **o**bvious, and **u**ndeniably **p**ainful, it should be perfectly clear to a novice what each movement is designed to achieve, not just in joint damage but all of the self-defence.

A prime example of this would be instructing people on the benefits of putting their thumb deep into an aggressor's eye socket, the directions are *simple* to follow, the result is *obvious* and easy to achieve, the damage caused is *undeniable* and the *pain* level is clear, it follows the *soup* principle. If you apply this same approach to what can otherwise be a complex world of joint manipulation, it makes everything easier. Rather than getting stuck in the details of joint anatomy, look at a human body and see the obvious ways you could bend a joint against its natural movement pattern, the way which makes you feel nauseous to think about, and do that to the person attacking you. Stamping on someone's ankle to snap it inwards follows the soup principle, as does kicking a knee joint backwards.

When people first start learning *RBM,* any information related to injuring shoulder and hip joints is omitted, as these can be difficult to manipulate without a developed skill set, especially when an aggressor is standing. They require a higher skill level to create a joint explosion than other joints, especially when considering the realism of an attack. The elbow, knee, wrists, and ankles are preferential targets, because they are more exposed and vulnerable joints to attack. Requiring little skill to disassemble, they make it onto the *RBM* joint dislocation list. *But why would you want to dislocate a person's joint?* There are numerous reasons you may need to do this, an example would be an aggressor under the influence of Phencyclidine (PCP), whilst the drug doesn't always make people aggressive there have been plenty of cases of PCP being present as a factor in violent attacks, and it's a known pain response inhibitor. There are documented cases of people high on PCP slicing the flesh off their own face, others cutting off their own genitals, and the list of drug induced unpleasantness goes on.

If a person on PCP was attacking you, imagine using a palm to the face accompanied by a stern shout of 'NO', which is commonly taught in women specific self-defence classes, and ask yourself can you see this working? How about the fast strikes to the face, head and body taught in popular self-defence classes which appear to promote fitness as a priority, would this stop the PCP fuelled aggressor? If a person can do more harm to themselves than you're attempting to do with these sports based and reality void techniques, how do you expect to stop them? A man on PCP once ate his own eyeballs, that's the sort of chemical induced, bat shit crazy level of wrecking machine you may find yourself facing. In this situation an armlock is not going to seal the deal, no way. Throwing fast elbows to the face and head, then kneeing to the testicles will all be in vain, as will shouting no or stop!

Facing a PCP raging aggressor is a rare circumstance, but combined with the explosion of cheap highs available it's worth considering the zooped up ability people on drugs have. You need a plan B, and in this case *B is for break the structure*, because regardless of their pain threshold being distorted through drugs, if they cannot move towards you because their bone structure is damaged, they cannot harm you *(without a projectile weapon)*.

If gouging an eye is not enough to stop an aggressor, then something is seriously wrong, and you will need to go structural. Break something, incapacitate them by taking away their ability to move their limbs towards you. The joints/bones you should aim to damage if needed, from head to toe are:

- The Sternum
- Dislocated Elbows
- Dislocated Wrists
- Pubic Bone
- Dislocated Knees
- Dislocated Ankles and Broken Foot.

Another example of a situation where the dislocation or breaking of a joint is advisable would be in the case of a person who's been abducted. On seeing an opportunity they strike their captor rendering them unconscious, but they may be unaware of where they're being held or how far it is to safety. Should they start running, knowing the aggressor will regain consciousness at some point and possibly try to hunt them down? Or should they stamp on the kidnapper's ankles and knees, with damage to either target ensuring when the person regains consciousness, they're unable to follow?

Identify the target, lock on, and get there no matter what is in the way.

"Roger, Roger, what's our Vector Victor?"

Airplane [37]

The psychological obstacles in the way of you reaching the Hot Zone Targets were covered in Phase 1. This section is looking at a physically created barrier preventing you from being able to strike the chosen targets. The obstacle I am referring to is their force on your body, how they get in the way of you moving forwards and bashing a target. A lot of the time vectors are common sense, if

---

[37]

Airplane - 1980 Paramount Pictures

they are pointing a gun at you, the main objective is not to be in front of the gun, because it's where the potential vectors of the bullet exist, known as the field of fire.

When the barrier is physical pressure on the body from a person grabbing or holding you, it gets a little trickier to understand, especially if you've never been attacked. A situation like being pinned against a wall requires you to start considering vectors of force, and it's where an understanding of these vectors prevents you wasting time and energy by using unsuitable options to try and to solve the 'stuck against a wall' problem. This can get complicated, requiring a huge amount of text with diagrams to explain scalars, vectors, mass, magnitudes, directions, velocities and so forth, or we can keep it simple and direct, which is how *RBM* like to do things.

Pushed up against a wall, you need to navigate around a physical obstacle, the body of a human aggressor. You won't be able to step forwards unless you are bigger, heavier, and stronger than the other person, who will be using their weight and force to trap you against the wall. You will need to consider that even if you're bigger than them, in all likelihood their hands will be wrapped around your windpipe, so trying to move forwards will be increasing the force placed on your throat. They may have a weapon pressed on your neck and trying to move forwards means pushing against the weapon, which is a rather unpleasant and dangerous experience.

In this situation you're not going to be able to move forwards, because you're pushing directly against the force placed onto your body, the force vector. People in self-defence classes can be seen struggling when taught to step forwards against this barrier, being told if they cannot reach the target with their hands to kick the groin, as their leg will be longer than the aggressors' arms. This is playing Russian roulette with your safety, because whilst in the position of being strangled against the wall, a kick to the groin can go one of three ways.

Outcome one, you strike the groin successfully and they let go of your throat, hold their injured area, and fall over. Fantastic!

Outcome two is not so great. You manage to strike the groin but without enough force to injure them, now they're really angry and know you intend to fight back, they immediately raise their violence level.

Option three is worse!
With option three, you miss, or telegraph the kick causing them to initiate a SAM Axis flinch response, they instinctively throw their hips backwards to avoid the attack. This doesn't sound that bad, until you realise the way the aggressor will generate force required for this evasive movement is by using you as a springboard. They will throw their weight forwards into their hands (the ones wrapped around your windpipe), to be able to propel their hips backwards. Not so great for you, as you have now indirectly crushed your own throat, and this is what happens when you don't understand vectors.

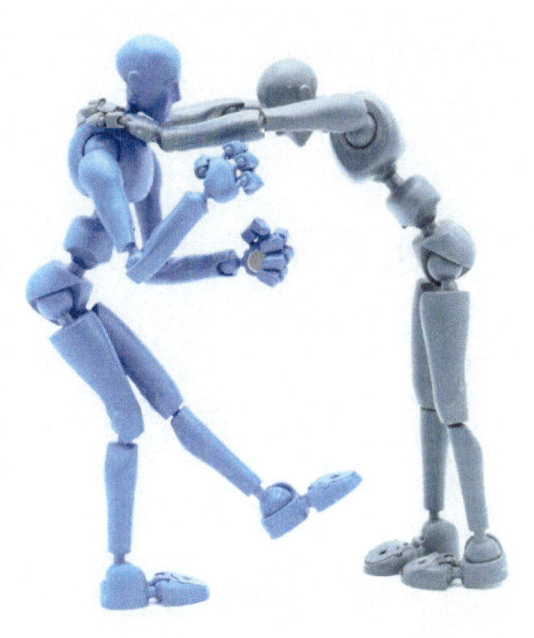

The way around this vector problem is to think of a person holding a long pole in their hands and pressing it onto you. Your aim is to be able to reach them, but you won't be able to move against the pole, it's a physical barrier, just the same as their arms when they've grabbed your throat.

You can't press forwards, but you can move sideways to step around the pole or twist your body to turn off the force vector, then proceed to move towards them so that you can reach the targets.

Treat their arms pressing on you, or any other force on you, the same as this pole to navigate around. Sure, their hands may still be on you, but you will have moved off the vector of force, enabling you to move forwards and strike a target. Also, you will learn how to fix their hands onto your body so when you move, their wrists will break.

The vector will tell you the way out, the escape route, it's whichever way you can move without feeling any pressure on you. You will become familiar with the feeling of which way to move when practising the *Solutions to Physical Threats Drills* with a practice partner.

Remember you have work tomorrow - The Safety Guidelines

The fundamental safety procedures:

Without trying to sound as though I'm hyping up the information you're about to read, it's dangerous! It needs to be, because it's used to stop a person who wants to harm you, by causing a serious injury to their body. For this reason, it's important you perform these drills slowly. I hope the text of roughly 35,000 words explaining why you don't need to train for speed has stuck with you, and you appreciate there's no need for fast movements when learning *RBM*. If you train for speed you will compromise on the most important details of the movements, and you will start to sacrifice driving through the target. In a real threat, speed will come from the urgency to find a way to survive, speed will come from fear, <u>but accuracy and efficiency will come from correct data loading.</u> Fast movements when learning will jeopardise your drill partners safety, so move slowly.

- Warm up prior to starting the data load to minimise the risk of injury
- You minimise risk for your drill partner by moving slowly
- Work with a drill partner who will mimic reactions, but they must be mindful of the urge to resist or assist your movements
- When in the role of the *aggressor*, attack the space your drill partner is in when simulating the attack, not the space they are going to move into. Remember you only have the luxury of knowing where they will move because you are both moving slowly, and you know in advance
- Avoid going past the anatomical limit of the joints, otherwise it snaps, pops, and causes screams
- Remove your jewellery to avoid tearing the skin
- Lack of concentration leads to injury, concentrate fully on what you are doing
- Do not verbally communicate with each other, this information is for when negotiation is off the table, so don't confuse the brain by mixing this striking data with verbal communication. You can include de-escalation techniques, but only to the point where the physical threat is being replicated by your partner, then stop talking and start hitting. Slowly!

Solutions to Physical Threats

- **What to do when grabbed!**
- **A Punch!**
- **A knife!**
- **Being Human, it's about doing the right thing**

If you've completed the drills outlined in the text up to this point, you'll have perfected moving forwards and striking different targets from different angles on your stationary drill partner, which was covered in the target coding drills and the zonal drills. If you haven't completed this yet, I suggest you do so before continuing any further, to maximise the efficiency of the following information.

Now it's about putting your ability to strike targets into practice whilst the person attacking you isn't standing still and they're a very real threat to your health. There's no point in only being adept at striking mannequins, you need to learn how to influence movements and deal with movement. Ideally, you will be able to find a drill partner to optimise the benefits of the self-defence data load. While the descriptions and illustrations will explain the concepts, there's no substitute for the eureka moments of finding out how it works when working through it with a partner. Just remember, this works, so move slowly and show consideration towards the safety of the other person when learning.

To fully benefit from the *RBM* information, you use physical movements to load the data into your brain while adopting the principles of a solution orientated mindset. Spend as many hours on the physical movements of *RBM* as possible so you never need to think of it again. Through repetition you'll have the information and the principles instilled in you, you will become an illustration of the principles in how you operate under threat, and in life.

The following *Solutions to Physical Threats* drills aren't for you to memorise and hold in your thought process as set responses, they aren't designed to be replicated move by move as a response to a specific threat. It's important you realise they are only laid out in patterns as a consistent way of loading the data into the Hippocampus, for storing the information in the memory banks. The drills are essentially a big database of potential answers, answers which can be jumbled up and used in any order needed as a solution to a real threat. A mish mash of movements your subconscious super-computer will piece together at the time, picking whatever is the most efficient and effective route to take. Remember; the ethos of this self-defence method is taking the initiative, working dynamically in creating a bespoke solution to a threat situation, not attempting to force a set response to fit as an answer.

There isn't any focus on gun scenarios or multiple attackers included in this book, but this doesn't mean *RBM* is short of information for these threats, it simply comes down to a basic fact there's only so much you can put in one book and what can be learnt without face-to-face instruction. What's included, is information for the most commonly occurring violent attacks which people are most concerned about, and it's important to start with this as it gives you a solid foundation of knowledge and ability.

The following *Solutions to Physical Threats* drills will outline set routines which have been carefully constructed in a unique format to maximise your learning process. You will be given solutions to different threats and shown how to implement these movements from the various starting positions you may find yourself in, from both a physical and psychological perspective. Physically, it's important to start from each of the different flinch postures to gain familiarity with them, seeing these merely as a starting point, not where things aren't going to plan with the attack being out of your control/influence. Psychologically, your state of mind can change from being ready for conflict and having a target selected, to finding yourself in a mental flinch with complete uncertainty of what's happening in the blink/flinch of an eye. Even though the movements contained here are very simplistic, don't confuse this with rudimentary, because the amount of information behind the principles of the movements is vast, and highly specialised.

The following drills aim to instil the ability to get yourself moving immediately. Dragging yourself away from the urge to stand still and try to work out what's happening before moving, which is essentially a mini-freeze response. The drills are designed to form conditioned responses to limit the potential of this 'stand still and freeze' happening, by carefully working through the different elements you might find yourself in at a specific point of an attack. These are *Mind Set, Body Posture, Your Starting Position, and Angle of Attack*.

<u>Mind Set</u>

Previously covered were the *codes of awareness*, which are: *Ready, Engaged, Prepared* or *Zombie*. These codes of awareness will now be expanded into a range of psychological operating gears which you may find yourself in whilst under threat. This is essential information<u>, because your awareness level is not the same as your psychological mindset in a threat situation</u>. Awareness is knowing what's going on around you, the mindset gear is what's going on inside of you, a person might be perfectly aware of someone walking towards them with a knife, yet unable to move to safety because they are frozen to the spot. The mindsets will be categorised as follows:

Aware and Engaged*, a target has been selected, and action is taking place*

Caught by surprise *and trying to focus and work out what's happening*

Wanting to press pause *so you can 'left brain' think*

Freeze *– potential Zombie moment*

<u>Body Posture</u>

The drills will include solutions for the main physical postures you may find yourself in from the following categories:

1. *The Pre-emptive strike*, by its very definition must be in a situation where you are Aware and Engaged, and a target has been selected. You move and strike the target to eliminate the threat, not standing still and waiting for the inevitable attack
2. *The Green Response* is being aware a threat is real, and an attack is about to occur. Seeing the aggressor invading your space, you pounce on the attack, striking whatever part of them moves whilst on route to the target zones programmed into your Hippocampus
3. The *Yellow, Orange, Red, and Black Flinches* will replicate the postures you may find yourself starting from when your SAM Axis reflex initiates a response to a threat

There is a direct correlation between the mindsets and the physical postures/actions you will be adopting.

Mind Set	Physical Action
Aware and Engaged, *a target has been selected, and action is taking place*	*The Pre-emptive strike*
	The Green Response
Caught by surprise *and trying to focus*	*Yellow Flinch*
Wanting to press pause *so you can 'left brain' think*	*Orange Flinch*
	Red Flinch
Freeze	*Black flinch*

<u>Your Starting Position</u>

The most likely physical positions you will find yourself in are standing, sitting or on the floor. You can expand on these if you think of any other situations you may want to cover, such as in a bath, on the stairs etc, but this text will focus on the most likely position attacks begin which are standing. You can add in starting from a seated position, laying on the floor etc as you progress.

Angle of Attack

The drill will cover the most likely potential of being attacked from the front, the side, and the back where applicable.

Each drill will cover the following;
- Encouraging you to move prior to the attack, preventing you from falling into the *'stand still and wait to see what the attack is going to be'* format often found in self-defence, which is a freeze encouraging, non-action principle taught in many systems. Upon sensing danger, if you realise a physical altercation is unavoidable you might as well get moving off the spot towards an exit, or towards a target immediately. Your task is get moving, whilst you shift your mind set into the gear of Leave or Eliminate, not standing still where the likelihood of freeze increases every millisecond.
- Explain how your body postures will change if you flinch, and what you're most likely to do when caught by surprise, and ultimately how to factor this into your self-defence system and base your responses around this.
- How and when to use a *1, 2, 3* clearing space principle to drive into action, moving off the spot while you get your mind into the right gear to strike a target. Moving and striking to prevent the left brain driven Doom Spiral from initiating. In a nutshell, not standing on the spot and being easy to hit or stab.

There's one principle which needs to be said in isolation to the others, due to its significance in your learning process. This is the principle which is to be used at any point from the beginning of Drill 1, all the way through to the Drill 8:

If at any time you forget what you're meant to be doing, and have a mental block: abandon the drill and strike any target!

Your mindset supersedes the importance of the movements, always! So, ditch the drill and strike a target, don't stand still trying to remember the drill.

If something unexpected happens with your drill partner, such as they're bent over instead of being upright, or they fall to the ground, or they grab you with a different hand etc. and for some reason the movements outlined in the drill don't fit the picture you are seeing, abandon the drill and strike a target.

Resist the temptation to stop and think, and don't try to force a drill to work if the situation changes and it's no longer viable. An incredibly important skill is being able to abort all focus on a target as soon as it's no longer viable and moving your attention immediately to a new zone. The ability to be dynamic in your responses in a threat environment is far more important than the drill, the only purpose of the drill is to load data, you can always add extra repetitions and get the drill right later. What you don't want to be doing at any time is trying to fit a square peg in a round hole because of the format of a book. You change, adapt, and strike a different target. Because I'm not there to monitor this and reinforce the importance of continuous movements, you will have to keep this at the forefront of your mind.

The first drill is based on what to do if a person is attempting to grab you, or they've managed to grab you. Please note, when working through the drill the aggressor will have their arms bent, which is a stronger physical structure than if they had their arms straight. They will be shouting and spitting in your face wanting to dominate, intimidate and threaten you. It's not a common occurrence for people to attack as though they're a zombie from Scooby Doo. In reality, you won't find yourself being strangled at arms-length by an aggressor, so don't let this unrealistic attack posture creep into your practice.

The upside for you, is the more realistic structure of strangulation brings their targets closer to you, and you will be able to reach them. Exactly the situation where the *Break Something in Case of Emergency Escape Targets* come into play. These are the reserve options, the ones where you won't need to move off the spot to be able to damage them, they can be broken without moving your mass. If you feel completely pinned, you can whack these. In case you can't remember, they are:

- Eyes
- Eardrums
- Jugular Notch
- Vagus Nerve
- Groin.

What to do when grabbed!

The conflict won't always start with their hands on your body, often a threat is detected from a distance, which if left unopposed will progress to the point where they do manage to grab hold of you. Drill 1 will cover the various stages of an attempted grab from the front. Drill 2 will focus on what to do if they've managed to grab you.

Drill 1 doesn't cover an attempted grab from the side or the back, because you will most likely be unaware of this attack due to restricted vision in areas they are approaching from. With no physical contact being made during the 'attempted grab' phase of their attack, the back and side angles offer minimal triggers to lead you to spring into action prior to the grab.

Solutions to Physical Threats Drill 1 - An attempted grab

The main sequence of movements for Drill 1 which you will repeat, is as follows;

a) Stand facing your drill partner.

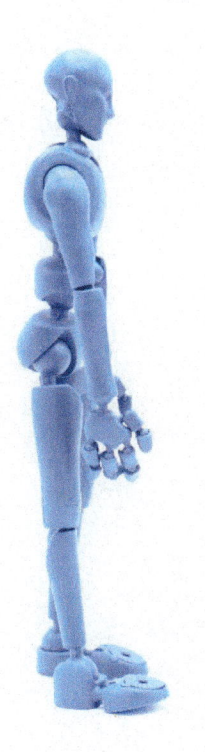

b) Step forwards with your right leg, grab them with your left arm around the back of their neck or head if possible, basically grab anything. Simultaneously drive the fingers or thumb of your right hand into their eye. Causing an injury and creating the instinctive reaction of them wanting to step back and bring their hands to their face to protect the injured eye.

c) Keeping hold of them with your left hand, you step with your left leg and use your right palm to the ear to perforate the eardrum. This target when struck successfully will cause the aggressor to fall to the ground or to kneel, due to the balance mechanism being damaged through the perforation of the eardrum.

d) Still holding onto them with your left hand, step forwards with your right leg and strike with your right forearm to the Vagus nerve. When struck, the Vagus nerve will cause a loss of consciousness.

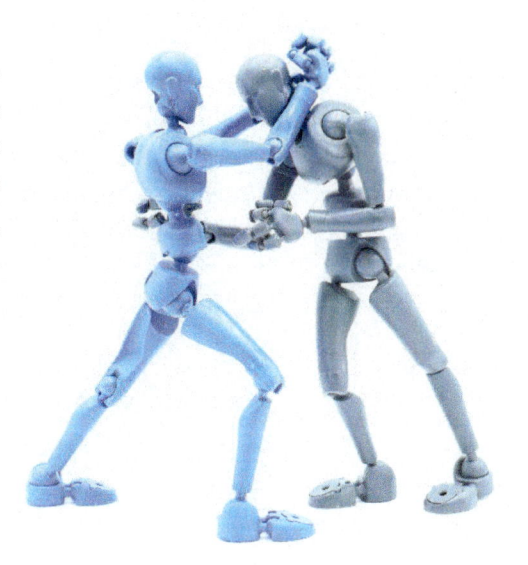

Remember, you're always aiming for the first move to hit the target and the problem going away, but the reason for you moving forwards and striking the aggressor again is to cover the possibility of missing the target, things don't always go to plan. Once you have struck the initial target zone 3 times, it will have disappeared because you've demolished it, or it disappeared because the aggressor has turned away to try to protect the area. You will now proceed to attack a different zone, because the initial zone is no longer available. Progressing to a new zone in the drill is continuing to load targets into the Hippocampus and instilling in you the sense you must keep moving until certain the threat is removed, it's not overkill, its data loading. Therefore, the next targets you will strike will be:

e) Use your left heel to stamp to their foot or ankle, driving through the joint to cause structural damage. Not stamping on their toes and annoying them. Two very different outcomes.

f) Use your right heel to stamp to a knee, driving the joint backwards so their leg moves beyond the range of motion when straight. Alternatively, you could stamp through the side of the knee.

g) Use your left shin to strike to the groin, driving through the pubic bone to cause structural damage. You aren't aiming to only hurt any dangly bits which may or not be there, but smashing straight through the pelvic girdle.

Initially your drill partner will be compliant, standing still and letting you strike the targets, while you will slowly familiarise yourself with these movements. Once you're ready to continue, the scenario then becomes more realistic, it becomes 'live' by adding in some physical and mental obstacles for you to overcome.

Drill 1A
Mindset - **Aware and Engaged**, a target's been selected, and action is taking place
Your Starting Position - **Standing**
Angle of Attack - **Front**
Body Posture - **A Pre-emptive Target Strike**

Your drill partner will stand at a distance of around 5 metres away, and start walking towards you, displaying one or more of the signs of aggression covered in the earlier section. You're aware of an impending attack, but instead of standing still and allowing the freeze potential to grow, you move off the spot:

a) Move off the line with your left foot, stepping across yourself to the right. If you use your right foot and go left or any other combination it doesn't really matter, but to keep a consistent pattern for the data load, try to stick with the left foot moving towards the right at first. Your movement brings the proxemics element into play, causing some turbulence in the aggressor's brain by moving off the spot and forcing them to track you, disrupting their plan of attack. Another benefit of moving off the line of attack is that it's taking a little bit of steam out of their approach, they lose some momentum when they change direction to track you. In addition, even though this scenario is describing a single aggressor it's wise to always assume there's more than one threat and moving off the spot as soon as possible is always advisable and has positive permutations when relating to multiple aggressors.

b) Keeping them in your peripheral vision, you take another step using your right foot, continuing your arc around them. The bodyweight is now on the right foot, on the outside of your circling motion.

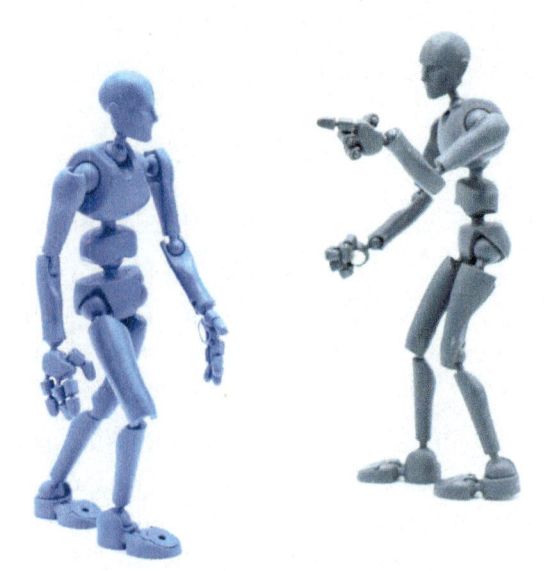

c) This enables you to launch in towards the attacker with your left leg, driving your left hand into their face, forcing their head backwards. This is a breakaway technique being used as what will be referred to as an *'in or out'* technique. Its purpose is distraction to create an opportunity to leave, so you can get *'out'*. Alternatively, if this isn't an option, the distraction gives the opportunity to follow up with a meaningful strike to a target and eliminate the threat, therefore creating the way to get *'in'*. The palm to the face will be a trigger for a flinch response in the aggressor, momentarily taking the power out of their attack, as they're no longer fully focused on their plan to hit you at that precise moment.

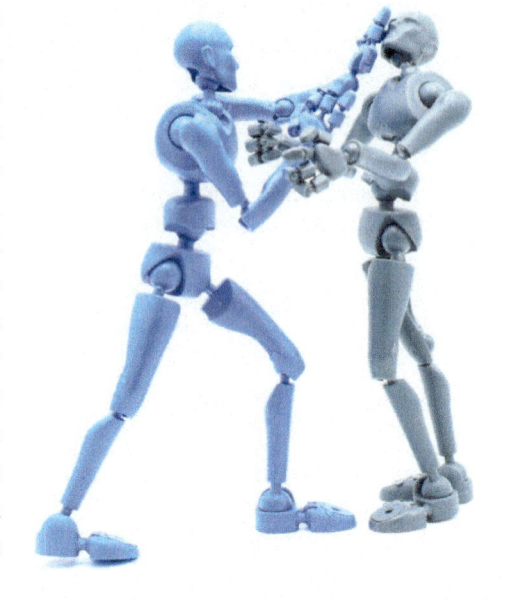

Please note, this palm to the face will not stop an aggressor who is intent on causing you harm by itself, which is how it's often presented in a lot of self-defence systems. This is purely to be used as an 'in or out' strategy.

d) Leave, run like the wind, but if this isn't an option, progress immediately to the next step of striking the targets outlined in Drill 1.

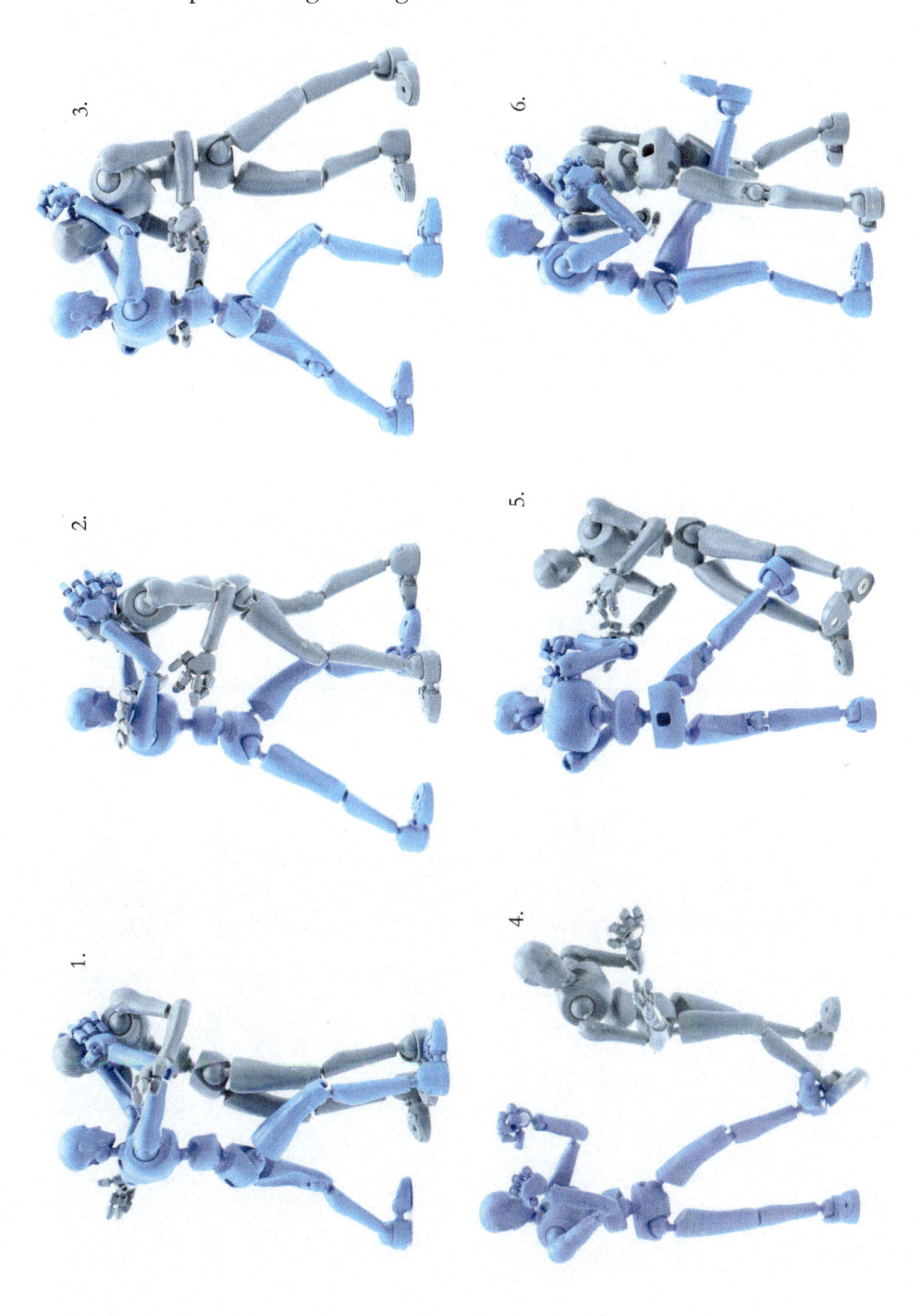

There is the option of having the hands up and trying to calm the situation whilst moving off the spot, using your verbal de-escalation techniques, and putting your palms up in a non-threatening manner. But throughout all of this, your mind is focused on two things, either leave or strike a target.

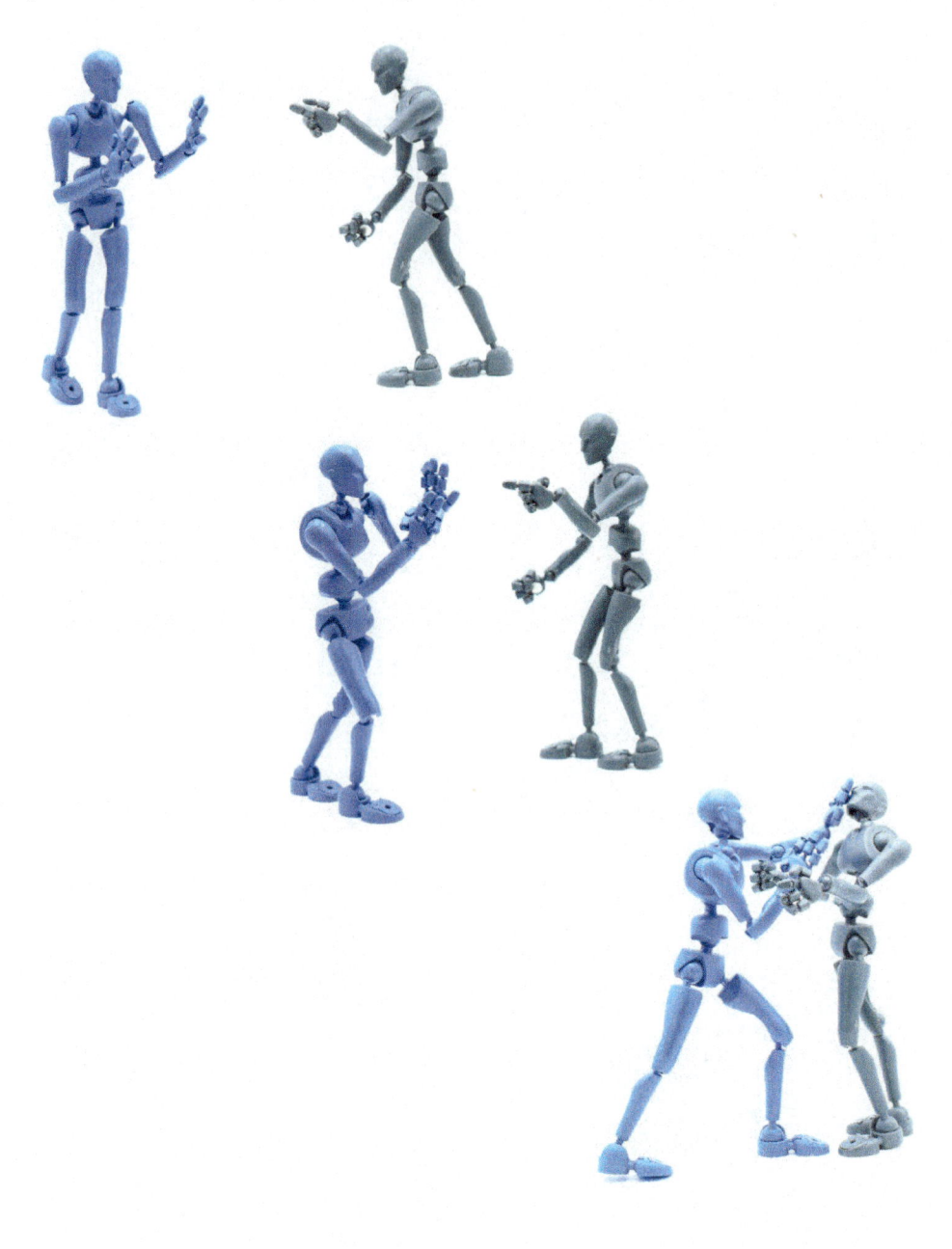

The Principles of Practice for Every Drill!

- The data load for *Drill 1A* is complete, stick to this format to get the information hardwired into the memory banks through repetition and operant and classical conditioning.

- Now mix it up, changing the leg you start with, change the arms and legs used to hit the targets, change the order of the targets (but still staying zonal), once the data is in the brain, avoid seeing it as a set routine.

- Repeat this without any concern as to what leg is leading or what arm you're using, do it to the point where you know you're hitting targets in a way which feels natural to you and disregard any importance of how it looks. Place no value on anything other than the fact you're moving off the spot and causing chaos for the person attacking you.

- The concept of moving and hitting targets in their zones is a parameter set for efficiency, but within this is a fluidity which doesn't require left hemisphere processing of remembering set patterns. Adhere to the principle of one zone for three strikes but hit whichever targets you like, in whatever order you feel is easiest within that zone, you can even strike the same target three times. After these three strikes, focus then switches onto a different zone, and the same principle applies within this new target area.

- *Alongside expecting and understanding your own flinch responses, you must anticipate their defence mechanisms.* This means your drill partner is going to introduce flinch responses, they're going to try to protect themselves by covering up while you're attempting to strike the target. They will perform either the yellow, orange, red, or black flinches as a response to you attempting to hit the target. They will also start to reach out with their hands to try and push you away, holding you at distance from them. If you strike all over the body, they will keep flinching away from you, however if you stick target zones you will find they get compressed, you will over run them by the third strike, and smother their attempts to evade the constant bombardment to the same target zone.

- Your drill partner has a valuable role to play in your development through presenting different visuals for you to act on, their role holds equal importance to what you're doing when loading data into your memory banks and developing your problem-solving skillset. Sometimes your drill partner will replicate a freeze response at any point, allowing you to successfully strike the target, either with the first move or maybe they freeze on the second or third movement. Other times they will SAM Axis finch, covering up or grabbing hold of you. They will mix up the responses, so you have to adapt to what you see each time.

- It's important both of you maintain a slow training speed during the drills, the drill partner will be in control of what responses you get, ensuring you adapt each time and not being able to stick rigidly to set patterns. If you move quickly, they won't have the opportunity to create these obstacles for you to navigate around.
- The drill partner has a high level of importance because your brain will always try to predict what will happen, and they can throw a spanner in the works by either freezing or flinching. Your job is to respond to this immediately and not stop and think about it. Immediately does not mean quickly, it means you keep moving with a smooth flow. Repeat the entire drill with your drill partner implementing this facet into the learning process.
- Keep your weight on them. After you have completed a movement, don't let them move away from you, there should be no break in contact. Grab hold of them and press your weight onto them prior to moving to the next target. Any gaps in contact, or at any time where you feel you aren't in control of their balance, is a time when they could strike you.
- *You now have the training process which will be applied to all further drills.*
    - Start with your drill partner being compliant while you get used to striking the targets,
    - Next, they start to initiate an attack.
    - Introduce the flinch or freeze response as an obstacle for you to navigate around. *But won't they fight back?* Not if you keep the pressure on them, constant attacks to one zone at a time overloading their brain, keep them mentally frozen while you are dropping bombs on the target zone. You must realise that *in the reality of facing a threat to your safety you will be moving quickly when striking these targets*, not giving the aggressor the opportunity to recover, no chance for them to act, and no time to reset.
    - Keep the pressure on their brain, keep taking pieces off the physical chess board.

<u>Drill 1B</u>
Mindset - **Aware and Engaged** and moving off the spot
Your Starting Position - **Standing**
Angle of Attack - **Front**
Body Posture - **A Green Response – GO!**

In this scenario, you're in a mental state of being aware of danger and switched on to the fact a conflict is close to occurring, you're primed and ready to strike because you've concluded that leaving isn't an option at this point. On the way towards the aggressor, you see an arm reaching out to grab you. Already in the mental gear of being ready for a physical conflict, you perform an aggressive movement called a Green Response. Striking anything that moves whilst you're closing in on the target zones. When you see something move, you hit it.

a) Start by moving off the line, causing disruption to the aggressor and at the same time kick starting your own psychological and physical strategy, rather than standing still and potentially freezing. This is a psychological move on the chess board, making them alter their angle of attack. Moving towards the aggressor closes the gap and in doing so, you restrict your thinking time, the thing which allows a greater freeze potential. You have a target picked, but on the way in the aggressor reaches out to grab you, and you aggressively move to intercept and you strike their arm with your forearms, as you're already primed and in fight mode.

b) At this stage, there may be a chance to slide past them and leave, but if this isn't an option, repeat all the steps of striking the target in Drill 1. Covering potentials is what the data load is based on, and now comes the obstacle of what if the other arm reaches forward.

Start to mix things up so you find it doesn't matter which arm they reach out towards you with. You can hit their arm inwards or outwards, and it's not important which side you step towards. You continue to find targets, the only difference will be changes to your visuals for target location, and you may simply want to start with the zone of the ankle, knee, and groin rather than the eye, dependant on what target zone you spot first.

You will realise there doesn't need to be a set correlation of movements between you both, you don't have to step left if they use their left arm or step right if they use their right arm, or find any other matching options. You move whichever way you feel is best, and work with whatever targets you see in front of you.

Repeat this process with your drill partner. As the person data loading the movements, you should decide which way you are going to move prior to the simulated attack, and deal with either arm as it comes at you without changing from your original thought upon seeing their arm. This isn't trying to hold onto a preconceived solution but reinforcing the principle of as long as you move, you will be positively influencing the situation, but if you wait to see which arm reaches forwards and attempt to match it with a set answer, you will likely freeze, or be too slow.

<u>Drill 1C</u>
Mindset - **Caught by surprise** and trying to focus
Your Starting Position - **Standing**
Angle of Attack - **Front**
Body Posture - **A Yellow Flinch**

Your awareness is as high as it can be as you go about your daily life. In a normal situation, observing the world around you without verging on the precipice of paranoia. Suddenly, an attack happens, causing you to make a SAM axis reflex. You jump out of the way of whatever flashed into your field of vision. This is where an evasive, protecting, defensive flinch happens.

a) In this surprised mindset, it's critical you don't stand still, pausing whilst attempting to try and mentally shift straight to a mindset where you're capable of target selection. You aren't in the seat of situational dominance yet, and the aggressor still has the capability to continue to attack you. To minimise damage and restrict time spent stationary, you use this physical flinch posture as a springboard to move off the spot by driving towards their mass. You will use what will be referred to as a *'1, 2, 3'* to clear some space, getting off the spot and giving yourself the necessary mental transition time to accept you're in a conflict and release the *Demolition Monkey*. This isn't trying to locate and hit a specific target, but instead it's just running straight through them with your fists flashing towards their face, causing them to engage their self-preservation flinch response.

The *1, 2, 3* replaces the palm to the face as a distraction tool, as the way in. However, you can follow up with the palm to the face as a bonus move, after all you're going to be generous and let them have all of you.

b) This 1, 2, 3 can open enough space to get out and leave, but if this isn't an option repeat the steps in Drill 1 where you're smashing targets to ensure your safety.

To gain familiarity and confidence, repeat with the inclusion of a yellow flinch on both sides and repeat with your drill partner putting their own flinches in, creating an obstacle for you to overcome.

*More data on the '1, 2, 3'

Is the *1, 2, 3* a perfect solution? No, the perfect solution if caught by surprise would be immediately identifying and hitting a target before any aggressor can throw another attack towards you, but this isn't realistic from what we know about the brain under stress. Whilst other options seem preferable, they aren't reliable, so when caught by surprise you're in a position where you must take a gamble.

Taking any of the potential flinches as a starting position, if you rush forwards towards them with the *'1, 2, 3'*, you move forward, you're moving off the spot and their attacks can miss. You're driving towards the threat and throwing your arms up towards their face and neck region, which could cause them to flinch and at the very least it will be a distraction. You're pulling yourself mentally away from a freeze and towards the mindset where you will be able to pick a target and strike it in a meaningful way. You could stay in the flinch posture, but then you will definitely get struck by the punch, definitely be stabbed or be hit by the bullet. It will also be easier for any other people who may be active in the attack to hit you if you are standing still.

I know people want more than this, they want the perfect, bulletproof, untouchable superhero option, but it would be a lie to say this exists. In my opinion, no matter how brilliant some solutions look in the training room, base it on what we know about brain schematics and realise it's unachievable to move from a surprised mindset straight to meaningful strikes every time. It may happen, you may throw an immediate forearm to the Vagus Nerve as a response, but for the times it doesn't happen, the *1, 2, 3* is the get moving, damage limitation plan.

Drill 1D
Mindset - **Caught by surprise** and trying to focus
Your Starting Position - **Standing**
Angle of Attack - **Front**
Body Posture - **Orange Flinch**

You're as aware as you can be in a normal situation, but you can't see everything all the time without suffering burnout and developing a paranoid disorder.

a) Something causes a SAM axis reflex to kick in, but this time, instead of simply evading the attack with a yellow flinch, some variable such as the proximity of an attack, or the perceived danger potential, causes you to involuntarily grab hold of the thing coming towards you. This is classed as an Orange Flinch.

b) As with the yellow flinch you avoid standing still whilst picking a target, you must move. Unlike the yellow flinch where you and the aggressor were separate entities, this time you are connected because you've grabbed them. Keep hold of the thing you have in your hand, and with the other arm start swinging towards their face/neck/ throat area with the other arm. You will be able to drive off either foot for this movement.

This isn't direct targeting, there isn't any thought placed on foot structure or timing of movements and striking. This is simply rushing towards them and throwing your fist or forearm towards the face and neck area. You could let go of their arm and rush at them with both hands as in the previous clearing space application. Mix them both in and see it for what it is, a tool for getting moving and not a targeted technique.

c) Repeat all the steps in Drill 1 where you are smashing targets. On occasion, strike the Vagus Nerve 3 times and ignore the other targets so you're only using your forearm and not the thumbs or fingers into the eyes. The reason for this is in case your hands have been damaged.

The Orange Flinch isn't a conscious decision, you would never choose to grab something which is moving because there is a risk of dislocating your thumbs or fingers, but you may grab hold because of the flinch response. If you dislocate your thumb or fingers whilst flinching, you won't be able to make a tight fist to punch, therefore you don't have an over dependence on punching within the *RBM* system. Even with damaged digits or hands you will be able to smash targets with your forearm, for this reason it's a preferred weapon to the fist.

Drill 1E

Mindset - **Wanting to press pause** so you can 'left brain' think
Your Starting Position - **Standing**
Angle of Attack - **Front**
Body Posture - **A Red Flinch**

Wanting to make everything stop to give yourself time to work out what's going on.

a) You find yourself in a wrestler's clinch, which is classed as a Red Flinch. If you let go, they will hit you, wrestle with them and you're working on strength and skill levels. Lift your back foot so you can kick them, and you will be dumped on your back on the ground.

b) Because of these factors, you have two options here, the first is to let go with both hands and rush through the middle, throwing your fists towards their face and neck as in the previous 1, 2, 3 clearing space movements. Or, stamp on them with your front foot to damage their base structure, hopefully breaking their tarsal bones or ankle. This is more of a driving step through the ankle than a high knee lifting stamp because you want one foot off the ground for as little time as possible when under attack, and lifting your knee up as high as possible isn't a great idea here. After this initial stamp towards the general area of their legs, you follow up with another two stamps. Again, not standing still and picking a deliberate target, but stamping in the vicinity of where their legs are in hope of getting lucky and injuring them or disrupting their base. They may flinch when they see your leg coming, this also compromises their structure. So, try a 1, 2, 3 using the feet.

c) After throwing your legs in their general area, you will have created the time to get yourself into acceptance mode, realising you are going to need to strike them. You will be able to lift your head up, look at the zone of the eye, ear and Vagus nerve and repeat the steps in Drill 1 where you are smashing targets.

*A Red Flinch posture is not relating to finding yourself in a clinch with a skilled wrestler or MMA practitioner, the positions are very familiar territory for people skilled in those arts. This is a solution for when you find yourself grabbed by someone, or you're holding someone in an attempt to momentarily stop them striking you. This isn't a position you should be hanging about in looking for the opportunity to implement a throw or a takedown, those are skilled movements. Get out of there, get moving and start hitting.

Drill 1F
Mindset - **Freeze**
Your Starting Position - **Standing**
Angle of Attack - **Front**
Body Posture - **A Black Flinch**

The threat of an attack and the danger this brings can cause you to cover up and hope it all goes away. The dreaded black flinch is a physical representation of the mental stress and turmoil being caused. If this happens, you may find yourself standing in an almost fetal position waiting for the blows reigning down on you to stop. But rather than hope it stops, drive into some space and get off the spot, pull yourself away from this physical freeze posture. It doesn't matter if you move in an illogical direction, just get moving and reset.

Drill 1 Conclusion

Stick to this format to get the data loaded into the database, using repetition of Drill 1 and the starting variables from 1A to 1F to achieve this. Then mix it up by changing the leg you start moving with and changing the arms used to hit the targets. Change the order of the targets (staying zonal), breaking away from it being a set routine, repeating this without any concern as to what leg is leading or what arm you're using. Repeat to the point where you know you're hitting targets in a way which feels natural to you, and disregarding any importance to how it looks, placing no value on anything other than the fact you're moving off the spot and causing chaos for the person attacking you.

Adhere to the principle of one zone for three strikes but hit whichever targets you like, in whatever order you feel is easiest within that zone, you can even strike the same target three times. Then switch your focus onto a different zone and the same principle of strike three times applies within this new target area.

Drill 2 will explore response options for when a person grabs you by the throat by either one or two hands. The main thing to realise here is nothing has changed the moment they grabbed you. It would have been much better for them to have struck you immediately, that would have had a physical impact greater than a grab, the grab is a psychological blow with a little physical impact.

If you can skip past the intimidation and the threat of what might happen and start moving, then you're in a good position because they made a move which wasn't as efficient as it could have been. When a person grabs you by the throat, be happy they haven't punched or stabbed you and get moving. This is a polar opposite mindset from the intimidation they're hoping to achieve with the action of grabbing you.

Solutions to Physical Threats Drill 2 - You've been grabbed

This drill offers a solution for when you've been grabbed and you're having to deal with the physical contact of a person holding you, and the movement restrictions this grab creates. Start Drill 2 with a compliant drill partner standing in front of you without any grabbing. The movements are:

a) Move your right foot towards them, your right forearm strikes their Vagus Nerve.

b) Grab hold of their head with your right hand and step forwards with your left foot, whilst driving your left forearm into the jaw and Vagus area. Keep hold of their head with your right hand, and step forwards with your right leg, driving your left forearm into the Vagus Nerve.

c) Move to the next zone. Grabbing their head with both hands, left shin kick to the groin, landing forwards, then attack the groin again with your right shin, again landing forwards.

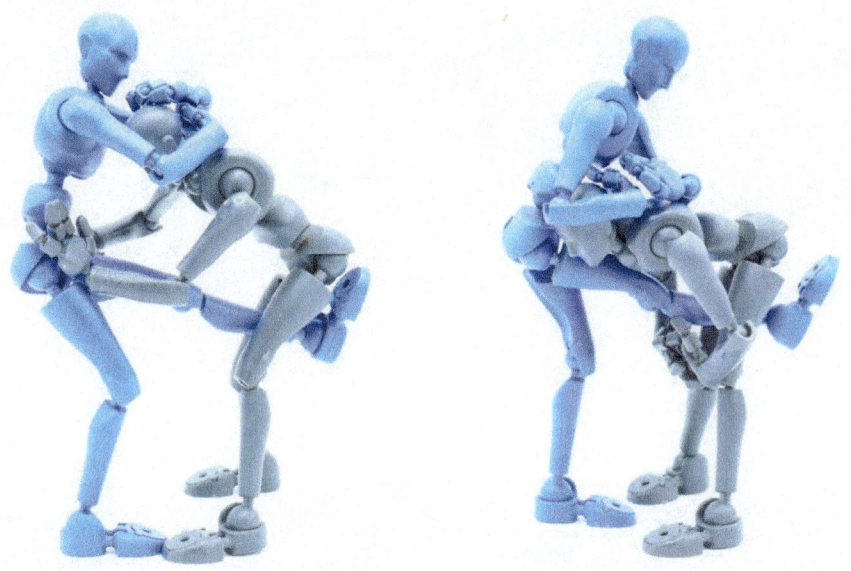

d) They will be bending forwards at this point, meaning the target at the base of the skull will have come into your field of vision. Step forwards, or across in front of them, with your left foot and drive your forearm downwards through the back of the neck.

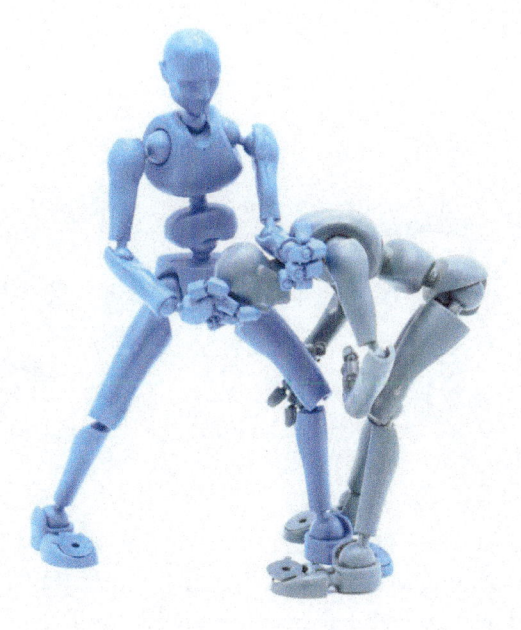

Here is the whole drill for you:

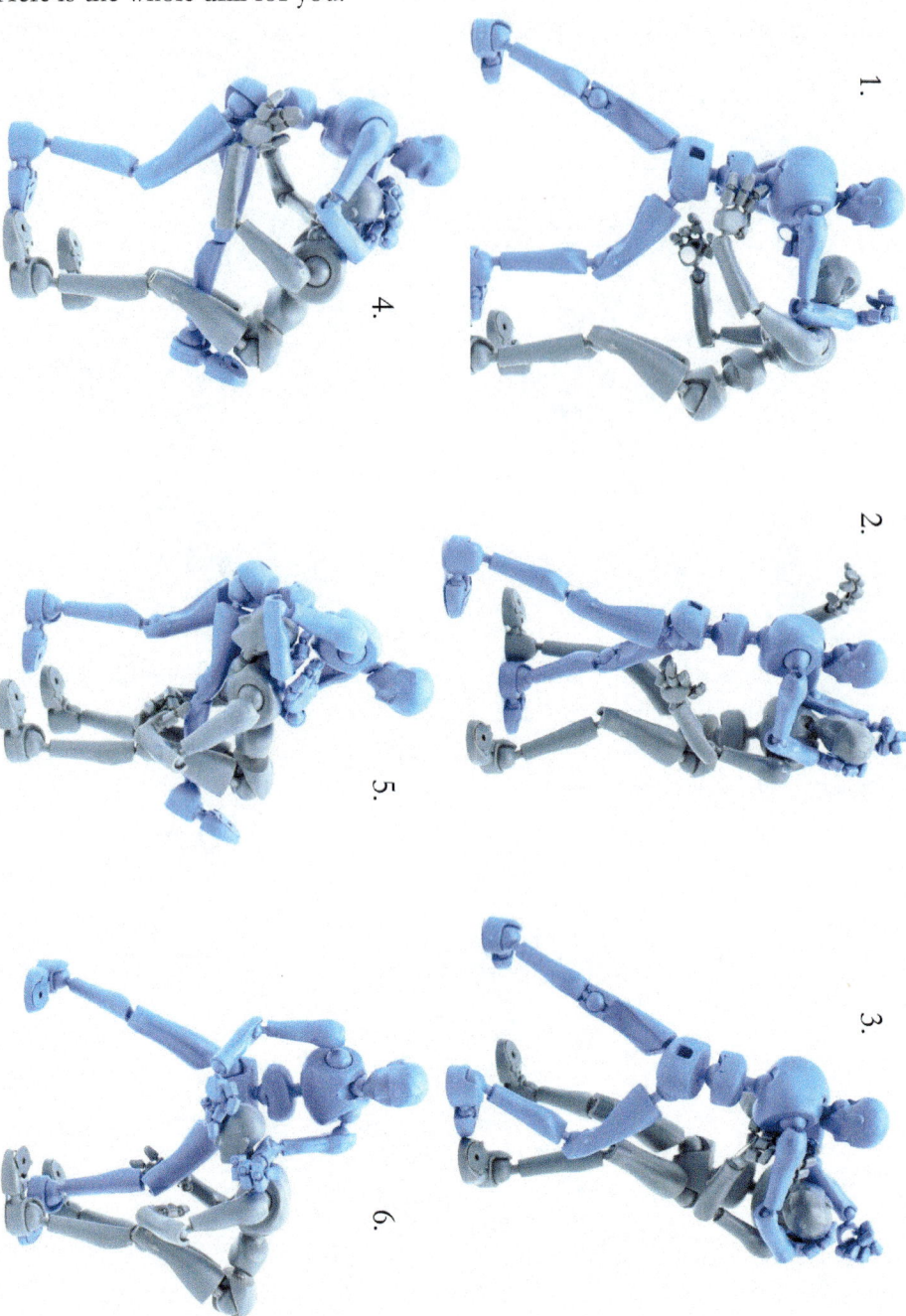

There isn't a pre-emptive target strike option for drill 2. The reason being, if you knew it was coming you would have moved off the spot and turned this into an attempted grab, which has been covered in drill 1.

Drill 2A
Mind Set - **Aware and Engaged** and moving off the spot
Your Starting Position - **Standing**
Angle of Attack - **Front**
Body Posture - **A Green Response – GO!**

To start with, the scenario will explore an attack where you are *Aware and Engaged*, the aggressor is shouting at you and they managed to get close enough to grab, but you were prepared, ready for the *Demolition Monkey* to launch an attack.

You've seen them close in yet you were unable to stop the grab, but you've picked a target. Mentally you're prepared and switched on to the danger, but you need to get moving because if you stand still you might partake in the introduction of their forehead to your nose, or they may have grabbed you with one hand ready to punch you with the other hand.

a) Grab hold of the wrist on your throat, trapping it onto your body. If it's both hands on your throat, pick one wrist to grab hold of. Move your right foot across yourself towards your left, moving diagonally to navigate around the vector of force being placed on your body with the pressure of their grab. As your right foot lands on the ground, your right elbow comes over the top of their arm. The reason for this is to stress and break the wrist joint on the little finger side, the Ulna. (if they have grabbed with their left)

Stressing the wrist joint will have a biomechanical impact as this will make them turn, preventing the punch from their other arm coming at your face. One of the key elements here is resisting the urge to remove their hand from your throat, because if you do this you will only be moving their hand around in mid-air when you step, therefore not causing any damage when you make your stepping motion. If the hand remains on your body when you grab the wrist and trap it, when you step the wrist will break.

You will know if you are doing this correctly with your drill partner, as when you move, they will need to move their feet to release the pressure on their wrist. At speed, the person won't be able to do this, and the wrist will break.

This grab and step across damages the wrist and influences the situation, creating the window of opportunity for you to use Drill 2 (or Drill 1) to strike the targets which end the threat.

Due to their hands already being placed on you, a yellow flinch is an unlikely occurrence in this situation. A yellow flinch would most likely happen with their hands on route towards you, and it would become an attempted grab which was covered in Drill 1, therefore you can progress to the Orange Flinch aspect of this drill.

Drill 2B
Mind Set - **Wanting to press pause** so you can 'left brain' think
Your Starting Position - **Standing**
Angle of Attack - **Front**
Body Posture - **Orange Flinch**

If caught by surprise when grabbed, you will instinctively reach for their wrist/wrists, not through choice but through a subconscious flinch action. This is another situation where a '1, 2, 3' will come into play, moving, and causing disruption rather than staying motionless and picking a target.

In *Drill 1,* this was implemented in the format of moving forwards and throwing your arms towards their face. This time you're going to feel the vector of force against your throat preventing you from doing this *(which is where a practice partner becomes so important).*

This time you're going to move in any direction where you feel you can navigate around this vector, the restrictive force on your body. Moving diagonally to the left or right of the person grabbing you will work, or even sideways can be an option. Another movement pattern people tend to forget is the you can drop your weight to move under the vector. Or combine them all, dropping your weight as you move diagonally forwards, and twisting your torso sideways as you move.

a) They grab you and you instinctively grab onto their wrists.

b) Moving either your left or right foot to move off the spot, twist your torso to influence the vector and stamp towards the foot and ankle area. If you miss it doesn't matter, you aren't deliberately consciously targeting at this point, simply attempting to move, causing some disruption whilst getting off the spot before any damage is inflicted on you. You do this clearing space movement 3 times and hopefully you got lucky and hit an ankle, foot, or shin, if not then things will have changed anyway because they will have moved their legs to avoid the attack to the area, which means the force on your throat has decreased and the vector is weakened. This 1, 2, 3 is to disrupt them whilst you're getting the *Demolition Monkey* in the driving seat, it's not to guarantee hitting a target.

c) Bring the back leg up to meet the front leg and then stamp again, and repeat this process three times as a 1, 2, 3 clearing space strategy.

d) Now implement Drill 2, either by stepping across yourself whilst holding onto their wrist and breaking it or going straight to the Vagus nerve if the pressure has been removed from your throat and you're able to move forwards.

A Red Flinch may happen if they grab you by the throat with one hand and the other hand is shaped in fist ready to smash you. You will hold onto the arm on your throat and reach forward to grab the other arm, ending up in a slightly different clinch in its appearance. The same rules for the Red Flinch in Drill 1 apply here, so apply the 1, 2, 3 clear space approach using your feet, and then implement striking the targets of Drill 2. (Or mix it up and use the pattern from Drill 1). The black flinch will be the same as in Drill 1, get moving in any direction to change the picture and give yourself something to work with.

Drill 2 outlines moving across to your left only because if grabbed by one hand it will most likely be the aggressors left hand, due to population dominant hand statistics. If they happen to grab with the other hand, you don't need to switch what you do, because depending on which hand they grab with, and which way you step across their body, one way will break the wrist and the other way destabilises their structure and opens the opportunity to strike a target zone. It's an alternative way in.

If they grabbed with the opposite hand to what has been outlined in the drill, then you will see something similar to this as you step.

The wrist won't break in this instance, but you will destabilise them and get inside the vector of force, right in front of the Vagus nerve and ready to go. With Drill 1 or Drill 2.

It doesn't matter which leg you use or which way you step, or what hand they grab with, but stay with the program at the beginning to give enough consistent repetition to load the data. After this, break away from the set pattern and move however you want to, with different hands grabbing and stepping different sides, mix it up and work with whatever targets you see in front of you.

Solutions to Physical Threats Drill 3 - Grabbed from behind

Being attacked from behind removes the option of a pre-emptive strike or a _Green Response_, because you're most likely unaware of the attack. Logic dictates you will be working from a flinch reaction when you feel the contact of the grab on your body.

The most likely grabs from the back in all probability will be them grabbing at your right shoulder to pull you around, so your face can receive the whopper of a punch they have as a gift for you. Due to most of the population being right-handed, they will most likely grab you on the shoulder with their left hand, ready to punch with their right. It doesn't matter which hand they grab with, but you may as well familiarise yourself with the most likely attacks to occur, statistically speaking.

The other way they would likely grab you, is best described as around the throat in an upright headlock pulling you backwards or throwing you to the floor. Sometimes the hand may be covering your mouth to stop you screaming and calling for help as they drag you off a pathway or into a vehicle.

Drill 3 covers the grab on the shoulder, and Drill 4 will cover the arm around the throat/hand on mouth.

Drill 3

Start facing your compliant drill partner to load the data, even though this sequence is for a grab from behind, initially familiarise yourself with the sequence starting face to face.

a) Stamp on their ankle with your left foot and drive through the joint. Use your heel to damage the ankle as though snapping a stick or crushing an empty soda can.

b) Move forwards, stamping to their knee with your right foot, landing forwards. This can either be snapping the knee backwards or causing it to cave inwards by coming in from the side of the knee joint.

c) Left shin kick to the groin, making sure you drive through the target and land forwards after the leg swing. This isn't a front kick, it's more of a straight leg swing.

d) They will bend forwards enabling you to grab their head. Move forwards with your right leg and press the head down and forwards towards the ground and pushing them backwards as you step, they will hit the ground easily. *(Note for the drill partner - at this point you will be pushed down onto the floor on your back, it's important you tuck your chin inwards and look towards your navel to prevent the back of your head hitting the ground, the aggressor won't have the luxury of this warning)*

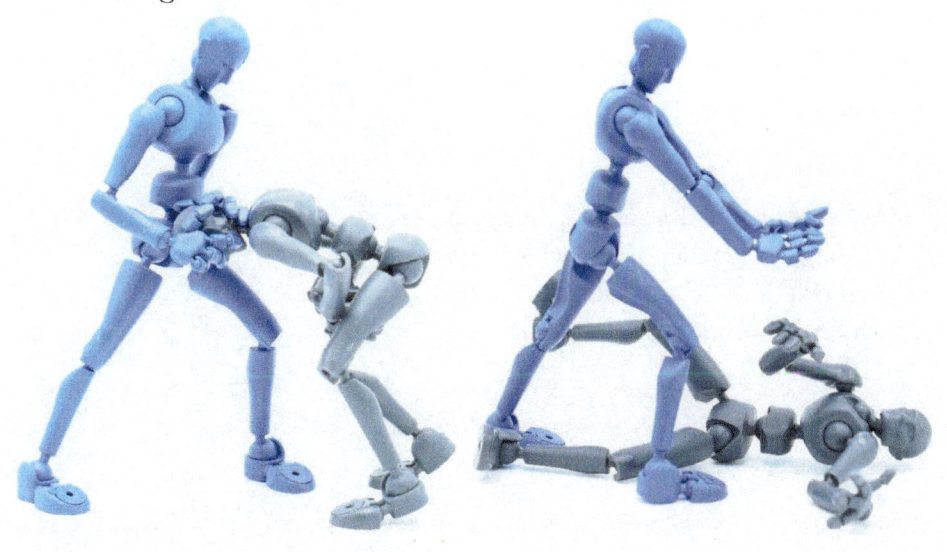

e) They're now on the ground, giving you the chance to familiarise yourself with targets available whilst they're on the floor, but potentially still a threat. Step forwards and stamp to the ankle.

f) Move forwards and stamp to the knee, further removing their capability to stand and pose another threat.

g) Move forwards and stamp to the groin, damaging the pubic bone which will structurally compromise the functionality of the hips and pelvis.

Here is the whole drill for you:

This is purely to load data into the brain on striking targets, it's unlikely after stamping on their ankle, their knee and kicking the groin, followed by dumping them on their back they will pose a threat whilst on the ground, but it's beneficial to teach yourself to be prepared to keep hitting. There's always the possibility a person who is intent on harming you somehow ends up on the ground without you landing a meaningful strike to a target, and rather than letting them get to their feet you should start hitting the targets whilst they're on the ground. You aren't taking part in an honourable duel or a competition, you are in fear of your safety.

<u>Drill 3A</u>
Mind Set - **Caught by surprise** and trying to focus
Your Starting Position - **Standing**
Angle of Attack - **Back**
Body Posture - **A Yellow Flinch**

a) Feeling their hand grab you on the shoulder, you will turn and bring your hands up unto a Yellow Flinch position.

b) From this point you will clear space and do a *1, 2, 3* with your arms driving towards their face.

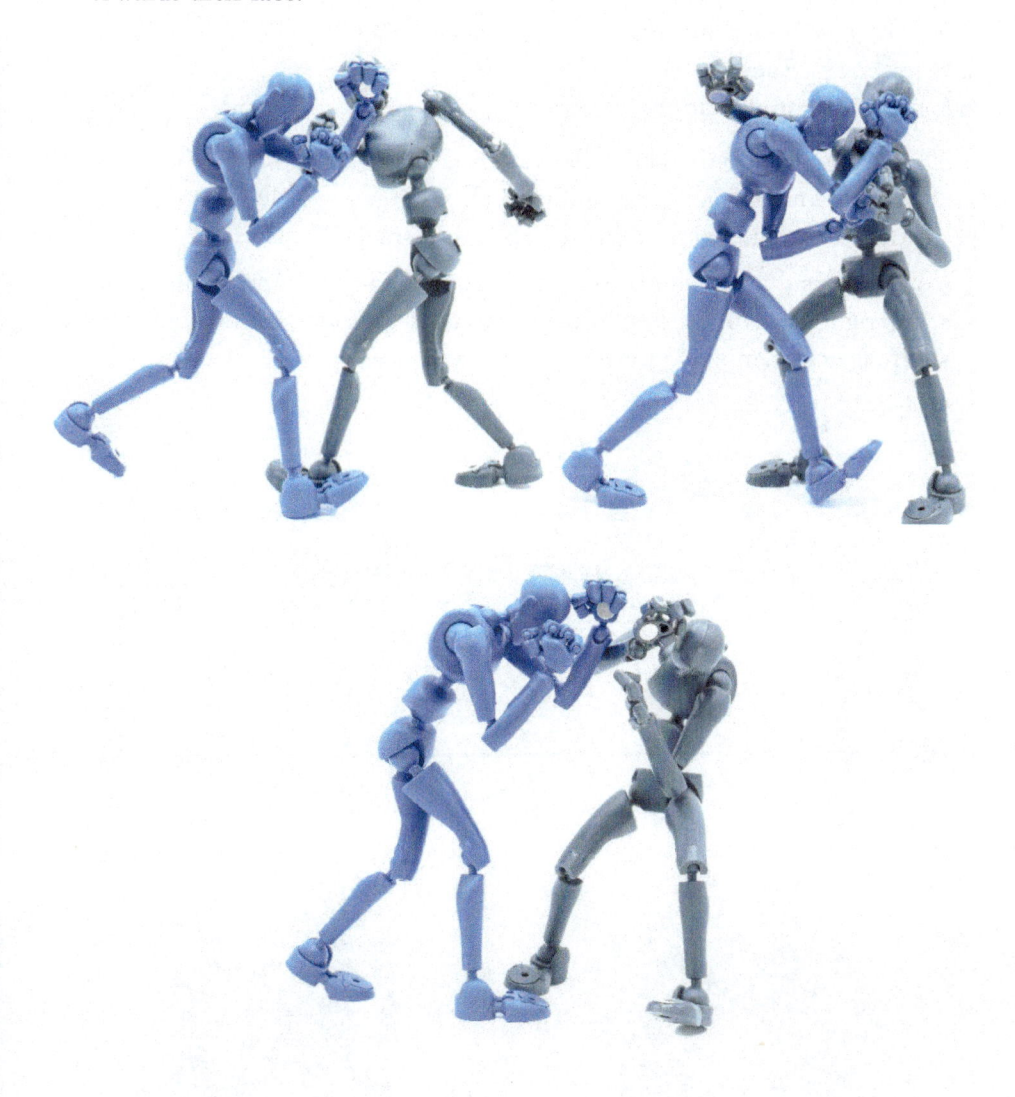

c) Now grab hold of them and put Drill 3 into action. (Or Drill 1 or Drill 2)

<u>Drill 3B</u>
Mind Set - **Wanting to press pause** so you can 'left brain' think
Your Starting Position - **Standing**
Angle of Attack - **Back**
Body Posture - **Orange Flinch**

There is a strong possibility you turn around and upon seeing their arm in front of you, you grab it. Either immediately grabbing it or lunging for it after the yellow flinch outlined previously. This is the Orange Flinch.

a) You turn and grab their arm, and follow this with the clearing space stamping towards their feet, bringing the back foot up each time so you are shuffling and stamping 3 times.

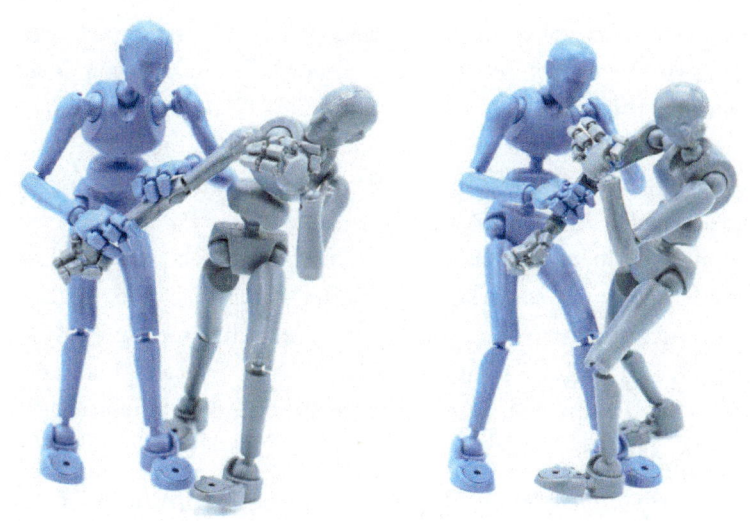

It doesn't matter which arm you grab or whether you are on the inside or outside of the arm, you keep hold and you start stamping. Once you have used the clearing space moves, you start hitting the targets as outlined in Drill 3.

Drill 3C
Mind Set - **Wanting to press pause** so you can 'left brain' think
Your Starting Position - **Standing**
Angle of Attack - **Back**
Body Posture - **A Red Flinch**

You turn around, and in a panic, you grab hold of them to try and stop everything from moving.

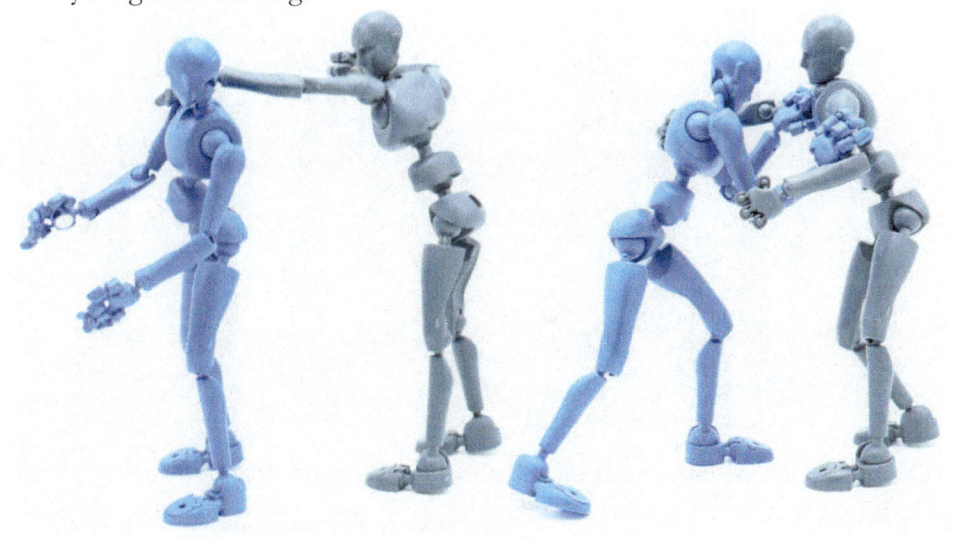

Get some space in your physical vicinity by either driving the arms to the face or using the feet stamping options. Either of these clearing space 1, 2, 3 strategies will get the job done.

Proceed to hitting the targets as outlined in Drill 3, then start to bring the option of Drill 1 and Drill 2 in to play as alternatives, finding they're all interchangeable after the 'way in' has been created.

Once you have the solutions for the front and back grabs and attempted grabs, the information is transferable to attacks from the side. With your drill partner, introduce side grabs and attempted side grabs and use the information you already have to find the solution. Include all the relevant flinches, and your drill partner will also throw in some freeze responses and flinch responses. Stay zonal and strike targets.

Solutions to Physical Threats Drill 4 - Grabbed from behind

This drill is concentrating on either an arm wrapped around the throat or a hand across your mouth from behind, a common and realistic threat. This holds different fears for different people, some worry they can't breathe, others worry they can't call for help with the hand across the mouth. With the arm across the throat people think they are trapped and unable to move.

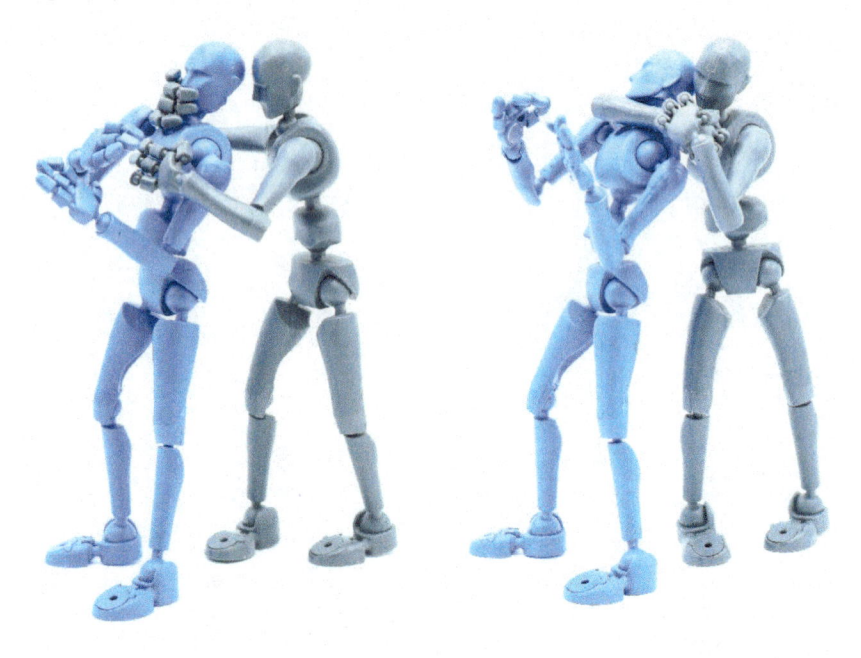

The pattern of movements to practice on your compliant drill partner is as follows:

a) Stand facing away from your drill partner, so they're around half a metre behind you. Move your left foot across and behind you, allowing you to turn and drive your thumbs into their eyes.

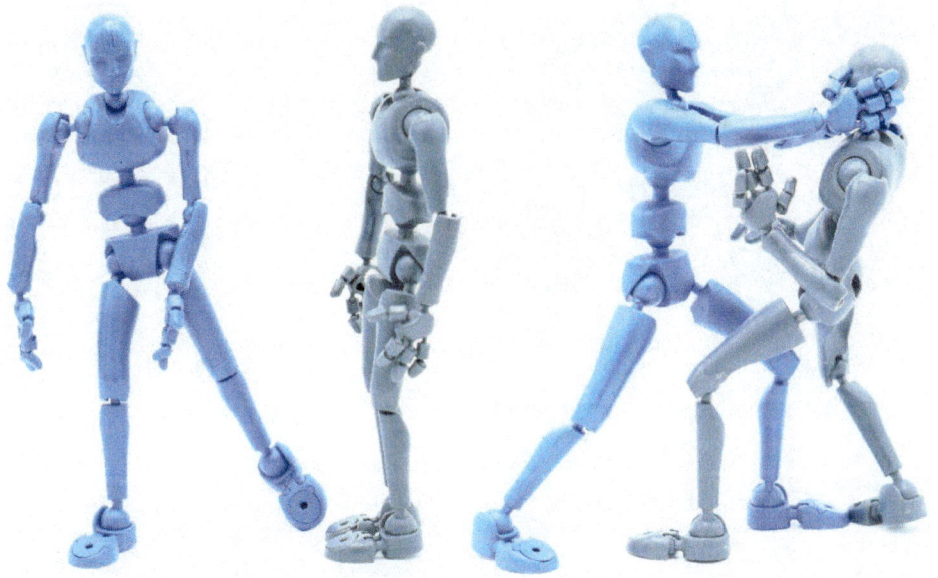

b) Keeping your thumbs pressed into their eyes, you will naturally want to use your legs to attack, so your right shin hits the groin.

c) Step and left shin to the groin, follow this with a right shin to the groin.

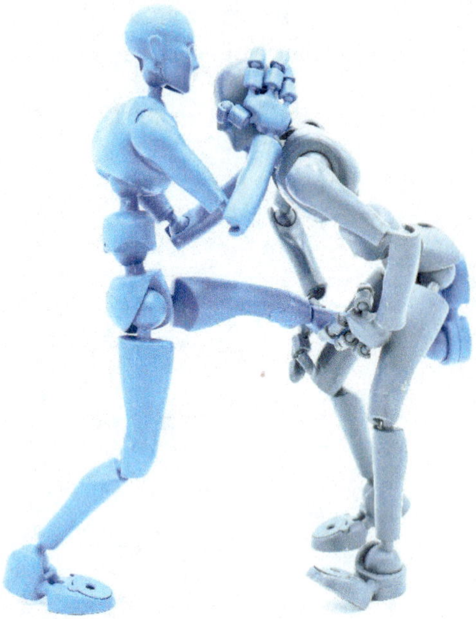

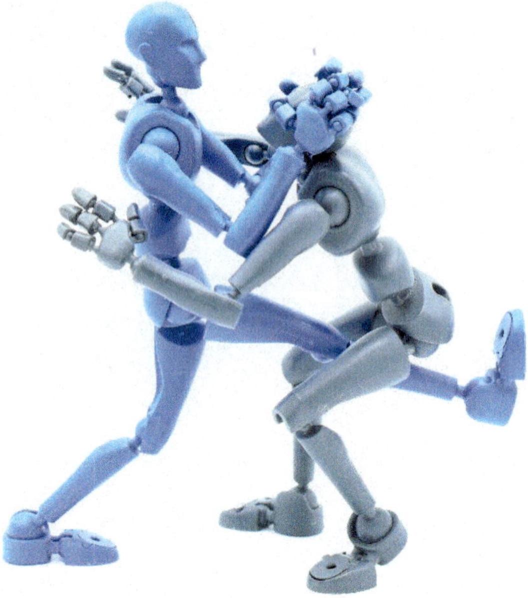

Here is the whole pattern for you:

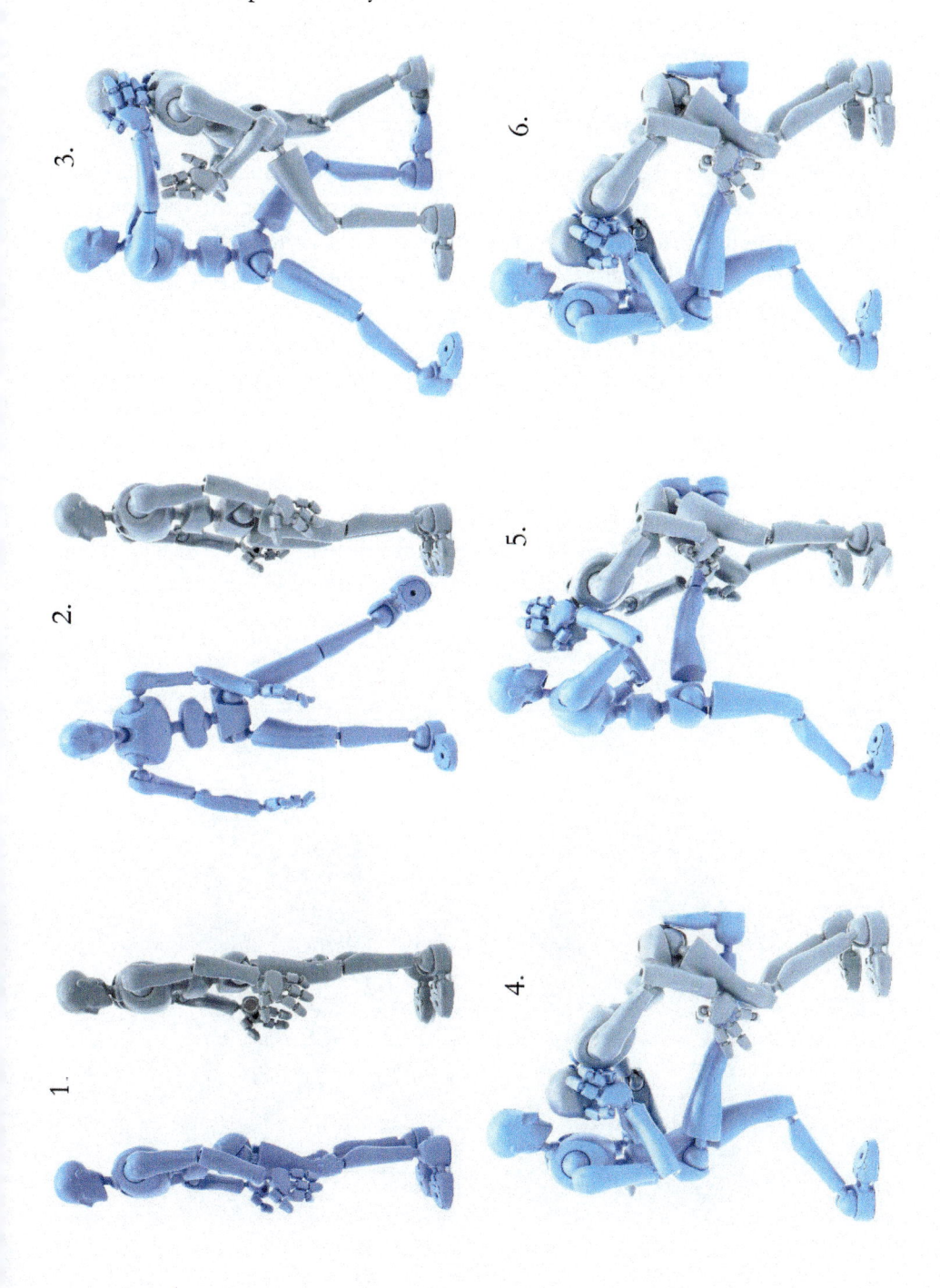

<u>Drill 4A</u>
Mind Set - **Wanting to press pause** so you can 'left brain' think
Your Starting Position - **Standing**
Angle of Attack - **Back**
Body Posture - **Orange Flinch**

A pre-emptive strike, a green response or a yellow flinch response are unlikely actions for this situation. Unless you're in the octagon competing in MMA, it's highly unlikely you'll be aware this attack is coming and be prepared for it. The yellow flinch will be overridden by your instincts to grab whatever is constricting around your throat or covering your mouth.

You need an entry technique, the 'way in' to get to the position where you can strike the target because your movements will be restricted by the arm across your throat or mouth. Even though you've been grabbed around the neck, you will still be able to move your hips and legs, so stamping backwards towards their feet and ankles is a good option. This is how you are going to cause disruption, attempting to get them to open that little bit of space between their body and yours, creating the half a metre gap that you started with when familiarising yourself with the movements on a stationary and compliant drill partner. The half a metre you will need to be able to turn and get to the target. You will use your stamp and shuffle technique.

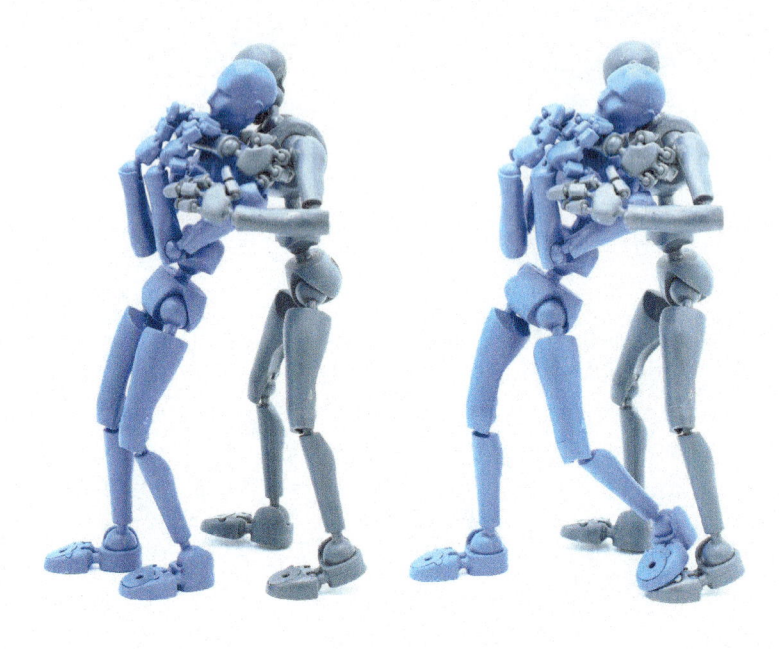

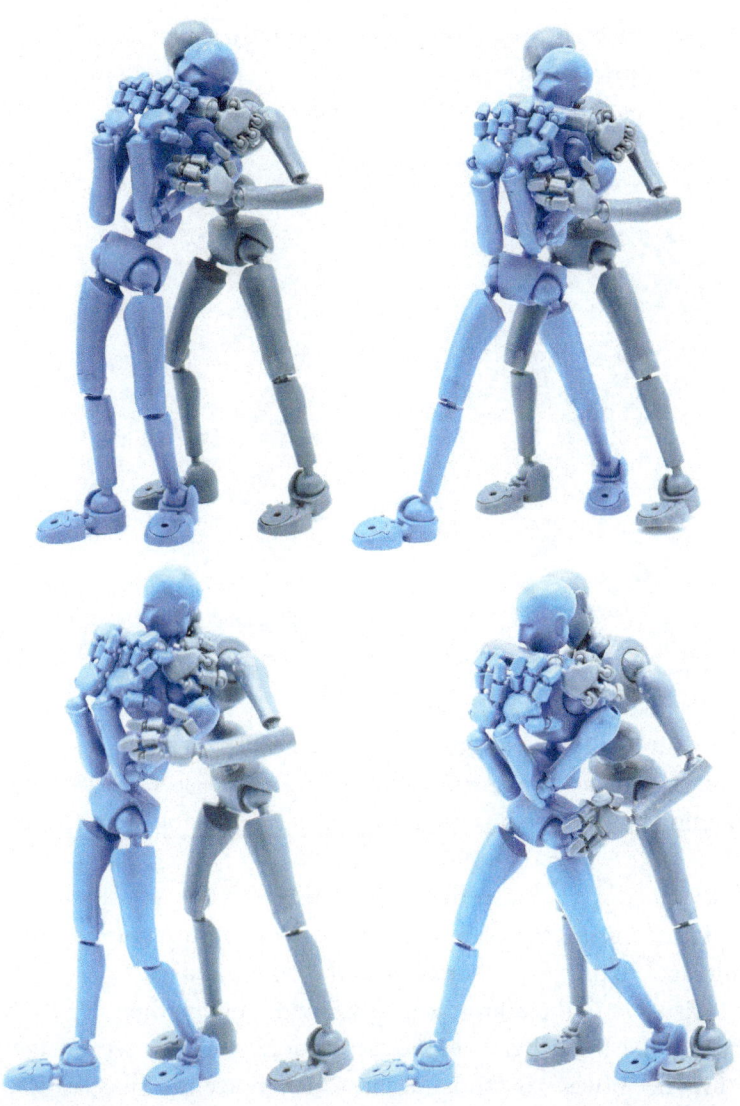

It's important here that you shuffle and stamp rather than alternating with your legs, because if you alternate you will be swinging the person who is behind you from side to side as your torso twists, which is how your body moves when using alternate legs to stamp. This isn't ideal because you will be competing against their bodyweight.

By using one foot for causing the damage, you will also decrease the time you are standing on one leg, because the closest foot to the aggressor will be the one moving each time, rather than a big backwards step using the front foot. By using the same foot to stamp, you will be dropping bombs to the same area which will help to increase the gap between your hips and the aggressors hips because they will need to move their legs to avoid your attack. You can always throw in a few elbows to the face before turning, and as you turn, then proceed to grabbing the eyes.

If you attempt to turn without disrupting their base, then you will feel their grip tighten as you turn inwards. *The backwards stamping is the all-important entry technique*, getting you to the position where you will be able to strike the targets of Drill 4.

If attacked in this way, you may have a mini- freeze, and the way to jump start the system is using the stamping on the foot to burn some hormones and jolt you into action, dragging yourself into the right mindset.

Fancy twists with their arm, squatting and pulling their leg so they fall backwards, and all the other complicated options you can see on the internet are great for the movies, but not the best idea to try in this situation. Stamp, make a gap, throw an elbow, and turn and get your thumbs into their eyes.

As a sidenote, it's not ideal to use your head flying backwards towards their face, because you might injure the top of your head on their chin or forehead if things don't go to plan, but it might be your only option because of how they've grabbed you, so it shouldn't be ruled out, just don't have it as your go to default action.

A Punch!

Don't stand still! Don't wait to see what attack they're preparing to launch. Pay attention to their body language, do they have a clenched fist, is their weight loaded onto one side ready for them to punch? Has one of their shoulders drawn back, showing they are winding up ready?

Rather than wait to see if it's a jab, a haymaker, a hook, or an uppercut, get moving. Move off the spot and disrupt how they are transitioning their mass ready to launch an attack. If you do this, the principles from the attempted grab of Drill 1 will apply here. But to give you additional choice and to expand your knowledge and skill base, here is a different option.

Solutions to Physical Threats Drill 5 - A Punch

Drill 5 with your compliant drill partner is:

a) Step forwards with your left leg and simultaneously drive the right forearm into the shoulder and Vagus nerve. Let your left arm track the movement of your right arm as it moves.

b) Step with your right leg and right forearm to the Vagus Nerve. Step forwards with your left leg and simultaneously drive the right forearm into the Vagus nerve.

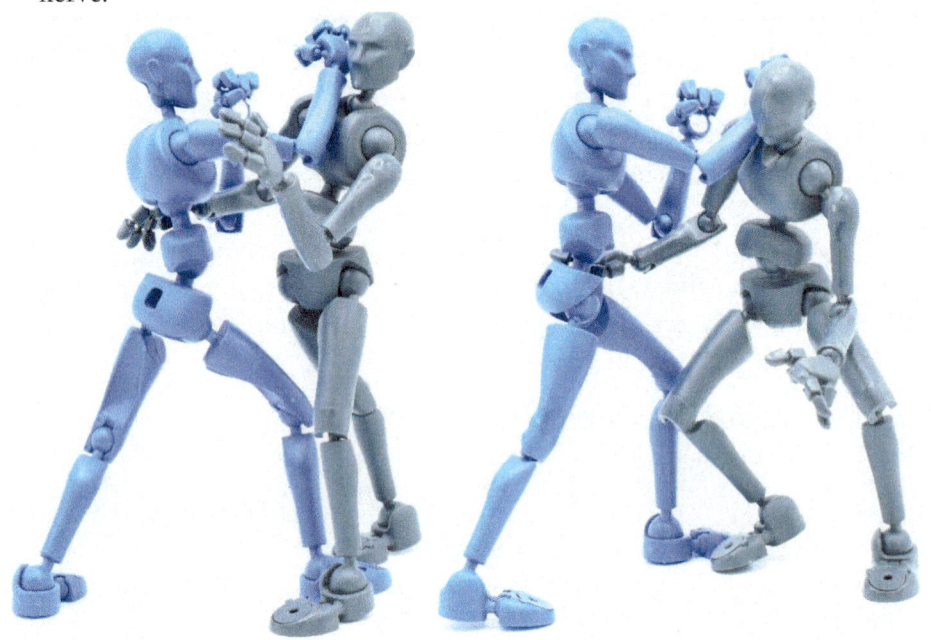

c) Stamp down through the ankle with your right heel.

d) Kick to the groin with your left leg, this will cause them to bend forwards. Drive your right knee into the jaw and Vagus nerve area, which has now entered the target field of vision.

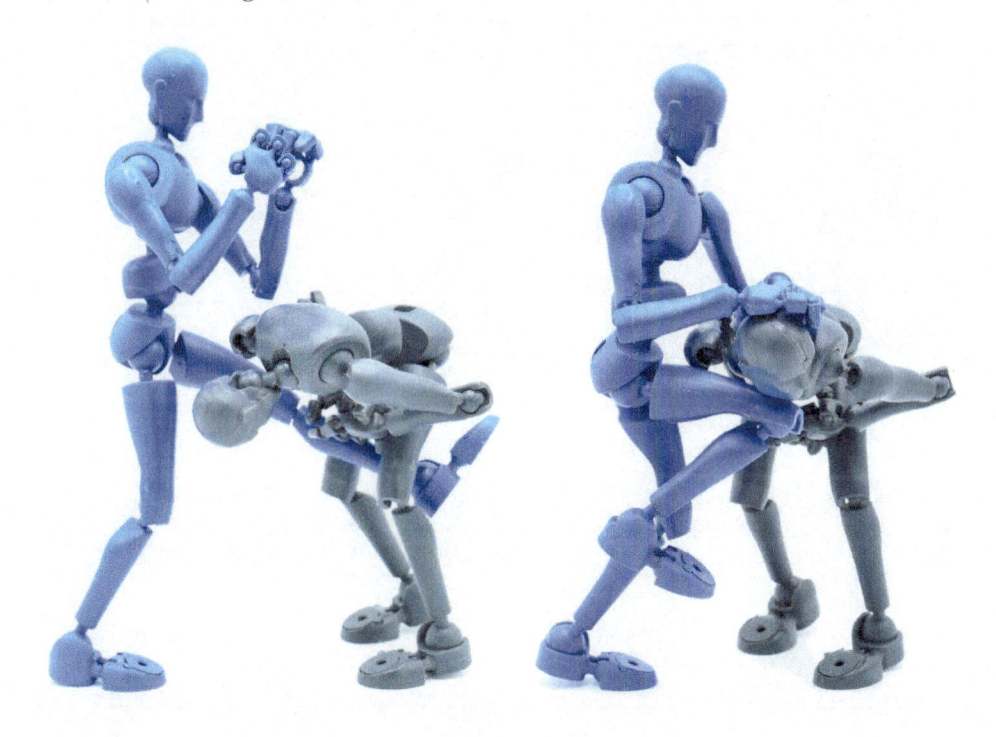

Drill 5A

Mindset - **Aware and Engaged**, a target has been selected, and action is taking place
Your Starting Position - **Standing**
Angle of Attack - **Front**
Body Posture - **A Pre-emptive Target Strike**

You're drill partner will stand at a distance of around 5 metres away, and they will start walking towards you displaying one or more postural signs they are winding up for a punch. If you get moving off the spot in your arc, then Drill 1 becomes a valid option as soon as your palm hits their face and prevents the punch from launching.

You're aware of an impending attack and you move off the spot:
a) Move off the line with your left foot. If you use your right it doesn't really matter, but to keep a consistent pattern for the data load try to stick with the left foot moving first. Take an extra step with your right foot.

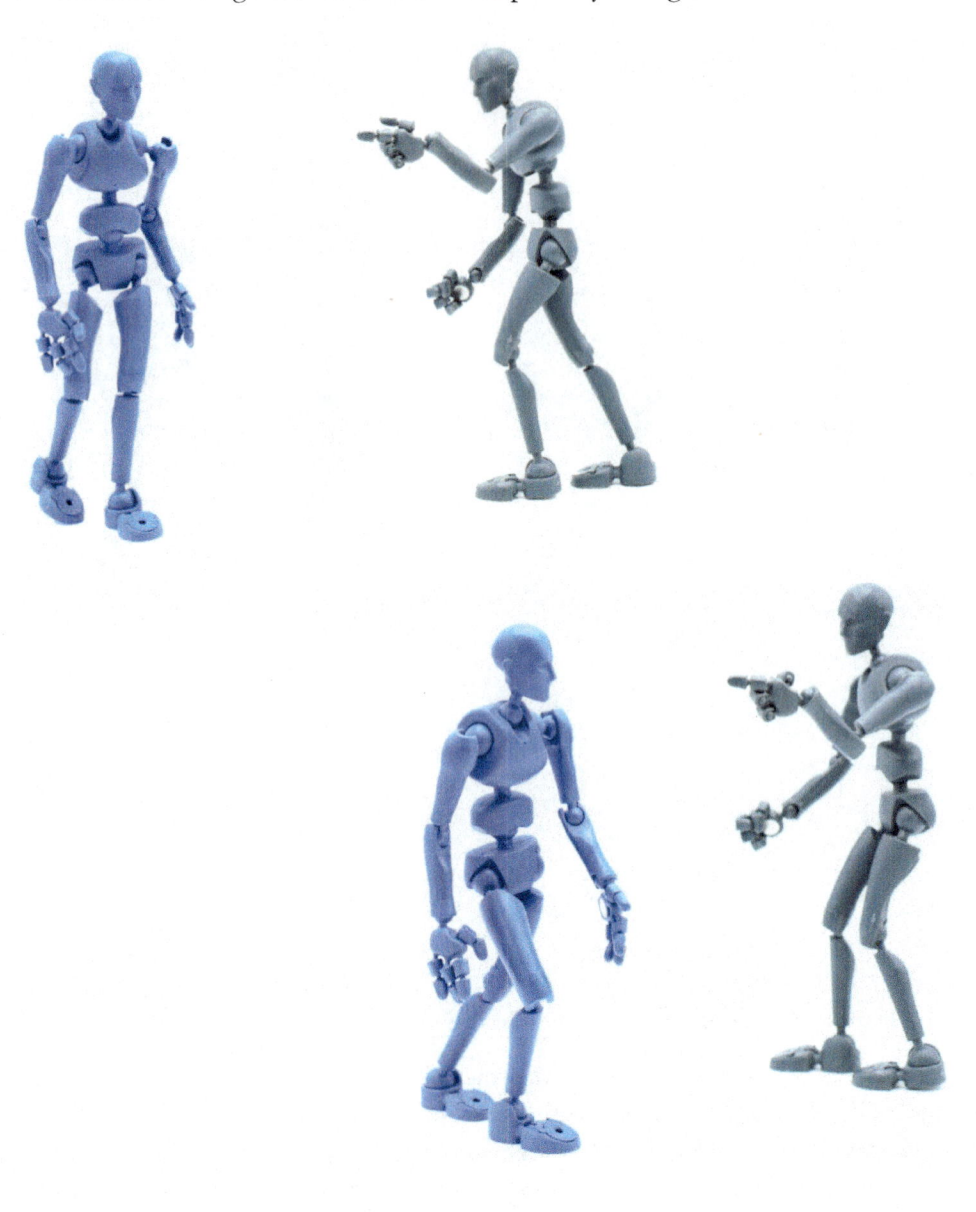

b) Drive towards them with your left leg, thrusting your left hand into their face, fingers curled and hoping for some contact with the eyes, then leave.

c) If leaving isn't and option, here is the full pattern for you.

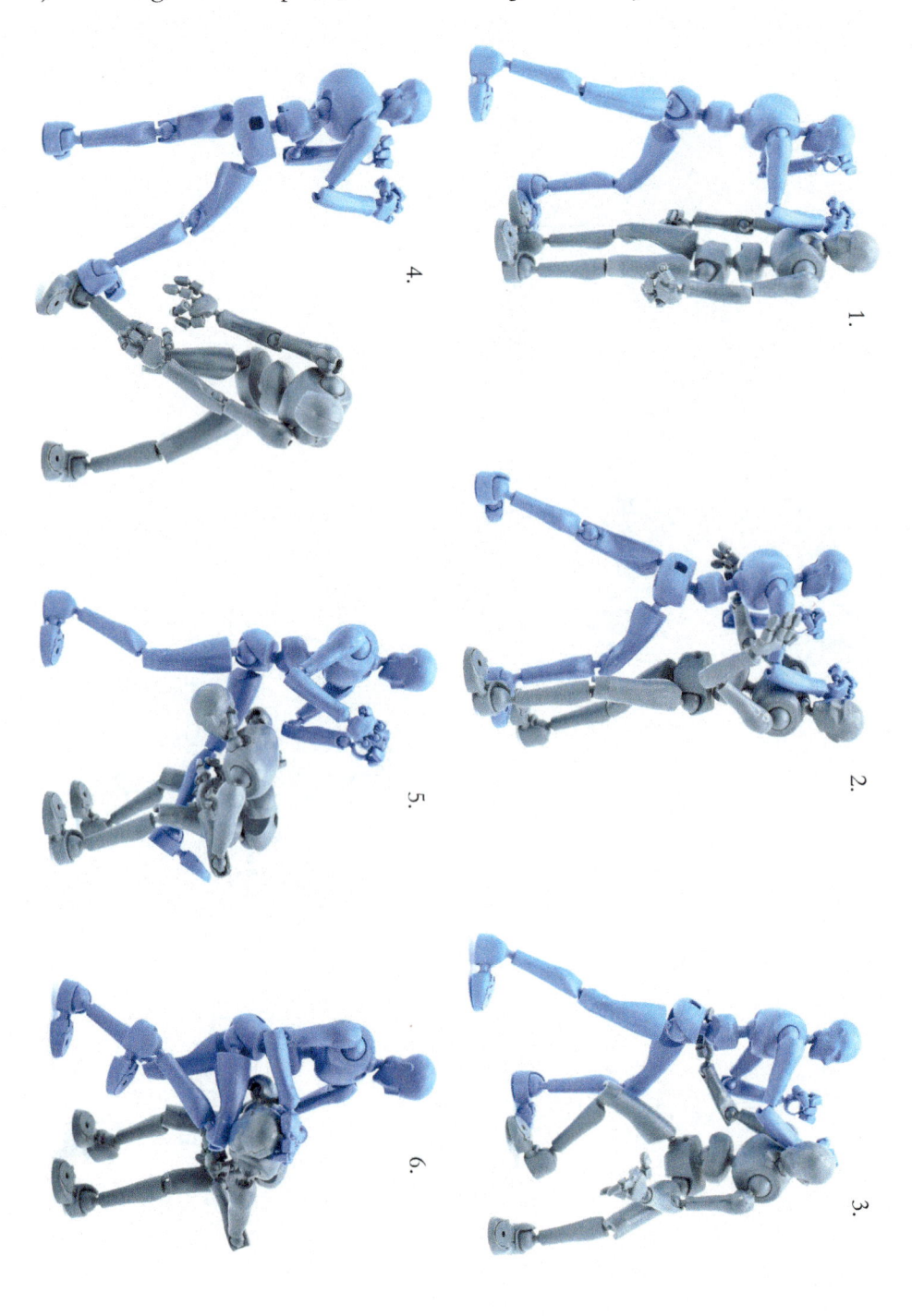

286

Drill 5B

Mindset - **Aware and Engaged** and moving off the spot
Your Starting Position - **Standing**
Angle of Attack - **Front**
Body Posture - **A Green Response – GO!**

On the way towards the aggressor, you see their arm drawing back ready for launching a punch. You perform an aggressive action by striking towards the area the punch will come from, not waiting for the punch.

a) You drive forwards, hitting their arm with your left forearm as the punch is thrown. But your main focus is landing your bodyweight on their upper torso, driving into the clavicle area. This will take the steam out of their attack and the power away from the punch as it halts their momentum. This is not a block, this is driving into the general area of the arm not waiting to meet it.

b) At this stage, there may be a chance to slide past them and leave, but if this is not an option use the steps in Drill 5.

Explore this on both sides, the drill partner will change the arm they use to punch, but you will keep moving towards the left hand side. This isn't to get you to stay with a set plan of attack, but to illustrate it doesn't matter which arm they punch with, if you get moving you can attack the punching or non-punching side. You can step to either side and they can punch with either arm. Regardless of the combination of movements, you will be able to hit the target zones. You don't need to wait to see which arm is punching and corelate the response.

Drill 5C, D, E & F

Yellow, orange, red or black flinch responses will be the same as in the previous drills. You will immediately start to clear some space using either your arms crashing towards their face, or if you have grabbed hold of them, use your feet to do the 1, 2, 3. After your flinch and clearing space option, you can implement Drill 5, repeating this enough to get the data load.

Then you can start to mix things up and use any of the previous drills, so your drill partner has no idea what response is coming their way, but move slowly to keep them safe. Changing the drill responses will build your confidence in the system. You don't have to treat it as a game of pairs, matching one answer to one type of attack.

Grabbing a fast moving arm isn't something you would choose to do, but you need to prepare the possibility of the instinctive orange flinch reaching out and grabbing the arm which is moving at speed towards you. Remember this instinctive grab can bring its own problems, because there is always the chance you may dislocate your thumbs grabbing a fast moving attack. Which is why Drill 5 is ideal for a punch, because the drill focuses on striking targets when you are unable to make a fist, or drive a thumb into the eye, or grab hold of them. It's structured to consist only of forearm smashes and using your legs.

A knife!

The 3 main principles when facing an attack with a weapon are:
- Disarm - taking away their ability to use a weapon to injure you, or taking the weapon away from them
- Retain - secure the weapon so it cannot be picked up and used by anyone else
- Use/or not use the weapon - whatever you deem the situation justifies

The first principle of disarm doesn't necessarily mean to take the weapon out of the aggressors hands, it means to take away their ability to use that weapon. For example, if you secure the hand holding a knife and follow this by breaking the aggressors ankle, it doesn't matter if the knife is still in their hand. You will be trapping the knife which is the retain principle, and preventing anyone else from using it. At this point you can push the knife towards the aggressor or any accomplices who may be present. Or refrain from using the weapon, it's your choice, as always.

Solutions to Physical Threats Drill 6 - A knife attack, Hitchcock Psycho style

A knife coming at you from over the top, plunging towards your face, neck, and upper torso is one of the most common knife attacks. Obviously use a rubber training weapon when practicing this drill and don't use anything which will cause injury.

a) With your stationary and compliant drill partner, grab hold of their weapon arm with your left arm, trapping their arm underneath your elbow and holding it tightly against your body. Hold tightly onto their arm with your left hand, really secure this against your body so when they pull their arm back, and they will, they may pull your whole body forwards, but their arm doesn't move away from you.

b) Your right arm reaches over the top of their arm and you use this to help in clamping their arm onto your body. It's all about fixing that arm, it doesn't matter if the knife is still in their hand if they are unable to move the arm to use it.

c) Stamp through their ankle with your front leg.

d) Bring your back foot up to meet the front foot and use your right heel to again stamp through their ankle, repeat this action another time.

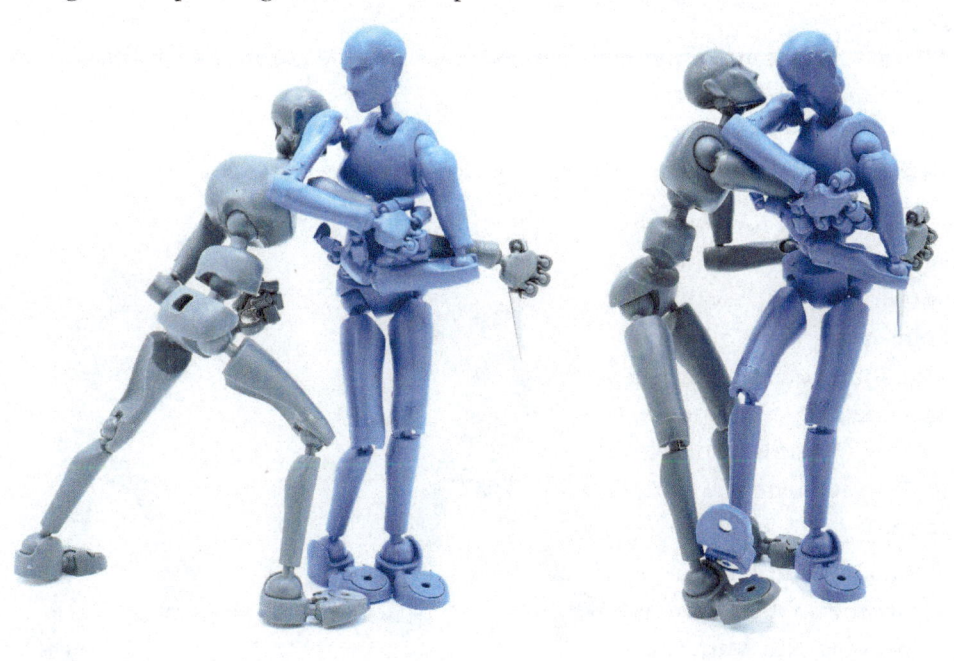

e) Step with your right leg and strike the Vagus nerve with your right elbow, then immediately return your right arm back to clamping down on their arm. Repeat this step and strike to the Vagus nerve three times, each time bringing the back leg up to meet the front leg before stepping forwards. This helps to maintain a good structure and balance.

<u>Drill 6A</u>
Mindset - **Aware and Engaged**, a target's selected, and action is taking place
Your Starting Position - **Standing**
Angle of Attack - **Front**
Body Posture - **A Pre-emptive Target Strike & A Green Response – GO**

On the way towards the aggressor, you see their arm drawing back with the knife ready to be plunged into you. You perform an aggressive response, striking towards the area the arm stabbing will come from.

a) Get off the line, move off the spot as soon as possible and start your arc.

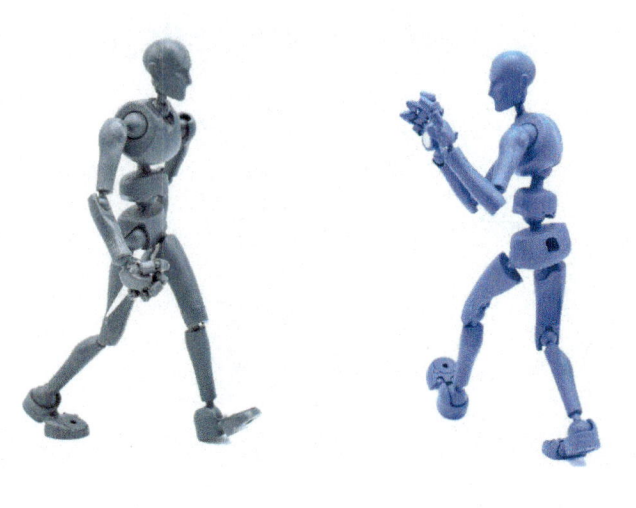

b) Draw them towards you by moving in your circle, this will make the angle of the knife attack more predictable for you.

c) Step forwards with your left leg, smashing down onto the arm and the torso, preventing the knife plunging into you.

d) Now immediately grab it, get over the top of their arm with your left arm and hold it against your body. Use your right arm over the top to assist in securing this threat against your body so they are unable to retract their arm and attempt to stab you again. Move straight into Drill 6.

Don't assume they will drop the knife when you strike their arm or hit targets, because sometimes a person will tape the weapon to their hands and wrists. Highlighting how simultaneously striking both sides of a person's arm to cause them to drop the weapon isn't covering all the bases of reality.

Here is the complete pattern for you:

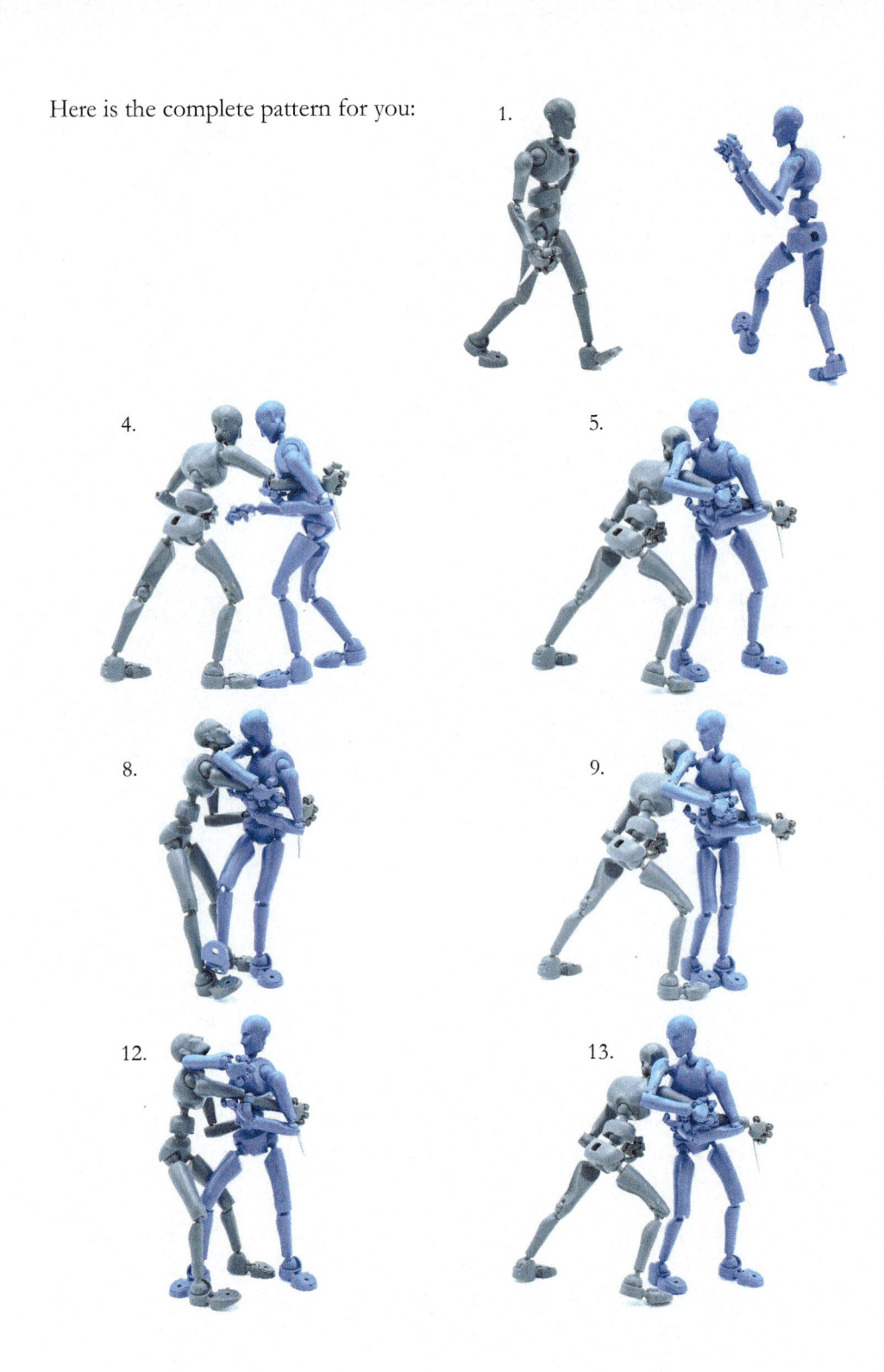

1.

4. 5.

8. 9.

12. 13.

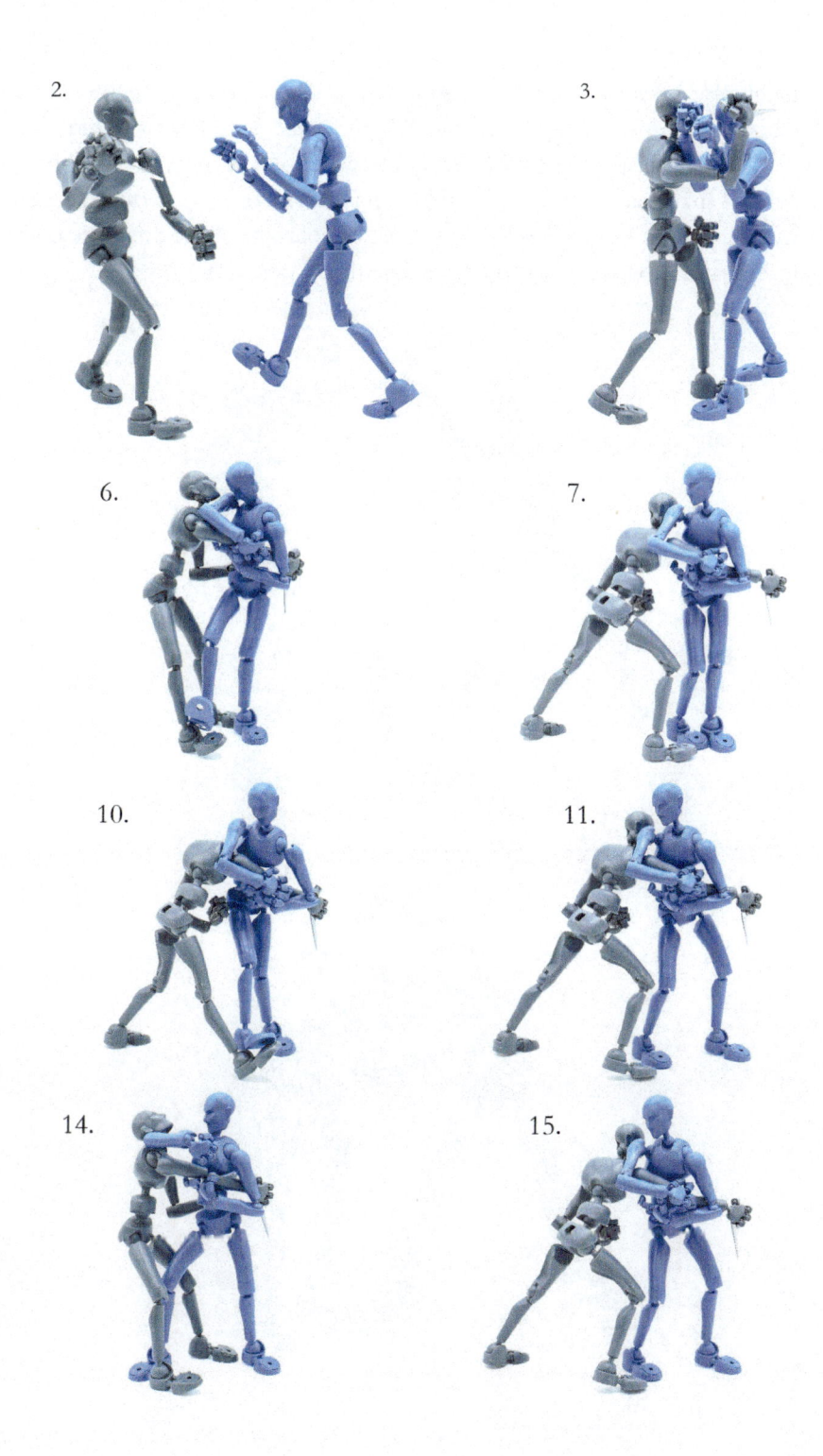

2.

3.

6.

7.

10.

11.

14.

15.

295

If caught by surprise by a knife and find yourself doing a yellow evasive flinch, this will immediately be followed by an orange flinch or a red flinch because you will desperately want to grab hold of the arm to restrict the movement of the weapon and to try and keep it away from you. For this reason, you will replicate the yellow flinch with your drill partner when the knife comes towards you, and move straight to the orange flinch position.

Get your right arm over the top of their weapon arm, stepping as you do this and pinning their arm against your body. Use drill 6 to eliminate the threat.

Once comfortable with this, move onto the yellow flinch followed by a red flinch. Again get your right arm over the top of their left weapon arm and pin it against your body. Use drill 6 to eliminate the threat.

Using your forearms and elbows to clamp their knife wielding arm against your body is specifically designed to avoid relying on your grip strength and ability to grip, because using your hand strength alone may not be enough.

If you've performed a yellow flinch, it's likely you will have defence wounds on your hands or forearms. These occur when you use your arms for shielding the vulnerable parts of your body from the knife attack. If this has happened, your hands will be slippery due to blood coming from the cuts to your hands and forearms, and this is one reason why you use the whole arm structure to pin their arm to your body and not grab their arm with your hands. You might lose your grip.

Solutions to Physical Threats Drill 7 – Knife pressed on your neck

The things I have seen other people teach, which will get you killed:

- Inconceivably, grabbing the knife! The instructions given were to grab the knife and twist it, using it as a lever. If you do this, they will pull the knife away from you and slice your hands.
- Knock the arm with the knife across your throat away from your neck or throat, which means you're basically slicing your neck, it's ludicrous.
- Simultaneously hit the outside and inside of their arm so the knife flies out of their hand, the least said about this approach the better, as this has already been highlighted as an issue if they have taped the weapon to their hands, and actually pulling this move off successfully under stress is a big risk.

<u>Drill 7A</u>
Mindset - **Aware and Engaged** and moving off the spot
Your Starting Position - **Standing**
Angle of Attack - **Front**
Body Posture - **A Green Response – GO!**

a) You're going to trap the hand holding the knife onto your body, nothing fancy, just a blind panic trapping of their arm to prevent them from moving the knife.

Throw a ball into a room of children and announce whoever had the ball after one minute wins some chocolate, and the winner, when they emerge from the bottom of the pile would be clutching the ball into their chest and clamping it with both arms.

This in essence is what you are going to do, hold the threat in the most structurally secure position you can. At first, this seems both alien and disconcerting, because you will want to get rid of the knife, you want the danger to go away. Even though it seems counter-intuitive to keep the knife close to you, it's the better option, because if you push it away they will thrust it straight back at you.

Your hands will instinctively raise and you will turn your face away from the knife, which is fantastic, as it creates a little bit of room to manoeuvre. You will bring both of your arms over the top of their arm, and pull down and into your body. Not down in front of you, because this will cause a loss of control over the arm with the weapon. The pressure is slightly down but mainly inwards, as though holding onto that ball to win some chocolate, pulling their wrist into you. At this point they may be able to push or pull with their arm, and you may be moved around as they do this, but that hand and knife will stay put, stuck to your body!

A closer look at the grab and pull down with an overhead view of trapping the arm against the body to get the knife off your neck:

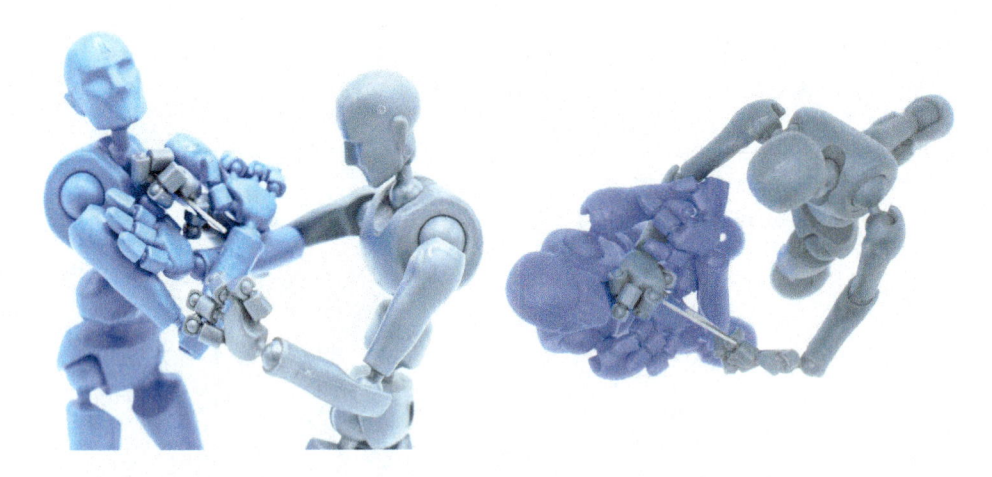

b) To maximise the impact of this trapping movement, as your arms come down onto their arm, you will step across yourself and twist your torso. It doesn't matter which way you turn, you will simply see different targets, but you will naturally be inclined to turn away from the threat of the knife.

Their primary concern will be getting that knife back! With their arm (weapon) secure and trapped against your body, your next move is stamping through their ankle to break their structure, taking away the ability to generate the power needed to pull or push the knife wielding arm. Breaking the structure will also restrict their ability to launch any other attacks such as punching you with their other hand or smashing their head into your face.

If they try and pull their arm away whilst you have one foot off the ground to do a big kick, it could end in trouble for you, because your balance is compromised and for this reason you will do the shuffle step. Bringing the back leg up to meet the front leg and then stamping with the front foot, limiting the amount of time you have one foot off the ground.

c) You shuffle step and stamp again, keeping your feet low and driving through the ankle rather than lifting your foot high off the ground.

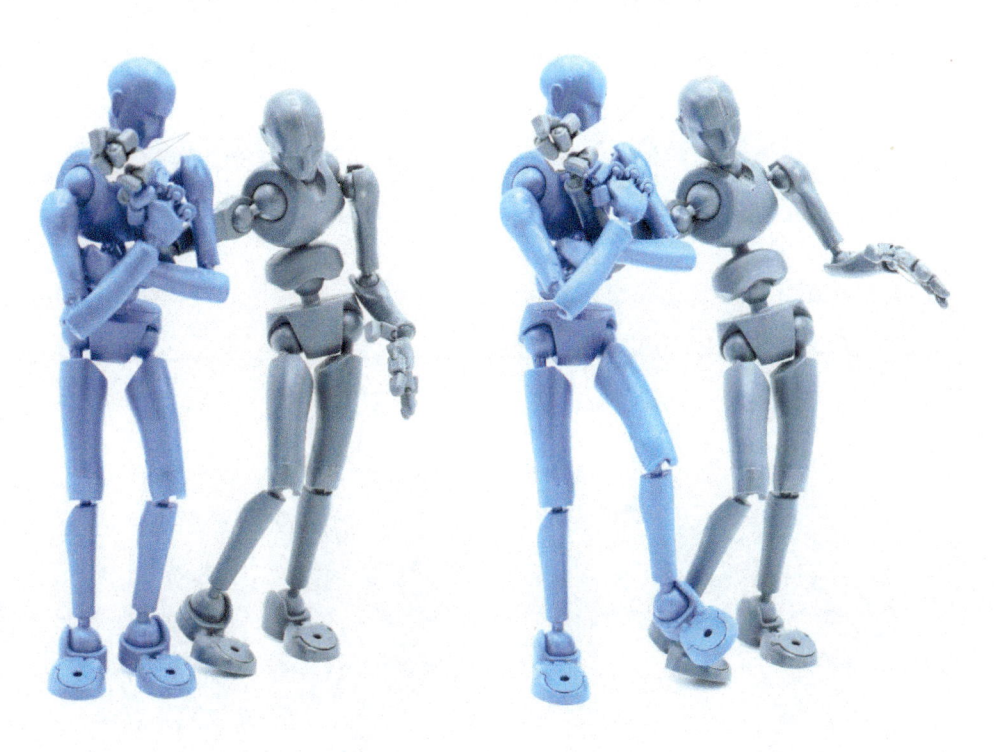

d) Shuffle step and stamp to the knee, disrupting their base by either causing structural damage or flinch responses from the aggressor.

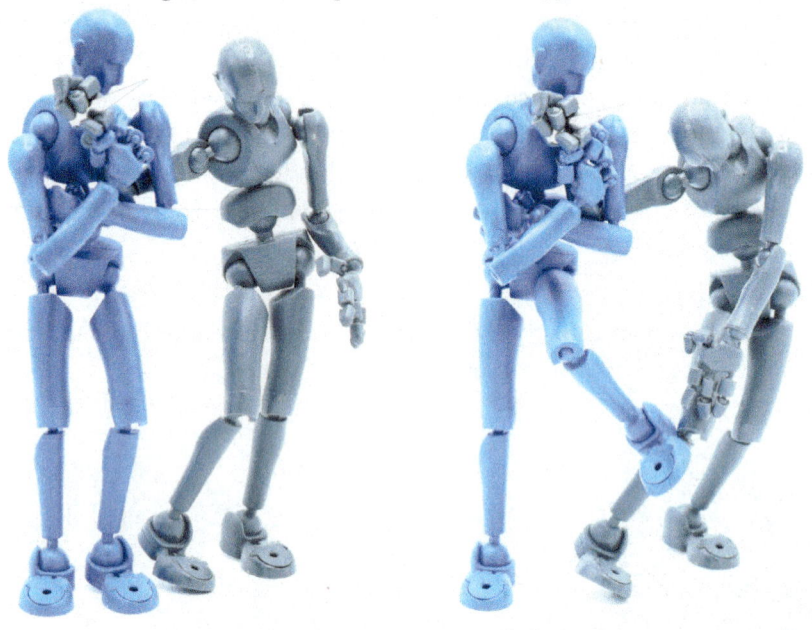

e) Turn towards them, twisting your torso and facing the aggressor, let your hands slide towards their wrist to control it, but still using your elbow and forearm to trap their arm. Twist the knife towards them, then kick the groin.

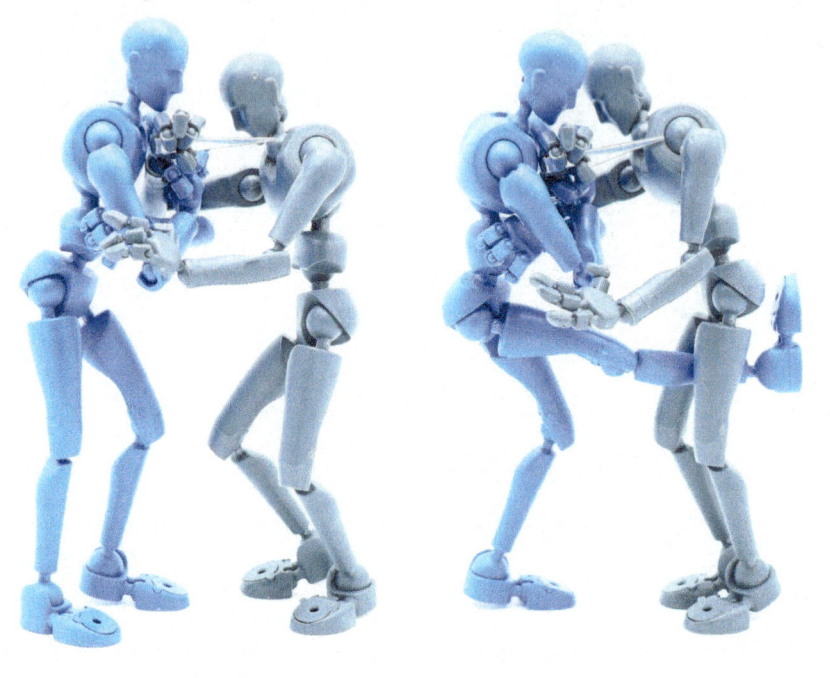

This situation will not have a pre-emptive strike because the knife is already pressed against your body. A yellow flinch is unlikely to occur because the threat isn't moving at speed towards you, it's static and already on your throat. A more likely flinch will be an orange flinch, grabbing the arm and attempting to push it away from you, not through choice but instinct.

At this Orange Flinch stage you will instinctively want to get your elbow over the top of their arm and trap it against your body, which will enable you to implement Drill 7 or even Drill 6. This will happen naturally through familiarity of what feels right, not having to think about it and find the corresponding response.

As with all these drills, they can be mixed and matched into what feels right at the time, this isn't a system of thought and pairing responses with attacks, the various drill solutions are interchangeable between different attacks.

Solutions to Physical Threats Drill 8 - A knife thrust at your stomach

No pre-emptive strike solution is included here, because people don't tend to telegraph this attack, this will at best, be a green response.

Drill 8A
Mindset - **Aware and Engaged** and moving off the spot
Your Starting Position - **Standing**
Angle of Attack - **Front**
Body Posture - **A Green Response – GO!**

a) Step to the side of the thrusting arm and smash down with both arms onto it as it comes towards you. It doesn't matter if you are on the inside or the outside of the arm

b) Expect them to draw the arm back in preparation to thrust again, so push off your back leg to leap forwards and smash the arm again as it draws backwards.

c) Now slide and hit repeatedly until the arm is knocked backwards back behind their hip.

d) Pounce onto their arm, getting your elbow over the top of it and clamping it into your torso.

e) As soon as you can feel you have disrupted their base and taken dominance of the situation, you will be able to implement Drill 6 or 7.

If caught by surprise, upon seeing the knife hurtling towards your guts, you will do an avoidance flinch, trying to swat away the arm coming at you. This will be followed by an orange or red flinch to stop that weapon slashing and thrusting all over the place. With your drill partner, practice the yellow flinch moving into an orange or red flinch. Follow this immediately by getting your arm over the top of their arm and implementing Drill 6 or 7.

Being Human, it's about doing the right thing.

When confident any threat to your life and any threat to your loved ones is over, you can make an educated guess the environment is safe and you can choose to switch your focus towards the aggressor's safety. I would say this would be more applicable in a home invasion situation than anywhere else, as if outside you may be exposed to further threats and you will want to get out of there immediately.

I know this may sound a little crazy, but when the threat is eliminated you can call for an ambulance to be sent along with the police. If trained in first aid you may decide to treat the injured person, *providing it's safe for you to do so*. Not providing any assistance which would enable the aggressor to be able to attack you again, but giving any emergency help needed to keep them alive whilst waiting for the medical assistance you called for.

During this time do not engage in any conversation with the person. Refrain from any interaction about the attack which took place and do not show any guilt or remorse about any injuries you have inflicted. You're only helping keep them alive if the injuries you inflicted are a threat to their life.

Looking after the organic motorhome
- *Warming up head to toe*
- *Bodyweight exercises for core strength*
- *Train like a Demolition Monkey*
- *Warming down & loosening the body*

You don't need to be strong to get your thumb into an aggressor's eye, and this section is *not* about stacking up on muscle in case you're attacked. Strength is a bonus of course, but the movements of *RBM* are designed to work without the factor of strength, because there's always the chance an aggressor will be stronger than you. The purpose of this area of information is purely to give a balanced approach to improving the condition of your organic motorhome, the one body you get for a lifetime of touring. Everybody benefits from using exercise to keep themselves moving and this can be achieved on a multitude of levels suitable for each individual.

Exercise can be used to help you keep going as long as possible, not just to make life last, but function well enough for you to enjoy your life. *RBM* isn't only focused on self-defence against a threatening person, it's self-defence against anything which threatens your life, with stress and illness falling into this remit. By increasing strength, flexibility, fitness, and co-ordination, your general health improves. The healthier the body, the more prepared it is and able to bat away the many illnesses waiting to grab hold of your immune system and give it a pasting.

There's an abundance of material on fitness training, stretching, nutrition etc. out there, and to try to cover this in detail is unrealistic, and certain elements require highly specialised knowledge. Instead *RBM* has a simple set of exercises to give a well-rounded approach to support the health levels of those who follow it. The *my style is better than yours,* debate on the topic of self-defence also occurs in the topic of exercise and there's so many different ways of moving the body it all too often leaves people confused and ultimately doing nothing, they basically have too much choice and freeze. What I suggest is you try something and see if it works *for you*, and if it does then keep doing it. If it doesn't, then change it.

Exercise is an unnatural phenomenon, our societies have developed far faster than our minds and bodies have been able to evolve, often creating an imbalance between people and their lives. When humans decided we were fed up with walking everywhere and opted to stay put and start farming, things started to change. The human diet altered significantly and as the years went past and the growth of technology took hold through industrial and electronic revolutions, less and less human physical output was needed and as the decades have passed, the daily level of physical demands for most people have diminished. Alongside the reduced level of physical exertion for most of the population in modern society, the introduction of central heating and draught free homes with double glazing is commonplace, with memories of ice on the inside of windows a thing of the past for most people. This means less fuel and energy is used by the body to stay warm when at home, impacting on the demands for calorie intake and the type of sustenance a person needs.

A luxury our ancestors didn't have, was readily available food to pick at without any calorific expense, and previously every calorie put into the body had an energy expense due to having to find it or catch it. The introduction of the fridge freezer changed this, being able to stock up with an excess of food and the frequent snacking of food readily available at your fingertips causes constant insulin spikes. Over stimulation of insulin via the pancreas brings with it heart disease and type two diabetes.

The digital age has left people mentally frazzled, the amount of data available today is staggering and the speed which information is thrust into the senses is something the human body and mind hasn't quite caught up with and adapted to yet. Our digital evolution has outpaced our neurological and emotional capacity to cope and this results in triggers of a data overload.

Exercise, by its design, is used to address these imbalances and bring with it some equilibrium. It's important when using physical movements to improve health that modern sports science information is used, but also making sure that our past isn't forgotten in the application of these physical movements. *RBM* approaches exercise with a view to achieving an increase in all round health and fitness by considering key elements which were present in our ancestors' lives. Things that when replicated through exercise, can help maintain good health for us today. The elements missing from our modern-day lives are:

1. The long, slow-paced movements of tracking animals and following the source of plant-based food as it's becoming available (this can be replaced by long duration & low intensity exercise, such as walking, slow paced cycling, or Tai Chi)
2. The patience to sit and observe your prey (replicated by meditation, or activities such as painting, knitting, crosswords)
3. The fast, frenetic chase involved in catching any of your meals which have legs (High intensity interval training HIIT)

4. The carrying of food & belongings, the building of shelters, and the manual tasks life would bring (This can be substituted by whole body weight training and core strength exercises)

Each of these facets when incorporated into your health regime will give a balanced exercise program. It will be artificial of course, as doing an hour of exercise in concentration isn't the same as completing various manual tasks throughout the day, which would have been the case in times gone by, but without reverting to that way of life you're instead aiming to replicate those demands as closely and as conveniently as possible.

As you're going to follow this without direct supervision in the room, you will need to monitor how you're performing the movements, it's important you keep yourself safe. The main guidelines are:

- If it hurts, then stop immediately,
- Don't do anything which you feel is going to aggravate any preexisting injury, or create any injury,
- Work within your limit and not anyone else's. You are training the body not the ego!

The information contained here does involve physical movement, for this reason it's important to highlight they do require some physical exertion which have the potential, however small, to cause physical injury. It's your responsibility to consult with a physician prior to starting, and regarding your suitability to participate in the RBM exercise program.

Warming up, head to toe.

Before taking part in any exercise its important to warm up to minimise the risk of injury. The purpose of warming up is moving the body in a way which gently lets the muscles know they're going to be asked to move further along their range of motion than if not taking part in exercise, and moving in a way which loads extra physical demands onto the muscles. There are some basic principles to adhere to:

- Slow and steady, the slower the better, unless indicated otherwise.
- Pay attention to how your body feels each day, you aren't a machine, your range of motion yesterday means nothing today.
- No pulsating/bouncing at the end of a moment, this can cause injury
- Remember to move in a controlled manner

The exercises for loosening the body and preparing yourself for exercise can also be used for general health and muscle maintenance. All movements are to be performed slowly and without any force. 5 repetitions for each movement is a good starting number.

<u>The Neck</u>
Moving the head slowly up and down, relax the jaw whilst doing this.

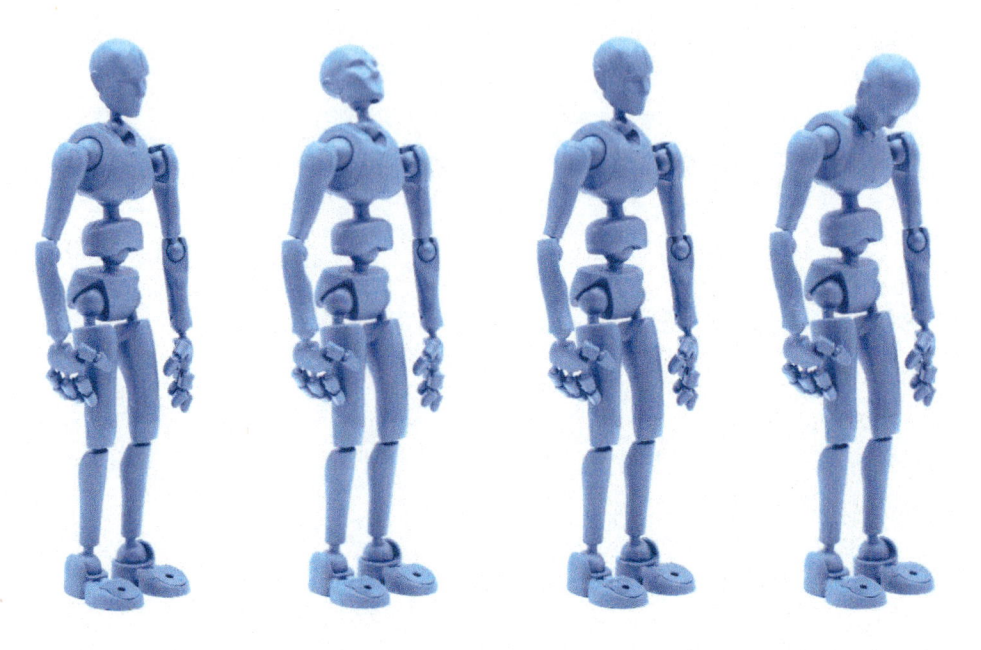

Turning the head side to side as though looking over your shoulders.

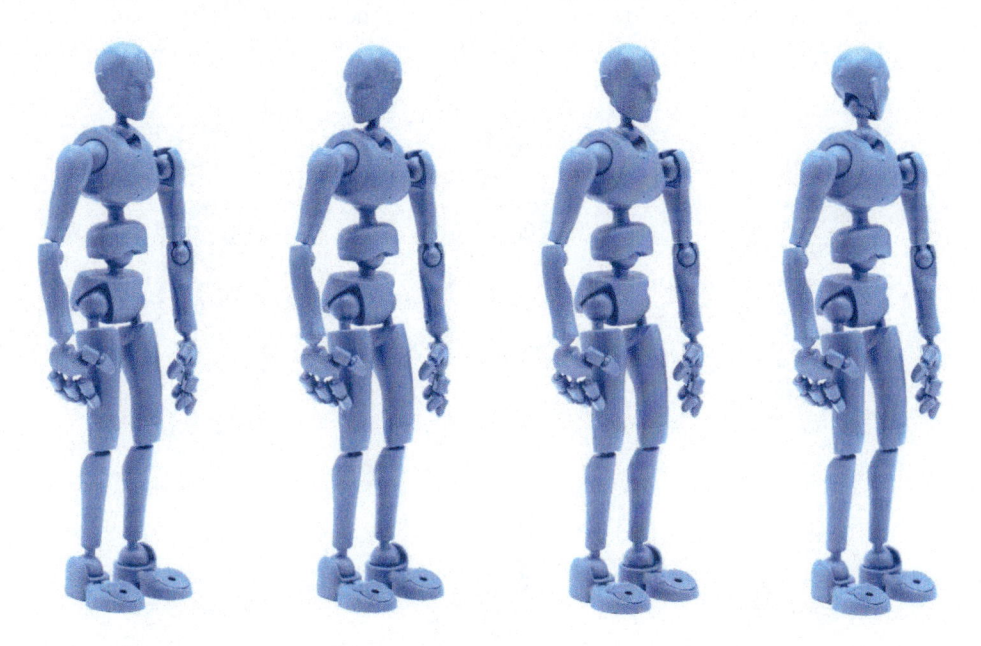

Half a circle, lowering and rolling the head from one shoulder towards the other. Relaxing and letting the weight of the head cause the movement.

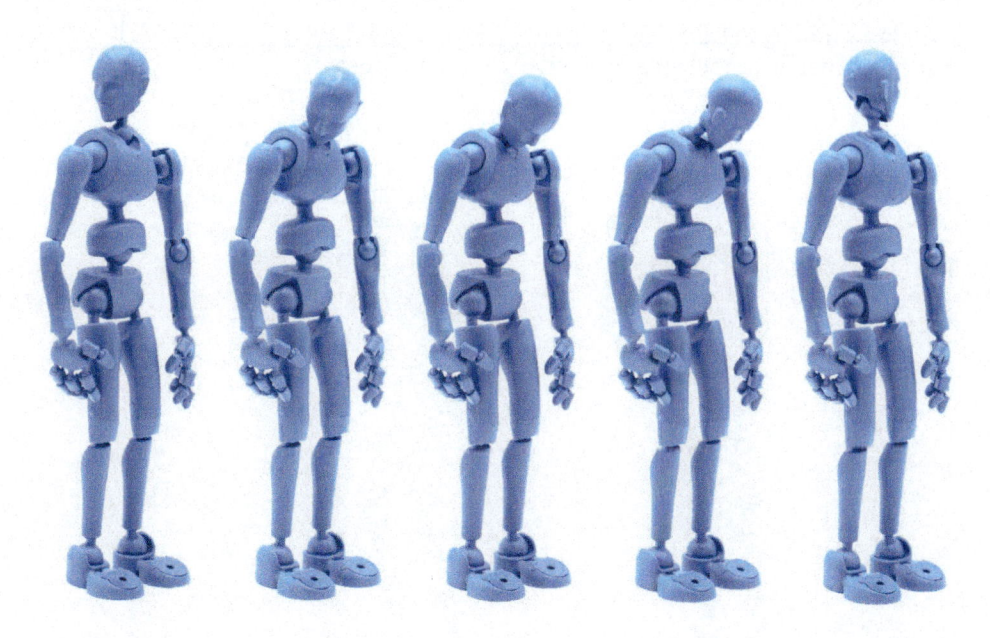

Tilting the head side to side, not dropping the head towards the shoulders, instead lifting the chin upwards towards the side and using the Atlas joint as a pivot point.

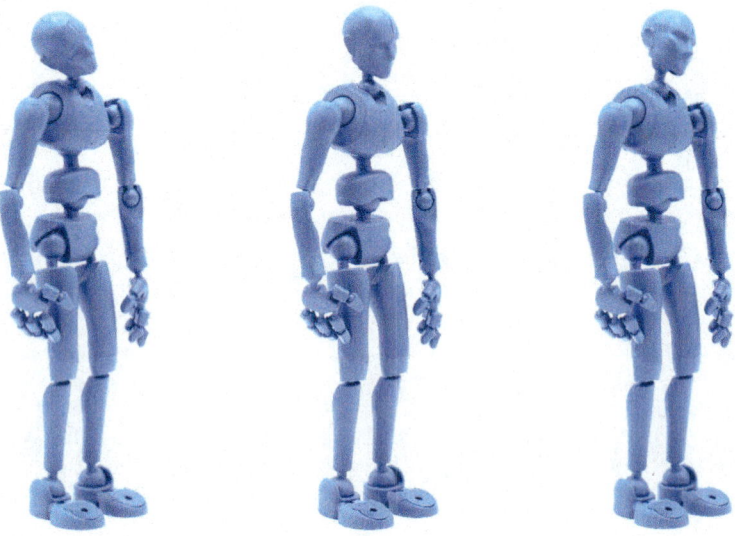

Shoulders & Scapula
Start with your palms facing inwards towards your face, lift and twist them away from you. Aim to get the back of the hands facing towards each other with your arms out straight to increase mobility of the shoulders.

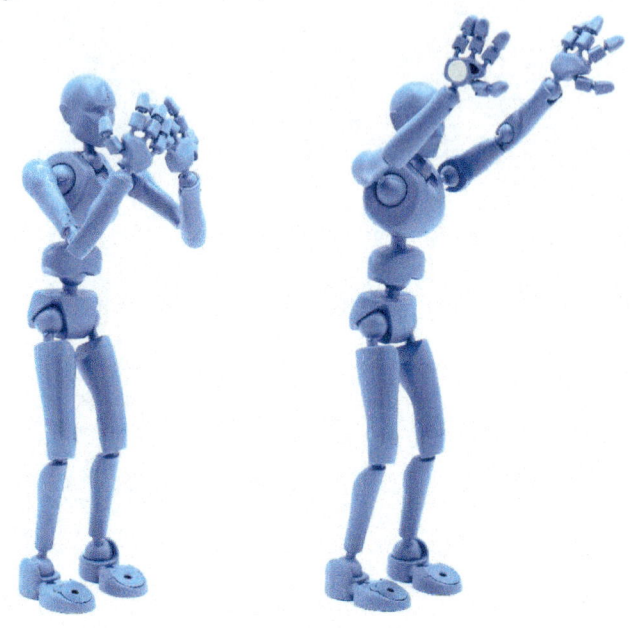

Shoulder girdle internal rotation & external rotation - slightly bend the body forwards with the knees also slightly bent. The arms are out to the side and hinged at the elbows, slowly lower the hands downwards, pressing them backwards. Follow this by lifting the hands upwards and pressing backwards. When lifting upwards avoid pressing the chest forward.

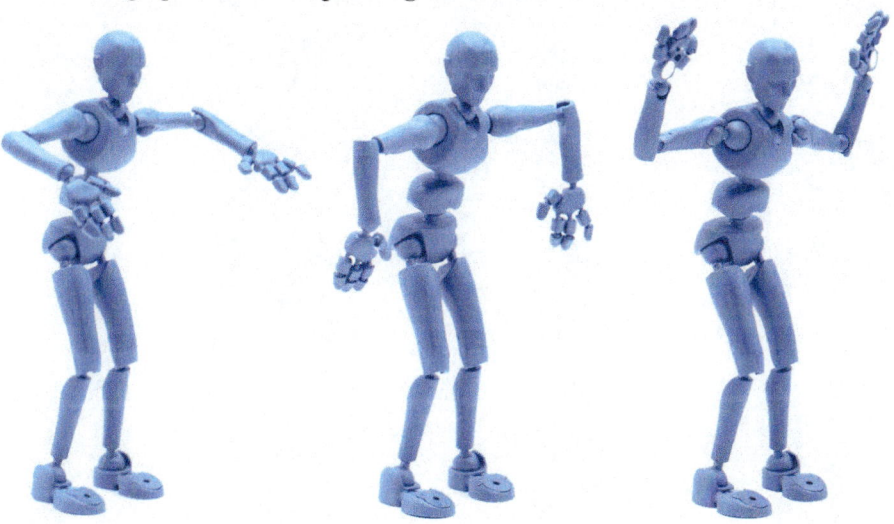

Scapula protraction and retraction - the arms are out in front of the body, with the elbows slightly bent and the thumbs touching. Open your shoulder blades (scapula) to press the arms further forwards. Then draw the shoulder blades together, pulling the arms towards you. The thumbs are touching through the whole movement.

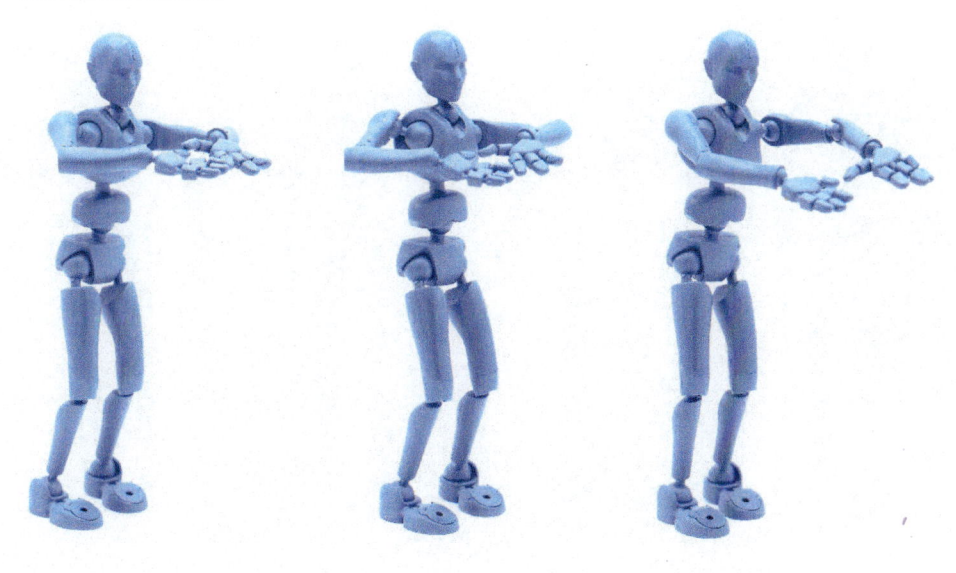

Spine

Twisting the spine - ensure the knees are slightly bent to protect the knees when you twist. Slowly and gently twist the spine side to side, aim to take your navel no more than 45 degrees each way to begin with. Avoid going past this point initially to prevent any shearing of the discs for those with any back issues

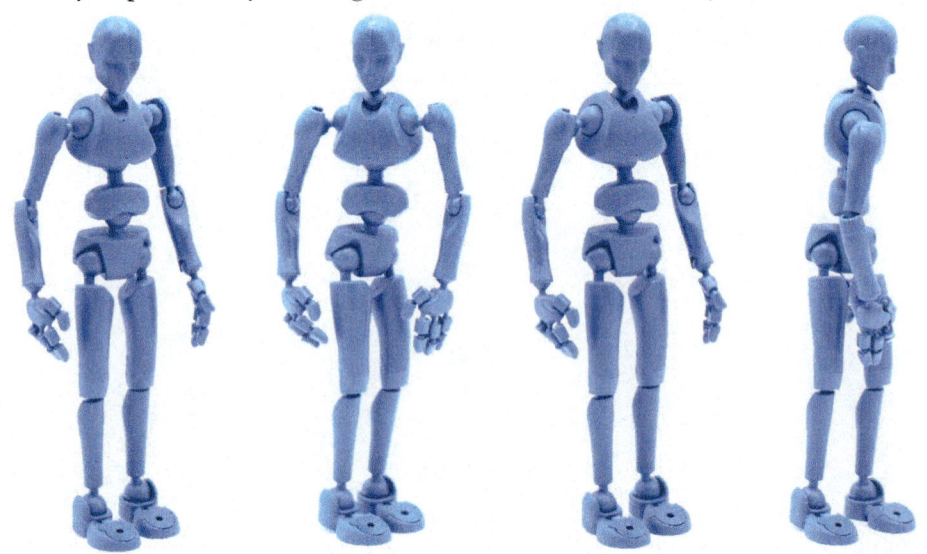

Sideways spinal movement - wave the torso from side to side as though creating a ripple down the spine, you achieve this by moving your hips. The aim is to mobilise the discs, not to reach down and stretch towards your knee, this can cause compression on the sacroiliac joint.

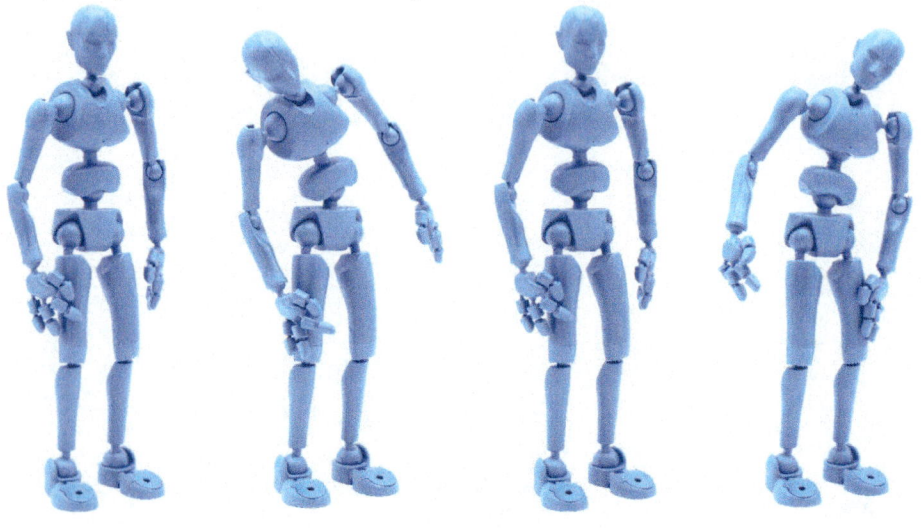

With the knees still slightly bent to prevent straining the hamstring and aggravating the Sciatic nerve, perform a roll down and roll up. As you lower down with a straight spine, look forwards to ensure the muscles are engaged and supporting the weight of the head, preventing it from overloading the lower back. Once down, you start to round the spine and stack the discs on top of each other to bring yourself upright, lifting the head at the end of the movement.

*Please note, this exercise is best avoided for those with low blood pressure.

Hips

Laying hip flexion - lay on your back on a mat or a soft surface. Focus on pressing the lower back into the ground and keeping this core muscle engagement active. Slowly lift one leg upwards and lower the leg back down to the ground. Aim for straight lines, try not to let the leg swing inwards or outwards as you lift.

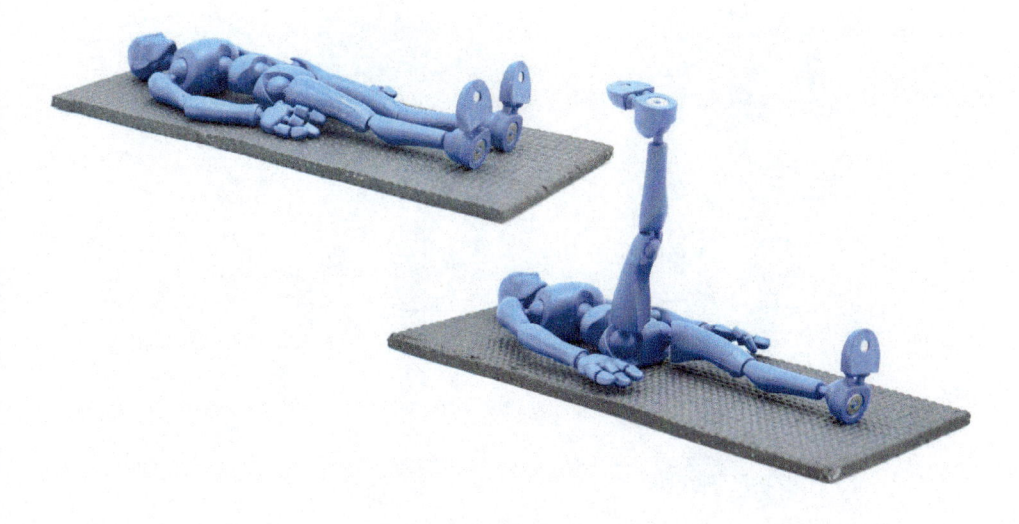

Side hip flexion – lay on one side, with the lower arm stretched straight out to the side along the ground. The top leg slides along the ground towards the outstretched hand. Resist the temptation to swing the leg here, it's a slow and controlled movement.

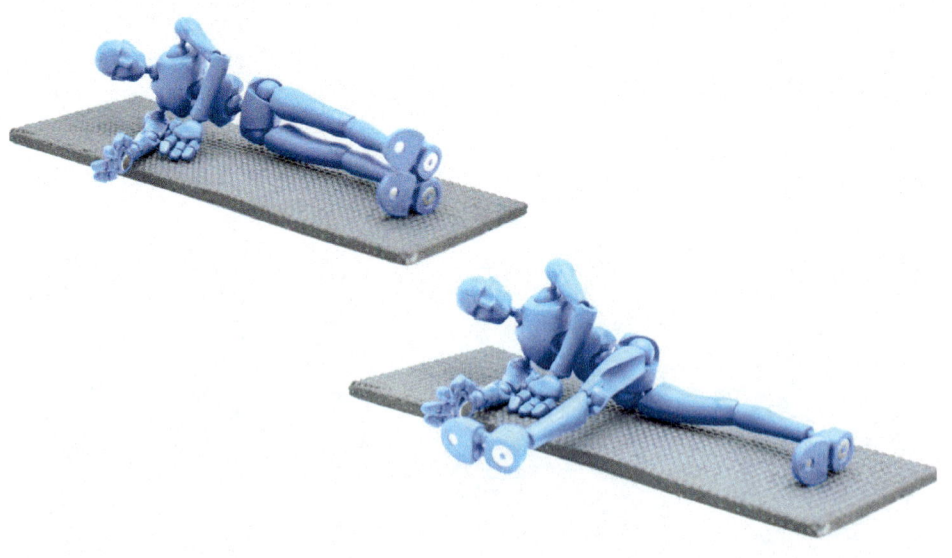

Standing sartorius isolation – turn one foot out to the side around 45 degrees. From this position, slowly lift the leg in front of the body. The knee of the standing leg stays slightly bent. You will feel this on the inside of the thigh.

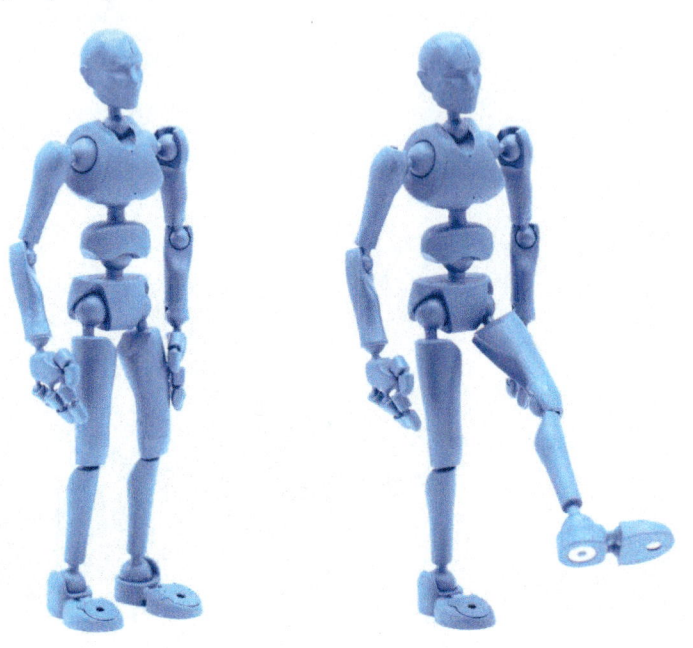

Hip hyperextension - laying on your front, bend one leg to a 90 degree ankle and lift the knee of this leg off the floor as though pressing the heel upwards. Use caution if you have any lower back compression issues.

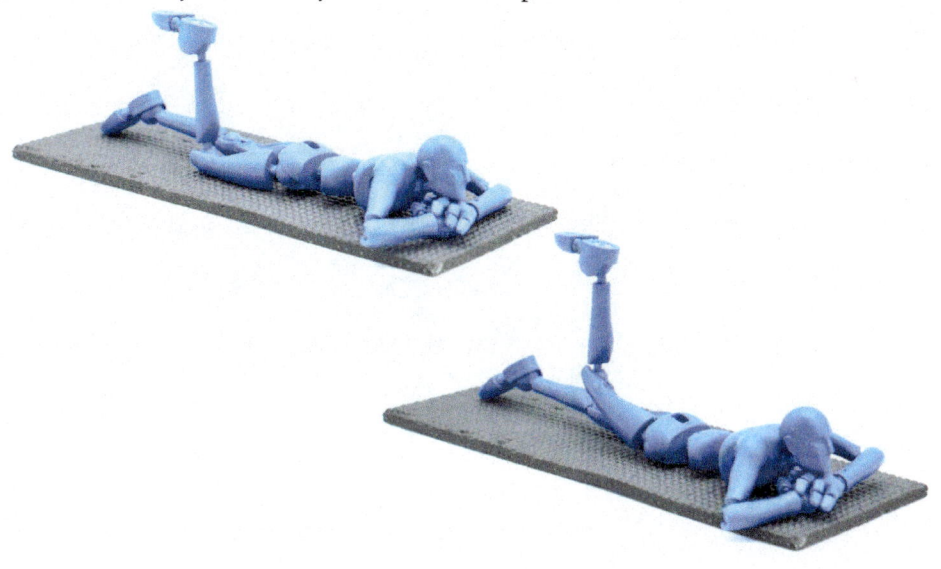

Hip abduction – laying on one side, lift the top leg upwards, pause, then return to the starting position. Avoid letting the top hip roll backwards. You're aiming for straight lines, no forwards or backwards deviation when lifting the leg.

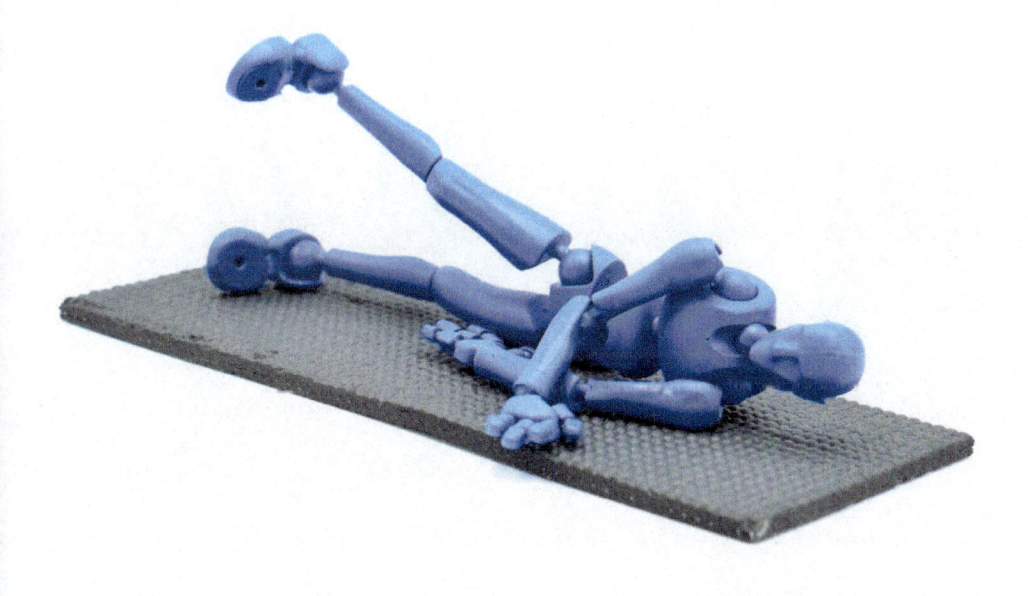

Hip adduction – Position yourself as in the previous exercise. The top leg stays up, and the lower leg is lifted to meet it. Lower the bottom leg down to the ground whilst keeping the top leg in the raised position and repeat.

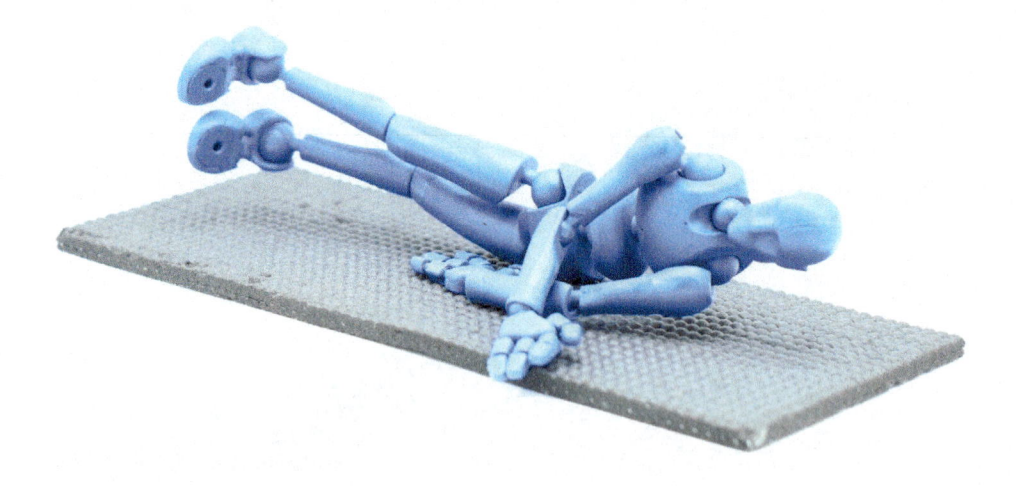

Internal & External Hip rotation – standing on one leg, bend and raise the other leg to bring the thigh parallel to the ground. Move the foot out to the side without lifting the pelvis. Return to the starting position and raise inwards.

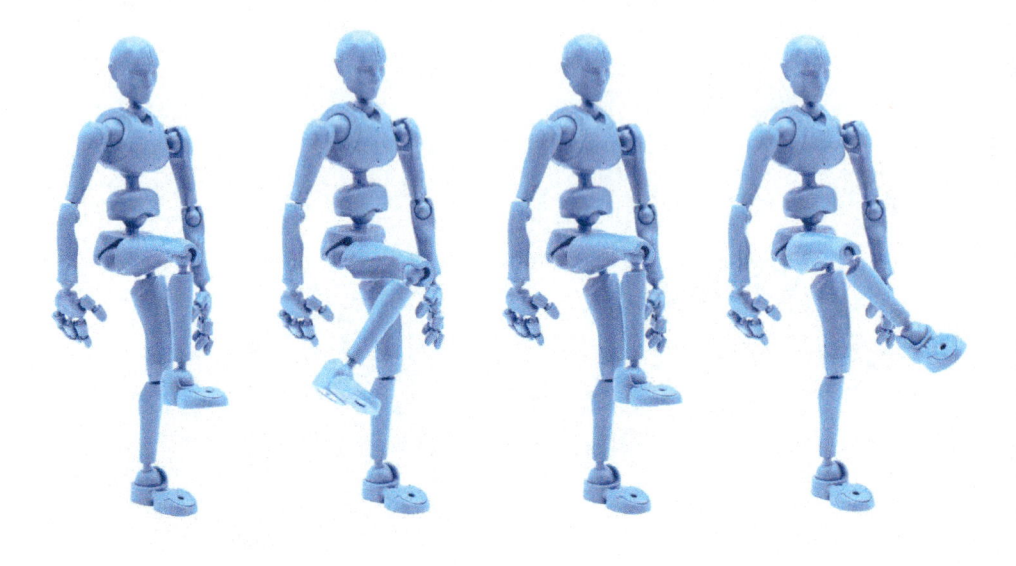

Knee

Knee extension and flexion - laying on a mat with one leg off the ground. The leg is bent to begin with, and you straighten the leg and bend it, working through the knee joint. Try not to let the thigh shift forwards or backwards as you straighten and bend the leg,

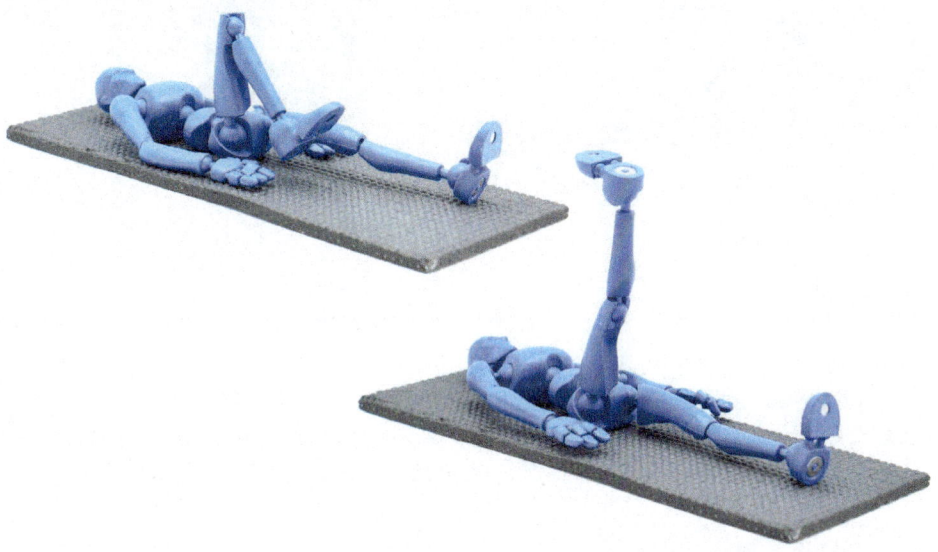

Internal and external knee rotation – Kneeling on a soft surface, one leg is placed in front of you. You begin by turning the foot placed in front of you outwards and then the foot returns to the central position, follow this by turning the foot inwards. The hands are simply to help keep the knee stationary as a guide, but no force is used with the hands to hold the knee in position.

Ankles & Feet

Ankle Supination & Pronation - sit upright with your legs in front of you. Aim to keep your toes pointing upwards at all times when rotating through the ankle joint, and avoid letting the feet wave by the toes pointing outwards or inwards. First, turn the soles of the feet inwards. Then return to the starting position before turning the feet to the soles face outwards and away from each other.

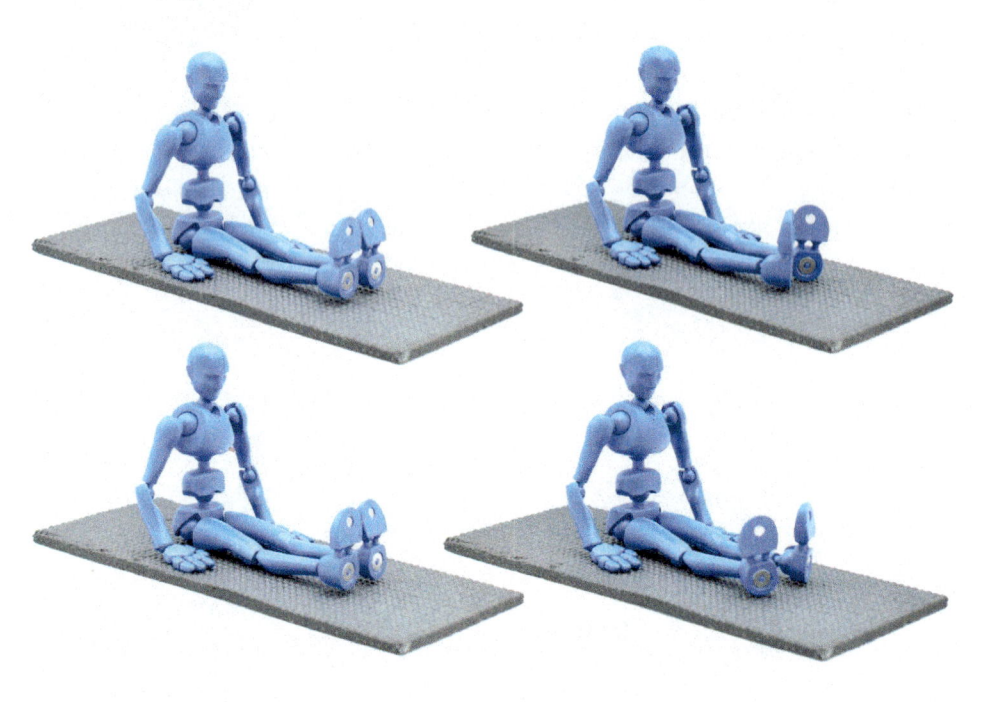

Plantar Flexion & dorsiflexion – standing upright with the knees slightly bent, raise up onto the balls of the feet whilst letting the arms swing backwards to act as a counter-balance. Making sure you keep the knees slightly bent at all times. Roll back onto the heels and lift the balls of the feet up off the ground, pulling them upwards towards the shins whilst swinging the arms forwards to counter-balance. Again, keeping the knees slightly bent.

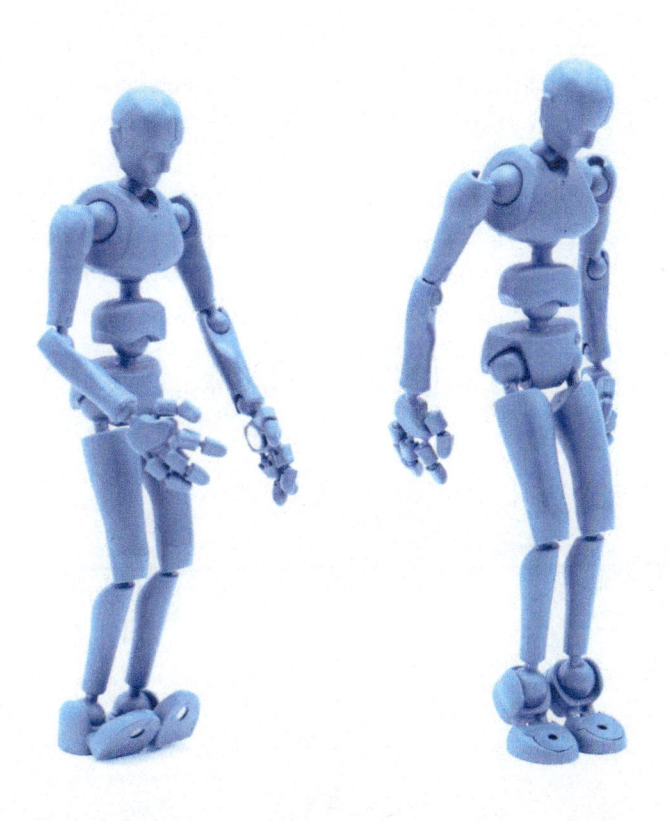

Bodyweight exercises for core strength

You aren't a robot, your body will be able to perform differently each day due to a multitude of factors, therefore you don't have to stick to a set number of reps for these exercises. Do what feels right for you.

Press ups

Basic press up. The staple of any exercise program is the humble press up, it's long been a go to exercise for good reason. Yet even though it's a commonly used exercise, it's regularly performed in a way which is detrimental to the shoulder joint. To prevent this, when lowering the body downwards, the elbows must be lowering down inwards and towards the side of the body and not sticking out to the side. The reason for avoiding this sideways emphasis is to protect the shoulder and the rotator cuff. If a press-up is too challenging, rather than starting on your knees and lowering down, place a foam roller on the ground underneath the thighs. Performing the movement on your knees can cause issues with the middle and upper back.

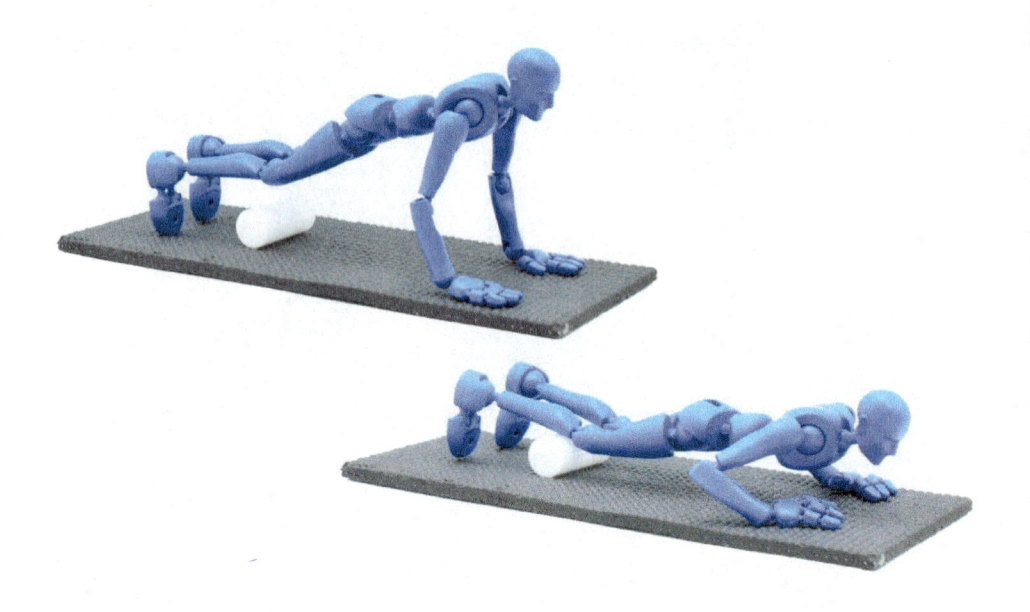

3 point press up - if you would like to increase the difficulty level, place one foot on top of the other leg. This creates a 3 point rather than a 4 point press up. Again, keep the elbows inwards when lowering, and there's always the option of the foam roller under the thighs.

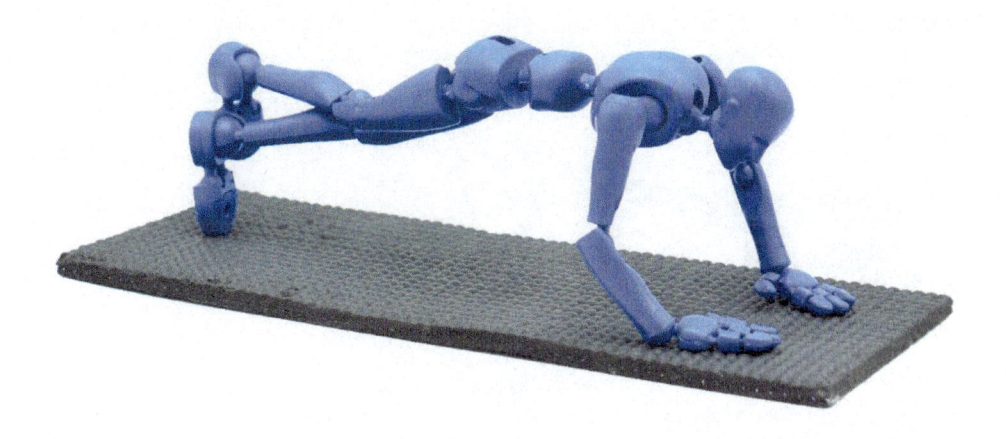

One arm press up- one of the hardest press ups when performed correctly. Not with the feet split apart or hips twisting, but instead the exact same movement as a regular press up but with one arm reaching forwards. A little tip, if this is the first time attempting this, it's quite nice to have a cushion on the ground underneath your head/face, just in case gravity wins.

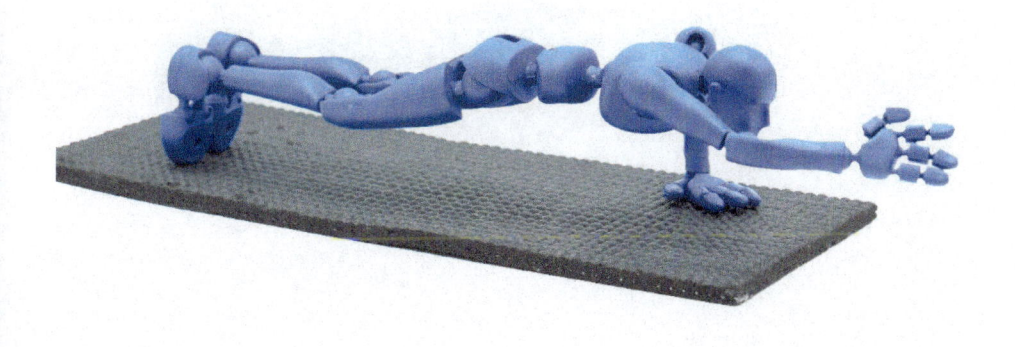

1 minute press up – for those who say they haven't got time to exercise, here's a solution. You start at the top of a press up, and hold this position for 15 seconds with the elbows slightly bent. After 15 seconds, lower to the middle position and hold this for a further 15 seconds. From here you lower the body so it's just off the ground and hold for 15 seconds. Then it's 15 seconds of flat out non-stop press ups!

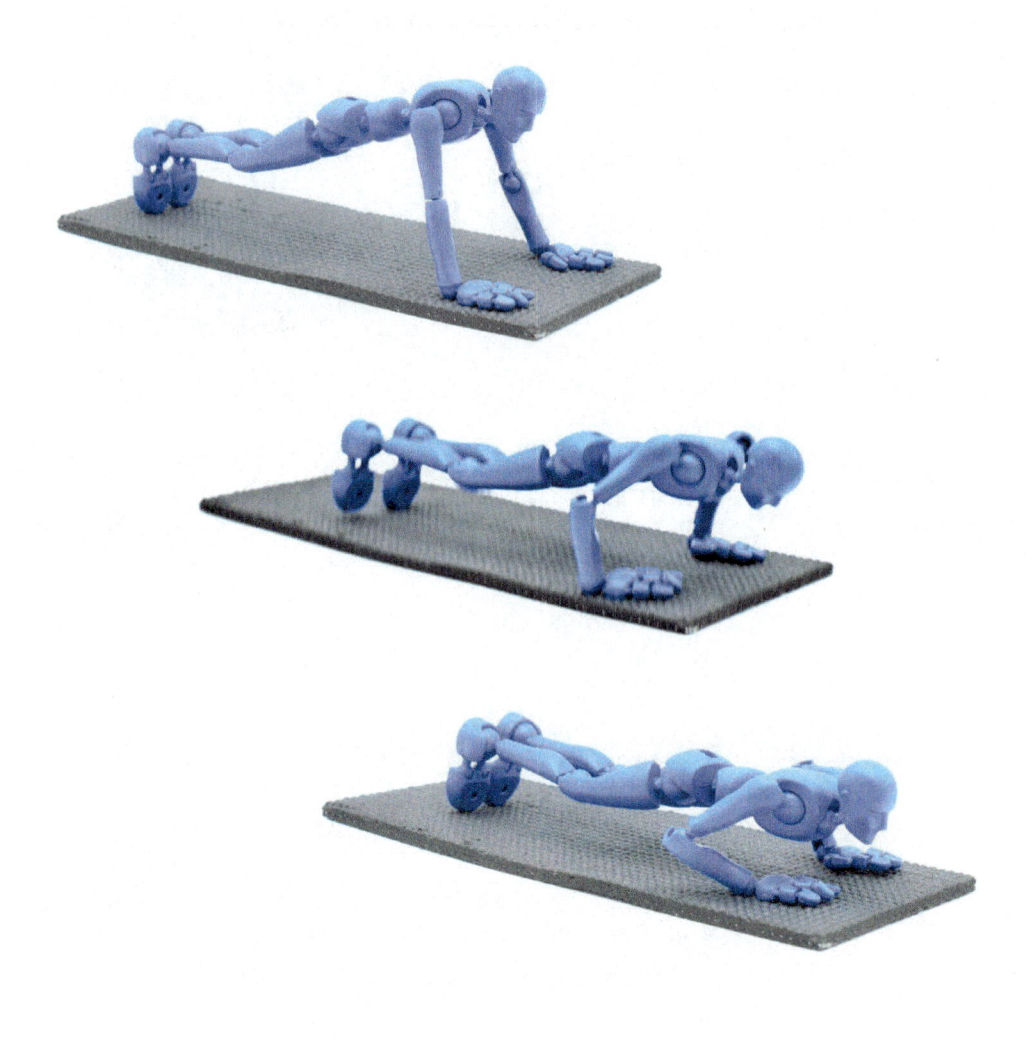

Sit up

Anchoring your feet underneath something will help you to perform a sit up, but it transfers a lot of the workload to the thigh muscles rather than keeping the focus in the targeted area of the abdominals. Letting your feet move forwards and backwards also shifts the workload away from the core, as does letting the feet raise up off the ground. To isolate the legs and target the workload directly to the abdominals, place your heels on the ground and feel as though you're squeezing a ball between your ankles. To prevent the shoulder muscles getting involved by generating momentum and pushing the arms forwards, you will place your hands in front of the body as though about to catch a ball. The arms will stay rounded with the elbows bent. This will limit the tension in the neck area which people often feel when performing a sit up.

From this starting position, you tense your core to start to curl the body up and forwards, try to maintain a slow and smooth pattern of movement. Only move through the first two thirds of the range of motion, as sitting all the way up can cause problems in the lower back. Sitting all the way up also lets the tension off the muscles, so the optimum way to perform the move is to slowly lift, stop before sitting upright, and slowly lower the body back down, without dropping to the floor. If you would like to make this easier, take the feet further away from the body. Another way to help is to hold a light weight in the hands, away from the body.

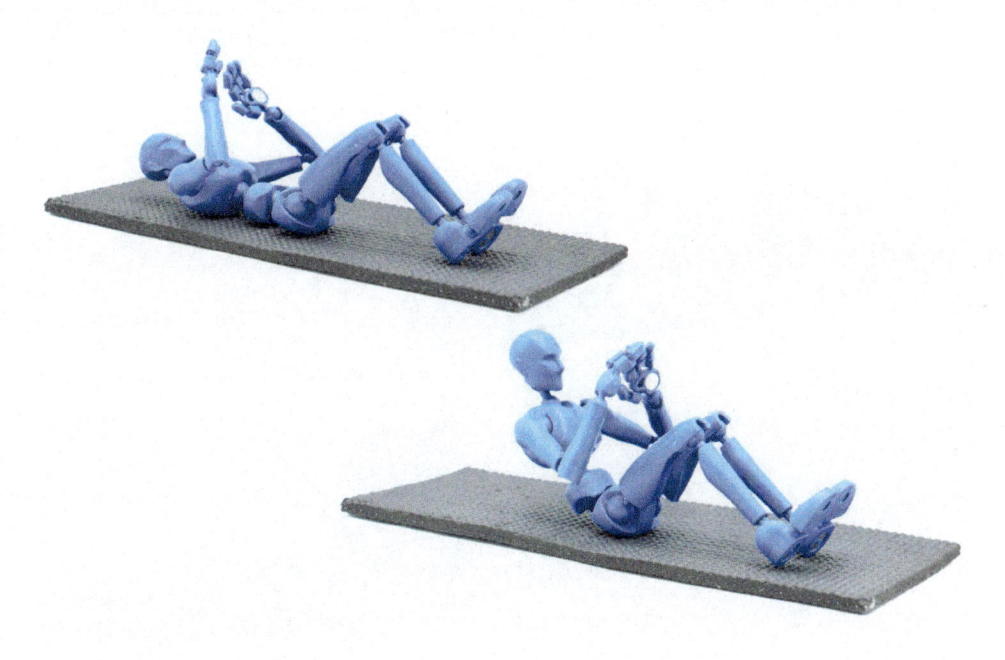

The halfway burn – if you would like to increase the intensity, you raise to halfway and pause. At this point, you start to make very small movements up and down, not bouncing, but controlled small movements. When you want to stop, you roll down to the ground. If at any point you feel this in the lower back, stop immediately and lower down to the ground.

Transversus abdominis – the muscles down the side of the torso, which need to be worked as well as the more commonly recognisable muscles at the front of the torso. To target these, you will perform a sideways sit ups.

Start laying on one side, with the lower leg bent and resting on the floor. If you straighten this leg you will likely get cramp, so remember to keep it bent. The top leg is bent with the foot placed on the floor as shown below. The arms are in front of the body. From this position you sit up sideways, taking the top shoulder towards the top knee. If this is too difficult then you can use the bottom arm to press on the floor to assist you in raising up.

Atomics! – Stability training is important, and any exercise which incorporates a balance element alongside strength is a winner. For this exercise, you start laying flat with the arms folded across the chest. As you sit upwards, you simultaneously bring the knees towards you, meeting with the elbows in the middle. Then returning to the starting position.

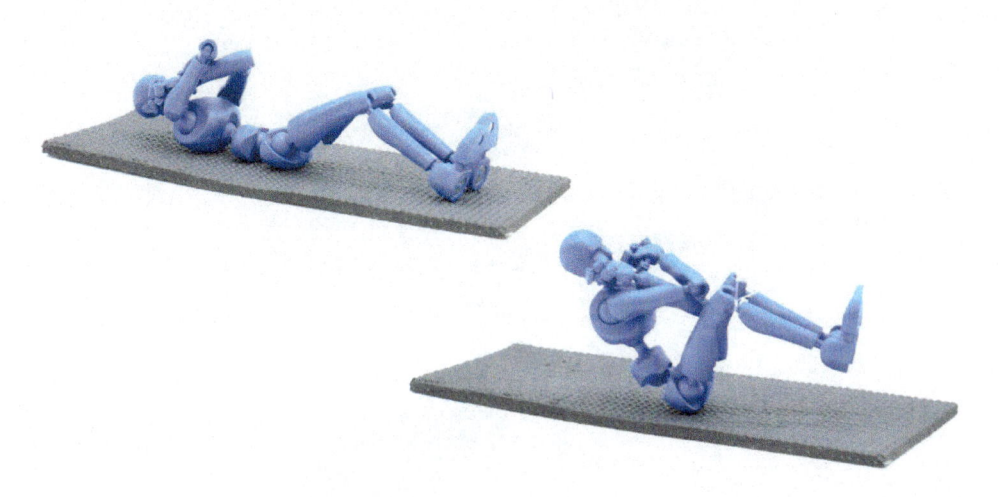

Plank

Basic plank – the arms are placed on the floor with the elbows directly under the shoulders. The knees are slightly bent and the core and glutes are engaged at all times. Tuck the pelvic upwards to stop the lower back from sinking. Relax the shoulders. Hold this position for a 15 second period when starting out. Build slowly.

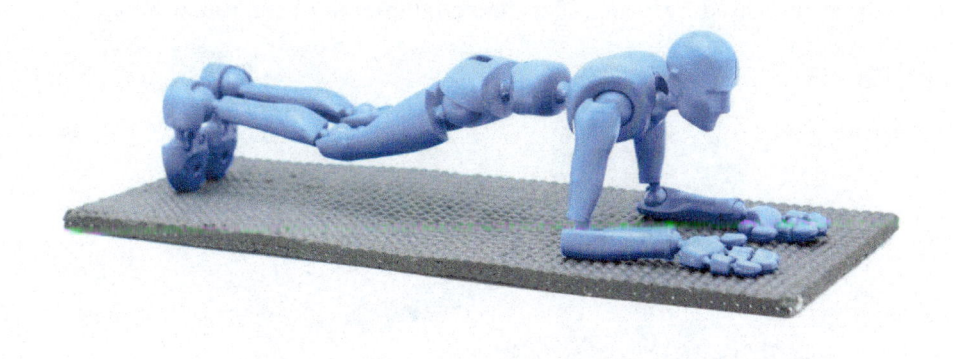

Side plank – the elbow is placed directly under the shoulder and you are resting on the edge of the foot on the lower leg, not the ankle bone. Lift the hips up and hold. You can increase the difficulty of this by using your hand instead of the forearm.

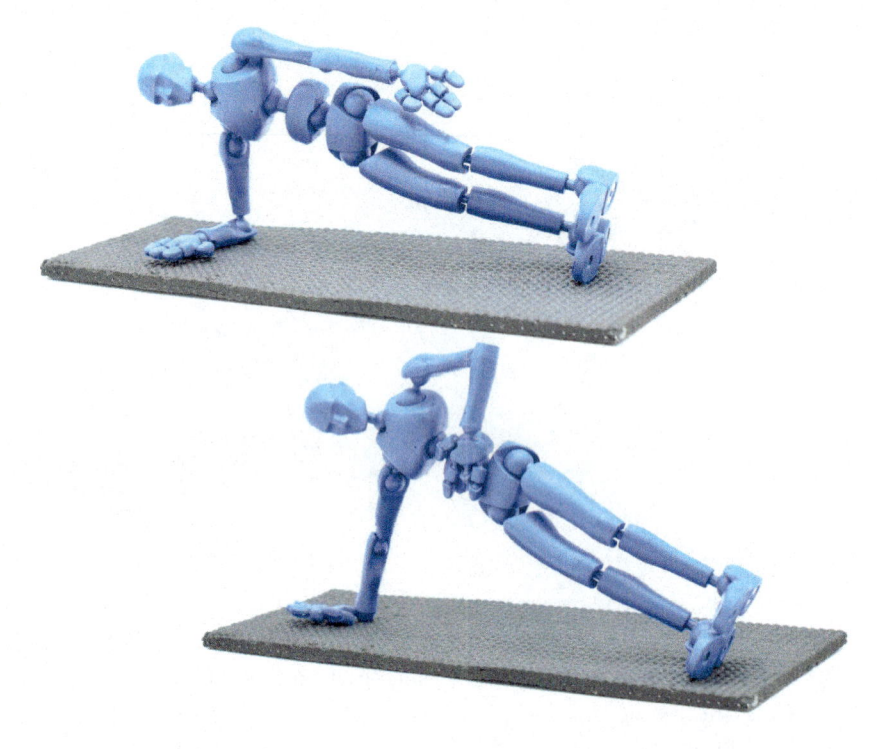

Side plank with leg raise – this challenges the body more than the previous exercise by lifting and holding the top leg in an elevated position. The difficulty level can be increased by changing to the hand instead of the forearm.

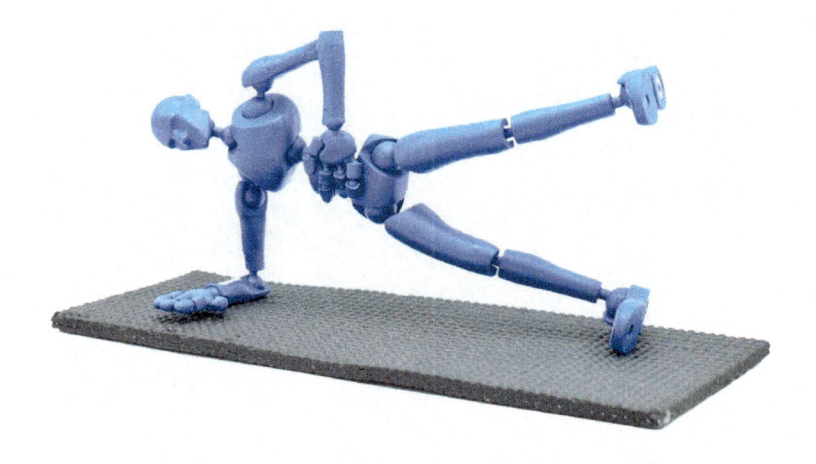

Front plank arm reach – from a standard plank position, reach forwards with one arm, before returning it to the starting plank position. Minimise the rotation of the torso. Repeat on the other side

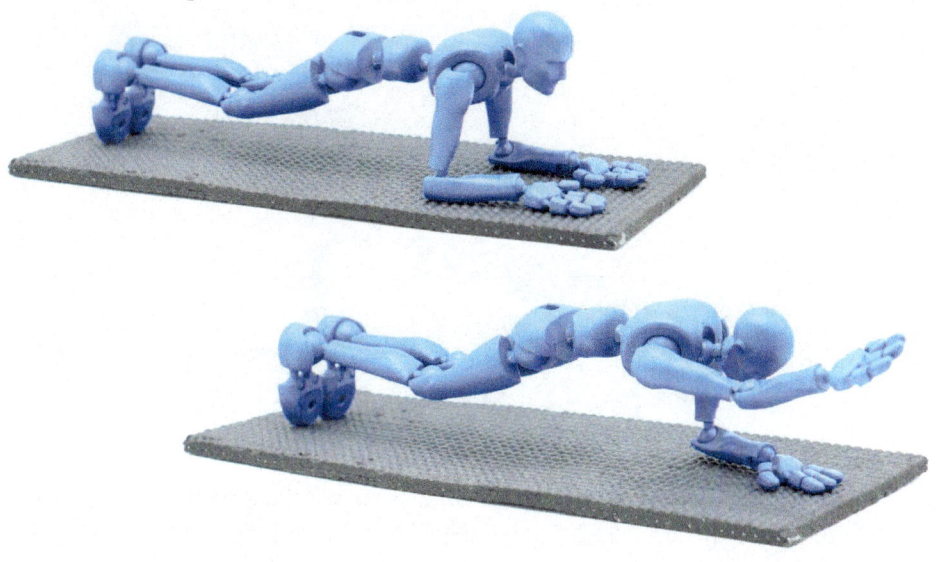

Next level planking
- from a standard plank position, reach forwards with one arm and lift the leg on the same side.

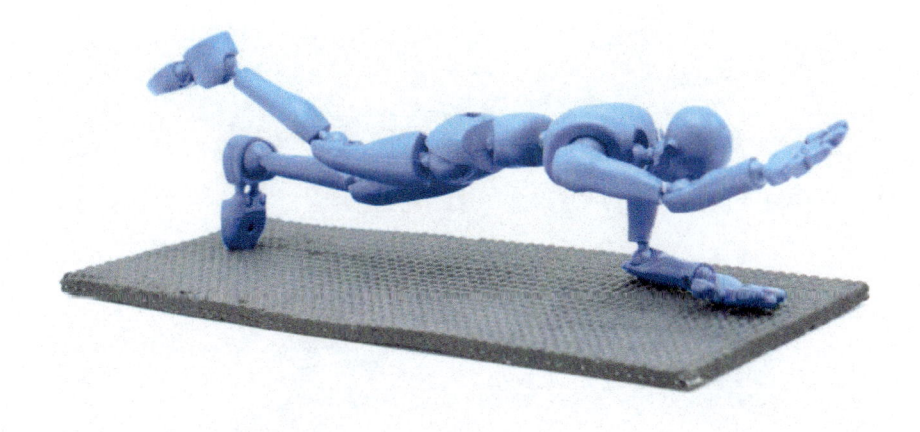

- Whilst in the reaching and leg lift position, you rotate the body into the leg elevated side plank position, rolling off the toes onto the edge of the foot.

- Now comes the stability challenge, you roll back onto the toes and return to the arm reaching and leg lift position, then stop and hold. You try to prevent your arm or foot touching the ground.

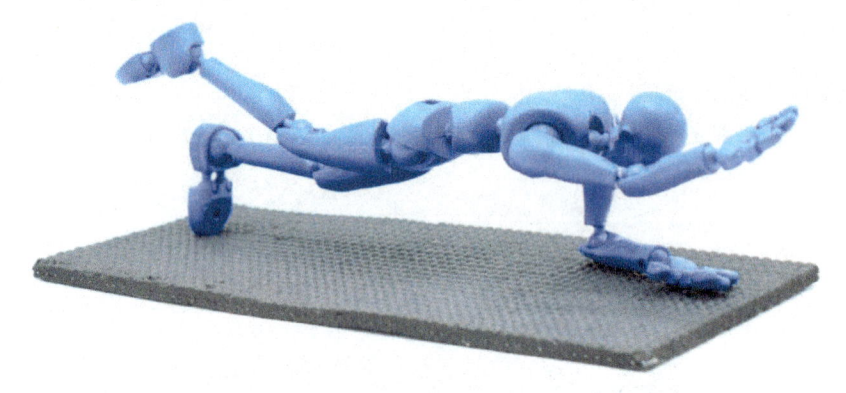

- Then return to the starting plank position.

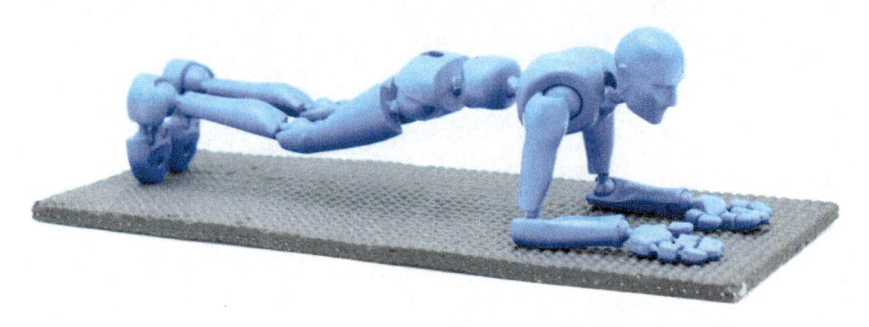

Squats & Leg Postures for Quads, Calves and Glutes

When it comes to working the muscles of the legs, it's important to have caution if you have low blood pressure, if all the blood rushes to these large leg muscles you may end up feeling light headed, so take plenty of breaks and monitor how you feel.

The squat – starting with the feet wider than shoulder width, bend the knees and squat until the thighs are parallel to the ground, the motion should be as if sitting on a bench. Raise to the starting position, without locking the knees straight. To increase the difficulty level use a resistance band.

Side step squat - starting with your feet shoulder width apart, step out to the side into the squat, this adds an additional degree of difficulty and stability to the previous exercise. Again, this can be performed with a resistance band.

Bridge – working on the glutes will help to support the lower back. Start laying on a soft surface, the legs are bent and the feet are flat on the ground. Tense the core muscles and lift the hips upwards into a bridge position. Lower the hips to the ground and repeat.

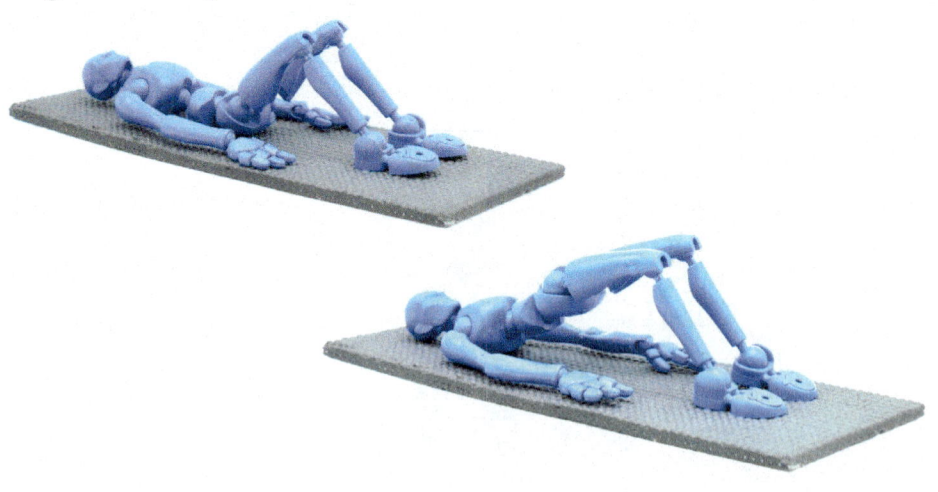

As previously explained, anything which challenges the balance alongside strength is valuable, therefore the next progression of difficulty is the single leg bridge. Assume the lifted bridge position and extend one leg outwards. Lower the hips almost to the ground, and raise back to the elevated position. Place the foot on the ground to finish and repeat on the other side.

Banded Glute bridge – taking the difficulty level up a level, the bridge but with a resistance band. Gently pressing the knees outwards as you lift. The one leg bridge can also be performed with a resistance band.

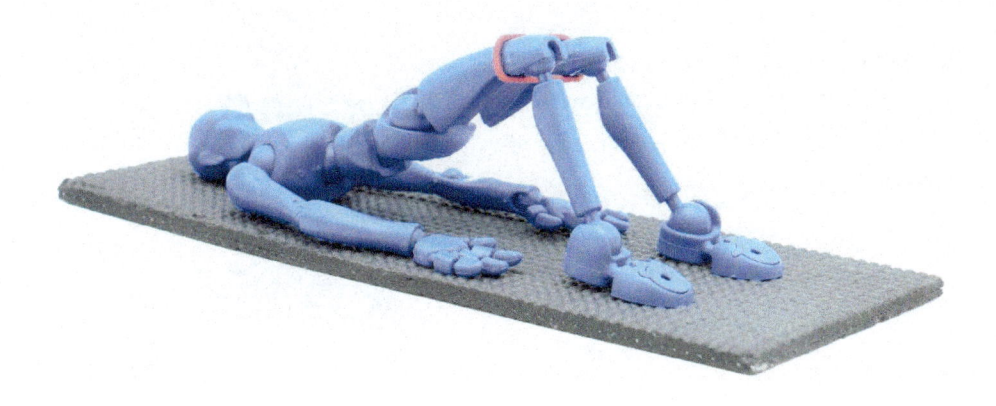

The Clam – laying on one side, the legs are bent and together. Use the heel as a pivot point and raise the top knee upwards. This can also be done with a resistance band, but start without one to get used to the movement.

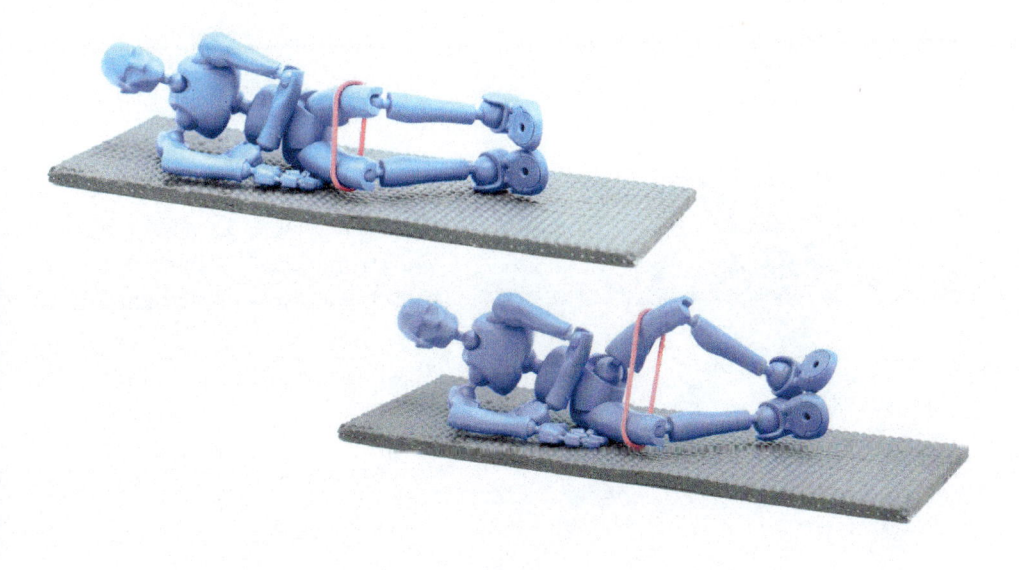

Standing postures for leg strength – these positions will work the various muscles groups in the legs. Hold each for around 15 seconds to begin with, progressing upwards to 1 minute for each posture.

A wide squat, aiming to get the thighs parallel to the ground, for an adult the foot placement would be wider than an exercise mat.

The big step – for those familiar with yoga, this is similar to the warrior position, but with both feet turned at a 45 degree angle. The front knee is bent and the back leg is also slightly bent at the knee. Build up to having the front thigh parallel to the ground.

The step across - the most challenging to explain. The front foot is turned out 45 degrees with the knee bent and the back leg is also bent. The bodyweight is placed so the front knee isn't directly above the ankle, but slightly behind, meaning the front shin is diagonally slanting backwards from ankle to knee. Repeat on the other side.

Standing on one leg – the standing leg is slightly bent at the knee as you shift your weight backwards, the other leg is raised off the ground.

The almost kneeling – start by standing with your feet shoulder width apart. Keeping this shoulder width distance, move one foot out in front of you. The front knee is bent and directly above the ankle. The back knee lowers and is almost touching the ground. The knee is directly underneath the hip.

This is the most challenging of all the standing postures and it isn't uncommon to see people put their hands across their face, chew their fists etc. just don't lean on the front leg with your hands. Repeat on the other side.

Train like a Demolition Monkey

If you want to move some weights around, a simple but effective routine is the *RBM 5's*. Five repetitions of each exercise shown, and at the end of it, you repeat the whole thing again until you have done five sets. Start with a light weight to get the body used to the movements, and gradually increase the load as you see fit, no pun intended!

Romanian deadlift
- Stand with your feet shoulder-width apart and shoulders back,
- Hold your weight (dumbbells or a barbell) in front of your thighs,
- Keep the core engaged and hinge forward at the hips, keeping your spine straight and sending your hips back as you bend forwards
- Your dumbbell/barbell should stop somewhere between your knee and the middle of your shin.
- As you lower, keep your shoulder blades drawn towards each other, try not let the shoulders round forwards
- When the weight is below your knees, thrust your hips forward and return to the starting position.
- Do not lock the legs straight at this point, they remain slightly bent throughout the entire exercise

Underhand grip bent over row
- Stand with your feet shoulder width apart, or with one foot in front as in a short lunge position.
- Both knees are slightly bent and remain so for the whole exercise

- Holding a barbell with your palms facing upwards. Lean slightly forwards.
- Your back stays straight and your elbows remain close to your body as you pull the barbell towards your chest by squeezing your back muscles.
- Slowly lower to the starting position.

Barbell biceps curls
Follow these steps to perform this exercise:
- Hold a dumbbell in each hand and stand with your feet as wide apart as your hips.
- Let your arms hang down at your sides with your palms forward.
- Pull your abdominals in, stand tall, and keep your knees slightly bent.
- Curl both arms upward until they're in front of your shoulders.
- Slowly lower the dumbbells back down.

Weighted squat
- Your feet are slightly wider than shoulder-width apart
- Stand with the bar across your chest, resting it in the crease of the elbows. You can do this with dumbbells resting on your shoulders.
- Press down with the heels, the ball of the foot and the little toe through the whole exercise
- Squat down by pushing your knees to the side while moving hips backwards
- Stick to only lowering until your thighs are parallel to the ground at the beginning to prevent injury
- Raise back up back up while keeping your knees slightly bent at the top of the movement

Warming down and loosening the body

Warming down and muscle maintenance after exercise is important as it helps to prevent blood pooling, which is where the lactic acid built up during exercise sits in the muscles and hampers recovery. Warming down will help to minimise the stiffness in the muscles and stretching exercises will help keep the elasticity of the muscles, which is beneficial to overall health. This elasticity is compromised if dehydrated, stressed, or muscles are overused.

STRETCHING

Head/Neck

Upper Trapezius – this muscle runs from the shoulder up to the neck and the top part of the back. If you tap the part of your body between your shoulder and neck, this is the upper trapezius. Stiffness in this muscle can result in headaches particularly around the temple and the eyes, pain between shoulder blades, and restrict motion in turning or tilting the head.

Sit in a chair and hold the chair underneath. Feel as though you are lifting the chair but keep the arm slightly bent. The head is tilted and slightly rotated. The other hand reaches over and holds the head and you gently press the head into the hand. Do not pull the head! This is a relatively small muscle so only hold this for 10 seconds.

Scalens – the muscles down the side of neck, if tight can cause numbness or tingling in the hand or arm. To elongate these muscles the movement is the same as the stretch above but without rotating the head to the side, the head is only tilted whilst the other hand holds it. Hold for 10 seconds.

Sternocleidomastoid – Tightness in this muscle can cause headaches at top of head. This movement is best done seated, place the index and middle finger of one hand onto the bumpy knuckle on the collar bone. Gently tilt the head up and away to the opposite side of the fingers. Be very gentle as it's a small muscle. You will feel this from the jaw down to the collar bone, sometimes you may feel this radiate across into the cheek. Hold for only 10 seconds at most.

Suboccipital – the muscles fanning out across the top of the neck just underneath the back of the head. Stiffness in these muscles will cause difficulty putting the chin onto the chest, and may cause headaches on the bottom of the skull or top of head.

To stretch these muscles, a towel or a strap is placed around the back of the head and held out in front of the body with the shoulders relaxed and the elbows pointing downwards. You tilt the head downwards as though looking at the ground in front of you. Gently press the head back and upwards into the strap/towel. No pulling with the arms. Hold for only 10 seconds

Shoulders
Infraspinatus - this is the usual suspect for the cause of pain in the shoulder. The muscle runs from the back towards the outside of the top of the arm. Any issues with this muscle can cause a stabbing pain in front of the shoulder, a pain that radiates down the arm into the forearm and hand. Also pain when lifting or lowering your arm.

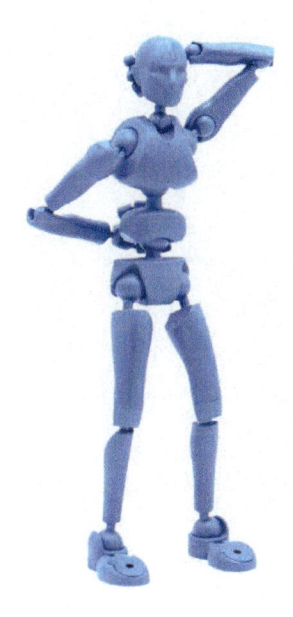

To work this muscle, be gentle because it's a small muscle and can be easily overstrained.

Place one palm onto the back of neck, and the back of the other hand onto the small of the back. Engage the muscles by gently pressing the hands onto the head and back, and then slowly press the shoulders backwards.

Supraspinatus – the muscle across top of shoulder which threads under the collar bone. If tight it will cause local pain when raising the elbow above the shoulder, and pain on the outside of the shoulder. To combat this use the stick stretch, easy to do but difficult to explain.

Start holding a stick upright, and let it fall to the outside of your arm, twisting your wrist away from you.

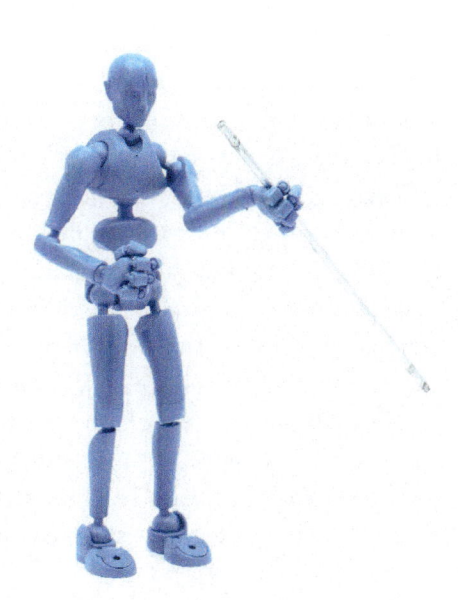

Next, you grab the lower part of the stick with the other hand. Rest the stick so it falls from the top hand and touches the arm just above the elbow on the upper arm. You position the stick so it's at a 45 degree angle across the body

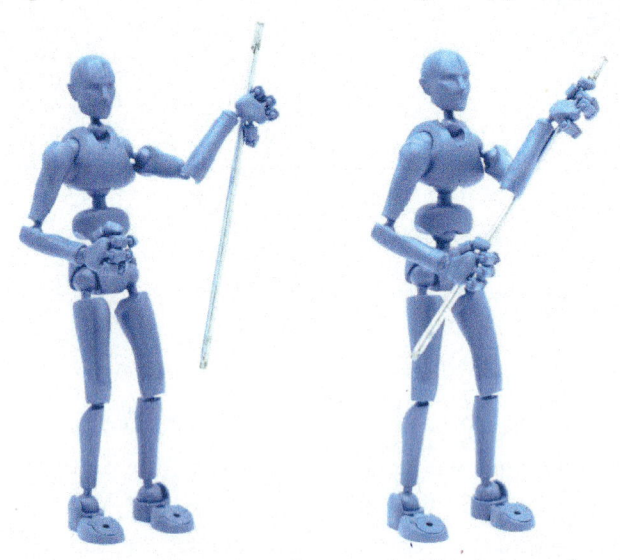

At this point you are ready to start the stretch. The bottom hand gently pulls and the top hand resists. Try to keep the little finger of the top hand on the stick. If you don't feel the muscle working, then the stick may be too close to the body so move your arms further forwards.

Teres Major – this runs from the shoulder blades to the upper arm and can create pain down the arm and numbness in the fingers. If you have a loss of strength when the arms are raised above the head, this is the muscle to work on.

Lean against a wall with the feet about a foot away, the arm closest to the wall is bent with the palm placed onto the back of the head.

The other hand grabs hold of the elbow, and you gently pull the elbow away from the wall, and resist this by pressing the elbow towards the wall.

This is all done whilst lengthening the latissimus dorsi muscles by bending the upper body away from the wall. The hips stay in contact with the wall but the body is in a banana shape.

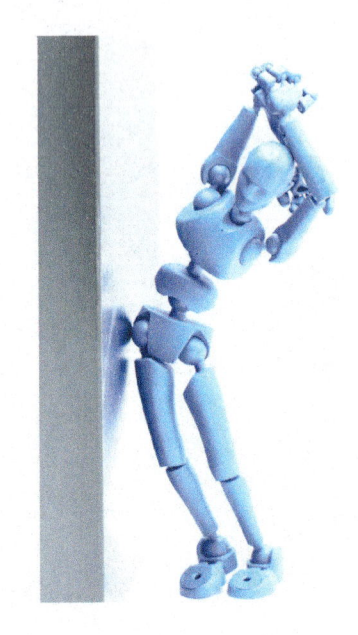

Pectorals

Pectorals Major – a large muscle spanning the whole chest area, reaching the upper arm above the bicep and into the armpit. Tightness in this muscle can create pain or spasms between shoulder blades, pain across sternum, pressure across the chest and numbness or tingling in the arms.

Standing in a doorframe, or next to a post. Move the foot furthest away from the upright forwards so your hips are level or almost level to the upright. The arm closest to the upright is placed with the elbow level with the diaphragm. The elbow and palm are pressing against the frame, the core muscles are active. Bend the front leg more to increase the stretch.

Pectorals Minor – runs from the collar bone down to ribs, underneath the Pectorals Major. Symptoms of this muscle being tight are linked to tennis elbow, and difficulty taking deep inhalations. The stretch for this muscle is the same as the previous stretch, but the elbow is raised to eye height instead of the height of the sternum.

Upper Back/Scapula

Middle Trapezius and Rhomboids, the muscles for whole scapula(shoulder blades). Tightness here will cause pain and muscle aches across the shoulder blades. Also aching towards the front of shoulder and numbness between shoulder blades.

Using a doorframe or a post, hold onto the upright with the hand placed lower than shoulder height. The arm is rounded, keeping the elbow bent, and you pull towards you. You will feel the muscle across the shoulder blade engage.

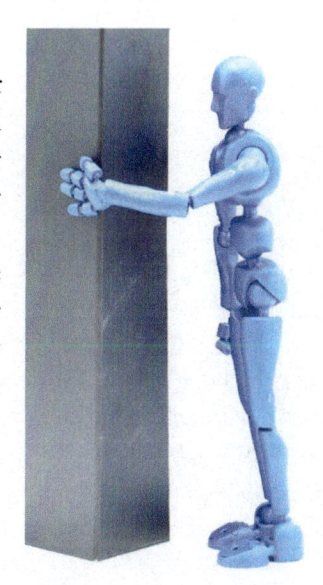

Lower Back & Hips

Latissimus Dorsi – fanning across the lower back from underneath the shoulder blades down to the small of the back. This muscle can cause pain or aches in the lower back and it make it difficult to work with your hands directly above the head.

Sit down with one leg across the other thigh, the arm on the same side of the bent leg reaches up and across the body.

The next movement for the Latissimus Dorsi begins by kneeling on the ground, with the hands directly underneath the shoulders and the knees directly underneath the hips. With one arm, reach through the gap between the opposite leg and arm. Rest the shoulder and head onto the ground and relax.

Quadratus Lumborum – this muscle runs up the lower back, and if tight can cause a pain or ache in the lower back. To lengthen this muscle, lay on one side with the bottom leg straight out. The top leg is bent, with the foot placed on the ground in front of you. Lean on the forearm and press the edge of the foot on the straight leg into the ground. Increase the stretch by bringing the hand closer to the body.

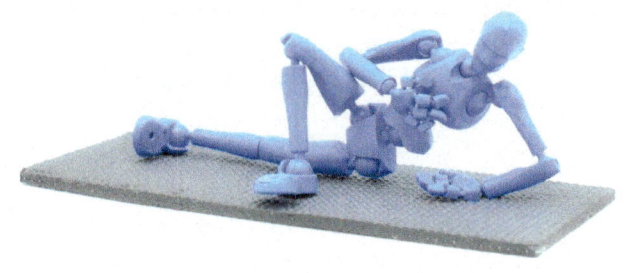

Legs

Gluteus Maximus – the largest muscle in the body, running across the buttocks to the thigh bone. This muscle can cause an ache or pain in small of the back, plus the back of the leg or outside of the leg. To target this muscle, lay on your back with one leg placed on top of the other. The foot is pressed into the thigh to activate the muscle, and keeping this pressure with the foot, you lift the other foot off the ground and curl the legs towards you.

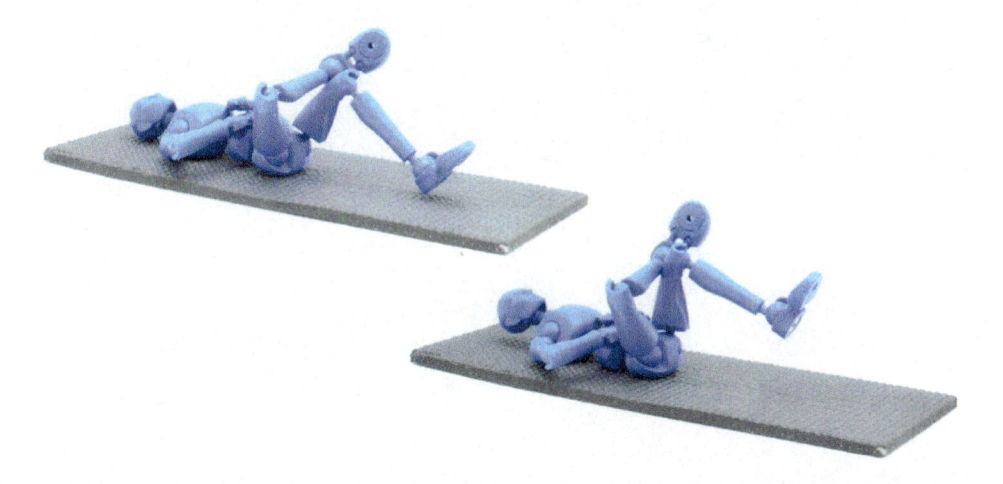

From this position, there is the option of lowering the legs to the side.

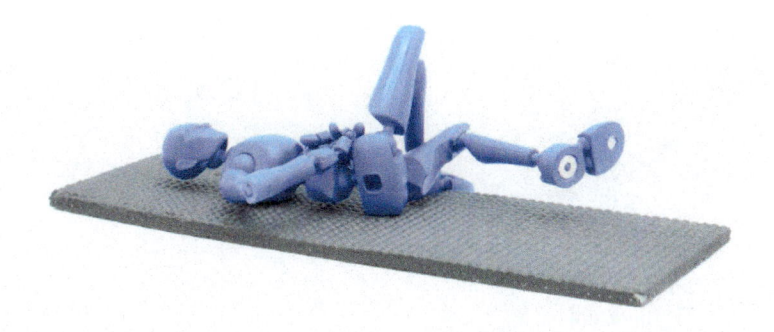

This stretch also works the Piriformis, which can cause pain on the outside of the knee which is known as runners knee, even in those who don't run.

Gluteus Medius & Minimus – the smaller muscles in the buttock, these can give the sensation of false sciatica, which is numbness and pain running down the back of the leg. The way to target this is by threading your leg underneath the body. You start kneeling on the ground, moving one leg out behind you and bringing it back in, repeating the movement several times to warm up the hip.

From this position, almost straighten the leg which still has the knee resting on the ground, and thread the leg which you have been moving forwards and backwards underneath the body.

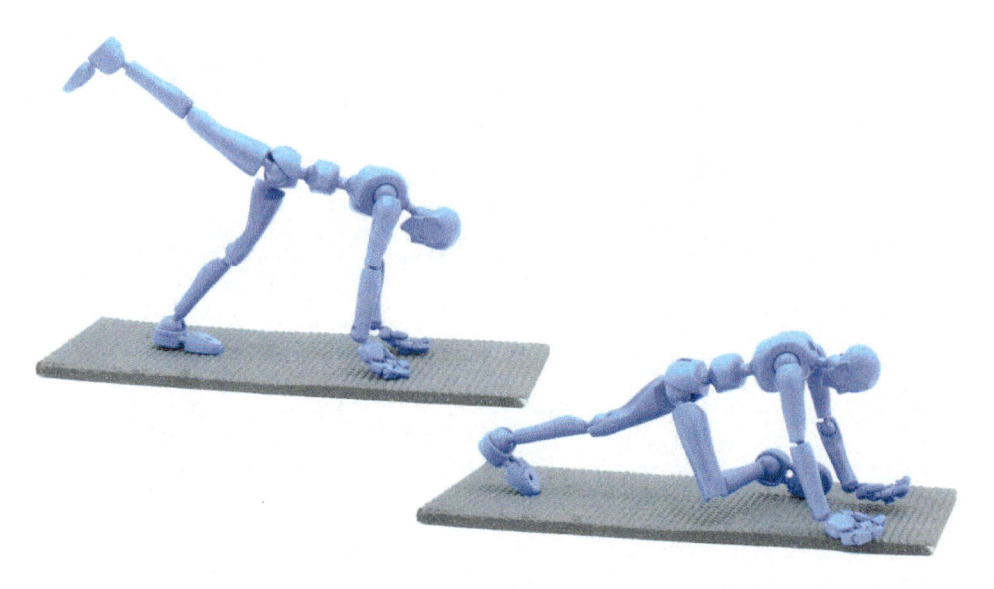

Next, you place the leg on the ground, trying to keep the shin parallel to the diaphragm. But be careful this doesn't place any tension into the knee joint.

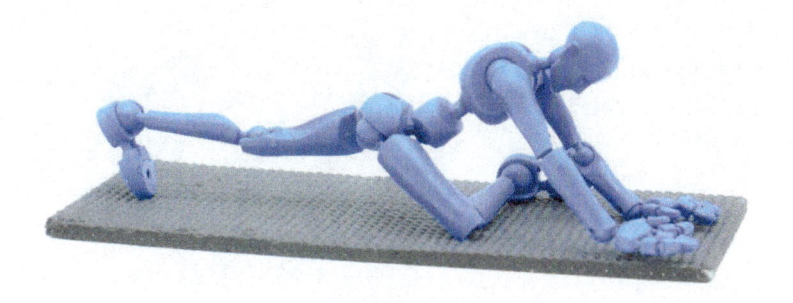

Finally, lower the body down and slide your back foot away from you.

Rectus Femoris – is the muscle running straight down the middle of the thigh. It contributes to pain in the lower back, and pain across the patella.

The stretch for the Rectus Femoris, starts by kneeling with one foot in front of you and one knee in front of a wall. It's a good idea to place a cushion or a rolled up mat under the knee to provide some cushioning. The foot against the wall has the toes upwards and the body remains bent forward at this point.

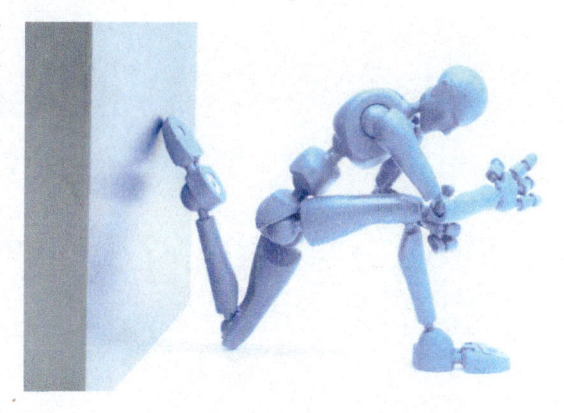

Now you press the foot against the wall and maintain this pressure as you raise the upper body to an upright position, and shift the hips back towards the heel of the foot against the wall.

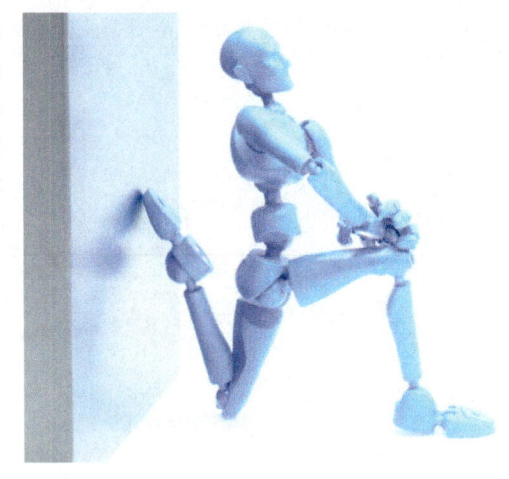

Ultimately, you want to work towards being able to place the knee closer to the wall and to reach up and behind you with the arms. However, the most important part is keeping the pressure onto the wall with the foot.

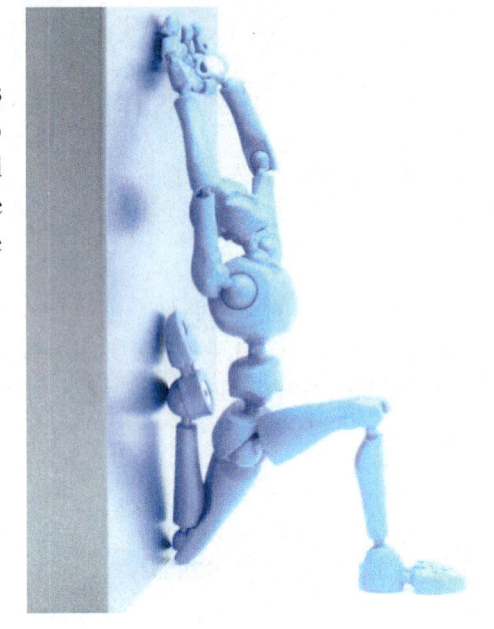

Hamstrings – running down the back of the thigh, tightness will cause difficulty in bending forwards, it also contributes to a shortened walking or running stride which indirectly creates shin splints. Often people experience cramping on the back of the leg, or the side of the thigh if the hamstrings are tight.

Stand next to a table, and place one leg on the surface with the leg straight. The standing leg is slightly bent and placed behind you as much as possible. You press the heel downwards on the table.

Gracilis – the long adductor down the inside of the thigh, which can cause pain on the inside of the knee. Lay inside a doorframe with one leg bent and pressing against the doorframe. The other leg is straight with the heel resting against the wall. Let the leg lower down to the side as much as possible, and then engage the muscle by lifting it back up a few centimetres and holding it in place.

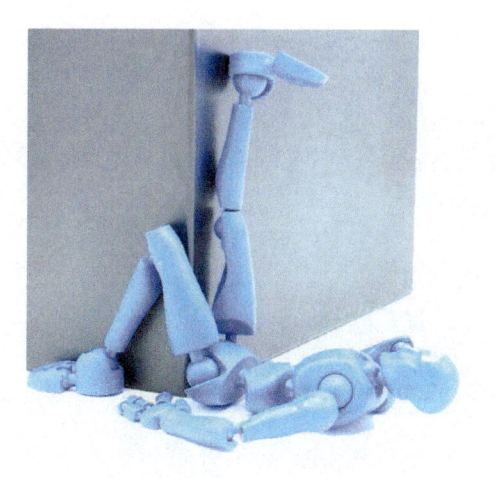

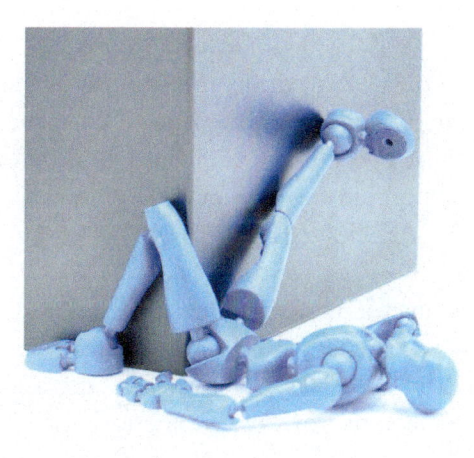

Gastrocnemius – the large part of the calf muscle. If tight will cause localised aching in the calf. To loosen this muscle you rest your left leg across a foam roller.

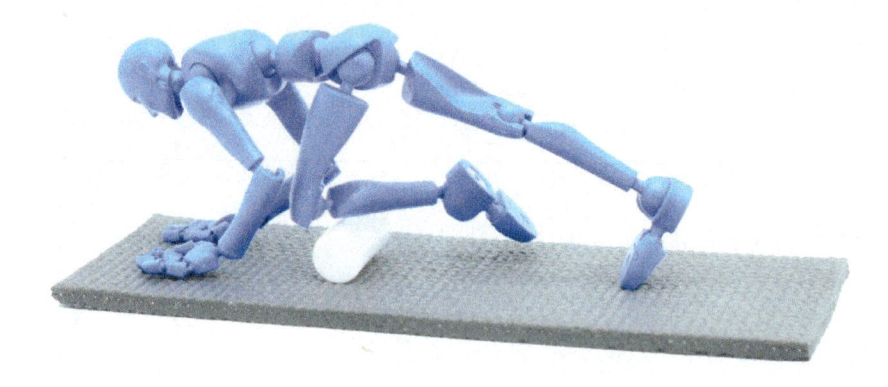

The right leg is now placed across the left calf muscle and into the back of the knee. Circle the toes of the left foot, this circling of the ankle will help to loosen the calf muscle.

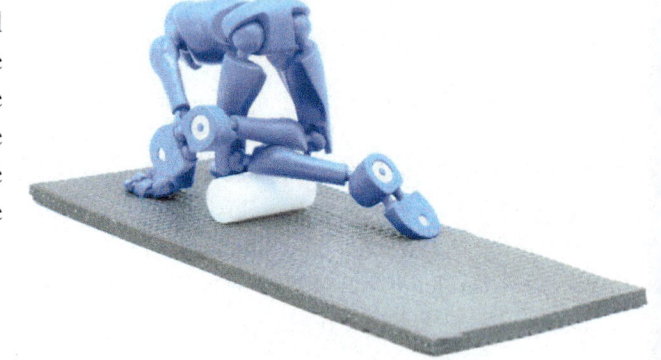

Soleus – the smaller muscle of the lower leg, found underneath the larger Gastrocnemius calf muscle. Tightness will cause an ache or pain in the calf, in the arch of the foot and tightness in the Achilles tendon.

Standing facing a wall, one foot is pressing against it and positioned so the ball of the foot is in contact with the wall with the foot slightly elevated. Press the foot into the wall as you bend your front knee to increase the stretch.

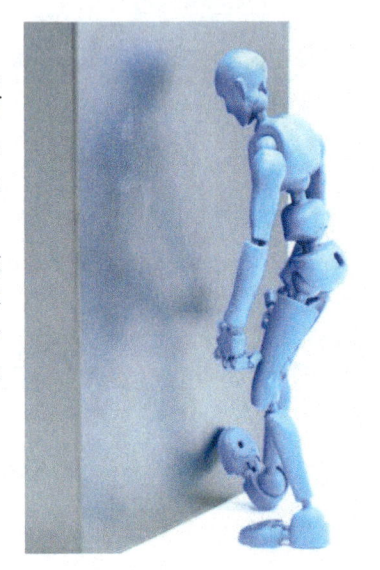

Tibialis Anterior – the muscle running along the shinbone, this causes aching along the shinbone and across the ankle. Place the front of the foot on a bench behind you, the hand on the same side reaches back and presses down on the heel to extend the ankle. Simultaneously resist by pressing the toes and the top of the foot downwards into the bench.

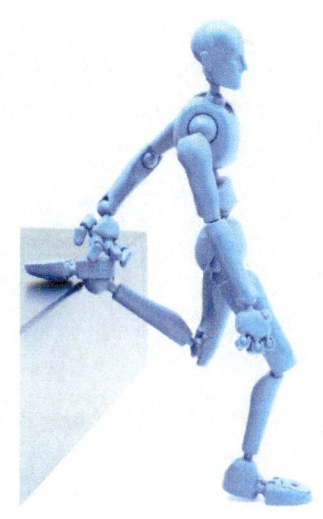

FOAM ROLLER

Foam roller work helps with muscle maintenance, muscle elasticity and recovery. The important thing to remember about foam roller work is not to overdo it, too much or doing it too intensively can cause inflammation rather than reduce it. A good rule of thumb is it shouldn't be painful, it may have a sense of discomfort, but it shouldn't be painful. The rule to be applied to all foam roller work is you never roll over a joint and you never roll the neck.

Calf Muscle

Resting one leg on the roller so it's positioned under the calf muscle, the other leg is bent with the foot placed on the floor. The hands are on the ground behind you. You shift your hips forwards and backwards to roll along the calf muscle. Have a mixture of the toes pointing upwards, out to the side and inwards to ensure you reach all of the muscle. Roll from just above the Achilles tendon and stop just at the top of the muscle before you reach the knee. To increase the intensity, rest one leg on top of the other, with the legs crossed at the ankle.

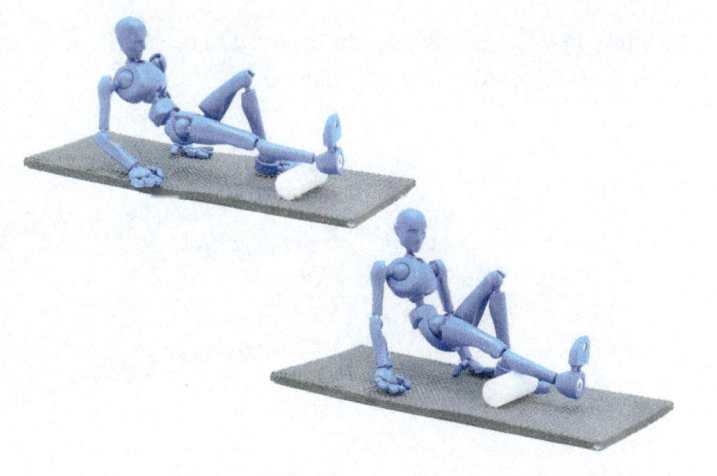

The Hamstring

Very similar to the movement for the calf muscle, but with the roller placed underneath the upper leg. You start just above the back of the knee and roll right up to the glutes.

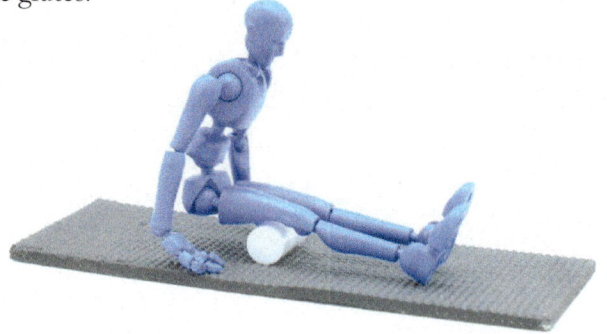

The IT band (Iliotibial band)

To roll the IT band it's advisable to start with one foot on the ground in front of you, and using your hands on the floor to take some of the weight off the leg on the roller. Otherwise, this can be very painful. Start with the roller just above the knee and roll to just underneath the hip joint.

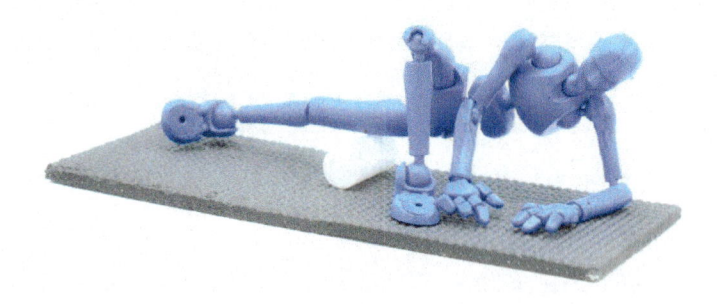

Ideally you will progress to the point where you have both legs stacked on the roller and it doesn't cause any pain at all.

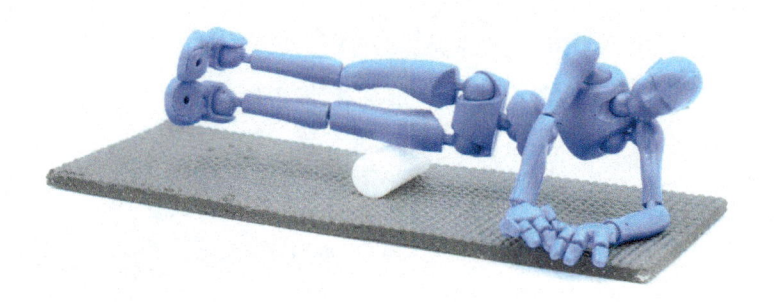

The Quads

Facing downwards with the roller under the thighs, the legs are bent and your arms are taking some of the bodyweight. You start with the roller just above the knees and use your arms to move the body so that the roller reaches the top of the thighs.

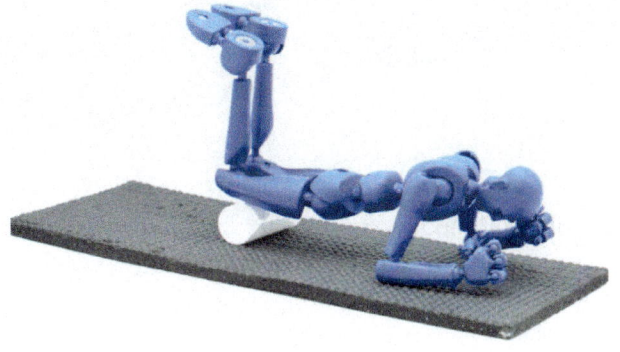

The Scapula

To start, you will need to set up the roller in the correct position, placed diagonally across the mat.

Lay across the roller with your arm reaching outwards and palm upwards. The roller should now be parallel with the scapula. Using your legs you move the body forwards and backwards to roll over the scapula.

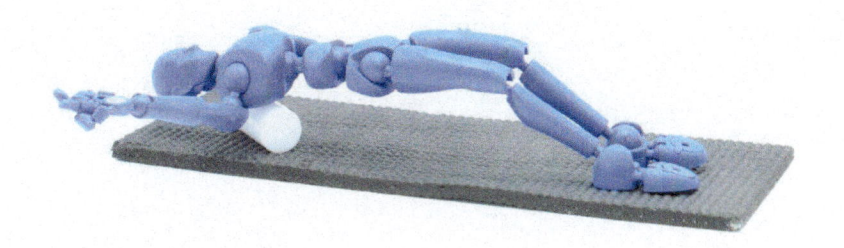

Spinal roll
Set up the roller so that it's running down the middle of the mat.

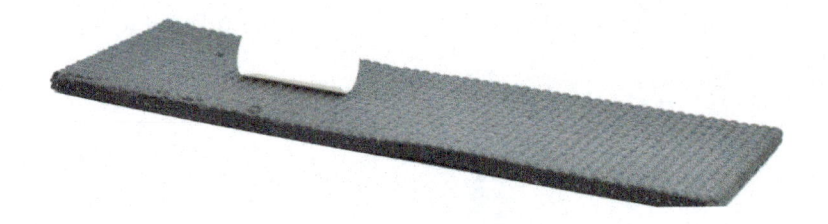

Lay on the roller with your spine on the roller lengthways. Keep your feet and hands on the ground for balance and gently move the body side to side, just a few inches each way to target the muscles near the spine.

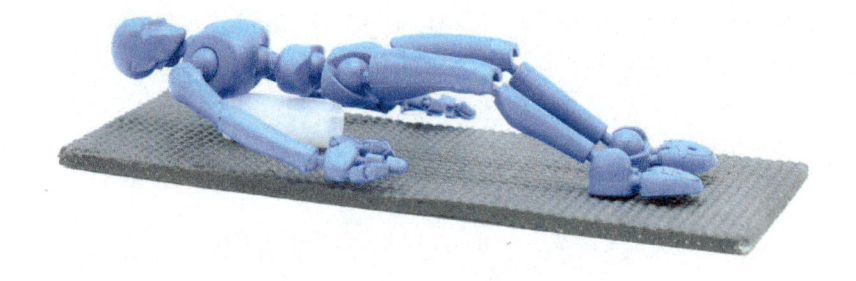

Over to you...

We all face an undefeatable opponent called time, and at some point time will decide to draw the curtains for each of us. This is out of our control of course, but what we do have power over, is how we live our lives up to that point, and also how we clock out when our time comes.

No self-defence system is fool proof, and no system can guarantee you come out on top in a violent attack. They can however, provide value through their ability to increase your chances of survival if faced with a violent aggressor. They also have the potential to develop what I think is the most important aspect of any self-defence system, your resilient mindset. Harnessing a tenacity to survive and to protect your life until the very end, and choosing to take control of your options, because if faced with the threat of violence you have two choices, do nothing, or fight back with everything you have. This mental fortitude can be applied to all areas of your life,

Rather than growing old in your mental approach to life, you can resist and fight back by having fun every day, keeping hold of the enthusiasm and joy you had as a child. Every day was the best day ever when you were young, tap into this feeling again and push back against time. Moving and maintaining your flexibility and strength helps to fight against illness and disease, this doesn't mean training like an Olympic athlete, but instead looking after the organic motorhome by walking, cycling, stretching etc. which will not only help to keep you here longer, but to be able to do the things you enjoy. Keeping the circulation going, filling the lungs with fresh air and the joints mobile, is an investment in buying you extra time. Learn new things and keep your mind fresh instead of sitting in a chair watching TV and withering away. If you become ill, fight it with all you have, never give in, your life is precious and every extra moment you can be here counts.

Taking time to relax isn't *'doing nothing'*, or *'wasting time'*. A boxer will sit on a stool and rest between rounds, gathering their thoughts, calming their breathing and getting their energy levels back up. Spending time doing a mental spring clean and breaking the stress response cycle is the equivalent of this. Take a break and get ready to move again, and when the bell rings and life throws another round at you, demanding your energy and focus to be poured into something, you will be ready to hit it head on with full force. Don't underestimate the importance of relaxing.

Regularly pay attention to your mental health, checking in with how you're feeling. Strength and courage are shown by speaking out and asking for help when needed, it's not a weakness. Use the breathing techniques to find a sense of stillness in your everyday life, the biggest threat to your health is a lifetime of stress and the techniques in phase 2 will help to restrict this.

This book gives you the theory to support a practical approach to self-defence and your approach to a stress reduced life. Reading it isn't enough, you must put the hours in to load the data into the memory banks and re-program how you respond to threats and stressors. Complete the drills in phase 3 until you're able to confidently create solutions on the fly with your drill partner. Commanding this ability and the confidence which comes with it is of high importance.

Extracting the solution focused, pro-active mindset out of the self-defence and establishing it as a full time operating state, is the number one target of *RBM*. No more rumination, no more worrying about things which haven't happened or may not happen, but looking at the facts and working with what's in front of you.

Now it's over to you to do these things, to live the principles and stay safe, and of course be happy!

For further resources, please visit www.RBMdynamics.com

References

References: Questions I am asked first, answered first

1. UK Government Crown Prosecution Service Source: Information taken via the www.cps.gov.uk website for the UK Government Crown Prosecution Service.
2. East Anglian Daily Times: December 2008, Will Clarke, http://eadt.co.uk/1.191251

References - The Mechanics of the Mind Under Stress:

3. Paul D. MacLean 1990: The Triune Brain in Evolution: Role in Paleocerebral Functions
4. Michio Kaku 2015: The Future of the Mind: The Scientific Quest To Understand, Enhance and Empower the Mind
5. Matthew White, 2011: Atrocitology: Humanity's 100 Deadliest Achievements
6. Richard M. Restak, 1995: Brainscapes: An Introduction to What Neuroscience Has Learned about the Structure, Function, and Abilities of the Brain
7. Jonathan H. Pincus: Base Instincts: What Makes Killers Kill?
8. Vaillant, GE (1992), Ego Mechanisms of Defense: A Guide for Clinicians and Researchers, Washington, DC, American Psychiatric Press
9. Col Lt Dave Grossman, 1996: On Killing: The Psychological Cost of Learning to Kill in War and Society
10. Vaillant, GE (1992), Ego Mechanisms of Defense: A Guide for Clinicians and Researchers, Washington, DC, American Psychiatric Press
11. STRESS AND THE GENERAL ADAPTATION SYNDROME; BY: HANS SELYE, M.D., Ph.D., D.Sc., F.R.S.C. Professor and Director of the Institute of Experimental Medicine and Surgery, Universite de Montreal, Montreal, Canada, British Medical journal, June 17,1950

References - Stay Safe and Feel Empowered:

12. Fig. 14 Accident and Emergency Attendances in England - 2018/19, Table 16, Distribution of accident and emergency attendances in England in 2018-2019 NHS Digital
13. Jeff Cooper, 1989: Principles of Personal Defense, Published by Paladin Press, a division of Paladin Enterprises, Inc., ISBN 0-87364-497-2 I
14. Dave Putwain 2012: A Psychologists Casebook of Crime, ISBN-10: 0415253004
15. Oxford English Dictionary, OUP Oxford; 3rd edition (19 Aug. 2010)
16. Dr Michael Craig: 2009 Altered connections on the road to psychopathy, Institute of Psychiatry at London's King's College Hospital
17. Radford University/FGCU Serial Killer Database
18. Oxford English Dictionary, OUP Oxford; 3rd edition (19 Aug. 2010)
19. Wensley Clarkson, 2015: Legal Highs - Inside Secrets of the Worlds Newest and Deadliest Drugs
20. Boyd, John, R., The Essence of Winning and Losing, 28 June 1995 a five-slide set by Boyd.

References – Building a Mental Stress Defender:

21. Monkey: 1980 Nippon Television Network System
22. Phebe Cranmer 1991: Defensive Behaviour and Autonomic Reaction to Stress CV Reactivity, The Development of Defense Mechanisms: Theory, Research and Assessment. (1991) New York: Springer-Verlag
23. Dennis Tueller, 1983 How Close is Too Close? SWAT Magazine

References – Where do you drop the Thunderfist Bombs

24. Hick, W. E. 1952: On the rate of gain of information . Quarterly Journal of Experimental Psychology.
25. Hyman, R (March 1953). "Stimulus information as a determinant of reaction time". Journal of Experimental Psychology
26. Eran Chajut and Daniel Algom 2003 :Selective Attention Improves Under Stress: Implications for Theories of Social Cognition 2003 Journal of Personality and Social Psychology, Copyright 2003, American Psychological Association, Inc.Vol. 85, No. 2, 231–248
27. Eran Chajut and Daniel Algom 2003 :Selective Attention Improves Under Stress: Implications for Theories of Social Cognition 2003 Journal of Personality and Social Psychology, Copyright 2003, American Psychological Association, Inc.Vol. 85, No. 2, 231–248
28. Eran Chajut and Daniel Algom 2003 :Selective Attention Improves Under Stress: Implications for Theories of Social Cognition 2003 Journal of Personality and Social Psychology, Copyright 2003, American Psychological Association, Inc.Vol. 85, No. 2, 231–248
29. Eran Chajut and Daniel Algom 2003 :Selective Attention Improves Under Stress: Implications for Theories of Social Cognition 2003 Journal of Personality and Social Psychology, Copyright 2003, American Psychological Association, Inc.Vol. 85, No. 2, 231–248
30. Eran Chajut and Daniel Algom 2003 :Selective Attention Improves Under Stress: Implications for Theories of Social Cognition 2003 Journal of Personality and Social Psychology, Copyright 2003, American Psychological Association, Inc.Vol. 85, No. 2, 231–248
31. Eran Chajut and Daniel Algom 2003 :Selective Attention Improves Under Stress: Implications for Theories of Social Cognition 2003 Journal of Personality and Social Psychology, Copyright 2003, American Psychological Association, Inc.Vol. 85, No. 2, 231–248

References – The Mental and Physical Obstacle Course

32. Dennis Tueller, 1983 How Close is Too Close? SWAT Magazine
33. Exercise on self-worth placed in footnote
34. Elton Mayo, Hawthorne and the Western Electric Company, The Social Problems of an Industrial Civilisation, Routledge, 1949.
35. A. H. Maslow, A Theory of Human Motivation, (1943) Originally Published in Psychological Review, 50, 370-396.
36. A. H. Maslow, Motivation and Personality published 1954
37. Star Wars: Episode IV – A New Hope Lucasfilm 1977
38. Airplane - 1980 Paramount Pictures

39. UK Government Crown Prosecution Service Source: Information taken via the www.cps.gov.uk website for the UK Government Crown Prosecution Service

Appendix 1

The following information is taken from the CPS Offences against the Person, incorporating the Charging Standard: [38]

Section 18 Assault – Grievous Bodily Harm (GBH) – Wounding (with intent)
Grievous bodily harm means serious bodily harm. It is for the jury to decide whether the harm is really serious. However, examples of what would usually amount to really serious harm include:
injury resulting in permanent disability, loss of sensory function or visible disfigurement; broken or displaced limbs or bones, including fractured skull, compound fractures, broken cheek bone, jaw, ribs, etc; injuries which cause substantial loss of blood, usually necessitating a transfusion or result in lengthy treatment or incapacity;
serious psychiatric injury. As with assault occasioning actual bodily harm, appropriate expert evidence is essential to prove the injury
Section 18 assaults are always dealt with by the Crown Court (rather than the Magistrates Court) and can carry a maximum sentence of life imprisonment.

Section 20 Assault – Grievous Bodily Harm (GBH) – Wounding (without intent)
It is not possible to attempt to commit a section 20 GBH offence. An attempt to cause grievous bodily harm should be charged as an attempt section 18 because, as a matter of law, if a suspect attempts to cause really serious harm, he must necessarily intend to do so. Similarly, if a suspect attempts to cause a serious wound of a kind that would clearly amount to grievous bodily harm, the offence would be attempted section 18.
Where the evidence demonstrates that the suspect intended to cause an injury that is substantially more serious than that (if any) which was in fact caused, prosecutors should consider the circumstances of the case as a whole as well as the relevant sentencing guideline to determine the appropriate charge. Because of the distinction between the definition of a wound and that of grievous bodily harm there is an argument for saying that it is possible to attempt a section 20 wounding - for example where an offender intends to cause an injury that would break the continuity of the whole of the outer skin but would not cause really serious bodily harm. It is unnecessary to consider this possibility in any further detail because in such circumstances, it is likely that either an attempted section 47 or an offence of common assault would be the appropriate charge in accordance with this Charging Standard.

Section 47 Assault – Actual Bodily Harm (ABH)
The offence is committed when a person assaults another, thereby causing Actual Bodily Harm (ABH). Bodily harm has its ordinary meaning and includes any hurt calculated to interfere with the health or comfort of the victim: such hurt need not be permanent, but must be more than transient and trifling: (R v Donovan 25 Cr. App. Rep. 1, CCA).

---

[38] CPS Offences against the Person, incorporating the Charging Standard, The Crown Prosecution Service

It is an either way offence, which carries a maximum penalty on indictment of five years' imprisonment and/or an unlimited fine not exceeding the statutory maximum.

As stated in the Common Assault section of this Charging Standard, the factors in law that distinguish a charge under section 39 from a charge under section 47 are the degree of injury resulting and the sentencing powers available to the sentencing court. Where the injuries exceed those that can suitably be reflected by Common Assault - namely where the injuries are serious - a charge of ABH should normally be preferred.

In determining whether or not the injuries are serious, relevant factors may include, for example, the fact that there has been significant medical intervention and/or permanent effects have resulted. Examples may include cases where there is the need for a number of stitches (but not the superficial application of steri-strips) or a hospital procedure under anaesthetic. But there may be other factors which are also relevant, and these will need to be carefully considered when deciding whether or not the injuries are serious.

Psychological harm that involves more than mere emotions such as fear, distress or panic can amount to ABH. In any case where psychiatric injury is relied upon as the basis for an allegation of ABH, and the matter is not admitted by the defence, expert evidence must be called by the prosecution (R v Chan-Fook 99 Cr. App. R. 147, CA)

For those cases where charges of either Common Assault or ABH are potentially available, police officers and prosecutors should refer to the Common Assault section of this Charging Standard. This provides clear guidance on the instances where Common Assault will be the appropriate charge.

This offence is capable of being racially aggravated under the Crime and Disorder Act 1998. refer to Prosecuting cases of Racist and Religious Crime, elsewhere in this guidance.

Section 39 Assault – Common Assault

An offence of Common Assault is committed when a person either assaults another person or commits a battery.

An assault is committed when a person intentionally or recklessly causes another to apprehend the immediate infliction of unlawful force.

A battery is committed when a person intentionally and recklessly applies unlawful force to another.

It is a summary offence, which carries a maximum penalty of six months' imprisonment and/or a fine not exceeding the statutory maximum. However, if the requirements of section 40 of the Criminal Justice Act 1988 are met, then Common Assault can be included as a count on an indictment. Refer to Summary offences and the Crown Court (Criminal Justice Act 1988 sections 40 and 41; Crime and Disorder Act 1998 section 51 and Sch.3 para.6, elsewhere in this guidance).

Where there is a battery, the defendant should be charged with 'assault by beating'. (DPP v Little (1992) 1 All ER 299)

Common Assault or ABH?

In law, the only factors that distinguish Common Assault from Assault occasioning Actual Bodily Harm (contrary to section 47 of the Offences against the Person Act 1861) are the degree of injury that results and the sentence available to the sentencing court. But this latter factor is only relevant in the Crown Court. The magistrates' court is able to pass exactly the same maximum penalty for both offences, namely six months' imprisonment.

Where (as will often be the case) battery results in injury, a choice of charge is available. It is very important that such decisions are made on a consistent basis and having regard to the two key factors:

1. The level of injuries that have resulted; and
2. The likely sentence that the court will pass.

Although any injury that is more than 'transient or trifling' can be classified as actual bodily harm, the appropriate charge will be one of Common Assault where no injury or injuries which are not serious occur.

In determining the seriousness of injury, relevant factors may include, for example, the fact that there has been significant medical intervention and/or permanent effects have resulted. But there may be other factors which are also relevant, and these will need to be carefully considered when deciding whether or not the injuries are serious.

It should be borne in mind that Parliament created the offence of Common Assault specifically to cater for those assault cases in which the injuries caused are not serious.

The offence of Common Assault carries a maximum penalty of six months' imprisonment. This will provide the court with adequate sentencing powers in most cases. ABH should generally be charged where the injuries and overall circumstances indicate that the offence merits clearly more than six months' imprisonment and where the prosecution intend to represent that the case is not suitable for summary trial.

There may be exceptional cases where the injuries suffered by a victim are not serious and would usually amount to Common Assault but due to the presence of significant aggravating features (alone or in combination), they could more appropriately be charged as ABH contrary to section 47 of the Offences Against the Person Act 1861. This would only be where a sentence clearly in excess of six months' imprisonment ought to be available, having regard to the significant aggravating features.

However, to reiterate, the presence of such significant aggravating features will not automatically mean that a charge of ABH should be preferred. The key determinant is the likely sentence that the court will pass.

CPS Offences against the Person, incorporating the Charging Standard, The Crown Prosecution Service

Printed in Great Britain
by Amazon